WITHOUT FIDEL

A DEATH FORETOLD IN MIAMI, HAVANA, AND WASHINGTON

ANN LOUISE BARDACH

SCRIBNER
New York London Toronto Sydney

SCRIBNER
A Division of Simon & Schuster, Inc.
1230 Avenue of the Americas
New York, NY 10020

Copyright © 2009 by the Eloise Company

First Scribner hardcover edition October 2009

SCRIBNER and design are registered trademarks of The Gale Group, Inc.,
used under license by Simon & Schuster, Inc., the publisher of this work.

For information about special discounts for bulk purchases,
please contact Simon & Schuster Special Sales at 1-866-506-1949
or business@simonandschuster.com.

The Simon & Schuster Speakers Bureau can bring authors to your live event.
For more information or to book an event, contact the Simon & Schuster Speakers Bureau
at 1-866-248-3049 or visit our website at www.simonspeakers.com.

Manufactured in the United States of America

1   3   5   7   9   10   8   6   4   2

ISBN 978-1-4165-5150-8
ISBN 978-1-4165-8007-2 (ebook)

For my father, Emil Bardach,
who lived long and left too soon

CONTENTS

PART I:
THE LONG DYING

PART II:
THE FIDEL OBSESSION

CONTENTS

PART III:
RAÚL'S REIGN

ACKNOWLEDGMENTS

This book is the outcome of a long conversation begun in 1992—when the first of four assignments from *Vanity Fair* magazine sent me to Miami and Havana. In Cuba, there have been scores who have contributed to my reporting over the years—in their homes, on the streets, and through notes and messages sent to me, sometimes through third parties. I leave their names unmentioned here except for one who has recently passed on and for whom there will no longer be an inconvenience. Carlos "Chino" Figueredo, a retired general of immense heart and inner conflict, was crackling smart and great fun. He lived through the best and the worst of the Revolution—and embodied both.

In the U.S., I am greatly indebted to all my colleagues who serve on the Cuba Study Group at the Brookings Institution, led by Vicki Huddleston and Carlos Pascual. Vicki, Daniel Erikson, Paul Hare, and Carlos Saladrigas have been particularly generous with their insights. For medical expertise, I am grateful for the counsel and research of the esteemed surgeon Leon Morgenstern. Don Bohning's work on the history of the CIA substation JM/WAVE was another great resource. Likewise, George Kiszynski, Luis Rodriguez, and D. C. Diaz of the Joint Terrorism Task Force were immensely helpful in navigating the murky demimonde of exile militant groups. The National Security Archive and Peter Kornbluh ferreted out scores of documents, many cited in Part Two.

In Miami, I have ongoing debts to Efraim Conte, Jane Bussey, Rosario Moreno, Joenie Hilfer, Lissette Bustamante, Jorge Tabio, and most especially Salvador Lew, who so generously introduced me to his many friends. Quite often it was edifying to recall the reflections of the late José Luis Llovio-Menéndez.

Always there has been help, hospitality, and fulminations from my stateside Cuban chorus: Gustavo, La Vivien, and Conchi, while Heine Estaron often had the right word or date. My former students cum assistants, Anneliese Vandenberg, Bailey Ash, Mareisa Weil, and Jonathan Vanian, saved many a day. Several courageous friends read early drafts—Eduardo Santiago, Susan Bridges, Bree Nordenson, Linda Jones, Libby Straight, and Ralph Thomas.

Special thanks to my wise and patient attorney, Tom Julin of Hunton & Williams, for vetting this manuscript, and to the *New York Times* counsel George Freeman, who, with Tom, fought the good fight for more than four years against intrusive government subpoenas.

At Scribner, this project was born out of the imagination of Colin Robinson, ushered in by Nan Graham, and carried across the finish line by the terrific Roz Lippel. The eagle-eyed Kathleen Rizzo caught more than her share of snafus. My agent, Tina Bennett at Janklow and Nesbit, routinely performed small miracles, ably assisted by Svetlana "no drama" Katz.

I owe a good deal to a small army of editors, who over the years bravely tackled my Miami/Cuba journalism—the genesis of much of my thinking for this book. They include several editors at the *Washington Post*'s Outlook, the *New York Times* news and opinion pages, *Vanity Fair,* Joy de Menil at *The Atlantic*, David Plotz at *Slate,* and Tina Brown at *The Daily Beast.*

My mother, who bravely perseveres, has taught me endless life lessons. And always there is Bobby, who makes it all possible.

FAMILY TREES

FAMILY TREE OF
FIDEL CASTRO RUZ

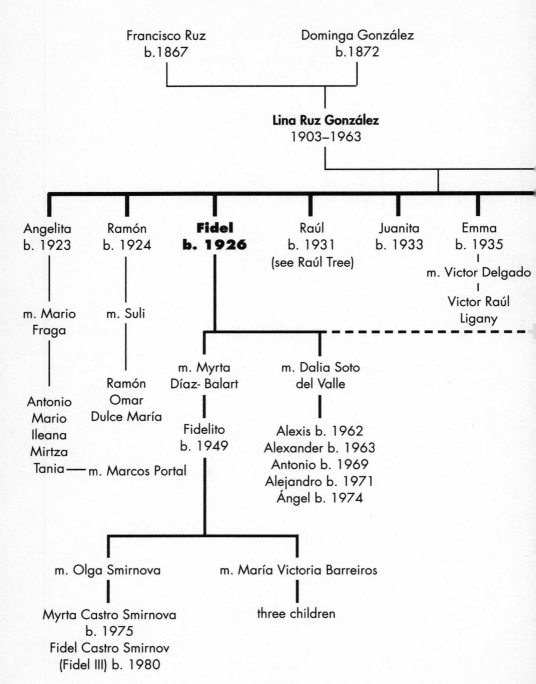

Francisco Ruz
b.1867

Dominga González
b.1872

Lina Ruz González
1903–1963

Angelita b. 1923	Ramón b. 1924	**Fidel** **b. 1926**	Raúl b. 1931 (see Raúl Tree)	Juanita b. 1933	Emma b. 1935

m. Victor Delgado

Victor Raúl
Ligany

m. Mario
Fraga

m. Suli

m. Myrta
Díaz- Balart

m. Dalia Soto
del Valle

Antonio
Mario
Ileana
Mirtza
Tania —— m. Marcos Portal

Ramón
Omar
Dulce María

Fidelito
b. 1949

Alexis b. 1962
Alexander b. 1963
Antonio b. 1969
Alejandro b. 1971
Ángel b. 1974

m. Olga Smirnova

m. María Victoria Barreiros

Myrta Castro Smirnova
b. 1975
Fidel Castro Smirnov
(Fidel III) b. 1980

three children

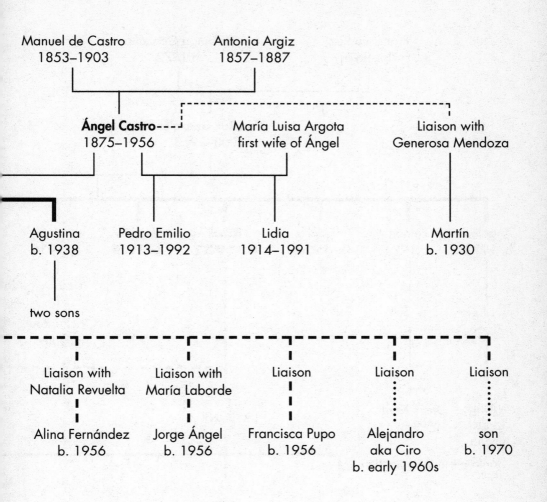

Manuel de Castro
1853–1903

Antonia Argiz
1857–1887

Ángel Castro
1875–1956

María Luisa Argota
first wife of Ángel

Liaison with
Generosa Mendoza

Agustina
b. 1938

Pedro Emilio
1913–1992

Lidia
1914–1991

Martín
b. 1930

two sons

Liaison with
Natalia Revuelta

Liaison with
María Laborde

Liaison

Liaison

Liaison

Alina Fernández
b. 1956

Jorge Ángel
b. 1956

Francisca Pupo
b. 1956

Alejandro
aka Ciro
b. early 1960s

son
b. 1970

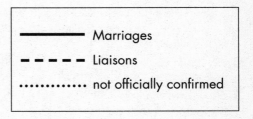

————— Marriages

– – – – Liaisons

·············· not officially confirmed

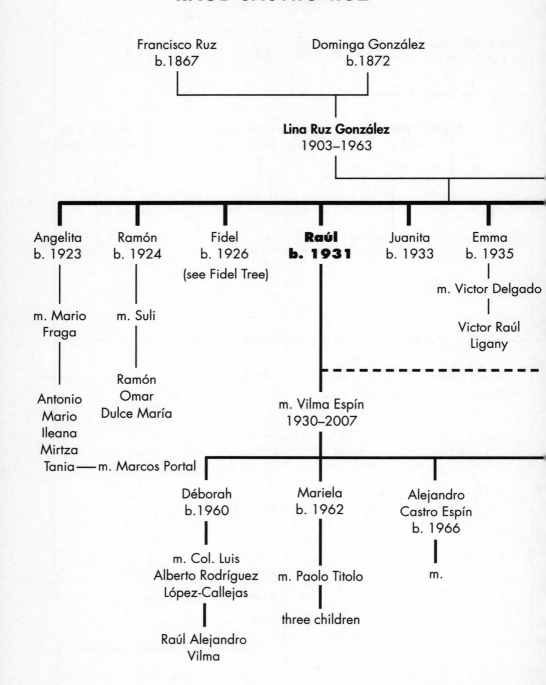

FAMILY TREE OF
RAÚL CASTRO RUZ

Francisco Ruz
b.1867

Dominga González
b.1872

Lina Ruz González
1903–1963

Angelita
b. 1923

Ramón
b. 1924

Fidel
b. 1926

(see Fidel Tree)

**Raúl
b. 1931**

Juanita
b. 1933

Emma
b. 1935

m. Victor Delgado

m. Mario
Fraga

m. Suli

Victor Raúl
Ligany

Ramón
Omar
Dulce María

m. Vilma Espín
1930–2007

Antonio
Mario
Ileana
Mirtza
Tania——m. Marcos Portal

Déborah
b.1960

Mariela
b. 1962

Alejandro
Castro Espín
b. 1966

m. Col. Luis
Alberto Rodríguez
López-Callejas

m. Paolo Titolo

m.

three children

Raúl Alejandro
Vilma

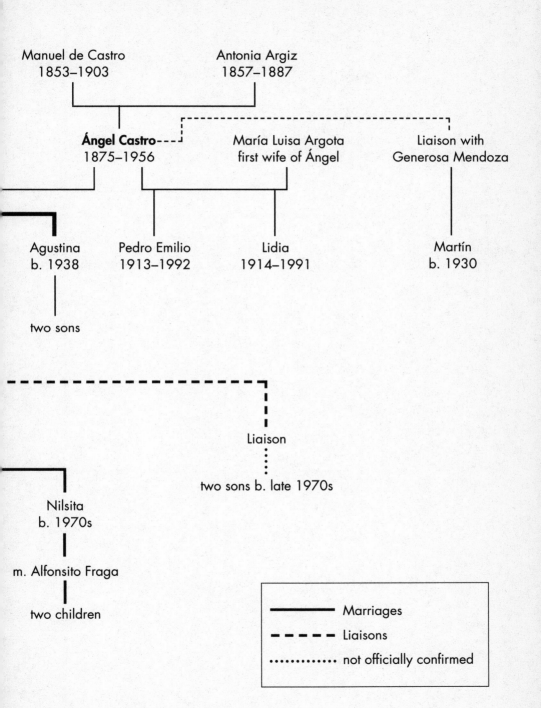

Manuel de Castro
1853–1903

Antonia Argiz
1857–1887

Ángel Castro
1875–1956

María Luisa Argota
first wife of Ángel

Liaison with
Generosa Mendoza

Agustina
b. 1938

Pedro Emilio
1913–1992

Lidia
1914–1991

Martín
b. 1930

two sons

Liaison

two sons b. late 1970s

Nilsita
b. 1970s

m. Alfonsito Fraga

two children

———————	Marriages
– – – – –	Liaisons
··············	not officially confirmed

PREFACE

What began as a chronicle of Fidel Castro's final chapter and the transition that would follow his anticipated death, evolved into a very different book. After all, Castro didn't die, even though by his own account, he had been mortally stricken on July 27, 2006. He then endured a series of botched surgeries and life-threatening infections that would have felled any other. But through sheer grit and, no doubt, a healthy sprinkling of vengeance, Castro lived on, refusing to surrender, retreat, or die.

For the next three years, cosseted in state-of-the-art hospital and convalescent suites, Castro could reflect on his life with some satisfaction. He had achieved the goals that most mattered to him, not least of which was his personal and political survival. And he had lived to see the fiftieth anniversary of the Revolution he had fought for in the hills of Oriente.

Equally satisfying to him, as well, was the array of sympathetic leftist governments installed throughout Latin America. While struggling with the indignities of collapsing health, Castro could find solace by merely casting his eye across a map of the hemisphere. There were the diehard socialist *compañeros,* Hugo Chávez of Venezuela and Evo Morales of Bolivia, followed by a second tier of allies, Luiz Inácio Lula da Silva in Brazil, Cristina Kirchner in Argentina, Rafael Correa in Ecuador, Michelle Bachelet in Chile, and the recent additions of stalwarts Daniel Ortega in Nicaragua and Mauricio Funes in El Salvador. The latter, along with Costa Rica, re-established diplomatic relations with Cuba in 2009, the last holdouts in Latin America to do so. The final coup was an apology Castro extracted from President Álvaro Colom of Guatemala, who "officially ask[ed] Cuba for forgiveness" for his country's role as a launching pad for the Bay of Pigs invasion in 1961.

There were other auspicious signs that favored the Cuban strongman. In October 2008, the United Nations General Assembly voted for the seventeenth consecutive time to condemn the U.S. embargo of

Cuba—this time by a vote of 185 to 3. Castro would also have relished George W. Bush's inglorious return to Crawford, Texas, having failed to implement his much-touted plan of "regime change" to bring democracy to Cuba.

The inauguration of President Barack Obama, in itself, was a game changer. Soon after, a poll by Bendixen & Associates concluded that the attitudes of Cuban-Americans had undergone a sea change—with 67 percent now in favor of lifting travel restrictions to Cuba for *all* Americans, an eighteen-point leap from three years ago.

Because of the ever-changing facts on the ground, this book evolved from an investigation and meditation on Cuba's Marathon Man to a trilogy: Fidel's near death and protracted finale; his enemies and their fifty-year war to dislodge him; and the meticulously planned succession and early reign of his brother Raúl.

The first section, *The Long Dying,* chronicles the story of Castro's greatest battle: pushing back at death's door with the nimbleness (or luck) of Lazarus. The reporting involved permeating the hermetically sealed bubble around the fiercely private and officially retired Castro through contacts with family members, doctors, and colleagues. With some of his health restored, the phoenix-like *Comandante* could not resist meddling in affairs of state. To this end, Castro created two new roles for himself: Fidel the Wizard, pulling the strings from behind the curtain, and as his country's Pundit in Chief, to whom attention must be paid.

Part Two, *The Fidel Obsession,* is the saga of Castro's most dedicated enemies and their unique relationship with the political leadership of Miami and Washington. By virtue of political and personal longevity, Castro lived to see many of his foes fall before him. His most daunting challenger, Jorge Mas Canosa, the powerful exile leader and founder of the Cuban-American National Foundation, died of cancer in 1997.

However, two former schoolmates of Castro persevered, becoming his most indefatigable would-be assassins. In the end, Luis Posada Carriles and Orlando Bosch matched Castro in grit and determination, but not in strategy or wiles. Nevertheless, their lifelong quest to eliminate Castro—notwithstanding significant civilian casualties—was not without admirers. Among them were some supporters of three Bush administrations, two in the White House and a third in Florida when Jeb Bush was governor. Castro loathed and, to a degree, feared the Bush family—viewing them as allies of his most committed enemies.

The overt and covert actions to topple Castro began as a parallel story of the Cold War. Thereafter, *la lucha*—the struggle—would continue, nourished by a scorched-earth ethos, an anti-Castro industry, and inconsolable heartbreak.

Part Three, *Raúl's Reign,* is the story of Raúl Castro's halting entrance to center stage in Havana after his brother succumbed to infirmity. I have focused on the political and personal history of Cuba's new leaders—with particular scrutiny of Raúl and his inner circle—their background, their ideology, and the differences that mark Raúl from his older sibling.

Drawing on almost two decades of covering Cuban and Miami politics, I have sought to provide some historical and cultural context throughout on what is certainly the most contested piece of real estate in the Western Hemisphere. The unique political ecosystems of the twin capitals of Cuba—Havana and Miami—have each done their part in fostering and ensuring a half century of hostility between the world's premier superpower and a Caribbean island. I have also made some brief detours into a few arenas that, to my thinking, have preternaturally infused Cuban political culture: informing, spying, alcoholism, and suicide.

Rarely appreciated is the fact that Cuba has led the hemisphere in suicides for centuries—a macabre phenomenon dating back to the Spanish conquest. Pervasive spying and snitching are also century-old traditions that were ramped up to a Stasi science after the Revolution. These will likely prove to be the most corrosive feature of the Castro legacy.

For the benefit of the new reader, it has been necessary to recapitulate some of the history and material from previous articles and books of mine, notably *Cuba Confidential.* The charts of the Castro family, Raúl's government, the political players, and timeline will hopefully further assist navigation for those new to the Cuban waters. Because this is neither a history of Cuba nor a biography of Castro, readers seeking more background might look toward any of the estimable volumes or writers cited in my endnotes.

On a general note, when a source in the text is not identified, it is not by oversight. Identification in Cuba, and to a lesser degree in Miami, and even Washington, is not without peril. It is one of the many obstacles in reporting on Cuba; another, of course, is the government's refusal to provide or verify any information they do not want reported. This ranges from the Castros' work schedules to quotidian family information, to data on sensitive topics such as prostitution. As imperfect a process as this may be, in my experience the more reliable information has never come from the government—including the two most famous Castros—but rather from former officials, family members, and the words and thoughts of ordinary Cubans, witnessing their history unfold.

On January 1, 2009, Fidel and Raúl Castro celebrated a half century of rule. Two weeks later, Barack Obama became the forty-fourth president of the United States. To the Castro brothers, however, Obama was simply the eleventh batter to step up to the plate. All told, not a shabby record for a brother duo from the two-horse town of Birán, Cuba. These are big numbers—and ones that beg a certain reckoning. This book, I hope, will offer some answers and reflections on the diplomatic train wreck that has passed for U.S.-Cuba relations and what the future may look like for both countries.

The fifty-year, high-stakes showdown between Washington and Havana is likely to culminate not in a final glorious duel but in a resignation born of fatigue. And there will be indisputable winners and losers—mostly losers—as the Obama administration wades into the troubled waters of the U.S.-Cuba relationship.

In heralding the new administration, Raúl Castro tossed out a provocative proposal, indeed a trade: Cuba would send fifty-five of its most high-value political prisoners, mostly human-rights activists, to the U.S. in exchange for the return of *Los Cinco Héroes,* the five Cubans convicted of spying in Miami in 2001 who are lauded by the Cuban government as martyrs. "Let's make a gesture for a gesture," declared Raúl Castro. "If they want the dissidents, we'll send them tomorrow, with their families and all. But let them return our Five Heroes." (In June 2009, the Supreme Court declined to hear an appeal of their case.) The rhetoric came straight out of the Castro playbook—equating spying with dissidence. It was also trademark Castro strategy at work: get your players back while exporting your enemies.

Fidel Castro was a pyrrhic warrior with an epic commitment to battle, regardless of the cost. His legacy is a complex one: a tattered country but a proud people. While one can snipe at the eroded state of the Revolution's declared triumphs of health care, education, and sports, Castro's undisputed gift to his country was nationalism. His credo was simple: Cuba would bow to no one.

Castro articulated his nationalist philosophy during his first visit to the U.S. in 1959, declining U.S. aid if tied to any conditions. Cuba would not be a beggar country, he proclaimed, regardless of deprivation or suffering. (In a peerless Castro syllogism, he justified the Soviet Union's patronage as a symbiotic "strategic relationship," while refusing to cash a single check for the U.S. lease on Guantánamo, granted a laughable $4,085 a year as negotiated in 1934). Nor would he accept humanitarian aid for the devastating hurricanes of 2008 if not given directly to a government agency. Never mind that damages from the withering storms topped $10 billion or that a half million Cubans lost their homes.

Castro's refusal reminded me of an afternoon I spent in a crumbling Vedado apartment in Havana in 1994 with José Rodríguez Feo, the great Cuban intellectual and former aristocrat who stayed behind and supported the Revolution. The engine that propelled Castro, Rodríguez Feo explained to me, was not his brain but his pride. "He destroyed this country," he said, "because of his pride."

Until 2009, U.S. forays into engagement with Cuba were a lot like a *New Yorker* cartoon by Robert Mankoff. The 1994 cartoon depicted an imperious businessman standing behind his desk, dodging a lunch date with a phone caller. *"No, Thursday's out. How about never?"* went the caption. *"Is never good for you?"*

Matters shifted four months into the Obama presidency when Washington began a tiptoe retreat from fifty years of policy informed by the Cold War. The insistent saber rattling and ultimatums of megaphone diplomacy suddenly ceased, supplanted by quiet and cautious negotiations.

The new Washington policy makers abandoned their traditional reactive role for one that was proactive. A good example came in March 2009 when the Castro brothers purged some fifteen key government players followed by confessional apologies from its victims. Typically, such reactionary moves prompted a reentrenchment and condemnation from the U.S. This time, Washington played its cards more shrewdly. In April, an undisclosed meeting was arranged between Thomas Shannon, assistant secretary of state for Western Hemisphere affairs, and Jorge Bolaños, the chief of Cuba's Interests Section in Washington. It was there that the U.S. expressed its hopes and concerns. Soon after, the administration announced it was lifting restrictions on travel and financial remittances for Cuban-Americans to the island, fulfilling a campaign pledge. The Obama team had grasped the wisdom that more visitors and contacts with Cuba, not less, were more likely to facilitate democratic change.

Days later, Raúl Castro responded in kind. "We have sent word to the U.S. government in private and in public that we are willing to discuss everything—human rights, freedom of the press, political prisoners, everything." As was his wont, Fidel soon contradicted his younger sibling, suggesting that human rights would not be on the agenda and that détente was not all *that* imminent. "There is no doubt that the president misinterpreted Raúl's statements," he wrote in his next "Reflections" column, before throwing water on the geniality and good cheer that marked the exchanges between Obama and his brother. Fidel then fired off a series of qualifiers, one being that Cuba would continue to charge a hefty tax, roughly 20 percent, on remittances sent from exiles. It was, he insisted, a necessary redistribution of wealth for Cuba's neediest.

Regardless of Fidel's reflexive naysaying, there was movement, albeit back and forth, but favoring the latter. Suddenly, the atmosphere was oxygenated and the scene was set for Barack Obama's groundbreaking invitation for a rapprochement with the island. "The United States seeks a new beginning with Cuba," Obama proclaimed in his opening comments at the Summit of the Americas on April 17. "I know there is a longer journey that must be traveled to overcome decades of mistrust, but there are critical steps we can take toward a new day."

How many steps will be taken on this journey depends on several factors. Among them are the amount of diplomatic capital the Obama administration is prepared to spend, the degree of economic desperation in Cuba, and the actuarial tables for Fidel Castro.

Just one thing is certain: after a half century, the "Age of Never" has ended.

Ann Louise Bardach
July 2009

PART ONE

THE LONG DYING

"I will be dignified until the last day of my life."
—Fidel Castro, 1954 letter
to his half-sister Lidia Castro

CHAPTER ONE

The Pursuit of Immortality

The dying began on July 27, 2006. It was not scheduled, nor was it supposed to end this way. Certainly, it would have been hard to imagine a final coda less appealing to Fidel Castro—a proud and prudish man who zealously guarded his personal privacy. But there it was, splayed across the front pages of newspapers and websites five months after his near-death following emergency surgery. There, too, were chapter and verse of virtually every inch of the intestinal tract of Cuba's Maximum Leader—from the hepatic flexure straight on to the end. For Castro, an obsessive autocrat and micromanager of matters big and small, nothing could have been more distressing. His steely control over his island fiefdom had been threatened; the moat around his personal life had been breached, and his patient confidentiality violated. Indeed, Fidel Castro had been sidelined as the master of his own fate.

A new portrait—that of a frail octogenarian clinging to life—had supplanted his carefully crafted persona of the vigilant *guerrero* (warrior). And with his infirmity, Castro's fierce grip on the largest island in the Caribbean finally began to loosen.

Disbelief and wonder transfixed millions of Cubans on both sides of the Florida Straits. Could it be that Fidel Castro was mortal? But as befitted a movie star dictator—and the world's longest-reigning head of state—Castro would take his time leaving the stage. That exit, with periodic finales, was fated to be a marathon: a personal epic one might be tempted to call *The Fideliad*.

On July 26, 2006, Castro participated in the usual anniversary celebrations of the Cuban Revolution. The centerpiece of the festivities was, as always, a commemoration of the failed attack he had led on the Moncada military garrison in 1953 in Santiago de Cuba at the eastern end of the island known as Oriente. Outnumbered ten to one, almost half of Castro's 134 guerrillas had been captured and killed, and some

3

brutally tortured. It was at Castro's subsequent trial that he famously declared, "Condemn me, it does not matter. History will absolve me."

The first stop of the 2006 commemoration for Castro was in the historic city of Bayamo, where in 1953, a second division of his troops had attacked the army garrison. The visit raised the odd eyebrow, as Bayamo had never been enshrined in post-revolutionary texts to the extent of the Moncada barracks. Some Castro critics pointed to the fact that he had not been part of the Bayamo attack and that the three leaders who led the raid had broken ranks with their obstinate comrade soon afterward. But there was no denying Bayamo's historical significance, most notable during the country's long independence wars from Spain. The Cuban national anthem, "El Himno de Bayamo," also known as "La Bayamesa," famously declares, *"Que morir por la Patria es vivir"*—"to die for the homeland is to live." Castro would gloss the sentiment still further, spinning it into the revolutionary slogan of *Patria o Muerte*—Country or Death.

Shortly after 7 a.m., presumably to spare him from the blistering summer heat, Castro delivered his annual "Triumphs of the Revolution" speech in the city's Plaza de la Patria. Some one hundred thousand of the faithful were bused in from neighboring towns, and stood waving small paper Cuban flags. There were fewer of Castro's usual improvisational riffs and even less passion; the speech ran a mere two and a half hours, brevity itself by his standards. Still, when many in the crowd dropped their flags, Castro egged them on: "It is good exercise, so keep on waving them."

Castro gave an even briefer recitation in nearby Holguín. And as the day wore on, it was clear that *El Comandante* was not himself, but visibly uncomfortable, piqued and coughing. In fact, he was in crippling pain. "I thought that would be the end of it," he later reflected. Hours later, he was flown back to Havana and rushed to CIMEQ hospital (Center for Medical-Surgical Studies), Cuba's foremost medical facility.

The next day, July 27, he underwent extensive intestinal surgery. The operation—a surgical shortcut that Castro insisted upon—failed. Abscessed material leaked into the peritoneal cavity, which led to peritonitis. Matters quickly worsened as systemic blood poisoning set in. For the next week, Castro hovered between life and death. The odds of anyone, never mind a man inches from his eighth decade, surviving such a surgical catastrophe were slim.

Undeniably, Castro had been blessed with an auspicious destiny—cheating death over and over and driving his foes (about one million of his countrymen) into exile. He savored with rich satisfaction the idea that he had swatted away ten American presidents as if they were so many pesky flies: squaring off against Eisenhower, besting Kennedy, ignoring Johnson, and charging straight on through Nixon, Ford, Carter, Reagan, Bush, and Clinton. It was a run that ended with a most satisfying finale, facing off against Barack Obama after dispatching the one he most reviled, George W. Bush. Relentlessness, a chess master's ability to see several moves ahead, and a genius for public relations appeared to have been embedded in Castro's DNA.

His had been a life of "the best laid plans," but now his fate was in the hands of others. A week earlier, Castro had made a last-minute decision to attend the Mercosur Summit in Córdoba, Argentina, at the urging of his devoted friend, Venezuelan president Hugo Chávez. Castro enjoyed a busy calendar of activities, including a visit to the childhood home of his martyred comrade, Che Guevara, in the town of Alta Gracia.

But the Argentine sojourn concluded with a raucous confrontation with reporters during a photo op of Summit leaders. A Cuban-American television journalist, Juan Manuel Cao, peppered Castro with queries about the fate of a prominent neurosurgeon denied a visa to leave Cuba. "Who pays you?" fumed Castro, erupting into a tirade captured on videotape.

After he fell ill, one insider at the Ministry of Health speculated that Castro's burst of canine fury with the insistent reporter had brought on a fresh and furious bout of diverticulitis. The painful, recurrent intestinal infection had dogged him since the 1970s and reportedly first required surgery in the 1980s. (Diverticulosis is a relatively common condition of the aging colon, characterized by outpouchings—or diverticula—in the lining of the colon, or large intestine. When the diverticula become infected, bleed, or rupture, the condition becomes diverticulitis, which can be exceedingly painful and potentially life-threatening.)

Consistent with the pattern of some sufferers, Castro's attacks often followed events that filled him with frustration or severe stress. The colon or gut, sometimes referred to as "the second brain" by psychologists, is susceptible to mental duress. (About 95 percent of the neurotransmitter serotonin and direct nerve connections to the brain reside in the colon.)

Though the sudden severity of his condition may have caught him by surprise, Castro was not unprepared. He had known for some time that another intestinal surgery was in his future—sooner rather than later. He had even contacted his former wife, Myrta Díaz-Balart, and asked her to come to Havana for support during the operation.

Castro almost certainly suffered from a condition sometimes known as "'malignant' diverticulitis," a variant form of the most severe diverticulitis of the sigmoid colon. The condition is not cancer. However, it often has a similar progression, with comparable morbidity and mortality rates. For those over seventy-five, it can be particularly vengeful. According to a report authored by Leon Morgenstern, MD, director of surgery at Cedars-Sinai Medical Center for thirty-five years, "This form of the disease pursues a relentless course of chronic sepsis, recurrent fistulization, and eventual death due to one or more complications of the disease."

Consequently, Castro's chosen handlers could deny that he had colon cancer with its implied finality. But in truth, Castro's illness, which cascaded into multiple complications, was equally challenging. It was just a matter of time.

Few had devoted as much thought and resources toward scripting their final days and legacy as the Cuban commander in chief, who approached his mortal end with the same obsessive zeal he had lavished on his life. As a young man, Fidel Castro ordained that he would live and die with pride and honor. He wrote his half-sister Lidia from prison when he was just twenty-eight years old, "I have enough dignity to spend twenty years in here or die of rage beforehand. . . ." Then he assured her: "Don't worry about me; you know I have a heart of steel."

From childhood onward, Castro cultivated the image of himself as an icon of endurance: honing his stamina and discipline, maintaining ramrod-perfect military posture, and working without rest. "I made myself into a revolutionary," he declared proudly in 2005. For decades, his enemies insistently prophesied his imminent demise—only to recant. "Immortal—until proven otherwise," became the ghoulish quip heard around Miami's Calle Ocho, Eighth Street, the Mecca of Cuban exile life. Certainly, if vengeance were the fuel of immortality, Castro would have lived forever. "I cannot think of a worse loser than Fidel," his good friend, the novelist Gabriel García Márquez, once observed.

Survival—simply staying alive—and the suggestion of immortality were central to Castro's iconography. He cheerfully floated the wildly hyperbolic estimate that he had survived 631 assassination attempts. In fact, the number of serious plots, as opposed to the hare-brained ones, did not exceed the realm of double digits. Nevertheless, gamy survival was as much a political act of defiance as a personal quest. A soldier, a warrior, Castro was shown always in uniform, the sentinel forever on guard against his island's enemies. Castro preened and exulted in the fact that he had defeated the hopes and schemes of a half century of White House occupants.

A master of propaganda, Castro was a peerless mythmaker. Of central importance was the myth of his own indomitability. To that end, Castro decreed that his family, personal life, and health were strictly off-limits. The government's airtight control over information mandated that such quotidian matters as Castro's marital and paternity status, even his daily schedule, were taboo for public consumption. In 2003, seeking to quell rumors of his declining health, Castro invited the maverick director Oliver Stone to film him having an electrocardiogram for Stone's documentary *Looking for Fidel*.

But those close to him knew that Castro had long battled a host of infirmities, from the nuisance of dermatitis, and the indignities and chronic pain of diverticulitis, to high blood pressure, elevated cholesterol, and a series of small strokes. In the past decade, he had become fastidious about his health and diet and traveled with his own medical entourage, along with emergency resuscitators, defibrillators, and oxygen tanks. Often he was accompanied by his cardiologist, Dr. Eugenio Selman Housein-Abdo, or another specialist well acquainted with his medical issues. As an added precaution, a twenty-four-hour state-of-the-art emergency room was installed on the fourth floor of the Palace of the Revolution, the scrupulously guarded bastion where Castro has his offices and where the Council of State meets.

Personal information about the Castro family has leaked out incrementally, sometimes through the testimony of high-level government defectors, but more often through the indiscretions of family members, neighbors, and hospital employees. Much of it travels via Radio Bemba, literally Radio Lips, as the lightning-quick transmission of word-of-mouth news is known. It has proven on occasion to be remarkably accurate, reaching many ears on and off the island.

On July 28, Radio Bemba rumbled to a roar when a convoy of three cars—two white Ladas with Fidel's signature black Mercedes sandwiched between them—raced up Avenida del Paseo and parked outside the Palace of the Revolution. Built by Fulgencio Batista for the country's Supreme Court, the palace adjoins the offices of the Communist Party's Central Committee. Castro's primary doctor leapt from the center limousine and hurried inside the building. "People talked about how unusual it was to see his cars like that," said one *habanera* who happened to be passing by at the time.

For three days, a murky quiet cloaked Havana. The news blackout was in eerie counterpoint to the squads of government officials seen scurrying between the offices of the Central Committee and those in the Presidential Palace. The silence broke dramatically on July 31. At 9:15 p.m., the nightly newscast was interrupted for an unprecedented breaking news bulletin. The camera then cut away to Castro's faithful aide and personal assistant, Carlos Valenciaga. Looking dour and drawn, the thirty-three-year-old Valenciaga read a prepared statement, purportedly written by Fidel Castro earlier in the evening.

"Because of the enormous effort involved in visiting the Argentine city of Córdoba to attend the Mercosur meeting . . . and immediately afterward attending the commemoration of the 53rd anniversary of the attack on the Moncada and Carlos Manuel de Céspedes barracks, the 26th of July of 1953, in the provinces of Granma and Holguín, days and nights of continuous work with hardly any sleep have caused my health, which has withstood all tests, to fall victim to extreme stress to the point of collapse. This has caused an acute intestinal crisis with sustained bleeding that has obliged me to undergo a complicated surgical operation . . . [which] will force me to take several weeks of rest, away from my responsibilities and duties."

The missive went on to declare a *temporary transfer* of power to several high-ranking ministers, with the most crucial responsibilities going to his seventy-five-year-old brother, Raúl, the head of the Armed Forces. The other appointed custodian was Carlos Lage Dávila, Cuba's economic czar, and one of the younger members of the Politburo at a spry fifty-four years of age.

Though the televised statement was meant to reassure the world of the stability of both Castro's health and his government, it had the opposite effect. Many Cubans, long inured to unreported news on Castro's health or personal life, translated the announcement as meaning that *El Máximo Líder* was indeed dead. No one—anywhere—had any doubt that Fidel Castro was grievously, if not mortally, ill.

Before Valenciaga had finished his remarks, the island, Miami, and Washington were electrified with speculation. *Habaneros* scooted into hallways and huddled with neighbors or lunged for their phones to rehash and decode the announcement with relatives and friends. Those lucky enough to have internet access cranked up their third-generation computers to any available phone line and searched for non-Cuban news reports.

To outside appearances, however, Havana, Santiago, and other major cities on the island were suffused with a stony calm. The streets were filled not with revelers but with police and soldiers who shooed residents back into their homes, dispersing even small groups of stragglers. Dubbed "Operación Caguairán" by Raúl Castro, who oversaw its maneuvers, the government's response was a long-established contingency plan to ensure order and stability in the event of just such an extraordinary occurrence. The plan was named for the caguairán tree, indigenous to Cuba, and renowned for the rock-hard core of its trunk. Previously, it had been a favored epithet Castro used to describe himself. "This popular mobilization, in silence and without the least boasting, guaranteed the preservation of the Revolution from any attempted military aggression," Raúl Castro said of the operation in an interview with the state-run newspaper, *Granma,* months later. He added that it was a necessary precaution, lest certain unnamed forces in Washington "turn crazy."

The mobilization, said to involve up to two hundred thousand enforcers manning the streets, would remain on alert throughout 2006. "Never before, except during the Bay of Pigs [1961] and the Missile Crisis [1962], had Cuba undertaken in its national territory such a mobilization of its troops on such a scale," editorialized *Granma,* an indicator of how seriously the Castro brothers had planned for such a transition. In July 2008, Raúl Castro affirmed that the operation remained in effect: "Today defense preparedness is more effective than ever, including Operation Caguairán—which continues successfully."

Roberto Fernández Retamar, a member of Cuba's Council of State and an author, congratulated the country and tweaked its northern nemesis on the seamless transition from Fidel to Raúl Castro. "They [the U.S.] had not expected that a peaceful succession was possible," Retamar crowed to reporters in August of 2006, in an implicit acknowledgment that the reign of Fidel Castro was coming to a close. "A peaceful succession has taken place in Cuba."

Some revolutionary-minded Cubans expressed heartfelt sadness to journalists. Others fretted that the disappearance of their titanic leader brought as much uncertainty and fear as it did hope. For the silent majority of discontented Cubans, Fidel was an authoritarian strongman, but he also was a known entity, a fact of Cuban life. "He is the devil we know," said one resident of the well-groomed Havana neighborhood of Miramar. Most Cubans, however, kept their true thoughts to themselves. Certain sentiments were best expressed by a shrug, a roll of the eyes, or with the trademark Cuban wave of the hand by the side of the head, signifying "whatever."

For many, the news came not a minute too soon. Fidel Fatigue was epidemic from one end of the island to the other, from the humblest sugarcane *machetero* to overworked, underpaid doctors, to Central

Bank employees; it even afflicted delegates of the National Assembly and seeped into the nooks and crannies of the Communist Party. Whether wishing him well or ill, a quiet excitement gripped Cubans as they waited for the next chapter of their collective lives to be revealed.

In Miami, several hundred jubilant Cuban-Americans raced over to Versailles Restaurant on Calle Ocho to celebrate what they believed to be Fidel's obituary. Some chanted *Cuba sí, Castro no!* while others sang salsa queen Celia Cruz's signature *sonero,* a Cuban ode to survival, called *"Ríe y Llora"*—"Laugh and Cry."

They were not alone in thinking that *El Comandante* had met his Maker. A prominent Geneva banker on the board of the banking behemoth UBS, with firsthand knowledge of Cuba's numbered Swiss bank accounts, was likewise convinced that Castro had died. Some of Cuba's funds and Castro's accounts had long been handled by the Geneva branch of HandelsFinanz—later bought by HSBC Guyerzeller Bank. "He's a cadaver," the banker told a close friend, noting that government funds, controlled by Castro, had been transferred, presumably to his brother Raúl, during the final days of July 2006.

As Cuba's Maximum Leader, with his myriad roles as the president of the country, president of the Council of Ministers, Council of State, and the Communist Party, as well as commander in chief of its Armed Forces, Castro had full access to all of the country's accounts and holdings. The boundary between the personal and the political, in his case, did not exist. When the Swiss banker was asked why he was convinced that Castro was dead, he responded, "The money would not have been moved, unless he was dead or facing death."

Castro's personal wealth was among the most sensitive of topics to him. In May 2006, *Forbes* magazine ranked Castro as the seventh richest world leader, with an estimated $900 million fortune. It was the first time Castro had merited a spot on the top ten list, a ranking hotly coveted by many a capitalist climber. But Castro—who declared himself a socialist in 1961 and who long prided himself on a spartan, unostentatious lifestyle—was mortified. "We estimate his fortune based on his economic power over a web of state-owned companies, including the Palacio de Convenciones, a convention center near Havana; CIMEX, retail conglomerate; and Medicuba, which sells vaccines and other pharmaceuticals produced in Cuba," wrote *Forbes,* noting that Castro "travels exclusively in a fleet of black Mercedes." There was one especially snarky, unattributed aside that "former Cuban officials living in U.S. assert that he has long skimmed profits," followed by the cursory disclaimer that "Castro insists his net worth is zero."

The report infuriated Castro. Immediately, he restricted the use of the Mercedes (some two hundred said to have been a gift from Saddam Hussein), directing officials to drive the graceless Russian-made Ladas and other less showy cars. He soon appeared on his favorite television show, *Mesa Redonda* (Round Table), and railed against the financial magazine for four hours. "What do I want money for now if I never wanted it before!" he declaimed to his sympathetic host, Randy Alonso.

Castro had previously threatened to sue *Forbes* for listing him in its annual Billionaire's Edition. "The revenues of Cuban state companies are used exclusively for the benefit of the people, to whom they belong," declared a 2004 statement released by the government. "I'll have the glory of dying without a penny of convertible currency," Castro assured Ignacio Ramonet, his co-autobiographer, claiming that his salary was a meager $30 a month.

Castro's protestations were not without merit. True, he was the son of a wealthy land tycoon, but he was also among the least materialistic of statesmen. Part of the Fidel enigma was that he did not spring from the traditional mold of Latin American *caudillos*—political bosses—with their depthless hunger for all that glitters. There were no chandeliers or disco yachts in the Castro lifestyle. Indeed, in the pantheon of Hispanic strongmen such as Argentina's Juan Perón, Venezuela's Marcos Pérez Jiménez, and Mexico's Carlos Salinas de Gortari, Castro lived in relative austerity. In this respect, he emulated his parents, who, despite their wealth, maintained a lifestyle of striking simplicity grounded in the demands of ranching and farming. "His are the habits of a soldier-monk," Ramonet noted in Castro's memoir, *My Life*. Filmmaker Saul Landau, who spent extended periods with Castro in the 1960s, described him as "part Machiavelli, part Don Quixote, with a philosophy that was half Marxist and half Jesuit."

In 1955, as Castro prepared to leave prison following his two-year stint for the assault on the Moncada, he wrote his half-sister Lidia, who was organizing his future living arrangements.

Regarding material comforts, if it were not essential to live with a minimum of material decency, believe me I would be happy living in a tenement and sleeping on a cot with a box in which to keep my clothes. I could eat a plate of malanga or potatoes and find it as exquisite as the manna of the Israelites. I could live extravagantly on 40 cents a day spent wisely, despite the high cost of living. I am not exaggerating, I speak with the greatest frank-

ness in the world . . . it is possible to lack everything and not feel
unhappy. Thus, I have learned to live.

Of course, Castro had the very best of whatever he desired and
famously indulged his bon vivant cravings for fine food and spirits. In
2009, Juan Reinaldo Sánchez, a former member of Castro's personal
security team for seventeen years, regaled Miami television viewers with
"true tales" about a vast complex designed for *El Comandante* and his
family in Havana as well as a private key off the island's coast with
a helicopter pad and private marina. Nevertheless, Castro lacked the
acquisitive, materialistic nature of a classic *caudillo*. It was power, not
treasure, that had always interested him. And in this sense, the Marxist
of the Tropics had all that he wanted. Cuba was his.

Following his disastrous surgery in late July, Castro battled for life and
breath in a private intensive care wing of CIMEQ. Then, in the early
days of August, to the astonishment of his medical team, the Cuban
leader pushed back against death's door. Still, more surgeries would
be required to keep him alive, and the Cuban titan would never be the
same man.

Few were allowed access to Castro's hospital suite. Among them was
his longtime friend and trusted right hand, Chomy, aka Dr. José Miyar
Barruecos, who handled Castro's e-mail and whose relationship with
Castro dated back to the early days of the Revolution. Castro's rarely
seen spouse, Dalia Soto del Valle, the mother of five of his sons, visited
regularly, as did Castro's first wife, Myrta Díaz-Balart, mother of his
eldest child, Fidelito.

Another visitor, according to one Miami savant, was Father Amado
Llorente, Fidel's beloved teacher from his prep school days at the Jesuit-
run Belén school in the early 1940s. The suggestion was that Llorente
had administered last rites to his former student. Just eight years older
than his pupil, Llorente had been a champion and confidant for the
ambitious but troubled teenaged Fidel. In 2002, Father Llorente told
me of a student hiking trip to the western province of Pinar del Río in
which the priest nearly drowned while crossing a rising river. "When
Fidel saw me go under with the current, he threw himself in the river to
rescue me," Llorente recounted. After young Fidel hauled his teacher to
safety, he exclaimed: "'Father, this has been a miracle! Father, let's pray!
Three Hail Marys! Let us thank God!' So indeed, at that time Fidel Castro believed in God." The elderly padre did not return calls, nor would

the vows of confidentiality required of a priest allow him to confirm such a visit, if, indeed, it had taken place.

Miguel Brugueras, a senior government official who served as ambassador to Lebanon, Argentina, and Panama, was among those allowed to visit with Castro in those early months. A devout *fidelista,* Brugueras solemnly told close friends after his visit that "Fidel will not recover from this." Castro did not have cancer, he said, but his condition was nonetheless "terminal." Consequently, Brugueras stepped down from his government post, viewing his political future as bleak. "He was not a *raulista,*" explained a family friend. Ironically, Brugueras would die within the year, while Castro soldiered on.

Many among the elite of Havana, known as the *nomenklatura,* were convinced that Castro had died during the first week of his hospitalization. That rumor was silenced only when two of his sons showed up in mid-August 2006 at a soirée in El Vedado, the upscale *barrio* bordered by the Malecón, the grand boulevard that shoulders Havana from the waters of the Atlantic. Antonio and Alexis Castro surprised many by their appearance at the home of Kcho, a popular artist/sculptor who was throwing a birthday party for his own father. The attendance of *los hijos,* however, was proof positive that Castro had slipped from the grip of the Grim Reaper. "They would not have been there if Fidel was in danger of dying right away," said one attendee, who added that Castro's health was on the minds and lips of all present. "Of course we all wanted to know but no one dared to ask them about it."

A few weeks later, Antonio Castro, an orthopedic surgeon and the doctor for Cuba's national baseball team (he was subsequently named vice president of the Cuban Baseball League in 2008), was more forthcoming with his U.S. counterparts at a conference for the World Baseball Classic. When solicitously asked about his father's health, the amiable Antonio shrugged sadly, and said, "It's terminal," adding, *"Lo que el Viejo tiene—es fulminante."* "What my old man has—is insurmountable." Antonio's American colleague surmised that *El Jefe* had cancer, the illness whispered about among the *nomenklatura.*

Not long after, a CIA spokesman weighed in, saying the Cuban leader had cancer and predicting that he would not live to see 2007. Of course the intelligence agency's pronouncements on such matters were rarely accurate. Their famously spotty track record on Castro and Cuba went back a half century, beginning with their underestimation of Castro's popular support in the late 1950s and their disastrous strategy for the Bay of Pigs invasion. There would be decades of other miscalculations. Throughout much of the 1990s, the CIA's National Intelligence Estimates had predicted that a military coup was likely—and that Castro's days were certainly numbered.

"Fidel's health was a cottage industry at the CIA," said Jim Olson, former chief of counterintelligence at CIA headquarters in Langley, Virginia, who noted that the Cuba Desk had been among the least successful at the Agency. "I remember when we saw him with the Pope [in 1998] and thought, 'Oh my God, he does look good.'"

Not everyone at the CIA agreed. One analyst was so keen to see the end of Castro that he argued that "regime collapse" was imminent. "By making such a case, the development of a constructive policy for engagement or succession was undermined," complained a former National Security Council official. At one point, a senior analyst told the State Department's Cuba Desk that he had identified a missile emerging from a Cuban silo in surveillance scans during the late 1980s, thus requiring a threat-and-attack assessment. However, according to a State Department official, when experts studied the pictures, it was clear there were no such missiles. In 2004, the CIA embarrassed itself further and announced that Castro had Parkinson's disease, arguably the one ailment he didn't have.

More credence was given to the casual indiscretion of Brazil's President Luiz Inácio Lula da Silva that Fidel Castro had cancer and that his condition was exceedingly grave. "He has colon cancer," a retired Cuban diplomat told me in 2007, seconding Lula's contention. "That is his central problem. It is a secret that they have held very tightly." But government sources, speaking off the record, emphatically denied that the Cuban leader had cancer.

It was Castro's great fortune to have lived long enough to reap the benefits of numerous surgical advances and a crop of newly minted wonder drugs—none of which had existed five years earlier. While most were imported from Europe, a few had been developed in Cuba's own biotechnology labs. By not succumbing to grave illness until 2006, Castro was able to buy time—time that was not for sale even ten years earlier. Like Ariel Sharon, the Israeli leader who clung to life for more than three years following a massive stroke, Castro reaped the perks of twenty-first-century medical technology. But unlike Sharon, whose problems were from the neck up and who remained in a vegetative state, Castro's infirmity stemmed from the core of his being. Most of his colon, gallbladder, and other abdominal viscera had been excised; he had literally lost his guts.

Castro's travails proved to be a treasure trove for late-night talk show hosts whose writers found the news irresistible fodder for dozens of monologues. "As you know, the elderly Fidel Castro is recovering from surgery in Cuba," Jay Leno deadpanned. "I understand he was rushed to the hospital on Donkey One." Leno had other salvos: "A message delivered on Cuban television today said that Fidel Castro's condition is listed as stable." A ba-da-boom zinger followed: "which in Communist countries means he'll be dead by Friday." "He ran Cuba for almost fifty years," began another gag, "and political analysts are now debating what kind of changes the Cuban people will hope for. I'm gonna guess: term limits."

Throughout the summer of 2006, David Letterman, Conan O'Brien, Craig Ferguson, Stephen Colbert, and Jon Stewart reveled in Fidelschtick heaven. "Cuban dictator Fidel Castro is still in the hospital with a serious medical condition," Conan O'Brien opined, setting up his nightly riff. "Castro said that a half century of Communist rule seemed like a good idea, right up until the point he was rushed to the hospital in a '55 Oldsmobile."

Not surprisingly, Miami produced scathing, and sometimes hilarious commentary.

"We interrupt this deathwatch to say Fidel Castro is fine, actually," Ana Menendez wrote in her *Miami Herald* column. "That's the news coming out of Havana these days. And though it may frustrate and baffle most laypeople to hear that an elderly man with an artificial anus and a rapidly loosening grip on reality could make such a remarkable recovery, doctors are not surprised. . . . In fact, the phenomenon has been around for so long that the medical community has given it a name: The Hispanic-Dictator Paradox."

For comedians, columnists, pundits, and talk show hosts, Castro's long dying became the gift that kept on giving. Castro's continued presence even proved irresistible fodder to the flacks at the State Department. "It's like the old country song," remarked State Department spokesman Tom Casey, "How can we miss you, if you never leave?"

A segment of Havana's chattering classes insisted that Castro had been fighting cancer for some time. One version had it that his troubles went back almost twenty years to when he was rumored to have been successfully operated on for a small tumor in one lung. Another account, unverified but popular in Miami, was that Castro had been secretly operated on for cancer of the colon in a Cairo hospital in 1990.

There was more corroboration that Castro had been receiving treatment for respiratory problems. According to one former Cuban intelligence officer, Castro's problems stemmed from an accident he had had while indulging his passion for deep-sea diving. Castro famously could remain underwater for unusually long periods of time while snorkeling, alarming his companions. Evidently, on one occasion he remained submerged too long, then returned to the surface too quickly. The accident damaged his lungs, the intelligence colonel said. (In 1994, Castro visited Ted Turner and a small contingent of HBO executives at a protocol house in Miramar. Arriving with Castro was a doctor with a defibrillator in tow. Michael Fuchs, one of the HBO executives, said that the execs asked one of Castro's staffers why he traveled with a defibrillator. They were told that *El Comandante* had been scuba diving, an explanation they found wanting.)

There was more consensus that Castro had been stricken by a small stroke in 1989 and again in mid-1994, when he was said to have been rushed to a downstairs clinic in the Palace of the Revolution. Word spread quickly about his incapacitation, leading to a flurry of stubborn rumors in Miami and Washington that the Cuban strongman had died. It was also true that like both of his parents, Castro struggled with high blood pressure, high cholesterol, and related cardiovascular problems. To improve his lung capacity and boost his stamina, Castro, a devotee of all manner of cutting-edge, New Age medical therapies, frequented an oxygen chamber. Others insisted that despite the deadening heat and humidity of the Caribbean Castro sometimes wore a thermal undershirt under his *olivos verdes* to aid his circulation.

Prior to the mid-1980s, Castro had chain-smoked both cigars and cigarettes and lived with a fierce, almost reckless abandon. By all accounts, he led a life without limits: eating, drinking, and working around the clock; resting only when he passed out from fatigue. In 1964 journalist Lee Lockwood spent a day snorkeling with Castro in Varadero and then going out in the evening. "He was a gourmand . . . and he had a very lavish dinner," recalled Lockwood. "He smoked a lot—one cigar after the other—and smoked cigarettes in between." During another of his five-course feasts, Castro began his meal by eating a jar of yogurt, instructing Lockwood "that it prepares the stomach." Certainly Castro was partial to extremes. When not binging on food, he sometimes fasted for up to three days. By his early thirties, Castro was exhibiting symptoms of digestive tract illnesses.

Bernardo Benes, a Miami banker who helped negotiate a series of prisoner releases in 1978, had several all-night sessions with Castro—usually beginning at 10 p.m. and ending at 6 a.m.—in which the Cuban leader chain-smoked Cohiba cigars. "Fidel had just created the Cohiba *puro*," said Benes, referring to Castro's role as the official taster and developer of the famed cigar. Castro's love of smoking began in his early teens in Birán when he first smoked a *puro* given to him by his father, Don Ángel. Benes estimated that between the two of them, they inhaled two boxes, or fifty cigars, each night, using the floor as an ashtray.

Benes was surprised by Castro's habit of flicking his ashes wherever they fell, but followed suit. In a letter to his sister in 1955, Castro spoke of his indifference to housekeeping: "There is nothing more agreeable than having a place where one can flick on the floor as many cigarette butts as one deems convenient without the unconscious worry about a housewife, vigilant as a sentinel, setting the ashtray where the ashes are about to fall."

During a December 1984 speech, Castro uttered an unusual aside on his own mortality. "Fifteen years from now, it will be the year 2000, and that's not too far away," he told the crowd. "Well, it may be a bit farther for some of us who are here, and who are being stalked by the Grim Reaper," he said with a dry laugh, then added: "And those of us who are *staring* at the Grim Reaper."

One year later, after forty-five years of smoking, Castro announced that he had given up his cherished *puros*. Smoking within his immediate vicinity also became taboo. One motivating factor was the death in January 1980 of Celia Sánchez, his most trusted confidante, going back to their guerrilla days in the Sierra Maestra mountains. The indefatigable and devoted Sánchez, renowned for her good cheer and the plume of cigarette smoke emanating from her lips, died of lung cancer at age fifty-nine. It was an incalculable loss for Castro, who told me he thought of her as "the guardian angel" of the rebel troops. Regarded as the eyes and ears of Fidel, Sánchez was one of the few who was willing to tell him the unvarnished truth and, on occasion, to contradict him.

In 1994, Marvin Shanken, the publisher of *Cigar Aficionado,* pressed Castro on the subject of his having given up his coveted cigars. "You are saying that you do not smoke even in the privacy of your home by yourself?" Shanken asked incredulously. "No," Castro replied. "Not even a puff?" "No. No," Castro repeated. "Not even a little puff?" "Not one," Castro assured him.

It was the first clear signal that *El Comandante en Jefe* was confronting a health issue. Only a life-threatening experience, it was mumbled quietly, could have motivated a Cuban male of his generation—for whom the cigar was a personal and national symbol—to retire the lifelong habit. "No question about it," said Benes. "He had to have been told he had no choice but to quit."

• • •

Close observers noted that by 1990, Castro began to moderate his considerable food and alcohol intake, and budget more regular hours for sleep and rest. A nocturnal, Castro often worked in his office from four in the afternoon until four in the morning. He would then sleep for several hours. In 1993, he told me during an interview I did for *Vanity Fair* magazine that reports of his not sleeping were wildly exaggerated; he insisted that he usually slept about six hours, though he could make do with less.

Around this time, Castro became a health aficionado, a student of biochemistry, and an adherent of New Age diets, homeopathy, and several miracle drugs. Over the next decade, Castro's lifestyle would morph from that of a reckless libertine—heedless of conventional health concerns—to that of an obsessive neurasthenic.

Max Lesnik, a Miami exile radio host, who renewed his friendship with Castro in the early 1990s, said that Castro's health and stamina were hard-earned. "He's obsessed with health issues," said Lesnik, who's shared several meals with Castro in the last decade. Bernardo Benes had a similar impression. During one all-night meeting in the Palacio, Benes used Castro's personal bathroom. The hyper-curious Benes could not resist a bit of casual snooping. Inside Castro's medicine cabinet were "dozens of little bottles of medicines all lined up in a row," he said. "Fidel is a hypochondriac."

In the mid-1980s, Castro directed his government to establish a state-of-the-art biotech laboratory and research facility known as LABIOFAM (Laboratorio Biológico Farmacéutico). Under the directorship of Fidel's biophysicist nephew, José Fraga Castro, and his nieces, Gloria Castro and Tania Fraga Castro, both senior officials and medical researchers at the Ministry of Health, LABIOFAM won kudos for its pioneering work in biotechnology and pharmaceuticals. Cuba developed several important vaccines for meningitis, infectious diseases, and veterinary illnesses. Among its most acclaimed products was a cholesterol-control drug known as PPG. At my first meeting with Castro in 1993, he spoke glowingly of PPG's successful entry into the marketplace. (Ingestors of PPG sometimes benefit from the drug's Viagra-like side effect, prompting *habaneros* to dub it *para pinga grande*—for a big dick). Castro was always an avid student of science and technologies, but some insiders felt that his keen advocacy of LABIOFAM and its research reflected another more personal interest: eternal life.

By the 1990s, Castro's enemies began to despair that he would ever leave the stage. *"Bicho malo nunca muere,"* aging exiles would mutter at Versailles Restaurant, sipping *cortaditos*—"A bad bug never dies." Castro, of course, relished being their tormentor and cultivated and encouraged the myth that he could live—well, forever. He quietly delighted in the joke that became popular after he passed his seventy-fifth birthday: Fidel Castro is given a Galápagos turtle as a gift. He asks how long the mammal will live. About four hundred years, he is advised. Fidel shakes his head sadly, shrugs, and says, "That's the trouble with pets. You get attached to them and then they die on you."

Booze, the Achilles' heel of the Castro family, would be Fidel's last and most coveted indulgence. Unlike his brothers, Castro was a periodic drinker prone to go on benders and then jump back on the wagon. Yet, even when binging, Castro seemed remarkably functional to those around him. His consumption of spirits, and his ability to remain standing, duly impressed many.

"Fidel had always been a good drinker, even with the Russians, who are real pros," wrote Carlos Franqui, the journalist and ex-*fidelista,* in *Family Portrait with Fidel.* Franqui related how, shortly after the Cuban Missile Crisis of 1962, Castro skillfully leaked his complaints about the Russians to a *Le Monde* reporter, notwithstanding having consumed an ungodly amount of booze. While Castro's loquaciousness was legendary, he was also a spongelike listener, methodically taking the measure of his guests. Alcohol seemed only to enhance both tendencies. "That night it looked as if Fidel was going to get really drunk," noted Franqui, who was no slouch in the spirits department himself. "After all, the *Comandante* was tipsy. . . . Finally, dawn arrived and Fidel decided to go home."

In 1993, I watched Castro as he arrived at a reception at the Palace of the Revolution. He first stopped at the drinks table and knocked back a tall water-glass-sized mojito in a few quick gulps. He then stepped out to work the crowd, fully in command and at the top of his game.

Ted Turner has been visiting Cuba since 1982. "We spent all night drinking and smoking cigars," Turner said of his first visit. The two iconoclasts bonded instantly and found time to hunt and fish together, usually while drinking. "He told me CNN was invaluable to him," said Turner in 2001. "And I thought, if Fidel Castro can't live without it, we ought to be able to sell CNN all over the world. So the idea came from a commie dictator." Turner added that "Fidel ain't a communist. He's a dictator just like me."

Still, by 1991, Turner observed that Castro would falter on occasion. A self-described alcoholic who at the time had stopped drinking, Turner attended the Pan American Games as Castro's guest. According to one of his CNN colleagues, Turner was struck by Castro's acumen, as well as his vast consumption of booze. The CNN founder was one of the few to clock its ill effect upon Castro.

At a dinner in 1998 at a European ambassador's house, Castro's security detail requested that Chivas Regal scotch be available for him. But by the time Castro left dinner three hours later, he had drunk a considerable amount of white wine and brandy—and made requests for French red wine, Sambuca, and sweet vermouth. The ambassador and his wife found Castro to be an engaging and alert guest, all the more remarkable, they said, for the copious quantities of spirits he imbibed.

But by 2000, Castro had become far more serious about his health disciplines and had begun to limit his alcohol consumption. He also began lecturing Cubans about the perils of alcohol abuse, just as he had about smoking once he had quit. In 2002, the *Comandante* became an avid devotee of the most un-Cuban of diets, macrobiotics, the austere health regimen that favors brown rice and vegetables. Off-limits to him were two staples sacred to the Cubans and their economy: sugar and coffee. Castro would become an avid tea drinker and follow a rigorous food discipline devised personally for him by Dr. Concepción Campa. Known to colleagues as Conchita, Dr. Campa is one of Cuba's preeminent medical researchers. Moreover, she is a member of the Politburo of the Communist Party and an official in the Ministry of Health. Campa and Castro were hopeful that the new dietary regime would stem or alleviate his diverticulitis.

U.S. Representative William Delahunt, who led a congressional delegation to Cuba in 2002, recalled a dinner with Castro and the congressmen at the Palace of the Revolution. "Fidel spent at least an hour going on about the benefits of macrobiotics and organic farming," recalled Delahunt, a self-described "meat and potatoes Irishman" from Boston. "At the end of dinner, he invited me to a new restaurant specializing in macrobiotics and organic food. I got his point that it's better to have domestically produced food."

While pursuing alternative and Eastern remedies, Castro kept abreast of the latest medical research. The mini-hospital suite he had installed in the Palace was periodically upgraded with the latest technologies. On occasion, the facility provided emergency care for special visitors. In 2001, former assistant secretary of state William D. Rogers fainted at a Palace dinner with Fidel attended by business magnates David Rockefeller and Pete Petersen. The dinner had begun after 2 a.m. and followed two days of nonstop meetings and events. Mark Falcoff of the American Enterprise Institute was sitting next to Rogers. "We had been summoned to the Palacio around ten at night. Fidel gave a three-hour speech—really a monologue," recalled Falcoff. "Then he announced there was a dinner for us in the next room. Fidel again rose to give a toast, and around ten minutes later, Bill fainted and collapsed in his chair. But no one moved until Fidel realized what was happening."

Julia Sweig of the Council on Foreign Relations was struck by the speed with which Rogers was rushed upstairs once Castro took note. "A couple of doctors immediately attended to Bill, reviving him," said Sweig. "Then Chomy [Dr. Miyar Barruecos] came by with a clean shirt for Bill to wear. Shortly after that, Fidel arrived and stayed until it was clear that Bill was in good health, and saw us out."

Castro's regimen, balancing Western medicine with an Eastern diet, seemed to be working. In 2004, Castro addressed a conference of economists and poked fun at the Bush administration's transition plans for a Cuba *without* him. "The dead man is not dead yet!" he gleefully announced.

Few men have so zealously pursued longevity as Fidel Castro. The Maximum Leader's determination to survive into his eighties neatly dovetailed with his commitment to health care in Cuba. He saw to it that Cuban medical schools turned out doctors at a higher rate than any other country in the hemisphere. According to the World Health Organization, Cuba has one doctor for every 159 people, as compared with the U.S. ratio of one doctor per every 414 citizens. Some 31,000 work in 71 countries, according to the *Miami Herald,* bringing in $2.3 billion in revenue to the state, while 72,000 are employed on the island. Both friends and foes have argued that the doctors that Castro has dispatched around the globe are the country's largest export.

While Cubans are fastidious about grooming and hygiene, Castro seemed to have an unusual preoccupation with the latter that bordered on paranoia. Coupled with his fear of assassination, he was keenly alert to a possible threat to his life via the intestinal tract. For a dinner at a European ambassador's home in 1998 in Miramar, his security detail arrived earlier in the day to interview the hostess and secure the environment. The chief security official took the ambassador's wife aside and informed her that *only* Castro would have access to the downstairs bathroom during the dinner. All other guests—including her family—would need to use the upstairs bathrooms. "He then inquired as to what kind of toilet paper will be available to the *comandante*," she recalled in her memoir, *Cuba Diaries,* writing under a pseudonym. "He asks if it is Cuban toilet paper. I say it is. He asks me if we don't have a better quality toilet paper. I say we don't. The head of security asks me to take [our] roll, put it in a plastic bag, tape the bag shut, and leave it beside the toilet for the President." Likewise the soap for Castro's use had to be in its original, unopened packaging.

Delfín Fernández, a former member of Cuba's counterintelligence services, who defected in 1999, reported another bizarre precaution. According to Fernández, Castro's chief bodyguard, Bienvenido "Chicho" Pérez, told him that Castro had his underwear burned after just one use. Evidently he believed there were plots afoot to spray deadly chemicals on his jockey shorts during their laundering.

Castro long surrounded himself with a cadre of loyal commanders, who doubled as a small army of medical doctors. Among the most notable in his inner circle were Che Guevara, the Argentine medic-turned-revolutionary and his aide-de-camp, confidant, and personal doctor, René Vallejo. The father of Celia Sánchez, Castro's devoted friend, was a noted doctor in Manzanillo who frequently came to the aid of Castro's guerrillas. Chomy Miyar, his trusted aide who replaced Celia Sánchez after her death as Castro's doorkeeper and personal photographer, is also a doctor.

Carlos Lage, long Cuba's economic chief, and Fernando Remírez de Esteñoz, who headed Cuba's Interests Section in Washington and was a key player in the Secretariat of the Communist Party (until they were booted from the government in March 2009), were pediatricians. Other members in the Politburo who began their careers as doctors include José Ramón Balaguer Cabrera and José Ramón Machado Ventura—both of whom served as soldier-medics in the Sierra. Several of Castro's children have attended medical school as well.

Castro himself methodically assembled Cuba's most brilliant doctors and surgeons to serve as his personal medical team. As important as their medical skills were their loyalty, discretion, and willingness to be available on a 24/7 basis. Some, such as Rodrigo Álvarez Cambras (Quico), the director of the Frank País Hospital and a renowned back surgeon, became trusted confidants. Castro's personal cardiologist, Eugenio Selman, is a surgeon at the General Calixto García Hospital. Both men were committed to the Revolution and Castro's leadership and seamlessly mixed health care and politics, sometimes serving as unofficial ambassadors. The gregarious Álvarez Cambras told me he counted eleven heads of state as patients—including Castro, the late François Mitterrand, Mu'ammar Gadhafi, former Panamanian strongman Manuel Noriega, and, most famously, the late Saddam Hussein. During both the Gulf War and the run-up to the Iraq War, Álvarez Cambras sought to mediate a resolution with Hussein on behalf of Castro, who presciently feared the worst.

Others on Castro's deep bench of medical specialists included Julio Martínez Páez (Lulu), director of the Fructuoso Rodríguez Hospital; his niece Tania Fraga Castro, an expert in biotechnology research; Noel Gonzales, a cardiovascular surgeon at the Hermanos Ameijeiras Hospital; and Hernández Cayero, a specialist in vascular diseases.

In May 2004, Dr. Eugenio Selman helped organize a longevity conference in Havana in which 250 medical experts from Latin America and the United States participated. The doctor, who founded a "120-Year-Old Club" that promotes longevity, and who has a flair for public relations, told reporters during the conference that "[Fidel] is formidably well." Selman dismissed speculation that Castro had had "a heart attack once, that he had cancer or some neurological problem." In fact, Selman insisted that Castro was healthy enough "to live at least 140 years. And I'm not exaggerating."

Selman attributed Castro's long run to "good genes," a disciplined diet, and mental stimulation stemming from his boundless curiosity. "He is a widely cultured man. He is always reading, at every occasion. He eats moderately," the doctor informed reporters. "His health is [as] strong as iron—he has demonstrated that his whole life." Castro worked sixteen hours a day, Selman said proudly of his star patient, describing him as typically working longer than those decades younger than himself. In 2008, Selman published a book in Havana entitled *How to Live to 120 Years,* in which he cited many of the qualities of his famous patient as the secret formula for centenarian success.

But when the good doctor accompanied his celebrity patient in 2005, on a march past the U.S. diplomatic mission in Havana to protest American policy against Cuba, Castro was seen walking gingerly with apparent difficulty, as if experiencing discomfort. By then, Castro had endured one of the two widely publicized spills that instantly set off a blaze of succession scenarios. On June 23, 2001, during a three-hour speech in El Cotorro, a small town thirty minutes outside Havana, a visibly sweating Castro suddenly stumbled and fainted.

Three years later, in October 2004, while delivering another discourse in Santa Clara, Castro stumbled over a small step and tottered wildly off balance. Captured on video and replayed endlessly on late-night television, the Cuban leader seemed almost to fly forward, before landing face-down on the stage. The accident left him with a shattered kneecap and a broken arm, and required six months of recovery. Castro was so unsettled by the second fall that he insisted on appearing on the evening television news to assure his countrymen that *"estoy entero"*—"I am in one piece and fine."

Both stumbles were recorded by the Cuban photojournalist Cristóbal Herrera. The startling images won the photographer kudos and were seen around the globe. They were also acutely embarrassing to Castro and the government—which unsuccessfully sought to prevent their dissemination. Herrera was soon dispatched into exile—on assignment—then barred from returning to his homeland.

In June 2006, Dr. Selman was again extolling Castro's superb health, his excellent DNA, and rapacious curiosity. One month later, Selman's celebrated patient was in the hospital, unconscious and fighting for his life.

Around 1997, Cubaphiles began to take note of the fact that Castro had started to refer publicly to his brother Raúl as his *"relevo"*—Cuban for relief pitcher. It was an expression, however, that he had used privately to describe Raúl since the 1960s. But days after his fainting spell in June 2001, an event that sent Havana, Washington, and Miami into a frenzied state of alert, Castro officially ordained his brother as his heir, introducing him as his *relevo*. "He's the comrade who has the most authority after me," announced Castro. "And he has the most experience. Therefore I think he has the capacity to succeed me."

In fact, Castro had borrowed a page from Mexican politics, implementing a Cuban version of *el dedazo* or "the finger." Under the *dedazo* system, the president literally points to his successor, thus guaranteeing that power is preserved by his Party—and his secrets protected. From the moment Fidel went under the surgical knife on July 27, 2006, the powers of state were formally transferred to his brother "temporarily," until he recovered.

In late October 2006, rumors that Fidel had slipped from his mortal coil were so insistent and pervasive that the government arranged for taped footage of Castro to be shown on television. Castro was well aware of the perils of a public appearance. Even when he was robust and well, his every move was scrutinized as thoroughly as a specimen in a petri dish. I remember watching him officiate at a 26th of July event at the Che monument in Santa Clara in 2000. After dropping a small Cuban flag from the podium, he leaned over and quickly scooped it up. Then he quipped that if he stumbled, word of his imminent demise would soon be racing virally around the globe.

Indeed, the October 28 videotape, studied as intently as a Gnostic scroll, hardly made a convincing case that *El Jefe* was well. The footage showed an aging Castro walking stiffly. Some viewers said he appeared to be disoriented while others opined that it was proof that he was near death. Among them was the U.S. intelligence czar, John Negroponte, who prognosticated—wrongly—that Castro had "months, not years" to live. He was seconded in his fallacy by National Intelligence Director Mike McConnell a few months later, who assured the U.S. Senate that "this year will mark the end of the long domination of that country by Fidel Castro."

By the end of 2006, family members fretted to trusted confidants that Castro had dropped more than forty-five pounds and was still not able to sit up or eat solid food. Well-informed members of Havana's *nomenklatura* no longer believed that Castro would recover. Perhaps he could survive a few more months, went their thinking, but he would never regain his physical capacity or stamina. One more round of blood poisoning would finish him off, went the chatter from the deathwatch. From the other end of the island came word that a group of workers, vetted and selected by Santiago's Communist Party, were seen excavating a site on Pico Turquino. A popular attraction for locals and tourists, Pico Turquino is the highest point in the Sierra Maestra mountain range. Soon Radio Bemba had a breaking news bulletin: the peak, a favorite haunt of the young Fidel, was certainly the spot he had chosen for his burial.

For the *nomenklatura,* macabre parlor games evolved. The first guessing game involved predicting Fidel's final day on earth. The second was naming his final resting place. Some leaned toward burial in the Cemetery of Santa Ifigenia in Santiago, close to the mausoleum of José Martí. Others gambled on Havana's Plaza de la Revolución or on Cuba's most famous burial ground, the Colón Cemetery. But insiders shook their heads, pointing out that Castro had always been a proud son of Oriente, with little appreciation for the glories of Havana. Locals in Birán hoped he would be buried alongside his parents and grandparents at Finca Manacas, his birthplace. Indeed, in February 2009 the government declared the entire *pueblito* of Birán a national monument. It was an unlikely choice, however, as politics invariably trumped family in the Castro canon—even in the realm beyond.

"What happens to my remains is a matter of complete indifference to me," he assured me in 1994. He added that the governance of the country would proceed without a hitch and "not be halted for even a minute," indicating that a succession plan was fully in place even then. The smart money had it that Castro had decided against a burial or a monument that could be desecrated and had ordained that his ashes be spread near Pico Turquino in the Sierra, the site of his most glorious memories as a guerrilla revolutionary.

Officially, the Cuban-controlled media stayed rigorously on message with the mantra that Castro was recovering well and would return to his duties as *Comandante en Jefe,* his preferred honorific. In December 2006, Cuban officials assured a delegation of visiting U.S. lawmakers that Castro had neither cancer nor any form of terminal illness.

Then, quite suddenly, the hermetically sealed bubble around Castro was punctured. On Christmas Eve, a Barcelona newspaper, *El Periódico de Catalunya,* broke the story of a secret trip to Havana by the Spanish surgeon José Luis García Sabrido. The doctor, whose specialty is colon cancer, had previously treated Castro and was known to be sympathetic to the Cuban Revolution. Traveling with him, on a jet chartered by the Cuban government, was sophisticated medical equipment and a trove of medicines unavailable in Cuba. Previously the doctor had been sending supplies to Havana since the initial surgery and had been in phone consultation with Castro's surgeons. (A Cuban doctor based in Miami, who asked for anonymity, said he too had been delivering cancer drugs to Havana for some time, indicating that some were destined for Castro.)

Upon his return to Madrid, Dr. García Sabrido had no choice but to hold a news conference. "He does not have cancer," García Sabrido told reporters. "He has a problem with his digestive system. His condition is stable. He is recovering from a very serious operation." Then the good doctor carefully hedged, parsing his words. "It is not planned that he will undergo another operation, for the moment."

Just three weeks later, on January 16, 2007, the Spanish daily, *El País,* published a bombshell account of Castro's condition based on two medical sources who worked at the same Madrid hospital as Dr. García Sabrido. Contrary to the doctor's sunny assessment, Castro had barely survived three bungled intestinal surgeries. Not only did the surgeries fail, but Castro had been stricken with two bouts of peritonitis, a potentially life-threatening infection. The depth and nuance of medical details in the news story was impressive. It was also a stunning breach of patient confidentiality, but one that left little doubt as to its veracity—or that Castro had been mortally ill.

Castro's dire situation was, to a considerable degree, one of his own making. "The Cuban dictator and his advisers are the ones who decided on the surgical technique that led to the complications," the newspaper reported. Typically a patient with Castro's history of chronic and acute diverticulitis, which causes painful, infected pouches in the intestines, would have a colostomy. A standard colostomy procedure involves cutting out the infected segments of intestine, and then attaching an external bag to the patient. Once the patient has fully recovered, a second surgery is necessary to reconnect the intestines.

But Castro nixed having a colostomy, perhaps out of pride, machismo, or hubris—or some combination of the three. Hoping to avoid a second surgery, he decided upon a far bolder operation. Despite warnings of the risks involved, Castro opted for a surgery in which infected portions of the colon were removed and the colon was reconnected at the same time. "Attempted resection is fraught with difficulty and a potentially lethal outcome," warned a 1998 report by Morgenstern on surgery for malignant diverticulitis. Castro's surgeons knew this, but their patient had his own ideas. "No one could tell him no," said a trusted friend of Castro's, who was present at some of the discussions about the imminent surgery. "He would not listen to anyone because he could not bear the idea of it [the external bag]."

Around the same time, writer Saul Landau heard a similar account from a surgeon in Havana knowledgeable about Castro's care. "They told Fidel the risks of doing only one surgery, and he said no, he was willing to gamble," said Landau. "He made, as usual, a risky decision. He gambled and he lost."

The desired shortcut—in which the colon was attached to the rectum—ruptured, leaking fecal material and causing peritonitis. An emergency second surgery was necessary if Castro was to live. But then matters went from bad to worse. While attaching a colostomy bag, surgeons saw that Castro's gallbladder had become gangrenous, requiring a tube to drain the toxic material. The drainage tube to the biliary duct, which connected the intestines to the gallbladder, also failed. Yet another surgery was urgently needed to insert a second drain, this one manufactured in Spain. Castro was leaking more than a pint of fluids a day, resulting in "a severe loss of nutrients."

One UCLA colon surgical specialist said he was not surprised by such a grim outcome: "The sepsis, lack of nutrition, and systemic stress of a failed surgery followed by peritonitis can be lethal," he said. After a lifesaving colostomy was performed, Castro was deeply distraught. "Fidel was crying," one of the doctors who was present in the hospital confided to a friend. "He cried several times that first day. He was devastated."

For the next five months, Castro was fed intravenously. When Dr. García Sabrido arrived in December 2006, he found that "Castro was starving to death," said Landau.

"They had been feeding him only intravenously and not giving him food and he was wasting away." Solid food was then reintroduced into Castro's diet and he slowly began to gain weight and show signs of improvement.

Dr. García Sabrido was chagrined by the indiscretions of his chatty colleagues in *El País*. Moreover, he was now in bad odor with his legendary patient. For the next two years, the good doctor had no further comment.

Cuba's veil of secrecy was further torn a few days later when the irrepressible Hugo Chávez spoke incautiously, once more, about his friend. "Fidel is in the Sierra Maestra again," Chávez said. Then, reaching for a poetic metaphor, he added, "fighting for his life."

Cuban officials threw themselves into a frantic counteroffensive. They emphatically denied the reports coming out of Spain and summoned Chávez to Havana for urgently needed spin control. On January 30, 2007, Cuban television broadcast a new six-minute video, along with photos of Castro and Chávez embracing in Castro's hospital room. Like Lazarus, he had slithered back to the realm of the living. Castro wore his post-operative uniform—a blousy red, white, and blue tracksuit that replaced his army fatigues, and had the added advantage of concealing a colostomy bag. Sipping orange juice, Castro spoke of his recent infirmities. "I hadn't finished rehabilitating when the other [accident] came," Castro said, referring to his fall in October 2004 when he fractured his left arm and knee. He added that his ongoing illness was not "a lost battle." His Venezuelan comrade cheered him on: "Yes, it's not a lost battle," exclaimed Chávez. "And it won't be!"

Castro's interest in Venezuela went back decades. In the spring of 1948, as a student leader, he had traveled to Colombia. It was a transformative experience for Castro and culminated in his participation in street riots known as the Bogotazo, following the assassination of the populist presidential candidate, Jorge Eliécer Gaitán. En route to Colombia, Castro stopped in Caracas for four days and was dazzled by the beauty and bounty of the country. In a letter to his father, he wrote: "The city is about forty kilometers from the airport; the highway that leads from the airport to Caracas is truly fabulous because it crosses a mountain range with mountains more than 1000 meters tall. Venezuela is a wealthy country, thanks mainly to its huge production of petroleum. There you can build great businesses, but life is very expensive. As for its politics, currently the country is run admirably well . . ."

Always mindful of the country's strategic geography and economic wealth, Castro financed leftist guerrillas in Venezuela in the 1960s and '70s. In the 1980s and '90s, he brokered an amicable relationship with President Carlos Andrés Pérez. But he found his ideal disciple in Hugo Chávez, a patron infinitely more appealing and malleable than Cuba's Soviet overlords. Chávez was a charismatic strongman with Bolivarian ambitions, a twenty-first-century Juan Perón with oil. Fidel's successor would be his brother Raúl, but his heir would be Hugo Chávez.

The bond between the two strongmen transcended mutual geopolitical interests. Chávez had barely known his own father and thus meant it when he said, "Fidel is like a father figure to me." From 1999 on, the two men saw each other dozens of times—sometimes privately and unannounced. Indeed, Chávez has good reason to feel he owes his presidency, if not his life, to Castro's canny maneuvers.

In his memoir, Castro chronicled the crucial role he played during the attempted coup of the Venezuelan president in 2002. "'Don't resign! Don't resign!' I kept telling him," recounted Castro, who coached his beleaguered friend throughout the ordeal. Paul Hare, Britain's ambassador to Cuba at the time, recalled that when all was thought to be lost, Castro "asked the European Union to charter a plane to carry Chávez to safety to Havana." The country's vice president at the time, Carlos Lage, put it simply: "Cuba has two presidents: Fidel and Chávez."

In late February 2007, fueled by a gust of unexpected energy, Castro made a surprise thirty-two-minute call to Chávez's radio program, regaling his friend with anecdotes and jokes. Castro had begun to work the phones at odd times of the day and night, prompting some surprised recipients to refer to him as *El Fantasma*—The Ghost. One Castro friend who visited him often credited the *Comandante*'s recovery to his use of a hyperbaric oxygen chamber: three to four times daily, said the friend, for one-hour intervals.

A few weeks later, photographs were published in a Colombian paper of Castro strolling in the gardens of his hospital with his friend, novelist Gabriel García Márquez. "Fidel is a force of nature," said the Colombian writer, reminding naysayers: "With him, you never know."

By the early spring of 2007, Castro seemed to have found his footing in the realm of the living. Though achingly frail, with the shadow of death never too far away, Castro summoned his formidable will and commanded himself to live. He would tolerate a meager quality of life in exchange for survival. And as the days turned to weeks, Castro resumed his role as his country's über-manager, meddling in all matters of state.

Slowly the Maximum Leader began to morph from Commander in

Chief into Pundit in Chief. On March 28, 2007, *Granma* began publishing the "Reflections" of Fidel Castro. Over the next two and a half years, in staccato bursts—sometimes weekly, sometimes monthly—scores of essays and columns were written. Castro's topics were great and small: from the downside of biofuels to fulminations against George Bush, the CIA, and his most insistent would-be assassin, Luis Posada Carriles. There were 9/11 conspiracy theories and revelations about how Cuba had tipped off Ronald Reagan about an assassination attempt. Not all subjects were weighty or political. No subject was too quotidian for the great man's ruminations—even the pressing need to replace incandescent lightbulbs with fluorescent ones made it into his column.

It was not entirely clear whether Castro was writing solo or with ghostwriters or by dictation. It is likely that he was aided by one of his media specialists, such as Reinaldo Taladrid or *Granma* editor Lázaro Barredo, both dedicated propagandists, who often crafted media platforms, messages, and books in the state's interest. Whatever the level of assistance, Castro's unique rhetorical flourishes and pungent diction were evident in his columns that ran in the state-run newspaper and were posted online. Notwithstanding the downward spiral of his health, he had not lost his sense of humor or caustic sarcasm. When President George W. Bush offered some wishful thinking in 2007, that "One day, the Good Lord will take Fidel Castro away," the Cuban wordsmith was ready with a one-two punch. "Now I understand why I've survived the plans laid by Bush and the presidents who ordered my assassination," Castro responded gleefully in his next "Reflection." "The Good Lord has protected me!"

The Cuban titan became a gifted puppeteer—no longer visible onstage, but deftly pulling the strings of power from the wings. He was now Fidel the Wizard, hidden behind the curtain of Cuba's Oz. On his good days, when his pain and discomfort were endurable, there was nothing and no one to stop him: the world would be hearing from him. As far as Fidel was concerned, the Revolution was his; it was a cradle-to-grave operation. And perhaps, beyond.

CHAPTER TWO

The Family

Gossip is the national pastime of Cuba, followed by baseball and sex—although the order could well be reversed. However, speaking out of turn about Castro's personal life guaranteed would-be offenders banishment from the inner circle. Secrecy was the watchword, for political and personal reasons. "He was always very private," his sister Juanita told me in 2002, "very reserved about his personal problems and all that. He was not a bragger."

Reporters also paid a steep price for any incursion into what Castro deemed his zone of privacy. I learned this firsthand in March 2007, when I arrived at José Martí International Airport in Havana. As I had on several previous occasions, I arrived with a Cuban tourist visa. As a full-time reporter, I am allowed by the U.S. to travel to Cuba without restriction under the general license granted to journalists. But getting a Cuban *visa de prensa* can take months, even years, as requests make their way through Havana's *burro*-cracy. Rarely are visas outright denied; instead, reporters find themselves in a nonresponsive, limbo zone that can last years. Not surprisingly, reporters often resort to traveling as ordinary tourists. The *Miami Herald,* long denied a single visa, responds by sneaking reporters—usually young and relatively unknown ones who write without bylines—into Cuba.

During my twelve trips to the island, I sought to spend as much time as possible outside Havana, doing what could reasonably be called "tourist activities," while seeing firsthand how the majority lived. Several times, I drove to Oriente or Trinidad on Cuba's southeast belly or to Baracoa, where the lush beauty of the emerald-green island was first appreciated by Columbus when he landed there in 1492. If I wanted or needed to interview a government official, I would then apply for a press visa at the International Press Center on 23rd Street in Havana.

"*Mírame,*" the immigration official seated in the glass booth barked at me as I stepped forward. "Look at me." It is the customary rude greeting accorded to all visitors arriving in Cuba, not *"Bienvenido,"* or *"Wel-come."* The official then perused her computer for a standard check for scofflaws, would-be assassins, or enemies of the state. Cuba's airports and its Customs and Immigration are entirely under the control of the Ministry of Interior, known by its acronym MININT, for Cuban Intelligence.

In my twelve previous trips to Cuba, there had never been a problem. For this particular trip, I had even sent an e-mail informing the press officer and "ambassador" in the Cuban Interests Section, which substitutes for an embassy in Washington, of my plans and itinerary, after meeting with them a month earlier. The Customs official looked up at me and said, *"Espera allí"*—"Wait over there." While my two traveling companions were allowed entry, I was told to stay put.

For the next twelve hours I was detained in Havana's dreary, over-air-conditioned airport. With its harsh fluorescent lighting, mindless music, and blaring television sets, the José Martí terminal can feel like an over-size interrogation cell. Initially I was told that I had to remain on the Arrivals floor—outside Immigration Control and within sight of airport MININT officials and their adjoining office. I was also told I could not make a phone call or speak with other passengers. A chilly gloom descended upon me as one MININT official after another shrugged his shoulders. They would not confirm that I was on the *lista negra*—blacklist, saying only, *"No paso"*—that I could not pass through.

The following day, I was escorted onto a plane returning to Cancún, Mexico. Exhausted and feeling poorly from the frigid all-nighter, I was out about $5,000 for canceled flights, hotels, and car rentals. It was six months before I found out who had pulled the plug on me—and why. *"El problema es Fidel. No le gustó su libro,"* a senior official in the government told a mutual friend. "Fidel did not like her book," he said, referring to *Cuba Confidential,* which was published in late 2002. Curiously, Castro was disturbed not so much by the political material in the book as the personal revelations about him and his family, in a chapter entitled "Castro Family Values." *"Porque de unas cosas personales,"* the official said. "Because of the personal things." One issue was perhaps the mention of his illegitimate daughter, Panchita Pupo, not previously known even to some of his own children. The official added that the situation was above his pay grade to rectify. The word would have to come from *El Jefe* himself.

Many Cubaphiles were surprised to learn I had been barred. It was well known that Castro avidly read all the major news accounts of himself and his country. Certainly I had written my share of tough reporting since 1992. But I was also the co-author of one of his favorites: the *New York Times* series on the anti-Castro militant, Luis Posada Carriles. Indeed, Castro read several long excerpts from the articles aloud at the forty-fifth anniversary of the Revolution celebration in 1998 that was aired on Cuban television and radio.

I was hardly the first journalist to be booted off the island. Following Castro's precipitous decline in July 2006, foreign reporters were literally rounded up. Among them were the *New York Times'* Ginger Thompson, who, having heard a report on the radio that Castro had fallen ill, had come in on a tourist visa from Mexico. A week after she arrived, Cuban officials tracked her down at her central Havana hotel and escorted her to the airport. "They took me directly to Customs and Immigration," Thompson said, ensuring that she could not leave the airport. When Eugene Robinson of the *Washington Post* arrived, he was put on the next flight back to the States.

Even having a press visa is not a guarantee in a country where the laws and rules are elastic, subjective, and sometimes capriciously enforced. In 1998, David Adams of the *St. Petersburg Times* arrived in Havana with a *visa de prensa* in tow. It was his first trip since his 1995 series on prostitution in Havana had so infuriated the Ministry of the Interior that Adams had been put on the media blacklist. He had been denied a visa to cover the Pope's historic visit, along with Peter Katel of *Newsweek,* and several other reporters deemed to be offenders.

All was fine until Adams checked into his room at the Hotel Nacional. "I was awakened at about 2 a.m. by uniformed MININT officials," recalled Adams. "They told me to pack my bags." When Adams explained he had been granted a press visa and was in the country legally, one of the officers took his press visa and hotel registration card, tore up the latter, and said, "Not anymore." "I was told it was no good." He was then hustled back to the airport and sent home. In Adams's case, there had been a communication failure between MININT and the Ministry of Foreign Affairs (MINREX), which dispenses the visas. Later that year, he won back his press visa and was allowed to resume covering the island.

Incredibly, the Cuban government is quick to cry foul when their reporters are denied entry to the U.S. They did so in September 2008, when two reporters for Cuba's *Prensa Latina* news agency, Ilsa Rodríguez Santana and her husband, Tomás Granados Jiménez, who have covered the United Nations since 2005, were denied re-entry to the U.S. after visiting the island. In a letter to the president of the United Nations Correspondents Association, the two expressed their pique and "strongest protest against such an outrageous and arbitrary act, which violates all standards regarding relations between the UN and the United States as the host country." Soon after, the two received their visas back.

The double standard on "freedom to travel" seems not to trouble the Cubans. Indeed, as Castro's health declined, the vise on information grew tighter and tighter. A list of all foreign reporters known to cover Cuba was drafted—said to exceed six thousand names—and given to airport officials around the country. Cuban press visas became scarcer and more precious than getting a seat on Air Force One. Reporters lucky enough to wangle a visa, which normally involved months of lobbying, begging, and no small expense, became exceedingly cautious in their reporting. The government had taken off the gloves, achieving a discernible level of self-censorship among the foreign press. The result was not comparable to what they enjoyed domestically but succeeded in curbing negative stories while serving notice to would-be violators.

Reporters are hardly the sole recipients of government inhospitality. According to one Canadian travel agent, who requested anonymity, it is not uncommon for "one passenger per flight," usually a visiting Cuban-American, to be detained upon arrival. The hapless travelers are typically sent back home on the next flight, regardless of having valid visas. Humanitarian groups and human rights organizations are also subject to the government's capricious vetting. In April 2009, Cuba denied visas to the U.S. Commission on International Religious Freedoms for a long-planned visit. Noting that even Saudi Arabia and China had allowed visits from the group, the commission's chair, Felice Gaer, speculated whether "the Cuban government had something to hide."

While foreign reporters learn that they venture into coverage of the Castro family at their own peril, state-employed Cuban journalists regard the realm as inviolable. Castro's personal domain was so forbidden that it was not until 2003 that state-run television offered its first glimpse of Dalia Soto del Valle, Castro's paramour since 1961 and the mother of five of his sons.

Following the same pattern as his own father, who did not marry his mother until after she had borne him seven children, Castro reportedly did not marry Dalia until 1980. In fact, many in the *nomenklatura* claim that Castro never married Dalia, but rather made her his common-law wife. "That's why she is called *la mujer de Fidel* [Fidel's woman]," observed writer Achy Obejas, "never *la esposa* [the wife]. Remember, the important thing in Cuban culture is to be wife Number One," not the second or third wife. Mistresses are an accepted fact of life among Cuban men of Castro's generation, and are even regarded as indicators of one's status. "It's the level of discretion that's the operative factor," said Obejas.

Bizarrely, all five of Dalia's sons with Fidel were given names beginning with the letter A. Three eldest sons, in a blaze of narcissism, were named with variations on Fidel's revolutionary nom de guerre, Alejandro, Castro's tribute to and obsession with Alexander the Great. (Alejandro is also the name of one of Raúl Castro's sons.) Alexis, the eldest, was followed by Alexander in 1963. Antonio, an orthopedic surgeon, was born in 1969; Alejandro in 1971; and Ángel, the youngest, named for Castro's father, in 1974.

In domestic and personal matters, Castro was courtly and discreet, not unlike his conduct with foreign visitors. While he enjoyed a multitude of romantic liaisons, remarkably almost none of the women involved have sought to publicize or to exploit their relationship to him. It is a tribute to his character that he created sufficient goodwill among his many *amantes* that they have resisted profiting from the relationship. One such affair was reportedly with the Venezuelan journalist Isa Dobles, who in the early 1980s had her own talk show that aired right before the evening news on Cuban television called *Isa Da la Hora* (Isa Gives You the Time). It was joked that "she played chess with Fidel every evening," a fanciful cover for the duo, according to one *habanera* whose family worked in Cuban Intelligence. (By the 1980s, Castro rarely played chess, claiming that the game and its glacial pace bored him, notwithstanding his celebrated jousts with Bobby Fischer in 1965.) Despite the fact that the outspoken Isa had a falling-out with the Cuban leader and was said to have been unceremoniously escorted to the airport in 1992, she never wrote a kiss-and-tell memoir.

Indeed, only one paramour, Marita Lorenz, who had a brief fling with Castro in 1959 after meeting him on a cruise ship captained by her father, has sought to enrich herself from her experience. Lorenz claimed at one point that she was forced to abort a pregnancy by Castro but produced no evidence to support her tall tale. She went on to be an advisor to Oliver Stone for his film *JFK*.

One of the few incursions into the Castro domicile came from a onetime girlfriend of Antonio Castro, Dashiell Torralba, who packed off for Miami in 2002, taking some home videos with her. For a reported hundred thousand dollars, Channel 23, Miami's local Univision affiliate, broadcast her video footage of the Dalia-Fidel compound known as Punto Cero, or Point Zero. The four-bedroom, sprawling home is off-limits to the public, protected within a high-security zone near Calle 160 in the posh western suburb of Havana known as Siboney. Castro maintained numerous other residences in Havana—and throughout the island—but Punto Cero is the family compound. Included on the ersatz video was two minutes of Fidel Castro padding around in his pajamas having some soup. But the video disappointed Castro's harshest critics. "Dashiell Torralba showed the upper-middle-class home that Fidel Castro calls home and, to say the least, it was nothing to write home about," opined one blog. "There was no fancy swimming pool, servants waiting on the ruler, and other common amenities of the ruling class." Torralba, who later worked at Macy's in Miami, was charged with credit card fraud in 2007.

When I asked Castro in 1993 how many children he had, he demurred, then relented and said, with a wry smile, "casi un tribo"—almost a tribe. He was not dissembling. Altogether, he had ten children. Along with Fidelito and his five boys with Dalia Soto del Valle, Castro fathered at least four other children, the offspring of several infatuations.

While not a fulsomely affectionate father, Castro met his obligations and kept an eye—however distant and roving—on his ever-growing clan. He attended financially to all his offspring and saw to it that they had providential opportunities. However, he did not tolerate ostentatious public displays of privilege, conspicuous consumption, or incompetence. When his eldest son, Fidelito, who headed the Cuban Atomic Energy Commission from 1980 to 1992, mishandled Cuba's nuclear power program in the mid-1980s, Castro had him fired. "There was no resignation," Castro said at the time. "He was fired for incompetence. We don't have a monarchy here."

On another occasion, he turned his fury on his son Alejandro. In the early '90s, Castro had reintroduced tourism but had ordained that hotels be off-limits to Cubans. When he discovered that Alejandro had accepted an invitation from European friends to stay in a hotel in Varadero, Castro had the hotel's manager fired. According to Alejandro's former wife, who later moved to Spain, Castro's son was so distressed by the incident that he moved out of the family compound at Punto Cero.

Fidel Castro fathered another son with an admirer named Maria Laborde, whom he met soon after his release from prison in 1955. Jorge Ángel Castro Laborde, born in 1956, is by all accounts a likeable, unassuming fellow with an extended family of his own.

According to a relative of Celia Sánchez, Fidel's confidante, another Castro son was born in the early 1960s, the offspring of a brief affair.

He is not known outside of a small circle and has received no public attention. The child was also named Alejandro, but perhaps to differentiate him from Dalia's son, he was nicknamed Ciro for Ciro Redondo. (A revolutionary martyr who survived the doomed Moncada assault, Redondo fought and died in the Sierra. A city was named in his honor in the central province of Ciego de Ávila.) His namesake, said one friend who attended school with him, had movie-star looks, with vivid green eyes and a complexion darker than the other Castro siblings. Young Ciro went into sports medicine after studying physical education, married a minor official in Cuban tourism in the mid-1980s, and settled into a comfortable two-story home, just west of Miramar.

There have been other children cited as Fidel offspring—all unconfirmed by the government or Castro. In 2009, Cuban intelligence defector Roberto Hernández del Llano appeared on a Miami television program and claimed that Castro fathered a child with the wife of an important official. According to Hernández, Rosana Rodríguez, the wife of Abraham Masiques, had a son named Fito born around 1970, who was in fact Castro's child.

Another child, Francisca (Panchita) Pupo, born in 1956, is Castro's daughter from a brief liaison with a woman from Santa Clara. "Lidia and Raúl looked after her in Cuba," said a family friend. "But she was never part of the inner circle." Pupo was given permission to move to Miami in 1998, where she has lived quietly and teaches school. She also enjoys a friendship with Juanita Castro, the only Castro sibling to break publicly with Fidel and the Revolution, fleeing in 1964. "I have been a guerrilla here in Miami," she joked. "Panchita's mother married a man who raised her," explained Juanita, who functions as the Castro family matriarch in Miami, "but Fidel took care of her support in Cuba. She is not bitter. She does not speak against Fidel. . . . After all, he is her father."

Most famously there is Alina Fernández, the daughter of the aristocratic beauty Natalia Revuelta. Fernández fled Cuba in 2003 and wrote a dishy, fierce memoir about life as Fidel's illegitimate child. Some in the Castro clan, including Juanita, suggest that Fidel is not Alina's father. Efraim Conte, a nephew of Celia Sánchez, seconded the notion, saying that Castro had made clear his belief to the Sánchez family that he was not the father of Alina. Others argue that there is sufficient resemblance between the two and point out that Castro would not have financially supported her if he had believed otherwise. Doubters, like the family of Celia Sánchez (who had an adversarial relationship with Alina's mother) and Juanita, believe that Castro did not dispute paternity in deference to Revuelta, who stayed behind and resolutely supported the Revolution.

But of all the women in his life, the relationship between Castro and Myrta Díaz-Balart, the mother of his first child, was the most pivotal. From their first meeting at the University of Havana in 1946, the relationship was fraught with passion, politics, and conflict. The ill will that would stem from the Castro–Díaz-Balart split not only poisoned relations between the two families, but played a remarkable role in the fifty-year stalemate between Cuba and the United States. One could well think of the Castro–Díaz-Balart saga as the House of Atreus or a Hispanic variant of the Hatfields and McCoys or simply as a five-decade running telenovela.

A beautiful philosophy student, Myrta was the daughter of a politically powerful family from Banes, a postage-stamp-sized town in Oriente that served as headquarters for the United Fruit Company. Myrta's father, Rafael, a well-connected lawyer who represented United Fruit, was also the friend and neighbor of an ambitious army colonel named Fulgencio Batista. After Batista seized power in a coup in 1952, he rewarded the Díaz-Balarts with two ministries. Myrta's father became Minister of Transportation and Communications, while her brother, also named Rafael, won the coveted appointment of Deputy Minister of the Interior (then known as Gobernación) responsible for intelligence, security matters, and the secret police. When his first child, Lincoln Díaz-Balart (the future congressman of Miami), was born, Rafael asked Batista and his wife, Marta Fernández, to be the child's godparents. Indeed, they waited until 1958 when the boy was four; the baptism was held at Batista's garish country estate, Finca Kukine.

Until Batista's coup, the younger Rafael had been Fidel Castro's good friend—so close that he had introduced his sister Myrta to him and stayed with them during part of their honeymoon in Miami. But Castro's sneak assault on the Moncada Barracks irreparably wounded his wife's family. Castro had ramped up a family feud over politics into a war with his in-laws. Initially, Myrta broke with her own family to support her husband, only to be told her sacrifices were insufficient. But Castro's pride was such that when he discovered that Myrta's brother had provided her with a meager government stipend, he turned against her, citing the paltry sum as an insidious attack on his honor. "I am ready to challenge my own brother-in-law to a duel at any time," he wrote one correspondent from prison in 1954. "It is the reputation of my wife and my honor as a revolutionary that is at stake. Do not hesitate: strike back and have no mercy, I would rather be killed a thousand times over than helplessly suffer such an insult!"

More than three decades of estrangement would follow. In late 1954, in the midst of their acrimonious divorce, Myrta left for the United States with five-year-old Fidelito, seeking reprieve and distance from her enraged spouse. Castro vowed to fight until death to win custody of his son. "I lose my head when I think of these things," he wrote his sister Lidia. "I will be free one day. They will have to return my son and my honor, even if the earth shall be destroyed [in the process]." Myrta got her divorce and initially retained custody. But Castro made it clear to his sister that he would never give up his claim. "If they think they can exhaust my patience, and that I am going to concede, they are going to find that I am wrapped in Buddhist tranquility and am prepared to re-enact the famous Hundred Years War—and win it!" Castro was successful—taking sole custody of his son in 1959, as part of the spoils of ousting Batista and seizing power. Myrta went into exile with her new family, in Madrid, Spain. "She would have loved to have got [Fidelito] out of Cuba," said her childhood friend, Barbara Walker Gordon.

Fidelito attended university in the Soviet Union—matriculating with a PhD in physics, and then traveled extensively. During this period, Myrta would have regular contact with her son, visiting with him on his trips to Europe. "They used to see each other all the time because he represented Cuba at meetings around the world," said Gordon. "He would fly into Madrid and have her come up and meet him whenever he was at a scientific meeting." On occasion, Myrta flew to various European cities for private rendezvous with her son, who sometimes brought his own children. She also began to make quiet, discreet trips to Havana. But in the early '90s, the visits came to a halt after father and son had a dispute.

In 1999, Myrta fretted to Barbara Gordon that it had been almost eight years since she had seen her son, although they communicated by phone and letter. "She was beside herself," said Gordon. "She hasn't been able to go back to Cuba. . . . It all has to do with this thing about [Fidelito] being under house arrest," referring to the falling-out between Fidel and his eldest son concerning alleged mismanagement of the nuclear reactor program headed by Fidelito. "She was very concerned about her grandchildren and her son," Gordon told me at the time. "She said, 'Don't ever say anything' She didn't want anything to interfere with her going to Cuba or having a relationship with her son. Because if anything got out, Fidel could make a fuss."

In 2000, Raúl Castro brokered a reconciliation between his prideful brother, Fidel's eldest son, and Myrta. "Raúl is the best one for her," Gordon said. "She told me that herself: 'He's the one who's taking care of my situation.'" The father-son relationship was further smoothed out when the academically inclined Fidelito assumed another position as a senior researcher and professor at the Cuban Academy of Sciences.

From 2002 onward, Myrta began spending a good deal of time in Havana with Fidelito and his family and back in the embrace of the Castro family. (Fidelito's eldest daughter, Myrta Castro Smirnova, born in 1975, is named for his mother; his eldest son, Fidel Antonio Castro Smirnov, born in 1980, is named for his father. Both are the children of his Russian-born first wife. Fidelito has three children, as well, with his second wife, the daughter of a general in the Cuban Army.)

Myrta's visits to the island infuriated her own family, the Díaz-Balarts, who had established themselves as players in Miami's politics, and deepened their mutual estrangement. So unthinkable were her long stays in Havana that her brother Rafael (until his death) and his sons, Mario and Lincoln, both congressmen from Miami, refused to acknowledge them. By 2007, Myrta was reportedly spending more time in Havana than Madrid, nestled in a comfortable home in Miramar arranged for her by Raúl Castro. Lourdes García-Navarro, a reporter for National Public Radio, is Myrta's niece through Myrta's second husband, Emilio Núñez Blanco, who died in 2006. Not long after, she saw her famously press-shy aunt in Havana. "She is as pleasant and friendly as an aunt would be," said García-Navarro. "But she's wary around reporters."

Indeed, her sojourns in Cuba could be seen as a final trophy for Castro. In a rare exception to Castro family privacy policy, Cuba released a photograph of a radiant-looking Myrta with her well-groomed, handsome son at the inauguration of the Nanoscience/Nanotechnology Summit in late 2008.

"I think she was the great passion of Fidel's life," said a former Castro mistress. Another friend recalled a dinner in which Castro shared a dream he had had about being with a princess, who appeared to be Myrta, leading her to conclude that "the love of his life has always been Myrta [because] she was the love of his youth."

Fidel Castro had never been especially sentimental about his birthday. Indeed, a few have questioned whether Castro was actually born in 1926—as he has claimed—or one year later, in 1927, a date suggested by a comment from his older brother, Ramón. Most scholars have opted for the earlier year, the date endorsed by his younger sister, Juanita. His mother vividly recalled her son coming into the world in the wee hours of August 13 at two in the morning, "Punto" she said— on the dot. From the gate, he was a handful: a larger-than-life baby, he sprang from the womb at twelve pounds.

While never fussing about his birthday, Castro relished the annual distress the date caused his estranged nephew, Lincoln Díaz-Balart. The Florida congressman, who is among Castro's most bellicose enemies, has the misfortune of having the same August 13 birthday. Notwithstanding his unsentimental nature, Castro knew that every year that he lived wreaked humiliation on his foes in Washington and Miami. To that end, plans for his eightieth birthday bash in 2006 had assumed the magnitude of a New Orleans' Mardi Gras monthlong blowout party.

But as Castro told me in 1994, "There are times when we really cannot be the masters of our own destinies." And so it was that Castro was confined to intensive care and his meticulously planned birthday festivities had to be scotched. Scores of foreign leaders and celebrities canceled their plans to jet into Havana for what had promised to be a star-studded, weeklong gala.

Instead, Castro spent his birthday in his hospital bed, an invalid connected to a drip of nutrients and antibiotics. A brief video was released of his brother Raúl and his Venezuelan protégé, Hugo Chávez, presenting a wan-looking Castro with a portrait of himself. Feeling it necessary to confirm the Maximum Leader's viability, *Granma* published photographs of him holding a telephone with a copy of the broadsheet dated the previous day, August 12. The photographic evidence was accompanied by a grim statement from the ailing leader: "I ask you all to be optimistic, and at the same time to be ready to face any adverse news."

It was a far cry from his seventy-fifth birthday, which he had also spent with Chávez. In 2001, a robust Castro celebrated his birthday with a champagne party in Caracas, while Chávez crooned "Happy Birthday." Then the swashbuckling duo—the oil sultan of Latin America and the Cuban ruler-for-life—embarked on a nautical tour of Venezuela's rain forests in Chávez's cabin cruiser.

Castro's birthday five years later was a cheerless affair. Returning to Venezuela after the 2006 birthday, Chávez spoke emotionally about his visit with his friend: "Fidel told me, 'Chávez, I already lived my epoch, I can die. I'm free to die, not you. You are a slave of life, don't let them kill you.'" Added the Venezuelan leader: "It will be a slow recovery because of the type of illness, which was serious at one point." Chávez's unscripted and unintentionally pessimistic remarks caused consternation in Havana, and not for the last time. Thereafter, Chávez was instructed to limit his comments to upbeat, alive-and-well assessments: the straight spin. A few weeks later, he insisted that Castro was having a rapid recovery. "He already sits up, writes, he has a phone, he gives orders, instructions," Chávez told his viewers on his regular Sunday television show.

But Chávez's account was belied by Castro's failure to appear at the Non-Aligned Movement Summit on September 11, 2006. Castro had spent precious political capital to win the privilege of hosting the NAM Summit, which functions somewhat like a Third World NATO for 118 countries. A few days before the summit, an event Castro hoped would burnish Cuba's image on the world stage, the government released a letter from him: "It can be affirmed that the most critical moment [of this illness] is behind me," Castro wrote with unusual candor and brevity. "Today, I recover at a satisfactory pace."

In time for the summit, a new billboard popped up around the island proclaiming, "Fidel Is a Country." No longer was Castro merely *Número Uno, El Jefe,* or *El Caballo*—now he was the very earth of Cuba. The billboards "seemingly appeared overnight," noted the Associated Press, "and have remained since then, suggesting that an entire nation of Fidel faithful will carry on his revolution after he's gone."

As befitted the world's longest-reigning non-monarch, Castro declared that his eightieth birthday would be rescheduled and celebrated on December 2, 2006. The date neatly dovetailed with the fiftieth anniversary of the landing of the *Granma,* the ship that carried Castro and his compatriots back from exile in Mexico to battle Fulgencio Batista. Castro hoped he would be reasonably fit and ambulatory by then, at least to make a public appearance, if only to wave to the crowd.

Expectations were high—and foreign dignitaries again queued up for the big event. A select cadre of reporters, fortunate enough to survive the capricious vetting by the Ministry of the Interior, were awarded visas and allowed to fly in. The celebrations centered on an elaborate military parade along the Malecón, Havana's oceanside boulevard.

The march was to culminate in a dramatic comeback appearance by Castro, who had prepared a speech to mark the occasion. As the procession began, one American television news producer was assured by high-ranking government officials "that Fidel was going to appear." In fact, she was told that "a special ambulance with a back brace had been imported from Canada"—a plank of sorts that would raise Castro and support him while he addressed the crowd.

Politburo and government officials were told to be in place at the parade site by 7 a.m. But as the celebrations concluded, Fidel had yet to be spotted. Finally, at the last moment, Raúl Castro rose to deliver the keynote speech—greeted by subdued applause. Muffled whispers spread through the restless crowd as it became clear that *El Comandante* was too ill to even attend.

One senior official later complained that he had been instructed to get up at 4 a.m. in order to be at the parade site on time. "And then, *El Viejo* didn't show up!" he lamented to friends. Castro's failure to make his highly touted appearance was a last-minute decision, leaving his handlers in the Ministry of Foreign Affairs scrambling with how to spin it. Castro later issued a note of regret explaining that he was "in no condition, according to the doctors, to face such a colossal gathering."

On October 21, 2006, a fresh blaze of rumors that Castro was near death, engulfed Havana and quickly raced around the globe. Some insisted that Castro was, in fact, already dead. Curiously, the date happened to be the fiftieth anniversary of the death of Castro's own father, Ángel. Fidel's illness, in fact, had a stark precedent in his family. His father had also suffered from intestinal troubles, and had died at the age of eighty of an ulcerated hernia. The ulceration had led to the same deadly infection, peritonitis, that had put the eighty-year-old Fidel in such peril.

Castro had a somewhat fraught relationship with his father. Ángel Castro had been born to an impoverished family in Galicia, Spain. At the turn of the century, he had come to Oriente, Cuba, as a young conscript to fight for Spain. Smitten with the lush tropical island, he returned when he was thirty years old determined to carve out a better life for himself. A *guajiro macho*—or what could be called a hick from the sticks— Ángel fell in love with the New World. He began by farming sugarcane on land leased from the United Fruit Company, land Ángel would later purchase. Through decades of ceaseless labor, the rough-hewn Castro became a wealthy *latifundista* and one of the largest landowners in Holguín Province. Eventually he amassed a thirty-thousand-acre spread, including forests, several streams, a sawmill, and a nickel mine. Almost all of Birán, including the few stores in town, was his.

According to Fidel, his father, like his mother, did not become fully literate until adulthood. In one letter to his father in 1948, Fidel reminds the elder Castro that "you must place a postage stamp on the letter," advising him how and where to write him: "my address is above on the left-hand side." Juanita Castro pointed out that "the personali[ties] of Fidel and my father are very similar. I remember my father as austere, reserved, strong character . . . [and] not expressive."

Fidel's mother, Lina Ruz, was the third of seven children whose parents had left the western province of Pinar del Río to resettle in Camagüey. As a young teenager, Lina Ruz took employment as a live-in domestic at the Castro *finca* in Birán, one hundred miles further east.

It was not long before the high-spirited, good-humored Lina attracted the interest of its *dueño*, Don Ángel. Ángel's wandering eye alighted on the teenaged Lina Ruz while he was married to María Luisa Argota, a schoolteacher and the mother of his two children, Lidia and Pedro Emilio.

Infidelity is as Cuban as sugarcane, and for several years, Ángel Castro juggled two families. For a period, both families lived on the vast grounds of Ángel's hacienda with Lina's children raised in a *casita*—a small house—on the grounds.

Ángel Castro was as hard-living as he was hard-working, indulging in occasional trysts that produced at least one other son. In 2006, the South Florida *Sun-Sentinel*'s Ray Sanchez reported on the existence of Castro's half-brother, who had never before been publicly acknowledged. Martín Castro, born in 1930, is four years younger than Fidel but two years older than Raúl. He is the son of Don Ángel and a young farmhand who worked for him named Generosa Mendoza. The amiable Martín lives where he was born—down the road from the Castro family *finca* in Birán.

"The dirty little secret of old Oriente," said Manzanillo native Eduardo Santiago, who left for Miami in 1969, "was multiple marriages or what others would call polygamy." Common-law marriage and adultery *en el campo* were hardly unusual. In the countryside of Oriente during much of the twentieth century, according to Santiago, the query *"Cómo está la mujer?"* or "How is your wife?" was often answered with another query: *"Cuál de ellas?"* or "Which one?"

Fidel Castro would follow a pattern similar to that of his father: marrying two women, the second after the birth of five children—while navigating through scores of lesser liaisons and siring a few illegitimate offspring. In this respect, he was his father's son.

Unlike Fidel, however, Ángel Castro recognized only his children with Lina Ruz and María Argota, the two women he married. In a 1939 letter to his brother Gonzalo Pedro Castro, who arrived with him in Cuba but went on to Argentina, he wrote, "My dear brother . . . I have turned 64. May God allow me a few more [years] to raise my kids; I have 9 [four boys and five girls]."

At some point in the 1930s, María Argota left Ángel's ever-expanding *hacienda,* with her children in tow, and moved to Santiago. She eventually settled in Havana. It was not until 1941 that Ángel and María Argota were actually divorced, despite the fact that divorce had been legal in Cuba since 1918. Weeks after getting his divorce, Ángel became a Cuban citizen.

It was another two years before Lina, with the help of Ángel's fellow Spaniard, Enrique Pérez Serantes (the bishop of Camagüey and later the archbishop of Santiago), was able to convince her stubborn lover to submit to a church wedding. The helpful priest also baptized Lina's brood, all of whom were born out of wedlock. By the time Pérez Serantes married the couple in December 1943, Lina had borne Ángel seven children, between the ages of five and twenty.

Although there was resentment between Ángel's two wives, it did not spill over to their children. For many years, Fidel's closest sisterly relationship was with his half-sibling Lidia, who was unceasingly devoted to him until her death. Lidia also remained close with her mother and bridged the relationship between her and Fidel. In a November 1954 letter, Fidel Castro asked Lidia to pass on "greetings to your mom." María Argota passed away in Havana in the early 1960s.

Lina Ruz evolved into a formidable woman: high-spirited, good-humored, and a ceaseless worker. Castro's signature inheritance from his parents was their ferocious work ethic. Lina was also a superb horsewoman and an excellent shot. But she was not a woman of culture. Nor did her sons develop more than a cursory interest in Cuba's fine arts. The culture exception in the family was Fidel's half-brother Pedro Emilio, whose mother, María Argota, was an educated woman.

After the Revolution, Pedro Emilio worked as a low-level official in the Foreign Ministry, but he never enjoyed the close relationship that Fidel had with Lidia. According to Alina Fernández, Pedro Emilio, a poet and classicist, had told her that he earned Fidel's loathing because "I am a rhyme maker, something that my half-brother considers a sure trait of weak, good-for-nothing types." Fidel may have forgiven older brother Ramón for his political apathy, Pedro Emilio pointed out, "but he will continue to despise me all his life."

"Fidel Castro is the son of a servant with his father," said Father Amado Llorente, Castro's favorite high school teacher at the Belén School. "So he hated [proper] society. He spoke to me about his mother not being the mother of the first two children of his father and this was difficult and complicated for him. . . . This was always a shadow over his life."

Ángel Castro recognized his own defiant, belligerent streak in Fidel—causing the two to clash on occasion. But he also recognized that Fidel was exceptional. He saw to it that Fidel attended the finest Jesuit schools in Santiago and Havana, assuring him entry into Cuban society and politics. Castro's good friend at the time, Luis Conte Agüero, recalled meeting Ángel Castro in Havana, and the aging gallego confiding in him, "Fidel is my favorite son."

When Fidel married the pretty and politically well-connected Myrta Díaz-Balart, Ángel paid for the couple's extravagant honeymoon in Miami. The newlyweds then traveled north by train to New York, where they enjoyed a suite at the posh Waldorf-Astoria on Park Avenue. Until his death, Ángel generously assisted Fidel financially.

In May 1955, Fidel and Raúl were released from the Isla de Pinos (Isle of Pines) Prison, their fifteen-year sentence for attacking the Moncada garrison having been reduced to less than two years due to a government amnesty. Raúl immediately returned home for a weeklong visit with their parents in Birán. "When Fidel was a prisoner, Dad suffered much during those two years," recalled Juanita. "Fidel promised to go [visit], but he never did." Ángel wrote presciently that he worried he would not see his rebel-leader son again.

In the 1990s, Fidel began to speak publicly about his father. In July 1992, Castro visited his father's family home in the small village of Láncara in northern Spain, following a summit in Madrid. "My father always wanted to return here," said an unusually expansive Castro, after having a few drinks at a city hall ceremony. "It took sixty years for me to fulfill his wish." In 1996, two days after his seventieth birthday, Fidel visited his birthplace and family home and spoke emotionally about growing up in Birán. He returned again after his seventy-fifth birthday. A tall, framed photograph of his father looking very much like the *guajiro* that he was—wearing a white *guayabera* and sombrero—was installed in his private office around the same time.

Soon after, Fidel committed the resources to establish his family home, Finca Manacas, as a historical site. The original two-story structure, built upon wooden pilings to allow cattle and horses to graze underneath, had burned down in 1954. It is unclear what prompted the fire, but the torching of sugar plantations and their homes by rebel soldiers was common during this period. A replica of the original building was built several years later. Visitors and tourists, who receive permission and tickets from the Holguín authorities, are now allowed to explore the property. Previously, the town of Birán had been erased from Cuban maps. Castro's childhood home appeared to be a case where his fiercely held personal privacy ultimately gave way to professional and familial pride.

On May Day 2007, Castro missed marching in the annual parade of workers for the first time in forty years. In June 2007, Castro's absence from the state funeral for Vilma Espín, Raúl's wife of forty-eight years, triggered a fresh wave of hushed whispers. Not only had Espín known Fidel since the late 1950s, she had served as Cuba's First Lady since the beginning of the Revolution. Nor did he appear—even to wave—at the October 8, 2007, festivities in Santa Clara, commemorating the fortieth anniversary of Che's capture.

And so it went: Castro, the movie-star dictator whose passion for the world stage was second to none, was too ill for a final curtain call, much less an encore. Instead, carefully staged photo ops or snippets of videotape with friendly leftist leaders like Chávez, Bolivia's *campesino* president Evo Morales, and Brazil's president Lula da Silva would be periodically released by the Foreign Ministry. The strategy was three-fold: to keep the baying press wolves at bay, to reward Cuba's socialist allies with the privilege of a photo op with *El Jefe,* and to provide Castro with a way of keeping his hand in the political pie.

There would be brief footage of Castro chatting with Wu Guan-zheng, a senior member of China's Communist Party, in April 2007, and two months later, a quickie video clip of his meeting with Vietnam-ese Communist Party chief Nong Duc Manh. Later in the year, Angola's president José Eduardo Dos Santos stepped up to the camera and gave the obligatory report that Castro was doing swimmingly well.

Castro regarded Angola as an ally—and a triumph for Cuba. He had committed fifty thousand troops to fight in Angola's civil war through-out the 1980s. At least five thousand Cubans had died, perhaps many more, with an untold number of wounded. But they had won their war, a victory cherished by Castro and credited by Nelson Mandela as being crucial to South Africa's subsequent liberation. The state-run weekly, *Juventud Rebelde,* ran a photo of the ailing Castro shaking hands with Dos Santos, who then delivered the requisite good news. "I saw him [Castro] recovering; he's strong, with good enthusiasm."

The pattern continued through 2009: periodic unannounced brief visits like Chile's Michelle Bachelet's drop-in at the end of February, another pow-wow with Evo Morales, and what was described as a "rev-olutionary lovefest," with three U.S. legislators from the Congressional Black Caucus in April. Just enough photo ops to maintain the illusion that the hemisphere's most famous strongman remained, well, strong.

While Fidel remained an ideological isolationist, Raúl Castro had slowly metamorphosed from rigid hardliner to relative pragmatist, advocating incremental reforms of the economy and other sectors. Consequently Raúl had come to represent a modicum of change to ordinary Cubans, struggling in their "lives of quiet desperation." But it struck many that every opening Raúl sought was quickly closed by his ailing brother—sometimes the very next day.

Throughout 2007, the brothers' sibling rivalry began to look increasingly more Oedipal—with Fidel undermining Raúl's authority at every other turn. In his scores of "Reflections," published in *Granma*, Fidel rarely mentioned Raúl but lavished praise upon Hugo Chávez, whom he sometimes called *"mi hermano."* "Fidel has subverted Raúl at every point," said one former Cuban diplomat in May 2007, who lamented that "he cannot do anything while Fidel is alive." When Raúl signaled an openness to negotiation with the United States early in his brother's illness, Fidel nixed the idea in his "Reflections" days later.

In what was widely viewed at the time as a blow to his brother, Castro installed Ramiro Valdés as the head of the newly minted Ministry of Information and Communications, with a vast mandate to manage all information technologies. One of the original *moncadistas,* Valdés was a full-throated hardliner who had served as the much-feared Minister of the Interior in the 1960s. He had retired from the Council of State in 1997, purportedly having fallen afoul of Raúl Castro. However, Valdés's 2006 appointment was just the beginning of a triumphant return to power, along with a robust reconciliation with Raúl. His reappearance also presaged the ascent of hardliners and *históricos,* those whose résumés included having fought in the Sierra with the Castros.

The battle lines were becoming apparent. On one side were men like Valdés, José Ramón Machado Ventura, and Juan Esteban Lazo Hernández, and the leadership of the Communist Party, also known as dinosaurs, or *talibanes.* On the other side were the so-called Reformers or Pragmatists, notably Council of State vice president Carlos Lage and Fernando Remírez de Esteñoz, chief of international affairs for the Communist Party and a member of the Secretariat. More often than not, Fidel tipped the scales in favor of the hardliners and *históricos,* favoring them to be the guardians of the state's institutions, which in turn would devotedly protect the Castros and their legacy. "While Castro knows that his regime must introduce some reforms if it is to survive, his sympathies lie with the *duros,* the hardliners," Edward Gonzalez wrote presciently in a 1996 RAND report for the U.S. secretary of defense. "He remains opposed to fundamental system change, in part for personal reasons—among them his strong aversion to capitalism [and] his fear that any dismantling of 'Cuban socialism' will tarnish his unique place in history."

In June 2008, Castro protested that he was *not* stirring the pot or fomenting intrigues. "I am not now, nor will I ever be, at the head of any group or faction. Therefore, it can't follow that there is infighting in the Party," Castro wrote in his column, composing the necessary fiction. In fact, he was in the final battle of an ideological war that he had waged for fifty years.

For his "Reflections" column at the end of May 2007, the Maximum Leader set aside his usual weighty concerns, such as imperialism, the threats posed by George W. Bush, and the like. Instead, Castro did something without precedent: he wrote about his own precarious medical situation. With unexpected and considerable candor, he confirmed much of what was published in the *El País* story.

> I shall digress now to tackle a topic which deals with my person, and I ask for your indulgence. . . . My compatriots were not too happy that I explained on more than one occasion that my recovery would not be without its risks. Generally speaking, there was talk about a date when I would make a public appearance, dressed in my olive green fatigues as usual. *Well then, it was not just one operation but several. Initially, it was not successful and this meant a prolonged recovery period.*
>
> For many months, I relied on intravenous procedures and catheters for the greater part of my nutrition, and I wanted to spare our people an unpleasant disappointment. Today I receive everything required by my recovery orally. There is no danger greater than that related to age and to a state of health which I abused during some of the hazardous times I lived through. Nowadays I do what I should be doing, especially reflecting and writing about issues which, to my mind, have some importance and transcendence. I have a lot pending. For the present, I do not have time for films and photographs that require me to constantly trim my hair, beard and moustache, and to get dressed up every day. . . . Let me simply say to everyone that my health has been improving and my weight is stable at around 80 kilos. . . . The rest of the time I am reading, receiving information, talking on the phone with many comrades and carrying out the rehab exercises that are necessary for my recovery. I cannot say or criticize everything that I know. . . . But I shall be true to the motto of never writing a lie.
>
> Fidel Castro Ruz
> 5:06 p.m. May 23, 2007

Two weeks later, Castro gave his first television interview since his surgeries in 2006 with Randy Alonso, the host of Cuba's *Mesa Redonda*. In a fifty-two-minute rambling session with his friendly interlocutor, a frail-looking Castro made the preposterous claim that the status of his health and recent surgeries had never been "a state secret."

A few weeks later, cheerleader Hugo Chávez dangled the idea of a surprise recovery. "Fidel keeps his uniform there and he looks out of the corner of his eye," Chávez told reporters after a visit with his friend. "I think we are approaching the hour when he will wear his military uniform again."

"I can say that I have enjoyed a certain privilege—like people who live to be one hundred," Castro told me in 1994, "not because anybody planned it but because of an accident of nature." Without doubt, Castro had been blessed with more than his share of luck. But as a consummate micromanager, he took pains to limit accidents—political and medical. Castro's refusal to leave the stage was hardly unique within the *caudillo* tradition.

In many ways, his personal style and autocratic rule were not dissimilar to that of Francisco Franco, Spain's brutal dictator of almost forty years. Both hailed from the rugged northern countryside of Galicia, Spain, a region renowned for its fierce and stubborn citizenry. "He is a Galician—*un gallego*," Castro's Belén schoolteacher, Father Amado Llorente, reminded me in 2002, emphasizing Fidel's father's birthplace. "A Cuban would already be tired of being in power. But not a *gallego* for whom it's 'until death,' just like Franco." Notwithstanding divergent political ideologies—Franco was a zealous anticommunist—the two men had a good deal in common. Both were willing to forge unpalatable and unpopular alliances with totalitarian states to shore up their power: Franco with Nazi Germany and Castro with the Soviet Union, patronage deeply resented by most Cubans.

There were other startling parallels. Franco's protracted, shrouded last days neatly foreshadowed Castro's. While Franco suffered from heart disease, his death was precipitated by peritonitis and sepsis, the same blood infection that delivered Castro to death's precipice on more than one occasion.

Franco first became grievously ill in 1974, and was forced to turn over his rule—"temporarily," he insisted—to Prince Juan Carlos. Like Castro, who initially only temporarily ceded control to his brother, Franco seemed to recover before succumbing to his final illness a year later. The Spanish government announced that Franco had died on November 20,

1975, at the age of eighty-two. It was a date that resonated with symbolism, being the day that José Antonio Primo de Rivera, the founder of Franco's fascist Falange Party, had been executed in 1936.

However, it is generally believed that Franco actually died days earlier. Another theory posits that doctors kept him alive under orders that Franco not leave his mortal coil until November 20. Franco's meddling with fate—stemming from his hope to leave this world with gravity and splendor—backfired and became the fodder of farce. His reluctant departure became a joke that would well outlive him. "Generalissimo Francisco Franco is still dead," Chevy Chase would intone with mock solemnity on the hit television show *Saturday Night Live*, as a running gag for the next year. Fidel Castro's long dying would prove equally compelling for late-night comedians.

Castro's attenuated leaving also wreaked havoc among journalists and news editors, as I could personally attest. The veteran war correspondent Martha Gellhorn found herself in a similar pickle three decades earlier. Gellhorn covered the Spanish Civil War with Ernest Hemingway and later married him. She wrote to her son in November 1975 that she had accepted an assignment from *New York* magazine to write "a huge piece" about post-Franco Spain. "This thrills me, the sort of journalism I love," she said. However, there was a problem, presaging the dilemma of legions of flummoxed reporters in 2006. "I am waiting for the old swine to die; but obviously he is being kept breathing (no more) while the Right tightens its hold on the country."

In 1968, Portugal's ruler-for-life, Antonio de Oliveira Salazar, slid out of his chair in his summer home, hit his head, and suffered a massive stroke. Although he was non compos mentis and required a ventilator to breathe until his death two years later, Salazar believed he was still running his country as he had since 1932. Dubbed the "dean of dictators" by *Time* magazine in 1945, Salazar presided over the Estado Novo ("New State"), the authoritarian right-wing party that he founded, which controlled every aspect of life in Portugal. Castro had similar aspirations with *El Nuevo Hombre*—his "New Man" initiative launched in the 1960s that sought to inject a socialist-soldier-citizen ideal into the Cuban consciousness.

Not unlike their peers in Cuba, Salazar's cabinet officials were too terrified by the remote prospect of a miraculous recovery to retreat too far from any of Salazar's policies. In the case of the Portuguese strongman, Salazar was, for all intents and purposes, brain dead. "He began by ruling without a heart and ended up ruling without a brain," wrote the journalist Carlos Alberto Montaner. "I fear that, in Castro's case,

history will repeat itself. . . . He is obeyed through fear, through iner-
tia. . . . That's what *caudillismo* is all about." Indeed, as long as his syn-
apses were firing, Castro let it be known, his would be the final word.

Authoritarian regimes are famously opaque about the final days of
departing rulers-for-life. The Soviets waited a week before announcing
the death of Leonid Brezhnev in 1982. Likewise the death of Tito, the
Yugoslavian leader, was prophesied for years and was a cliff-hanger for
months, before he finally passed on in 1980.

Castro was an avid reader and amateur historian and had studied the
final days of all the world's great players from Julius Caesar onward.
He decided that he would direct all matters of Cuba for as long as
blood was pumping to his brain. After all, he had commanded a revolutionary insurgency while a prisoner in solitary confinement, fifty years
earlier. Running the country from his commodious convalescent suite,
he assured himself, was simply another challenge.

It was whispered throughout 2006 that Castro's spouse Dalia and
other family members had asked him to resign as commander in chief
to concentrate solely on his health. They were not alone. Even some in
the government and Party mumbled the same—and not out of consideration of Castro's health alone. Many in the *nomenklatura* believed
that Raúl would be more pragmatic and less ideological than his stubborn brother and hence, more inclined to implement vitally needed
reforms.

But as the months turned to years, Castro could not bring himself
to resign, notwithstanding his counsel to journalist Lee Lockwood in
1965: "All of us should retire relatively young." In December of 2007,
he wrote that he still believed that "My elemental duty is not to cling
to positions, or even less to obstruct the path of younger people." However, he dashed any such hopes for a graceful exit, suggesting instead
that he would follow in the footsteps of the celebrated Brazilian architect Oscar Niemeyer, who continued to work at age one hundred. "I
think like Niemeyer, that you have to be of consequence up to the end,"
he opined.

When I asked Castro in 1994 when he would retire, he snapped, "My
vocation is the Revolution. I am a revolutionary, and revolutionaries
do not retire," then added, "any more than writers." Castro laughed,
pleased with his quip, but he was less sanguine when I quoted Thomas
Jefferson's admonition: "A revolution every twenty years." Wagging his
index finger, Cuban-style, he said he disagreed. "I think it is better to
have one every three hundred years. Life needs to renew itself," he said.

Castro went on to speak about himself as if he had been dispatched to Cuba by the gods. "I am not here because I have assigned myself to this job for a lengthy period of time," he said. "I am here because this job has been thrust upon me, which is not the same thing." As he spoke he seemed to convince himself of what he was saying.

On August 13, 2007, Castro's eighty-first birthday, Cuba's state media soberly reported that Castro's condition was "stable" and that he remained an active participant in the affairs of the country. Notwithstanding the report, his birthday was a gloomy affair for the star patient and all concerned. Indeed, no one believed the government.

Havana was buzzing about a bombshell story published a day earlier in *Reforma,* Mexico's leading daily. The page-one story contended that Castro had undergone another series of operations a month earlier—and was once again fighting off another round of peritonitis. One senior diplomat in Havana said the operations hopefully would prolong Castro's life, but doctors had no illusions that they would cure him. *El Comandante* continued to lose weight, the newspaper reported, and was no longer seeing visitors or deemed capable of taking long walks.

Certainly Castro was experiencing a challenging time. Not even Hugo Chávez went to Havana to celebrate his birthday as planned. Some pundits noted Castro's failure to call in to Chávez's weekly TV show a week earlier, as had been announced. Filling in for him was Carlos Lage, the executive secretary of the Council of Ministers. More telling were the unusually candid comments of Mariela Castro Espín, Raúl's daughter. A noted sexologist, who has played an increasingly public role since Castro's illness, Mariela seemed to suggest the end was near. "The concern that we all had about losing our leader," she said, "is now closer to us."

Toward the end of August 2007, newspapers in Colombia and Bolivia published stories citing military sources in Cuba who claimed that Castro had, in fact, passed on. The rumors had become so noisy that Chávez opened his Sunday television show by issuing a blanket denial. "Rumors are circulating that Fidel Castro has died, [but] Fidel is producing, he is writing." Then Chávez proclaimed: "All of us will die one day, but Fidel is one who will never die."

On August 24, a twenty-six-year-old Cuban-American blogger named Mario Armando Lavandeira Jr., who posts under the name Perez Hilton and specializes in teen celebrity gossip, recycled the Bolivian and

Colombian dispatches. Lavandeira flatly announced on his blog that Fidel was dead and that the Miami Police Department would be making an official announcement imminently. It was a story of pure confection by a young blogger who had blurred and conflated crucial details.

Miami officials *had* met that day—but simply to review their contingency operation, dubbed "Alpha-Bravo," in which they would secure certain neighborhoods near Calle Ocho for the anticipated blowout party once Castro was dead. Lavandeira was perhaps emboldened by his fellow exile compatriot blogger, Val Prieto, who had breathlessly made a similar claim on his "Babalú" blog: "Various sources inform that an announcement will come within the next few minutes from the Cuban government on Cuban TV and media." This was news to John Timoney, Miami's chief of police since 2003. A bemused Timoney told the *Wall Street Journal* that his forces had never gone on alert, adding drolly that "Since I've been here, Fidel has died four times already."

In a later post on his "PerezHilton" website, the would-be prophet offered a timeline. "The announcement of Fidel Castro's death will be made at approximately 4:00 p.m. Eastern. PerezHilton.com has just been updated exclusively." When 4 p.m. came and went, Lavandeira posted another update: "An official announcement is still expected today. We are hearing that law enforcement wants to wait until rush hour traffic is over in Miami."

Perez Hilton had made his name chronicling the comings, goings, arrests, and rehabs of teen queens Paris Hilton, Britney Spears, and Lindsay Lohan. And he was not deterred in his entry into foreign affairs by his bogus scoop.

> PerezHilton.com was the first media outlet in the world to break the news of Castro's death. We posted THIS ITEM on it last week!!!! A Cuban broke the story of the oppressive ogre's passing. We are soooo proud and happy!! . . . There's gonna be a big ol' party en Calle Ocho, mi gente!!

Indeed, he had something to crow about, having succeeded in getting his story picked up by several credulous mainstream reporters.

Soon there were rumors about the rumors. Depending on whom one spoke with, embalmers—from both Egypt and Russia—had arrived in Havana to attend to the deceased Castro. Never mind that Castro had already signaled in private conversations and with a few reporters (myself included) that he favored cremation. The rumors begat rumors, reaching critical mass by day's end on August 24. The

Miami Herald got in on the action with a story covering the rumor mill: "On Friday, the rumors heated up again for the third week in a row: Fidel Castro's death would be announced, first at 2 p.m., then at 4, then at 5." The *Herald* story told of callers on Ninoska Pérez-Castellón's daily talk radio show, *Ninoska en Mambí,* weeping tears of joy believing the Great Satan of Cuba had expired. La Ninoska, the indefatigable anti-Castro radio diva of exile Miami, consoled her call-in supplicants. "The moment will come," she said soothingly, "but this is not the moment."

"Don't believe a word. It's all a fabrication by the Miami crowd," a senior Cuban official warned Reuters News. He was right, of course. Nor was it especially hard to debunk the Perez Hilton–fueled rumor that had duped and embarrassed the mainstream media. For one thing, Ricardo Alarcón, the president of Cuba's National Assembly and their point man on U.S. policy, had gone on vacation and had not returned. Secondly, Foreign Minister Felipe Pérez Roque, had flown off to Brazil to attend a summit, then skipped off to Iran. Moreover, Raúl Castro had made a trip to Italy, a crucial partner in Cuban tourism, in which he toured a state-of-the-art golf course in Tuscany. None of the three—all major players in the Cuban political firmament—would ever have ventured outside of Havana had Castro been remotely close to death's door.

From the summit, Pérez Roque denied the rumors, insisting that Castro was still the captain of Cuba's ship. "He is being informed and consulted constantly," he assured the world. Still, both Alarcón and Pérez Roque backed away from their previous comments that Castro would soon return to office. No longer did they speak of Castro's imminent recovery.

On August 24, 2007, Castro was having a reasonably comfortable day and was watching his favorite show on television, *Mesa Redonda.* He was particularly interested in the show as it featured his old schoolmate Max Lesnik, the exile columnist and *bête noire* of the Miami establishment, discussing the one hundredth birthday of the Cuban reformer, Eduardo Chibás. (A popular political activist, Chibás famously shot himself after his radio show in 1951, one year before Batista seized power.)

It was at Chibás's funeral that a twenty-five-year-old Castro made his name, by leaping upon the grave and delivering a fiery denunciation of the Batisa regime. Castro owed much to Chibás—most notably, his own emergence as a political star to fill the void left by Chibás's death. There has always been one exception to Castro's aversion toward nostalgia: the Cuban Revolution. On this subject, his reminiscences have bordered on reverie. Castro could now lie in his private hospital suite, eyes closed, and simply remember. For comfort and reassurance, he possessed his own mental movie: an endless video loop of his own improbable victories as the great guerrilla revolutionary.

By 9 p.m. on August 24, 2007, Miami radio and television's rumor frenzy had devolved into a no-news meltdown. It was achingly clear that Fidel Castro Was Not Dead—Yet Again.

Castro could not resist celebrating his latest victory over "the Miami Mafia," as he designated his enemies who had settled in South Florida. Clad in his now familiar tracksuit, he arranged to be videotaped for a one-hour interview for Cuban television. Asked about rumors of his impending death, Castro smiled contentedly and responded, "Well, here I am!"

CHAPTER THREE

The Island and the Empire

In the late summer of 2007, the Pundit in Chief was feeling especially frisky—and prolific. In his weekly, sometimes daily, columns, Castro's new and preferred designation for his northern nemesis was now the Empire, an epithet that nicely synthesized the sinister with the snarky. On August 14, he entitled his "Reflections" column "The Empire and the Independent Island," a lengthy brief on the sorry history between the U.S. and Cuba, focused on the U.S.'s "constant craving to appropriate Cuba." There were numerous other offerings, including "The Empire and Falsehood" and "The Empire's Illegal Wars." In his column on August 27, Castro opined on the relative civility that had prevailed between Cuba and the United States when Jimmy Carter and Bill Clinton were presidents. "Enough of tales and nostalgia," he wrote, before turning his sights to the upcoming U.S. elections, proposing a certain winning Democrat ticket: "Today, talk is about the seemingly invincible ticket that might be created with Hillary for president and Obama for vice president." As it turned out, he wasn't far off the mark in suggesting that the two would eventually pair up.

Of course, Castro knew that any endorsement of a candidate from him could well be the kiss of death. He went on to scoff at the candidates' anticipated policies on Cuba. "Both of them feel the sacred duty of demanding 'a democratic government in Cuba.' They are not doing politics: they are playing a game of cards on a Sunday afternoon." But on the night of the 2008 election, when his musings could no longer damage Obama, he let his views be known. "Without a doubt, Obama is more intelligent, cultured and levelheaded than his Republican adversary," he wrote in his *Granma* column. "McCain is old, bellicose, uncultured, of little intelligence and not healthy."

Castro's most withering ridicule in his "Reflections" columns was invariably saved for his pet dartboard: George W. Bush. Of the eleven

57

American presidents he had faced off against, Castro found George W. Bush the most distasteful—and threatening. Intellectually, he dissed him as a lightweight; politically, he castigated him as "dangerous." His contempt never wavered throughout his infirmity. One column spoke of how Bush "had cheated" Al Gore out of the presidency in 2000. Following Bush's televised speech on the imploding financial markets in 2008, Castro again reached for his poison pen. "In any case, we must not be ungrateful or impolite," he wrote with rich sarcasm. "We have to thank Bush for his brilliant insight on political theory." Castro ranked Bush's final State of the Union address as the nadir in "demagoguery, lies and total lack of ethics," adding for good measure that "nobody can offer a more elegant criticism of the Empire than Bush himself."

The relationship between the Bush family and Cuba and Castro is long and complex. It is grounded in personal and economic interests that stretch back almost a century.

From the 1920s until his death in 1953, George Herbert Walker (the grandfather of George H. W. Bush) served on the boards of seven companies with interests in Cuba, mostly in sugar, rum, and railroads. As documented by journalist Kevin Phillips, the majority of the sugar companies merged into the West Indies Sugar Corporation in 1942, becoming the largest concern in Cuba, and one that was publicly traded on the New York Stock Exchange. Walker's son George Herbert Walker Jr., known as Uncle Herbie within the family, managed the family's sugar interests until their confiscation in 1959.

Growing up, Fidel Castro had vivid memories of the vast holdings of West Indies Sugar, whose land bordered his family's *finca*. "Those of us who were privileged could have shoes, clothes and be well fed; but a sea of poverty surrounded us," Castro said in a speech in 2002. "I remember that my father had over 24,700 acres of farmland. Of course, that meant hardly anything, as 284,245 acres surrounding our family's land was owned by the West Indies Sugar Company and the United Fruit Company."

It would be a historical stroke of irony that the Castro family plantation abutted the most successful sugar company in Cuba, in which the Bush family were major shareholders and George Herbert Walker Jr., aka Herbie, was a director until 1959. Ray Walker, Herbie's son who is known as one of the family's free thinkers, said he recalled "my mother and father going back and forth to Cuba and coming home with all kinds of things," but had no idea about the losses of the company.

Told that the company had a significant claim against Cuba, filed in the 1960s, Walker responded curtly, "I wouldn't be interested as it would not be good money."

In May 1959, Castro's fledgling government passed the Agrarian Reform Act, limiting private ownership of land to a thousand acres and expropriating all other land, notably that of the sugar companies. By the end of 1960, the nationalization of West Indies Sugar was complete. According to Kevin Phillips, "between 1957 and 1960, the assets of West Indies Sugar shrank from a value of $53 million to almost nothing." In 1966, the company registered a claim with the U.S. Foreign Claims Settlement Commission to seek compensation for "the taking of the Company's properties by the Cuban government." In 1997, West Indies Sugar certified its losses at $84.9 million (in 1959 dollars). "The Foreign Claims Settlement Commission awarded 6 percent interest per annum on all claims, to run from the date of settlement of the claim by Cuba," explained attorney Robert Muse, an expert and experienced litigant in claims against Cuba. While the commission did not specify whether the interest was to be calculated on a simple or compounded basis, the State Department calculates on the basis of the former. Should the claims ever be settled or paid, West Indies' losses would be about $330 million, with a considerable amount due to the Bush family.

There were other reasons Castro detested the Bush family. Prescott Bush, father of George H. W. Bush (#41), also had interests in Cuba. A U.S. senator representing Connecticut, who served in Army intelligence during World War I, Prescott was an early champion of and collaborator with the OSS (Office of Strategic Services), the precursor to the CIA. It was a passion that he passed on to his son, George H. W.

Throughout the 1950s, the CIA was carefully tracking the revolutionary fever sweeping the island. CIA chief Allen Dulles, a close friend to the Bush family, had come to believe that Cuba played a crucial role for American business and U.S. security. (Dulles also served on the Board of Trustees of United Fruit, the largest U.S. business operating in Cuba and Latin America. The law firm of his brother, John Foster Dulles, secretary of state under Eisenhower, represented the company.) Consequently, the Agency backed Cuba's thuggish dictator, Fulgencio Batista, notwithstanding some misgivings.

Former president George H. W. Bush became something of an expert on Cuban exile affairs. Indeed, several documents suggest that he was the FBI's go-to person on Cuba in the early '60s. A memo addressed to the State Department and written by J. Edgar Hoover on November 29, 1963, reports that the FBI had briefed "Mr. George Bush of the Central

Intelligence Agency" soon after the assassination of President John F. Kennedy on the reactions of hardline exiles in Miami and "those who did not entirely agree with the President's policy concerning Cuba." Hoover's memo stated that George Bush and an officer of the Defense Intelligence Agency had been briefed the day after the assassination because of fears that "some misguided anti-Castro group might capitalize on the present situation and undertake an unauthorized raid against Cuba, believing that the assassination of President John F. Kennedy might herald a change in U.S. policy, which is not true."

In 1988, when the *Nation* magazine published the memo, which soon bubbled into the mainstream media, a Bush family spokesman said that the person named in the memo "must be another George Bush." That assertion was undermined by a second memo dated November 22, 1963, that stated that "at 1:45 p.m. Mr. George H. W. Bush, President of the Zapata Offshore Drilling Company, Houston, Texas," called the Houston FBI station chief seventy-five minutes after the assassination of JFK to report that "one James Parrott had been talking about killing the President when he comes to Houston." The memo, which was declassified in 1993, stated that Bush, then president of the Harris County Republican Party, said "he was proceeding to Dallas," but would return to Houston the following day. "Bush stated that he wanted to be kept confidential." (Parrott was subsequently interviewed and found to have nothing to do with the assassination; he went on to work on Bush's 1992 campaign.)

Bush's company, Zapata Offshore, had been funded by George Herbert Walker Jr., Bush's beloved Uncle Herbie, who treated his nephew "like a son," according to one Bush cousin, much to the chagrin of Herbie's own children. George Bush served as Zapata's CEO from 1956 until 1964, crucial years of U.S.-Cuba turmoil. The company was never profitable but was strategically close to Cuba. It did, however, play a useful role in the Bay of Pigs invasion by allowing its oil rigs to be used as listening posts, and again during the Cuban Missile Crisis. *Barron's* magazine in 1988 identified Zapata as "a part time purchasing front for the CIA." In fact, the CIA's secret code name for its failed Bay of Pigs invasion by thirteen hundred exiles in April 1961 was "Operation Zapata." Conspiracy buffs inevitably point out that the two re-commissioned Navy ships used in the operation were renamed *Barbara* and *Houston*. The name Zapata, however, is the name of the peninsula on Cuba's southern belly where the CIA invasion force landed.

Further stoking conspiratorial theories, Castro repeatedly claimed that George Bush was a participant and/or a supporter of Operation

40. A shadowy CIA group of anti-Castro saboteurs, OP 40 specialized in guerrilla, covert attacks against Cuba in the early 1960s.

George H. W. Bush became director of the CIA in January 1976 and served through January 1977. Bush replaced William Colby, who had infuriated conservatives with his cooperation with the reform-minded Church Committee in 1975. Among other startling admissions, Colby told the Senate committee that the Agency had played a role in destabilizing Chile in the early 1970s. Colby also implemented major reforms at the CIA, including the prohibition of assassination as a policy tool, and became the first CIA director to institute congressional briefings on agency operations. Both actions deeply alienated the Agency's right flank, which enthusiastically backed the appointment of George Bush.

Upon being made CIA chief, George Bush installed Ted Shackley as deputy director of Covert Operations, the Agency's third most powerful job. Shackley had set up and run the Agency's JM/WAVE station in Miami (its massive substation dedicated to ousting Castro). He was closely allied with David Atlee Phillips, who ran its "propaganda shop," and who was formerly the agency's Havana bureau chief. By all reports, Bush and Shackley had a close relationship and a common philosophy that favored covert operations. Shackley later played a key role in the secret arms-for-hostages operation Iran-Contra.

However, Shackley was a divisive figure, and relations between Henry Kissinger's State Department and George Bush's CIA were painfully strained. The disconnect was so serious that, according to William D. Rogers, the assistant secretary of state for Inter-America Affairs at the State Department rarely relied on CIA intelligence. "The Agency was controlled by hardliners," said Rogers, who passed away in 2007. "They had an agenda, and the intelligence was lousy."

George H. W. Bush's name is emblazoned on the CIA's Langley headquarters not because of his brief tenure as its director, but because of his history with the Agency. As it turned out, Bush's fourteen-month directorship at Langley was remarkable in just one regard: it coincided with the worst spate of bombings and assassinations throughout the hemisphere by Cuban exile militants. As far as Fidel Castro was concerned, it was not for lack of trying that the Bush family had failed to depose him.

Upon assuming the presidency in 2000, George W. Bush deputized Castro's estranged relative, Representative Lincoln Díaz-Balart, as his point man on Cuba. The Miami Republican, along with his congressional colleague and fellow exile hardliner, Ileana Ros-Lehtinen, had gone the distance to ensure that Miami's canvassing board shut down the recount during the 2000 presidential election. Both were well rewarded by the new administration and both attended to the heavy lifting and horse-trading in Congress to ensure that anti-Castro programs were amply funded.

Of the two, Lincoln Díaz-Balart had the more personal connection to the Castro family. Indeed, he has been a lifelong satellite around Planet Fidel: the two men, of course, share a birthday, and Díaz-Balart had been Castro's nephew by marriage, his most ardent foe, and would-be successor. As George W. Bush's quarterback, Díaz-Balart dictated virtually all policy and staffing regarding Cuba. The excitable congressman had once suggested a military blockade of Cuba. Nor was he averse to an invasion of the island, and made no secret of his ambition to topple and replace his former uncle.

It had been the dream of his father, Rafael Díaz-Balart, that his eldest son would wrest control of Cuba from his former brother-in-law. Castro had humiliated the once powerful Díaz-Balarts, who had welcomed him into their family only to be driven into exile by him. "I will not live to see this [Castro's end] happen," Rafael told me in 2001, four years before his death, "but my sons will." Rafael had four sons, all men of considerable profile in Miami. Lincoln and Mario are both congressmen, José is a television anchor for the Telemundo network, and his namesake, Rafael, is a businessman. So deeply felt were these familial and political wounds that those who hazarded to break with the family's confrontational policies toward Cuba were viewed as threats to Lincoln's aspirations.

In 2001, the Cuba Study Group was created out of the detritus of the Elián González debacle, when Miami found itself on the losing end of a scorched-earth battle to keep the six-year-old child in the U.S. The city's exile leaders soon broke into two camps: those who leaned toward deeper hardline entrenchment versus a new breed of pragmatists willing to consider options other than confrontation with Cuba. The Cuban American National Foundation (CANF) would be sundered as it transited from the far right to a center-right path. CANF's militant flank had moved on to form the Cuban Liberty Council, which was backed by the Díaz-Balarts. The Cuba Study Group was conservative but pragmatic. It focused on economic and policy issues and was led by businessmen Carlos Saladrigas and Carlos de la Cruz, and Luis Pérez, a prominent Miami attorney, all lifelong Republicans. The men had come to believe, reluctantly over many years, that a more nuanced and realistic policy toward Cuba was necessary.

Such thinking did not sit well with the Díaz-Balart clan. Soon after the group's formation, Rafael Díaz-Balart asked to meet with Carlos de la Cruz and Luis Pérez. Referring to Saladrigas as *"el muchachito"* or "the little boy," the Díaz-Balart patriarch told the men that the Cuba Study Group was an unwelcome intrusion in exile politics. He added that his family viewed Saladrigas as an impediment to Lincoln's plan to be the next president of Cuba. "Tell [Saladrigas] he needs to wait his turn," the octogenarian Rafael warned the men. "In the meantime, we have no problem with him being in the [Cuban] Senate." Initially, sugar tycoons Alfie and Pepe Fanjul had signed on with the Cuba Study Group. But after being advised by surrogates of Díaz-Balart that their extensive business interests in Florida might lose some state and federal perks, the brothers reportedly stepped to the side.

In 2004, the Cuba Study Group released the results of a comprehensive poll showing a dramatic shift in attitudes among Cuban exiles. Its findings, consistent with other polls at the time, revealed that the majority of exiles favored diplomacy with Cuba and harbored deep misgivings about the U.S. embargo. The Díaz-Balarts responded by joining forces with Miami's exile radio czar Armando Pérez Roura of Radio Mambí, who functions as the Walter Winchell of Calle Ocho, and called for a protest march. "It was the first time in history," said Saladrigas, "that anyone ever called for a protest against a poll." Leading the march down Calle Ocho were Lincoln and Mario Díaz-Balart. Throughout the day, Pérez Roura crowed on the air that some three hundred thousand exiles had marched behind the two congressmen. In fact, aerial photographs suggested the number was several thousand. "This is what they do in Cuba," said Saladrigas. "It was an *acto de repudio* [acts of repudiation: demonstrations staged by the Cuban government] right here in Miami."

Regardless, the Díaz-Balarts and their allies were at the helm of U.S. policy toward Cuba throughout George W. Bush's term. For eight years, the Miami team argued for increased confrontation with the island—in order to "bring the Cuban people democracy."

From 2001 through 2004, Fidel Castro repeatedly voiced concern that George W. Bush was prepared to invade Cuba, at the behest of hardliners in Miami. Pre-emptive military strikes and covert actions, he often pointed out, were well regarded in the Bush family. George H. W. Bush, as Reagan's vice president, played a key operational role in the 1983 invasion of tiny Grenada, a disciple-ally of Cuba. In 1989, President Bush ordered the invasion of Panama and the capture of its president,

General Manuel Noriega, who was then jetted to the U.S., where he spent the next two decades in prison.

In 2003, excitement mounted among a segment of influential hard-liners in Miami that George W. Bush was ready to "liberate Cuba." A few Cuba hands felt that had the administration not been so diverted by the war in Iraq, a U.S. invasion of Cuba—similar to the military strikes in Panama or Grenada—was on the table. Believers cited the fact that the Department of Defense had been holding "simulation exercises" on Cuba. In fact, the U.S. has done gaming and simulation exercises since the Cuban Missile Crisis—with both the Cubans and Soviets as potential adversaries.

According to retired Air Force Colonel Sam Gardiner, who conducted simulations at Defense in 2002 and 2003, the purpose of the military games was twofold: "stability in Cuba and in Florida: the point being to intercede as early as possible in a refugee flow." Among the simulations explored, he said, were ones in which the U.S. is "invited" into Cuba or where the U.S. "acts preemptively to stabilize" the island following an immigration exodus. Other triggers or opportunities included a natural catastrophe, an economic crisis, and political collapse.

Those believing that a military foray into Cuba was under consideration gave credence to a report that the 82nd Airborne and Navy SEALs had been alerted for just such an intervention in late 2003. It was scotched, according to a military source who spoke with Steve Clemons of the Washington Note, after the Iraq War devolved into chaos, leaving U.S. troops stretched too thin.

But Castro was not taking any chances. According to University of New Mexico sociologist Nelson Valdés, military contingency plans to respond to a possible attack from the United States were drafted at a Communist Party meeting on July 15, 2003. "Cuban plans included concrete steps to be taken in case of Fidel Castro's incapacity or death, prior or during a U.S. military attack," wrote Valdés. The following year, the Bush administration enacted the harshest measures against Cuba since the Cold War, virtually criminalizing travel to Cuba for most Americans and severely limiting family visits for Cuban-Americans. Castro saw the measures as one more provocation, according to Valdés, and warned in an open letter: "In Cuba's present condition to confront an invasion, my physical absence by natural or other causes would not hurt our ability, in any way, to fight and resist."

In October 2007, Castro rallied sufficiently to have a live phone call with his publicist in chief Hugo Chávez. It had been prearranged that

Chávez would host his weekly radio/television show, *Aló, Presidente!* from Santa Clara, where the fortieth anniversary of Che Guevara's death was being commemorated. Chávez had toured the museum, the imposing statue of Che, and the mausoleum holding Guevara's remains, all duly and reverentially recorded by Cuban state television.

It didn't seem to matter that several of Che's descendants seem less than enchanted with tropical Marxism. Che's eldest son, Camilo Guevara March, is often in Paris, while his younger sister, Celia, obtained an Argentine passport and lives in Buenos Aires with her family. Che's namesake, Ernesto Guevara March, is a former punk rocker known to rail against Cuban consumerism. He has complained that the government denies him a passport to travel. "He's the one they always march out for all the Che events," said writer Achy Obejas. "But he'll say anything, so sometimes they kill the mike when he starts talking." One of Che's grandsons, Canek Sánchez Guevara, is a heavy metal musician who lives in Paris where he is active in opposition Cuban-exile politics. It has been left to Aleida Guevara, a Marxist and a doctor like her father, to carry the family banner and resolutely defend the Revolution.

Another son of Che is Omar Pérez López, born out of a brief infatuation the Argentine had with a saucily pretty Cuban journalist in 1963. According to journalist Michael Casey's book *Che's Afterlife,* Pérez is a poet and dissident who has not been recognized by Aleida's family. Pérez was a signer of the Third Option manifesto published in 1991, described as a "democratic alternative" for Cuba. For such insubordination, Pérez was sentenced to one year in a labor camp in Pinar del Río picking tomatoes. Ironically, the camp was created by Che in 1962 as a rehab for revolutionaries who went astray.

After his Che tour, Chávez met with Acting President Raúl Castro to put the finishing touches on a slew of sweetheart deals for oil production and refining, as well as tourism. Chávez also committed to finance a one-thousand-mile underwater fiber-optic cable from Venezuela to Cuba. A technological umbilical cord, the cable would provide the infrastructure for an information and digital superhighway, upgrading telecommunications and internet between the two countries. Venezuela's stipend to Cuba now hovered at $4 billion annually, including a hundred thousand barrels of oil per day.

Fidel Castro's hourlong phone call to Chávez was timed to follow the airing of a videotape filmed during their weekend meeting. In the taped segment, Chávez called Castro the "father of all revolutionaries," while his Cuban mentor was shown thumbing through Che Guevara's *Bolivian Diary.* Chávez then serenaded his friend with a revolutionary hymn to Che, prompting a flush of emotion from Castro. "I am very touched when you sing about Che," the ailing Castro responded. Like a besotted adolescent, Chávez exclaimed at one point, "there is electricity in the air!"

The televised conversation between the two Hispanic strongmen suggested that the successor of Fidel Castro would not be his low-profile, policy-wonk brother Raúl, but rather the region's other movie-star dictator. Chávez seemed to say as much. "Deep down, we are one single government, one single country," the Venezuelan told Cuban television earlier that day.

For the rest of 2007, Castro remained unseen except by family, doctors, and trusted friends and aides. "He's like brand new," insisted Ramón Castro, Fidel's eighty-three-year-old brother, known as Mongo, in a quickie exchange with the *Sun-Sentinel* at an animal sciences conference. Mongo Castro went on to express confidence that Fidel would continue to lead the country. He smiled and added a truism he knew only too well: "He does whatever he wants to do."

On December 6, 2007, Fidel Castro had his aide place a telephone call to the home of Elián González, "the miracle child" who had been found floating in an inner tube off Fort Lauderdale in 1999. The child's rescue became a cause célèbre in the Miami-Havana wars. After seven months of blistering legal wrangling, culminating with a rebuff to the child's Miami relatives from the U.S. Supreme Court, little Elián was reunited with his father and family in Cuba. It was the ideal battle for Castro, one in which he had the rare opportunity to occupy the moral high ground. For months his Miami foes were vilified in the national and international press—depicted as kidnappers of a hapless, helpless child. "With enemies like these," went the oft-heard refrain in Cuba, "Castro does not need any friends."

Whatever his affection for the precocious child, Castro recognized Elián as a political trophy. California's former governor and current attorney general Jerry Brown, who enjoyed several days with Castro in 2000, was convinced that the photogenic tot was being groomed by Castro for high political office, perhaps even the top slot, at some point down the road. Indeed, Elián and his family have been well taken care of—politically and materially. After his return, his father, Juan Miguel González, was rewarded with a seat in the National Assembly and the family was upgraded to a more spacious home in Cárdenas.

Elián's young father said he felt indebted to the Maximum Leader. "Fidel became part of our family," Juan Miguel explained in a documentary film about the Elián affair, speaking with palpable emotion.

The degree of indebtedness was in evidence when the miracle child gave his first speech at a televised anti-imperialist rally in Havana on April 24, 2005. The date was selected to commemorate the day the charismatic child was taken from the Miami home of his relatives by federal agents. The rally was held at an amphitheater known as the "Protestodrome" which was hastily built across the street from the U.S. Interests Section during the Elián War.

"Five years ago, I returned to my dad," the eleven-year-old Elián said, reading from prepared remarks. "When I saw him, I became very happy. I could hug him; I could see my little brother. That was the happiest day of my life." He went on to thank the American people and Fidel Castro, who was seated next to the boy's father. "I want to thank all those who made my dream of being a free child come true." The rally ended with a round of the Revolution's chant *Patria o muerte!*—"Homeland or death!" In June 2008, *Juventud Rebelde,* the state-run youth newspaper, announced that the former poster boy (for both sides of the Cuba war) had joined the Communist Party and vowed "never to let down Fidel or Raúl Castro."

Castro had been known to occasionally forget the birthdays of his own children, but never Elián's. In his infirmity, Castro had discovered the telephone. Previously he had been averse to extended discussions on the phone, presumably as a result of security concerns. On December 6, 2007, the fourteen-year-old was summoned to the phone in his home in Cárdenas. "I want to take the opportunity to tell all Cubans that I have just spoken to *El Comandante,*" the teenager told reporters later. "He is feeling very well. He wished me Happy Birthday."

In the minutes just before the clocks struck midnight on January 1, 2008, Cuban state television and radio read a holiday greeting from Fidel Castro: "During the course of the morning, the forty-ninth year of the Revolution will be left behind and we will have fully entered the fiftieth year, which will symbolize a half century of heroic resistance." The words were recited by a television news reader as photographs of the young, dynamic Castro flitted across the screen.

In fact, the fiftieth anniversary of the Revolution was still a year away. General Fulgencio Batista had fled Cuba—with much of the national treasury in tow—on December 31, 1958. But concern that Castro would not live to see the actual fiftieth anniversary prompted some actuarial fudging. Henceforth, it was decided that 2008 would be billed as "the fiftieth year of the Revolution."

The second anomaly of the new year was the total absence of augury in the *"Letra del Año"* ("Letter of the Year") concerning Castro. Every January, the high priests, or *babalaos,* of Santería, the dominant faith in Cuba, release their prognostications for the year. It is an event eagerly anticipated by Cubans, although it has long been known that even *santeros* and *babalaos* know the limits of political discourse. The *babalaos* had plenty to say, predicting several climate catastrophes, an upswing in crime, and an epidemic or two. But mindful of state limits on messages, even those delivered from the other side, they were mum on the topic most on the minds of Cubans.

"You'd better wash yourself with white flour and honey," Natalia Bolívar had advised me years earlier when I informed her that I had finally scored an interview with Fidel Castro. An authority on Afro-Cuban religions and Santería, Bolívar arched her eyebrows in mock innocence and wagged her index finger in front of her face, Cuban-style. "People say bad things happen to people after they're with Fidel," she said, in the sunlit, art-filled living room of her Miramar apartment. "They go kaput." Bolívar was informed by more than the spirit world. She had been a resistance fighter in the 1950s against Batista and, having been a former aristocrat of considerable beauty, had known Castro intimately. For many years, she has walked the razor's edge of so many who stayed and supported the Revolution only to be bitterly disappointed. *"Un despojo"*—a spiritual cleansing—she said, was what was advised. I asked who told her so. "I don't know," she replied, with mock innocence, waving her hand by the side of her head. "The *babalaos* say so."

While the *santeros* maintained their silence, the established pattern of periodic photos ops of the convalescent in chief continued throughout 2008. The ailing Castro would slide from view for weeks or months until the percolation of rumors roared to a fierce bubbling. Then poof! he would reappear to receive the embrace of a visiting foreign leader. On January 16, there was more photographic evidence to attest to Castro's viability. Pictures of Castro, wearing his trademark leisure suit and white Adidas sneakers, with Brazil's President Luiz Inácio Lula da Silva were released following a manic, whirlwind twenty-four-hour visit by Lula to the island.

A year earlier, Lula had let it slip that he believed Castro had cancer. But no more, at least not publicly. "My feeling is that Fidel is in impeccable health and that he's as lucid as he's ever been," the Brazilian socialist declared, adding somewhat improbably, "I think Fidel is ready to take on his historic political role in this globalized world." Privately, some in Lula's entourage allowed that Lula believed Fidel was in the final stages of cancer and was astonished that the Maximum Leader was still alive.

The visit by the socialist president, representing the richest and largest country in Latin America, was hardly a condolence call to an ailing dictator. Brazil's semi-public oil company, Petrobras, had its eyes on Cuba's offshore oil and natural gas resources. Additionally, the southern hemisphere's emerging superpower was hungry for Cuba's sugar to feed its profitable ethanol industry. In exchange, Lula happily signed off on credits and deals with Cuba worth one billion dollars. A few months later, during a visit to Havana, Brazil's foreign minister affirmed that his country hoped to become "Cuba's Number One trading partner."

The man who was in fact Cuba's Number One Partner swooped back into Havana for a surprise visit with his mentor on March 8. Chávez delivered the salubrious news that he had found Fidel "happy, splendid and full of ideas," but made no mention of the reason for his social call: the release of two high-profile hostages held by the FARC (Revolutionary Armed Forces of Colombia) who had just arrived in Cuba. Guiding Chávez's maneuvers with the guerrillas and his nemesis, Colombian President Álvaro Uribe Vélez, was, of course, Castro. (In November 2008, Castro "published" a book entitled *Peace in Colombia,* described by Culture Minister Abel Prieto as a "tribute" to Manuel Marulanda, founder of the FARC, who had died suddenly of a heart attack earlier in the year.)

Bolivian President Evo Morales arrived in Havana a few months after Chávez and reported that Castro had lost weight but was fully alert. "I found him thin but very lucid," Morales said of his two-hour conversation with the Cuban leader. "And as always, a very wise man."

But Castro's condition had slipped precipitously in May 2008, according to a *fidelista* who had fought in the Sierra. Following a visit with his former comrades in Havana, the retired revolutionary, who requested anonymity, passed on the grim tidings from Raúl's inner circle that "Fidel will not live through the year and probably not the summer." The former revolutionary's visit coincided with well-circulated reports that Fidel had undergone further intestinal surgery and was in an unstable and delicate condition.

But the indomitable Cuban rose again for another meeting with Hugo Chávez on June 16, dashing the hopes of his enemies. *Granma* reported that the two men had a three-hour "animated and affectionate" meeting. Later, a brief video of their meeting—minus the audio— was aired on Cuban television showing Castro thinner, paler, and with whiter hair, chatting with Chávez and his brother Raúl in a garden setting. They were the first images of Castro seen in five months, released to put the kibosh on the latest cycle of rumors of his death. "It is a difficult moment in the world," Chávez cautiously told reporters at Havana's José Martí Airport. "But fortunately, the Cuban Revolution, that is about to [celebrate] a half-century, and the Venezuelan Revolution, that is about to fulfill ten years, have become brothers and have united forces."

As if to dispel lingering suspicions, Chávez's visit was quickly followed by several other brief encounters with important officials. First up was Uruguayan President Tabaré Vázquez, a former doctor, who reported that the Cuban leader seemed to be alert and doing "very well." He was followed by He Guoqiang, a senior Chinese official, who laid the groundwork for a visit from President Hu Jintao, and also extended an invitation to Castro to attend the Olympics. Of course, both parties knew that Castro would not be at the Games, as much as he had hoped to attend. Through its embassy in Havana, China had been providing Castro with both traditional Chinese herbal medicines and modern pharmaceuticals, along with specialists in both arenas, since he had fallen ill. Photos of all of the *Comandante*'s visitors were duly snapped and released to the media as evidence of Castro's recovery and engagement.

The Bush administration chimed in with its own assessment of the Maximum Leader: "There is no doubt that Castro is dying," said one U.S. official, adding a priceless non sequitur of news no one could use: "We just don't know when."

There had been speculation and hope throughout 2007 that Fidel would decline to run in the National Assembly elections to be held on January 20, 2008. Such a graceful sidestep would have boosted and burnished his brother's authority. But alas for Raúl, word came down that Fidel intended to seek another term. One *habanero* said he sensed a dispirited collective exhalation throughout Havana at the prospect of more of the same dysfunctional limbo state.

By law, the Assembly's 614 members select the Council of State's 31 members, as well as the big-ticket jobs of vice president and president. However, there is only one slate of nominees, producing an electoral result that most regard as preordained and cosmetic. "The current electoral law, marked by its totalitarian character, does not guarantee the elemental right of citizens to freely elect people," said dissident Vladimiro Roca. As was traditional, Castro's home district of Santiago submitted his nomination to represent it. In his column, Fidel conceded that he was too weak to campaign. "I do what I can," he said, as if his election were not a foregone conclusion.

Fidel's absence from the stage for the preceding months had renewed speculation about his mental state. Renowned for his loquaciousness and speeches that sometimes ran four to seven hours, Castro had become strangely mute. "I write," he explained in his column. "For me, this is a new experience: writing is not the same as speaking."

Nevertheless, some maintained that the Maximum Leader had dropped a few of his marbles, due to his infirmities. His most embittered critics in Miami whispered that there were days when he was sounding a tad like the inmates at Mazorra, Havana's notorious mental institution. "No one seems to have explained satisfactorily the failure of Fidel to appear in public for twenty-two months," noted one seasoned European diplomat in 2008. "My own theory is that mentally he is in decline and that there is no way he could be viewed as a credible CEO. Some of his 'Reflections' are bizarre, even by his recent standards. So the Cuban government cannot risk a public appearance by him for fear that this would become obvious."

Although there had been no live footage of Fidel Castro for almost three years, the Castro brothers were getting work done. While Fidel posed for the occasional photo op, Raúl was closing deals. Whatever the tensions between the brothers, they had nailed down wide-ranging trade and investment accords that guaranteed Cuba's survival. They had hammered out an oil-for-life deal with Chávez and convinced Brazil's Lula da Silva to commit to an array of construction and agricultural projects. The Brazilian president had also signed on to have Petrobras, the world's leader in deep-water drilling, mine Cuba's newly discovered trove of crude oil in its northern waters.

It all came down to a sharp poke in the eye of the U.S. and its one-note policy of seeking to isolate the island. "Cuba is a country," lamented one U.S. oilman, "not a crusade." In March 2008, one hundred House members and twenty-four senators wrote Secretary of State Condoleezza Rice to express their dismay and fear that the U.S. had placed itself so far out of the game that it was approaching irrelevance: "Our policy leaves us without influence at this critical moment, and this serves neither the U.S. national interest nor average Cubans. After fifty years, it is time for us to think and act anew."

More embarrassment was served up in June 2008 when the European Union announced it was lifting sanctions against Cuba, despite American entreaties to maintain them. The restrictions had been in place since 2003, when Cuba locked up seventy-five dissidents and independent journalists. Almost fifty-five were still incarcerated at the time of the EU announcement. The policy change had been championed by Spain but resisted by the Czech Republic, Sweden, and Britain, which added the caveat that the Brussels-based body continue to lobby for full release of the political prisoners. Despite his victory and the humiliation of the U.S., Fidel Castro was not satisfied. He lambasted the EU's lifting of sanctions against his country as "an enormous hypocrisy" and one that was "disparaging." Many were left shaking their heads as to Castro's unhappiness about such a hard-fought, clean-cut triumph.

In fact, the post-Fidel transition had gone so seamlessly that Cuba announced in early 2008 that it was no longer interested in diplomacy with the U.S. until after George W. Bush was ensconced in his Crawford, Texas, ranch. Jorge Alberto Bolaños Suárez, the newly installed chief of the Cuban Interests Section in Washington, told the Associated Press that Cuba had put the U.S. on hold until January 2009. "I'm not concerned with what the current State Department says because we are waiting for what the next one has to say about Cuba," sniffed Bolaños. "The truth of the matter," said Kirby Jones, president of the U.S.-Cuba Trade Association, "is that Cuba does not need the U.S. They have simply moved on and done business with everyone else."

All said, not too shabby for a dying man.

It was not until February 19, 2008—nineteen months after his illness snatched him from public view—that Fidel agreed to budge and formally hand over power to his brother. Finally acceding to his own mortality and pressure to give his brother some much-needed elbow room, Fidel announced that he would step down. However, the passing of the torch was most notable for how it was handled. Certainly Castro had lost none of his capacity to surprise—nor his trademark genius for media manipulation.

Five days before the much-ballyhooed National Assembly pronouncements of who would reign and how, Castro quietly announced his resignation in the online edition of *Granma*. In a letter to the state-run daily, Castro said he would not accept a new term when the National Assembly met on February 24 to announce its appointments. "I repeat I will not aspire to nor accept the post of President of the Council of State and Commander in Chief," he wrote.

Castro's edict galvanized the international media. Cleverly released in the wee hours of the morning following a sleepy three-day Presidents' Day holiday weekend, it blazed through multiple news cycles in the U.S., then went global. It was pedigree Fidel, with his intuitive gifts for public relations. He had upstaged not only his brother as he passed on the crown, but also the National Assembly's announcement that had been scheduled for the same day as the Academy Awards. As Fidel was well aware, all eyes would be on Hollywood's glitterati—not Raúl Castro.

Of course, Fidel was only resigning, not retiring. In fact, *renunciar* has a tad more innuendo than its English-language equivalent of "resign." It can also mean to give something up and has a bit more wiggle room than, say, *resignarse*. In short, it was assumed that Castro would continue on as the wizard behind the curtain. "I am not saying goodbye to you," he wrote. "I only wish to fight as a soldier of ideas."

Just days later, Fidel was back—opining in his "Reflections" that he had wanted to take a ten-day break from his column, but that duty had beckoned: "I didn't have the right to keep silent for so long." There was one small, albeit notable, change. No longer was his column touted on the front page of *Granma* as "Reflections of the Commander in Chief," with an accompanying photo of him in his snappy olive-green fatigues. Now his essays were entitled "Reflections of Compañero Fidel," alongside a photo of him, with an inscrutable smile, one hand waving—perhaps to say good-bye. Also for the first time, his column ran on page four, at his request, as he pointed out.

Down the road, he tweaked his billing again, opting for a lighter, friendlier touch and entitling his column simply "Reflections of Fidel." On those good days when Castro was feeling his oats, there was nothing to stop him from meddling, with or without his grandiose titles. As long as he could speak and think, the world would be hearing from him.

Naturally, Raúl Castro was fully aware that the National Assembly would be naming him as his brother's successor. And by all accounts he was feeling upbeat and sanguine. On February 16, days before Fidel's *renunciado,* Raúl attended the wedding of the well-known artist Kcho—the painter's second trip to the altar. Wearing a long-sleeved white *guayabera,* Raúl Castro was in top form. Ray Sanchez, the *Sun-Sentinel*'s bureau chief in Havana at the time, attended with an invited guest and reported that an effusive Raúl was "posing for pictures, shaking hands with everyone, making jokes, kissing babies, even flirting a bit." Among the 150 guests at the Vedado wedding were Raúl's daughter, Mariela, along with several of Fidel's sons, Fidelito, Antonio, the doctor, and Alejandro, the son who had been dogged with problems with alcohol and controlled substances. But it was the seventy-six-year-old Raúl Castro who was front and center stage. At one point, he took off for a stroll with Kcho and his bride along the Malecón. It seemed, Sanchez said, that Raúl Castro was a man whose moment had arrived, and who was fully at peace with himself.

Quite a few were disappointed that the Castro brothers had not seen fit to appoint Carlos Lage to the presidency, as reformers, businessmen, and pundits had hoped. The popular pediatrician-turned-economic-czar, it was believed, would have moderated Cuba's economic policies, allowing more private businesses to flourish on the island. He was also an astute man. In 2007, he nailed the Bush administration's dilemma in a conversation with a foreign colleague. "The U.S. has a plan for when Fidel is alive and another for when he is dead," he said. "But they don't have a plan for in between."

Soon after his acceptance speech on February 24, for which he donned a smart black suit and silver tie, Raúl Castro picked up the phone for a chat with Hugo Chávez on the latter's live weekly television show. It had been widely whispered that Raúl Castro was wary of Chávez and that his inner circle found the Venezuelan to be undisciplined, and worried whether he was fully dependable. Chávez's fierce loyalty, after all, was toward Fidel and to his own ambition to become the next Simón Bolívar of the hemisphere. The Chávez-Raúl relationship was not helped by Chávez's quip during his Santa Clara visit for the Che commemoration in 2007 that Raúl "had practiced his first shot at Moncada," suggesting that Fidel's brother was a late bloomer.

But Raúl's phone call sent a clear, unambiguous signal that Chávez and Venezuela would remain Cuba's chief patron—at least for the time being. "Nothing is going to change," Chávez told Raúl on air. "I ratify my commitment to Cuba, the commitment of the Venezuelan people, of the Bolivarian revolution, to you, to Fidel, to the Cuban Revolution, to the people of Cuba." The two went on to sing Venezuelan folk songs—something Fidel Castro would never have done. Raúl jested that he would not be following in his brother's oratorical footsteps. "No speech of mine lasts more than an hour," he said. Brevity was a small but appreciated perk of Raúl's coronation—to the relief of many.

George W. Bush greeted the news of the historic succession in Cuba with his customary lack of diplomacy. He dismissed Raúl as "a tyrant [who's] nothing more than an extension of what his brother did, which was to ruin an island and to imprison people because of their beliefs." The State Department's Tom Casey chimed in, casually dissing Raúl Castro as "Dictator-Lite," sounding more like the *Wall Street Journal*'s strident partisan Mary O'Grady than a diplomat. The major economic powers in the hemisphere felt otherwise: "Raúl Castro taking over in

Cuba puts Latin America at ease," said Brazil's Lula. Mexican officials heralded the succession of Raúl as one of "great significance" as they prepared a host of new diplomatic and commercial ventures with Cuba.

Notwithstanding Casey's blitheness, there was a rippling of movement in the turgid waters between the U.S. and Cuba. For one thing, even the most orthodox hardliners on both sides privately acknowledged that change was inevitable and coming sooner than expected. There had been a flurry of moves by Raúl Castro, from the prison release of several dissidents to a series of economic reforms. *Miami Herald* columnist Andrés Oppenheimer predicted that Raúl's new slate of initiatives would be "change disguised as continuity."

But many fretted that the U.S. was losing any opportunity to affect Cuba's future, as the Castro brothers ramped up and solidified trade agreements with Cuba's allies in Latin America, Europe, and Asia. "We are moving towards being irrelevant," said Vicki Huddleston, former chief of the U.S. Interests Section in Havana. One State Department official conceded as much, saying that after eight years of nonpolicy under George W. Bush, "a lot of our policy muscles with Cuba have atrophied." He noted that improving relations with Cuba would "go nowhere with the Bush administration." Then he added helpfully, "We do have a statement prepared for the day he dies."

CHAPTER FOUR

Writing for History

The first obituaries for Fidel Castro were published in December 1956. It was then that the government of President Fulgencio Batista duped a gullible UPI correspondent named Francis McCarthy into reporting that Fidel Castro, and his brother Raúl, had been killed in an ambush. In fact, the thirty-year-old leftist rebel leader was hiding out in the Sierra Maestra mountains. Desperate to jump-start his revolution—and his life—Castro dispatched an emissary to find an A-list messenger.

After a grueling trek, slogging through the near-impenetrable Sierra, Herbert Matthews, a star correspondent for the *New York Times,* was told to wait in the wet and chilly woods. It was dawn before Castro, ever mindful of stagecraft, finally descended from the hills—thus establishing his standard operating procedure with the media: Always keep reporters waiting, preferably in the dark, for as long as possible. The result was a heroic portrait that landed on page one of the *Times.*

From the beginning, newspapers and networks have maintained a standing obituary of Castro. It seemed only wise. After all, several American presidents had decreed that his elimination was a desirable outcome. Then there were the legions of freelance assassins—embittered, hard-wired exile militants—determined to wreak vengeance on the man who, in their view, had hijacked their country.

In the mid-1990s, high-decibel gossip that Castro had barely dodged a rendezvous with his Maker prompted news organizations to freshen up their obituaries. Pundits prepared their sound bytes, ready to yammer for their allotted seventy-five seconds of live television. And again, on June 23, 2001, following Castro's famous *desmayo,* or fainting spell, and the improvised oratory of his panic-stricken foreign minister, Castro's obits were rushed back to the rewrite desk.

The Castro obit industry cranked up one more time in 2004 when Fidel fell facedown splat to the ground. By then, Castro had made some unusual concessions about his mortality. Subtle but crucial changes signaled concerns for his health and the future of his Revolution. On July 1, 2006, Cuba's Communist Party decreed that the twelve-member Secretariat would be restored, thus enhancing the role of the Party when the transfer of power occurred. The Secretariat had been disbanded in 1992 after the Soviets dropped out of the picture. Henceforth, it would serve as the Party's steering committee and ensure that the Party, and its majority hardliner members, would play a central role in the post-Fidel era.

A month later, when Castro underwent emergency surgery, the obit business roared into a frenzy and has remained on standby ever since. Over the next three years, Castro's obit would be revised monthly, sometimes weekly, at news bureaus around the globe. One reporter at National Public Radio lamented she had taped three Castro obituaries in the first year of his illness. In the second and third years of his infirmity, there would be many more revisions.

"We had to redo our obit several times," Anders Gyllenhaal, the editor of the *Miami Herald,* said a year after Castro fell ill. Tom Fiedler, the paper's editor from 2001 to 2007, told *Editor & Publisher* that "we had plans for Castro's death going back to the '90s. It was truly exhaustive, maybe more detailed than the Pentagon's plan to invade Iraq," Gyllenhaal told me in 2007. "We've had internal workshops here about it and had to make big changes twice. Fortunately, we had a dress rehearsal," he added, referring to Castro's close call in July 2006.

A year later, the *Herald* was not feeling so sanguine. A senior editor, Manny Garcia, discarded traditional newsroom etiquette and penned a dishy, ornery brief in which he compared Castro to a "kidney stone—a constant pain who never seems to go away." Garcia explained his pique. "You gotta understand that the Cadaver-in-Chief is our story and biggest challenge," he complained. "We sit in meetings, long meetings, going over possible stories. Phrasing. Tone. Length. We got at least five different versions of Fidel's obit, pegged to the time of day or night he dies. We built a Web page for the big day. . . ." For journalists covering Cuba, whom Castro had long held in insect-low regard, the long dying of the Caribbean strongman had become one more indignity to be endured.

The first attempt at a Castro biography appeared in April 1959, with a collection of his letters entitled *Cartas del Presidio* (Letters from Prison) with the subtitle *A Preview from a Biography of Fidel Castro.* Its cover featured the then-twenty-six-year-old Castro's mug shot taken after his arrest for the Moncada assault in 1953.

The book's twenty-one letters included missives sent to his wife

Myrta; his half-sister Lidia; the esteemed intellectual Jorge Mañach, who had elegantly glossed Castro's Moncada speech; his personal lawyer; a future mistress; and the father of a compatriot who had perished in the Moncada attack. The collection also included several letters to his trusted friend and political stalwart, Luis Conte Agüero, who published the letters and wrote the book's preface, a passionate tribute to the man he believed would be Cuba's savior. Two years later, Conte Agüero fled the country and copies of the book disappeared from the shelves. In 2005, I wrote a new introduction to the book, which was republished in an English/Spanish edition.

A celebrity inmate, Castro used his time in prison—about twenty-two months—resourcefully. He read and wrote ceaselessly and relentlessly plotted his political future. The letters amply demonstrate Castro's strategic thinking and natural leadership. They are an early indicator of his Machiavellian cunning and his genius for public relations. "We cannot for a minute abandon propaganda, for it is the soul of our struggle," he famously wrote his confederate Melba Hernández in 1954. Letter after letter illustrates Castro's ability to inspire others to do his bidding. Many of his correspondents appeared to have centered their lives on him, anxious to know his needs and eager to fulfill them. Some focused on his political agenda while others awaited instructions in public relations and talking points: "Maintain a deceptively soft touch and smile with everyone," he advised Hernández. "Follow the same strategy that we followed during the trial; defend our points of view without raising resentments. There will be enough time later to squash all the cockroaches together. Do not lose heart over anything or anyone."

The letters are an early map of Castro's political ambitions, along with lesser matters including his desired visits with Fidelito, his devolving marriage and subsequent divorce. Although Castro has never been regarded as a man of easy sentiment, the letters are filled with warmth and affection toward those he trusted. To those who opposed him, there were rages and rants.

There are disquisitions on all manner of topics, from his food preferences and public relations to his philosophical musings, including his esteem for the Stoic philosopher-statesman Cato, who chose to end his life rather than live under Caesar. For Castro's enemies, a casual homophobia eked from his pen: "Only an effeminate like [Ramón] Hermida, at the lowest degree of sexual degeneration, would resort to these methods, of such inconceivable indecency and unmanliness," Castro huffed in one letter, referring to the Minister of the Interior.

The most poignant aspect of the letters is the number of correspondents Castro lauded as devoted friends or heroes who would later break from him when he assumed power. Support for the Cuban Revolution had cut across all class and economic distinctions. Most believed that the removal of the corrupt and repressive Batista regime could only augur better things for Cuba. But in time, many came to believe they had been betrayed.

Many, like Jorge Mañach and Castro's own sister, fled into exile. Others were sent to prison or the firing squad. A few, like Miguel Ángel Quevedo, the gifted editor of *Bohemia* magazine, who had proved so helpful to Castro, took their own lives. Such was Quevedo's singular importance that Castro had beseeched Conte Agüero to bring the publisher-editor on board. "I beg you to visit Quevedo," he wrote, "and exhort him in this sense. . . . The simple publication of the charges will have tremendous consequences for the [Batista] government." In another letter to his wife Myrta, he reminded her, "Do not fail to give the article to Miguel Quevedo, now with more reason than ever."

On July 26, 1958, the fifth anniversary of the Moncada assault, *Bohemia* published Fidel's "Sierra Maestra Manifesto," laying out his fervently held belief in the necessity to unite the various factions seeking to topple Batista. On January 11, 1959, the magazine printed a special edition that sold more than one million copies. Quevedo's subsequent suicide note, sent to the renowned journalist Ernesto Montaner, is a searing indictment against his former friend. "Fidel is nothing more than the result of the clash between demagoguery and stupidity," he wrote before taking his life in Caracas in August 1969. "All of us contributed to his creation. . . . I die disgusted and alone. Condemned, without a country, and abandoned by friends to whom I generously gave financial and moral support during the most difficult days. . . . And now we are all victims."

It was inevitable that Fidel Castro would seek to have the last word. Make that roughly two hundred thousand final words—as is the case with *My Life,* Castro's voluminous and irresistible "autobiography." Published in the United States in early 2008, it is based on some one hundred hours of conversation with the journalist Ignacio Ramonet, spanning more than two years.

The book was first published in 2005 in Spanish under the title *Fidel Castro: Biografía a dos voces* (A Biography in Two Voices). Castro, however, regarded the English-language edition as being of greater significance. To that end, Ramonet informed his readers that Castro "totally revised and amended" the Spanish original. According to Ramonet,

Castro was still glossing the text in November 2006. That would mean that while the Cuban leader was dangling between life and death, being fed intravenously, fifty pounds thinner and barely able to sit up, he summoned his über-human will to rewrite his memoirs. "I wanted to finish it because I didn't know how much time I'd have," Castro explained to a friend.

With his pliant interlocutor, Castro does have the last word. After all, Fidel Castro was not spilling the beans with just anyone. Ramonet is an unabashed *fidelista* who addressed his subject as "*Comandante.*" "Few men have known the glory of entering the pages of history and legend while they are still alive," he wrote in his Introduction. "Fidel is one of them." High praise but true enough. Then the Kool-Aid kicks in. "He is the last sacred giant of international politics."

Notwithstanding his considerable experience and talents as a journalist, Ramonet functions somewhat as a literary Oliver Stone—whose cinematic hagiography of Castro produced two rosy portraits, *Comandante* and *Looking for Fidel.* Undoubtedly, scholars and historians will be in the debt of both Stone and Ramonet for their extraordinary access and the sheer scope of their materials: fifty hours of videotape and hundreds of hours of audiotape. Their tape transcripts, when edited by less partisan chroniclers, could be well worth the wait.

To their credit, Castro and Ramonet turned to the excellent translator Andrew Hurley in presenting their opus to English-language readers. He was an unusual choice, having previously translated several vociferous Castro critics, including Heberto Padilla, Jorge Edwards, and Reinaldo Arenas. Hurley wrote that he was a tad surprised to get the assignment and his notes are among the most interesting parts of *My Life.* Comparing his work as a translator to that of a defense lawyer, Hurley noted that "I saw, and see, Fidel Castro as one of the most 'censored' world figures in English . . . represented almost invariably by his enemies."

Hurley had to cope with the Maximum Leader's eleventh-hour revisions, which he described as Castro's desire "to present a less 'outspoken' or 'unbuttoned' image." He wrote that some of Castro's changes stemmed from wanting to revise a "'politically incorrect' statement" . . . [and thus] some of his more direct and uninhibited statements ended up on the cutting room floor." Hurley found the requested changes to be "historically interesting" because "they revealed Castro's mind at work *before* the super-ego of hindsight and counsel kicked in." So extensive were Castro's edits—"tens of thousands of changes"—that the marked-up, inky pages "looked like ants at a picnic," according to Hurley. Fortunately for historians and Cubaphiles, he relocated some of Castro's cuts to the book's endnotes.

Castro shared his own memories of the anxiety he felt during the revision process. "Never in my life had I thought so much," he told an interlocutor from *Granma*. "I had thought that it would be a quick thing, like the interviews with [writers] Frei Betto and Tomás Borge. And then I became a slave to the French writer's [Ramonet's] book. When it was at the point of being published without my going over it . . . I barely slept during those days." Castro goes on to paint an astonishing, and not especially flattering self-portrait—a man more preoccupied with his legacy than his own physical survival, who had summoned what may have been his final breath to micromanage his afterlife. "When I fell gravely ill on the night of the 26th and in the early morning of the 27th of July [2006], I thought that would be the end," Castro recalled. "And while the doctors were fighting for my life, the head of the Council of State's office was reading me the text, at my insistence, and I was dictating the pertinent changes."

Not surprisingly, Castro's prodigious gifts are well displayed in his autobiography: his formidable erudition, steely discipline, epic curiosity, and an astute grasp of history. A careful reader can even glimpse his flaws: the obsessiveness, colossal pride, and fierce willfulness. There are also telling, even chilling insights. Discussing an early betrayal when he was a young activist in Havana in 1952, Castro said he learned some crucial lessons that would harden his heart. "He was a *compañero*," he said of a cohort-turned-informer. "I trusted him. That's the mistake. You shouldn't trust someone just because he's a friend."

At times, it seems as if *all* of Castro's reflections are in his memoir—the history of Cuba, the collapse of the Soviet empire, Joseph Stalin, his mentorship of Hugo Chávez, U.S. politics, even Lee Harvey Oswald. Castro is never boring and presents himself as a man who never knew boredom. He sees the broader, global picture—especially in regard to history's strongmen. "Despite his terrible abuses and errors," Castro opines generously of Stalin, "one has to give [him] credit for an accelerated industrialization of the country."

For the English edition, Castro added a chapter devoted to all things French, perhaps to honor France's historically good relations with Cuba and himself. Castro lavishes admiration on former French president François Mitterrand and his wife, Dominique, Jean-Paul Sartre, and the works of Honoré de Balzac and Victor Hugo. In Castro's reading of history, Charles de Gaulle was "a genius"—as well as a soul mate of sorts. He saluted de Gaulle for what he called "his intransigence [and] defiance of the United States and the English." He even offers a shaky comparison between the Cuban and French Revolutions. And there are many interesting musings on his childhood idol and lifelong north star, Napoléon Bonaparte.

Also for the English edition, Castro added a new chapter on his family and background in which he is uncharacteristically forthcoming and emotional. He speaks of his mother, who died in 1963 at the age of sixty from congestive heart failure, with immense affection, sprinkled with hyperbole: "Without her, I assure you that I—who always loved to study—would be a functional illiterate. My mother was practically illiterate, and like my father, she learned to read and write practically on her own. With a great deal of effort and determination, too. I never heard her say that she'd gone to school. She was self-taught."

As Castro gazed backward on his childhood, he saw Lina Ruz as a *guajira* Renaissance woman—notwithstanding the misfortunes and austerity of her own life. "My mother, although she wasn't saying so every minute, adored her children," he wrote. "She was a cook, a doctor, a caretaker of all of us—she provided every single thing we might need and she was a shoulder to cry on for any problem we might have. . . . I never saw her rest one second the whole day."

But much is left unsaid or sanitized—from the excesses and failures of the Revolution to family secrets. Castro's account has his mother, Lina, giving birth to her firstborn, daughter Angela (named for the child's father), in 1923 when Lina was nineteen. Some Castrophiles contend that Lina was actually fourteen, having been seduced by Ángel Castro soon after she began working in his home. (Records document Lina's birth year as both 1903 and 1908, which could be the result of a typo, a careless registrar, or some historical fudging.)

Castro recalls his parents as almost hardscrabble pioneers, who through dint of their ceaseless labors became immensely successful. Both Ángel and Lina roamed the family *hacienda* on horseback, their rifles tucked into their saddles. "My father was a very isolated landowner, actually. My parents didn't go out and only rarely had visitors. There was no rich-family culture. They worked all the time. And our only contact was with the people who lived there in Birán," said Castro about his earliest years. He well describes the schizophrenia of being the offspring of wealth but not culture—of not hailing from what Cubans call *"una buena cuna"*—literally a good cradle, but meaning a good or proper family. "If I'd been the grandson of a rich family . . . I'd have had an aristocratic birth, and all my friends and all my culture would have been marked by a sense of superiority and all that. But in fact, where I was born everybody was poor—children of farm workers and extremely poor *campesinos*. . . . And my own family, on my mother's side, was poor, and some of my father's cousins, who came over from Galicia, were poor. . . . I lived with people of the most humble origins. . . . On the other hand, in Santiago and later in Havana, I was in schools for the privileged."

Ángel Castro, who donned a pistol, whip, and machete over his coveralls, was known to be both severe and generous with his three-hundred-plus workers and his own children. "There was also the fact of corporal punishment, a slap on the head or a belt taken to you," Castro said about his father. "We always ran that risk."

At the age of six, Castro and his older brother, Ramón, and sister Angelita were sent to Santiago to live and study with the family of their Haitian schoolteacher. It is probable that Ángel Castro's unusual domestic relationships necessitated moving some of Lina's children out of sight for a period. No doubt Lina believed as well that she was improving her children's opportunities. But it proved to be a harrowing, almost Dickensian experience for Castro and his siblings. The Haitian family, desperate for money, hoarded the stipend paid to them by Ángel Castro ("120 pesos a month, which at the time was a fortune"), and provided the Castro children with minimal food and study. "Because I was the son of a rich man, I was the victim of exploitation," Castro explained. "I gave myself my own lessons. Since then, I've always taught myself things." Asked if that experience damaged his feeling toward his parents, Castro answered with an adult's hindsight. "No, I loved them, at least respected them."

While Castro was a precocious, gifted student, he was rebellious and pigheaded from the gate. At one point, he and his brothers Raúl and Ramón attended grade school at the Colegio De La Salle, a Marist Christian school in Santiago. When their parents came to pick them up for the Christmas holiday, they were mortified to learn that their sons—Fidel in particular—were the terror of the school. The principal told the parents that their progeny were "*los tres bandidos más grandes que habían pasado por la escuela*"—the three biggest rascals that had ever gone through the school.

For punishment the three were taken out of their expensive school and returned to the family farm and grounded. There would be no more fancy out-of-town prep schools. In response, Fidel famously threatened war on his family. "I must have been eleven, because I was in the fifth grade, and that's when I said all those terrible things," he recalled. Castro confirmed the childhood anecdote that some journalists suspected was apocryphal: "I said I was going to burn the house down," he tells his Boswell, pointing out that the building "was made of wood." "But you didn't really intend to do that, did you?" queried Ramonet. "I'm not sure what I would have done," Castro mused, with a nod to the origins of his scorched-earth warrior character. "Most likely I wouldn't have. I mean, I was very, very angry, but I wouldn't have done it, I'm convinced. But I said I would, and I must have said it very seriously."

Castro conceded what his friends at the posh Havana prep school, Belén, would invariably point out: that there was a decided cultural deficit in his upbringing. "We were privileged, going to schools for the wealthy, the upper class, yet we had big gaps in art, painting . . . nothing at all about art." It would remain so throughout his life. Castro had tremendous talent and an insatiable interest in sports, science, politics, history, and military strategy but he never developed a passion for art, dance, film, or the *belles lettres*. He told me in 1994 that he spent his free time watching documentaries about science and astronomy. It would be left to his comrades Celia Sánchez and Alfredo Guevara, the Marxist intellectual who founded the country's prestigious film school, ICAIC, to foster and preserve Cuban culture in whatever ways they could.

While Castro's memoir seems to touch on just about everything, there are significant blanks in the narrative. George Orwell's admonition that "autobiography is the most outrageous form of fiction" comes to mind in some patches of his self-portrait. There is no mention of his sister Juanita's flight into exile. More tellingly, he is mum on the near-dozen children he has sired, and has nothing to say about his first great love, Myrta Díaz-Balart, and his second spouse, Dalia Soto del Valle. Nor is Ramonet much help. "It never crossed my mind that we should speak about Castro's private life, his wife or children," Ramonet tells readers to their palpable disappointment.

Put another way, Castro is the master of the verbal smoke screen, in the parlance of Zen Buddhism. He knows all too well, whether speaking or writing, that a blizzard of words can both tell a story *and* obscure simple facts and humble truths. After all, he is an accomplished story-teller and mythographer.

As it turned out, Castro was not alone in seeking to have the final word on his life. Published almost at the same time was *The Autobiography of Fidel Castro*—a thirteen-hundred-page tome written in Castro's fictional voice by Norberto Fuentes. Formerly Fuentes had been cozily comfortable with the Revolution and enjoyed unusual access to Castro. His disillusionment began, however, in the late 1980s and he defected in 1994. In an interview, Fuentes said he opted to omit "the usual things about the Revolution and Castro: a dictator, a murderer with blood on his hands. The idea is to understand a phenomenon, a force of nature, somebody who exists, who is with us, and who will be a part of history forever." Asked to list some of Castro's vices, Fuentes gave a generous appraisal: "He has a lot, but as he himself would say: why look at the sun's spots? There's no point in assessing Castro in terms of his vices; it is his virtues that count, his achievements as a leader."

My Life was not Castro's first attempt at writing history. In 2003, *Todo el tiempo de los cedros* (In the Time of the Cedars) appeared in Havana. The title referenced the grand and gracious cedar trees that flourished on the Castro *finca*. It is a sunny and flattering memoir of the Castro family written by Katiuska Blanco, who was afforded unprecedented access to family members, letters, and photographs. Its sycophancy is undiluted; it is even dedicated "to Fidel, who breathes life" and to his parents. Nevertheless, it is crammed with fascinating detail and both intended and inadvertent insights. Perhaps because of the latter, it disappeared from circulation not long after its publication.

Blanco quotes from a diary purportedly written while Castro was in solitary confinement in prison in 1954. One long, rambling missive is a veritable discourse on the philosopher Immanuel Kant—a free association that Castro would pick up fifty-five years later, after the election of Barack Obama. Moreover, and perhaps why it was included, the entry showcases Castro's intellectual deftness in navigating complex theory. One cannot help but wonder whether philosophy or physics might have been his true calling.

I had fallen asleep reading "The Transcendental Esthetic of Space and Time." Of course, space and time disappeared from my mind for a good while. Kant made me remember Einstein, his theory of the relativity between space and time, and his famous formula about Energy: $E=mc^2$; the relation that might exist between the concepts of one and another, maybe in opposition; his conviction of having found definitive criteria that saved philosophy from deteriorating, beaten by experimental sciences and the imposing results of his discoveries. Would the same thing that happened to Descartes, whose philosophy was unable to be proven because it contradicted the proven laws of Copernicus and Galileo, happen to Kant? But Kant does not try to explain the nature of things, but rather the means by which we reach nature; whether it is possible to know or not to know and accordingly when they are estimated or erroneous; a philosophy of knowledge, not of the objects of knowledge. Accordingly, there shouldn't be a contradiction between Kant and Einstein. Nevertheless, there are his concepts of space and time, basic points to elaborate his philosophical system. And is there room for contradiction? Clearly, it won't be difficult to make sure, but while I asked myself that question, just like many others that continuously besiege us, I thought of the limits of our knowledge and the immense vastness of the field that man has worked with intelligence and effort through the centuries. And the very acknowledgment of these findings saddens one. . . . In the middle of all this, I couldn't stop debating whether it was worth it to invest my time studying these things and the possibility of utilizing my findings to resolve the present evils.

Evidently, Fidel's fixation with Kant remained lifelong. In February 2009, Castro penned a bizarre rumination on Rahm Emanuel, President Obama's chief of staff. "What a strange surname!" he exclaimed, diving into another free fall, free associative discourse, this one in the form of a blog post. The name Rahm Emanuel, he mused, "appears to be Spanish, easy to pronounce, but it's not. Never in my life have I heard or read about any student or compatriot with that name, among tens of thousands. Where does it come from? I wondered. Over and over, the name came to mind of the brilliant German thinker, Immanuel Kant, who together with Aristotle and Plato, formed a trio of philosophers that have most influenced human thinking. Doubtless he was not very far, as I discovered later, from the philosophy of the man closest to the current president of the United States, Barack Obama."

In Blanco's family history, Fidel is the warmhearted, noble warrior who cherishes country and family. There are a few references to his younger sister Juanita, but no mention of the fact that she irrevocably broke with him and fled the country. On the death of Ángel Castro, Blanco writes that Fidel mournfully recalled his passing. "Fidel remembered what his old and sick father said often: that he would die without once again seeing his children." It would be followed by a letter from young Fidelito meant to dramatize Castro's conflicts between family and duty when he fled to Mexico after his release from prison in 1955 to escape threats on his life. "Now [Castro] understood his [father] well, because after leaving for Cuba, he underwent a similar situation. . . . He once again said farewell to his son Fidel Ángel, without knowing if he'd ever see him again. Fidelito, a six-year-old, wrote back how much he missed his dad."

Castro's mother, Lina, is presented as a paragon of maternal love and a vessel of selfless revolutionary fervor. In reality Lina was less than sanguine about the Revolution's radical reforms, most especially the nationalization of the Castro family estate. But in Blanco's account, Lina is the sacrificing Maríana Grajales, the lionized mother of the nineteenth-century revolutionary generals and martyrs, Antonio and José Maceo. In August 1958, she writes her son in the Sierra—sending her letter by clandestine courier.

Dearest Son:

I pray to God, whole-heartedly, that you are well and enjoying a perfect health and that your good fortune lives on. . . . Attached to this letter I am sending you a photo of your son and I. This picture was taken in the beginning of April, when I went to visit him; as you can see he is very big and very handsome. God willing, he will have your same ideals and great valor. . . .

Every day I pray to God that we will soon be able to hug, all of us together and full of joy, surrounded by LIBERTY that you love just as all Cubans. Every mother is proud of her children, even if her children are nothing more than just her children, but that is not the case with me, because in all of you I have more than just children. You are true heroes, the heroes of the youth and of the entire community that has their hope and faith instilled in you. For this reason, I feel twice as proud of my sons . . .

For the time being, I bid you farewell with all the love of a mother who desires to see you soon and who never forgets you.

May God bless you,
Lina

Two weeks later—just four months before he would claim victory from the Sierra, Castro responded to her.

Dear Mother:

I happily received your letter . . . [but] I will be very brief because of all the things that I want to discuss with you. I would have to write a whole lot or write nothing at all. There will be time when the war is over.

I am well and healthy, like I have never been, and the same goes for Raúl. I am able to communicate with him via radio whenever I want and everything is going well.

I already knew that Ramón was in Spain, and I also knew that about Agustinita's trip. Someday the entire family will once again reunite. You can send me news in this way [messenger] and you will receive letters from me frequently.

Send my greetings to all my good friends whom I have not mentioned, but whom I always remember. Many kisses to you from your son. Fidel

In counterpoint, and equally telling, to Blanco's gauzy, sentimental rendering of the Castro family are the book's fascinating album of photographs of the young Castro family. There are snapshots of the married couple, their children at play, at school, and as soldiers. But in none of those of Fidel, nor of his parents, does anyone wear a trace of a smile.

On July 10, 2008, Castro published an introspective essay on his life as a convalescent in a column he entitled "The Day Off." His most pressing activities these days, he said, were reading and writing and keeping up with the news of the world. But he had made the choice to free himself from his duties, he informed readers, so that he could spend the day with his friend Gabriel García Márquez and Márquez's wife, Mercedes Barcha. "I decided to rest," Castro wrote. "I invited them to have lunch, something that I have never done with any visitor in these almost two years." The luncheon turned into a sprawling five-hour affair in which Castro emotionally reminisced about his life and especially his childhood in Birán. "Never had I seen him so caring," remarked García Márquez afterward. Castro referred to the afternoon with his old friends as "the most pleasant" he had had since he fell ill.

One month later, on August 13, when he turned eighty-two, Castro informed his readers that he continued to adhere to the diet prescribed by his doctors. Then he made a small, revealing admission about his medical prognosis. He said he attended to his health regimen "not to add years to my life, but productivity to my hours." Castro's birthday came and went without any public or official celebration. Neither photographs nor video of Castro were released—spurring a new burst of sizzling gossip that he had significantly declined. Naturally, there was the annual birthday message from Chávez and another from Cuba's athletes at the Olympics in Beijing, who saluted Castro as their "team coach, greatest home run hitter, and unconquerable gladiator." But Castro remained out of sight.

The Maximum Leader was indeed out of sight, but not silent. In the first two weeks of July 2008, he published a record eight columns of "Reflections." "Fidel, even though sick, speaks more than his brother Raúl!" proclaimed the headline of an EFE article, which noted that

Raúl had given a mere two speeches since assuming the presidency and that neither had exceeded fifty minutes.

Fidel's absence from public view during his birthday week prompted the usual speculation, but also sober contemplation from his critics. "Only rarely had the will of one man had so much weight in a country," wrote the Havana blogger Yoani Sánchez. "His obstinate personality will be historic. . . . On the eve of the 50th anniversary of the Triumph of the Revolution . . . it can be said that there are two great truths about the experiment Castro began in Cuba: that it has not collapsed, as had been predicted by its enemies, and that it has not achieved its promised objectives, as its followers had forecast."

As he had so fervently hoped, Fidel Castro had lived to see the golden anniversary of the revolution he had brought to Cuba. The Cuban Marathon Man had been able to summon his vast reserves of grit and perseverance. But the degree to which he celebrated was unknown, because he was neither seen nor heard.

On December 31, 2008, a terse, one-sentence message was released, purportedly from Castro: "Upon the celebration in the next few hours of the 50th anniversary of the Triumph, I congratulate our heroic people." One week later, on January 8, the fiftieth anniversary of his triumphant march on Havana—an eight-day victory lap that began in Santiago—there was no photo op, no message, not even a column of his "Reflections." Indeed, the great event came and went in eerie silence.

Two visiting heads of state, both favored allies of Cuba, returned to their homelands empty-handed. President Rafael Correa of Ecuador and President Martín Torrijos of Panama had been told that they would visit with Castro. To many Cubaphiles, it was the coup de grâce signifying one gloomy conclusion. Correa later confirmed that he had been informed during his visit that Castro had suffered "a relapse and was in very delicate health," consistent with the progression of malignant diverticulitis. The fact that neither man met with Castro ramped up speculation. The Cuban triangle of capitals, Havana, Miami, and Washington, buzzed with word that Castro was at death's door or beyond. And this time it was not bloviators or bloggers driving rumors but seasoned diplomats and other Cuba veterans who made the case that something was quite amiss in Havana.

More than a month had passed since Castro had penned one of his frequent columns—back on December 15, 2008. The last photos of him dated back even further to November 18, when he met with Chinese president Hu Jintao. His meeting ten days later with Russian president

Dmitri Medvedev was also unusually low-key with no photographs released to the media.

At the same time, *Granma* had begun reprinting Castro's favorite speeches stretching back to 1959—sort of a greatest hits list. Renato Pérez Pizarro, who writes the *Miami Herald*'s "Cuban Colada" blog, saw the list as an attempt "to remind readers that Fidel then was young and full of fervor and promise."

The drone of chatter was amplified by reports from Cubans about an intensified and intrusive level of police on the streets. Throughout January, residents complained that access to the internet was blocked more often than not.

There was one more item cited by conspiracists on the Deathwatch. In December 2008, Carlos Valenciaga, Fidel Castro's executive secretary and longtime faithful aide, who had solemnly announced Castro's health crisis on television, suddenly fell out of favor—and out of a job. Not a few surmised that Valenciaga's downfall signaled that Raúl, not Fidel, was finally calling the shots. As it turned out, Valenciaga's head was simply the first to roll. Two months later, twelve of Fidel's most trusted officials would be sent packing.

Such was the roiling environment when Hugo Chávez, once again, lit the fuse under the fire. On January 10, 2009, Chávez told his television and radio listeners that his friend would not be seen again in the public eye. "Fidel in his uniform, who walked the streets and towns late at night, hugging the people, will not return," said Chávez. "That will remain in [our] memories." The voluble Venezuelan then reminisced about the last time the two had been together publicly—during their trip to Argentina in July 2006, only a week before Castro slid into mortal peril. "He walked to the door of the plane and we hugged," said Chávez emotionally. "*Dios mío,* I didn't think it would be the last time." Before he finished, he sought to reassure listeners. "Fidel will live forever—beyond the physical life."

By the time Chávez's Sunday show ended, Castro's obituary had been updated and readied for release around the globe.

But as he had done so many times before, Castro walked back from the grave, albeit with a good deal of assistance. On January 21, 2009, he rallied himself for a forty-minute unannounced chat with Argentina's president Cristina Fernández de Kirchner. The timing of the meeting was carefully chosen. Cuba had to move quickly to neutralize the spiraling rumors that Castro had died—before they became an article of faith. Still, the government did not want to upstage the inauguration of the new president in Washington. "He told me he had followed the inauguration of Barack Obama very closely," Kirchner told reporters later. "He had watched the inauguration on television all day. He had a very good perception of President Obama [as] a man who seems absolutely sincere. Fidel believes in Obama." The requisite photo op, which some cynics dismissed as "a Photoshop," was released. This one showed the Cuban leader looking solemn and cautious, wearing a black track suit with red trim, holding tightly to the arm of Kirchner.

The Argentine was escorted to the airport by Raúl Castro, who was peppered with questions about his brother's medical condition. "Do you think if he were really gravely ill that I'd be smiling here?" said Raúl, positing a convincing case. "Soon I'm going to take a trip to Europe," he said, referring to his upcoming trip to Russia. "Do you guys think I would leave here if Fidel were really in grave condition?"

In the spring of 2009, a somewhat rejuvenated Castro began spending more time at his Siboney home, where his doctors had created a state-of-the-art medical suite. Over the next few months, there would be sightings of Castro in his neighborhood—always surrounded by a security detail on foot and in Mercedes sedans. One passerby had seen him walking slowly, "shuffling," with evident effort, accompanied by Eusebio Leal, the historian who has supervised the restoration of Old Havana. The daughter of one neighbor told ABC News that "my mom says they always know when the *Comandante* is coming because bodyguards with AK-47s show up well before to check the area. Then he slowly walks by, usually in his track suit and with a couple more bodyguards. Sometimes he stops to say hello." According to the *New York Times*, on another occasion he was seen walking with his son Alejandro near CIMEQ, the highly regarded hospital not far from his home, where he made weekly visits presumably to clean and change his colostomy apparatus and, possibly, to have dialysis.

A few carefully chosen guests were even invited to visit him at his home. Three members of the Congressional Black Caucus had one such visit in April 2009 and said that Castro's spouse, Dalia, greeted them at the gate while Castro stood leaning against the doorjamb. Accompanying Castro was his old friend Chomy, formally known as José Miyar Barruecos.

Representative Bobby Rush, a former Black Panther, said his group was enchanted by the Cuban leader, who remained seated during their two-hour chat. He described Castro as speaking with the trio "as though we were old family members." When it was time for them to leave, Rush said, "he was very careful and deliberate when he stood up."

Prior to the visit, Castro had penned a favorable review of the new American president in his "Reflections" column that had concluded with a note of startling candor. "I am well but I insist that none of [my comrades] should feel constrained by my occasional 'Reflections,' *the gravity of my health*, or my death."

He offered further introspection. "I have had the rare privilege of observing events for a very long time. I receive information and I calmly ponder the events." Castro then made his first public acknowledgment that he was terminally ill. "I do not expect I shall enjoy such a privilege four years from now—when President Obama's first term has concluded."

"He will die like the Jesuit he was raised to be," predicted María Luisa Menéndez, whose family were devout *fidelistas* until they left in 1961. "Mark my words, there will be a priest next to him giving him the Last Rites."

Over the years, Castro had told the occasional visitor that his father's family roots were Jewish. Indeed, the Castros hail from the region of northern Spain where Jews predominated, and the name is not uncommon among Sephardic Jews. It is not unlikely that the family converted to Catholicism two centuries back. That said, Castro's intellectual roots and rigor were pure Jesuit. "He was educated by the Jesuits and remains an atheist Jesuit wearing fatigues instead of the frock," the Cuban journalist Ángel Tomás González told the *Guardian*. "That's why there was no problem between him and Pope John Paul."

It was Castro who decreed that Cuba was an atheist nation in 1962, chased the Church off the island, and banned the Christmas holiday until 1997. However, he never fully cut ties with the Vatican, although he was as suspicious and ruthless with the Church as he had been with any other potential threat. Thirty-five years after he asserted his dominion over the Church in Cuba, he negotiated a truce with the Vatican, resulting in Pope John Paul II's pilgrimage to Havana. Just prior to the papal visit in 1998, Castro reinstated the Christmas holiday.

For the Pope's historic mass in the Plaza of the Revolution that attracted a million Cubans, the top-tier Politburo members dutifully donned their best suits and sat quietly in the front rows. Behaving as respectfully as altar boys, Fidel's men made an evident effort as they sat before the Pope, their eyes wandering, their legs crossed. Only Fidel, dressed in his finest French suit, sat properly with his hands perched on his knees. "Only Fidel remembered," noted Menéndez, "that one never crosses their legs in front of the Pope."

The papal visit, however, had been blighted by the Monica Lewinsky scandal, which tore through Washington and into the headlines, disrupting Cuba's meticulously media-orchestrated plans. All the top U.S. anchors—Peter Jennings, Dan Rather, Ted Koppel, and Tom Brokaw—were instructed to return immediately to Washington. Cuban officials were visibly devastated by the turn of events and saw a sinister conspiracy at work. "This is the dirty hand of the CIA. It is clearly one of their tricks," an exhausted official with the Foreign Ministry told me at the time. When I explained that some evidence had emerged that the president had had an affair with a young woman, he looked incredulous, and said just one word: "So?" A conspiracy to rob Cuba of its papal moment it would be, as far as Havana was concerned.

Jorge Fernandez, a Cuban-American involved in Cuba's reconciliation with the Catholic Church, described Fidel as behaving like "Eddie Haskell [the ingratiating teenager of the 1960s TV series *Leave It to Beaver* fame] the whole time he was around the Pope. He could not have been more respectful during the visit." Fernandez had assisted the return in 2008 of the Knights of Columbus, hailed as "the right hand of the Catholic Church" by Pope John Paul II. With Fidel's blessing, God had been welcomed back to Cuba—within limits, of course. Recent polls, according to Orlando Gutiérrez, who tracks dissident groups in Cuba, indicate that 75 percent to 85 percent of Cubans believe in the Divine while some 60 percent are now baptized, figures that were in the single digits just twenty years ago.

During Castro's final illness, he redoubled his efforts to arrange a visit with Pope Benedict, whose emissary, Cardinal Tarcisio Bertone, would be Raúl Castro's first meeting with a foreign official as president. The Church today is the largest nongovernmental organization (NGO) in Cuba. Its adjunct, Caritas, has twelve thousand volunteers, who serve as one of the most reliable humanitarian groups in the country. Nor is the Catholic Church working the faithful alone. Pentecostals, Methodists, and Mormons have redoubled their efforts and converts. The Mormons now claim some thirty thousand members who worship at three hundred temples, albeit in some structures that are little more than *bohíos,* or shanties.

An especially warm welcome mat was extended to the Russian Orthodox Church. Castro shrewdly viewed the Church as a key element in his new strategic alliance with his former patron. On October 20, 2008, a notably thinner Castro, wearing a white tracksuit and Adidas sneakers, met for ninety minutes with Metropolitan Kirill, the Church's foreign affairs official who assumed the top slot of the Church as its Patriarch three months later. Kirill visited with Castro after consecrating a Russian Orthodox cathedral in Havana, then issued a clean bill of health for Castro: "He is in full command of his senses," said Kirill, "[which is] proof of his overall recovery and his inner strength. "In public, Fidel always has said he is a Marxist, but his evaluation of what is going on today in the world is a Christian evaluation," said Kirill, who presented Castro with the Church's Order of Glory and Honor. In his next commentary, Castro assured readers that his Russian visitor, and by inference the Church, "is not an enemy of socialism."

In his private life, Castro had declared himself to be an atheist or agnostic for most of his adult life, but he had been a young man of faith. "Physical life is ephemeral, it passes inexorably," he wrote consolingly to the father of a fallen Moncada comrade in 1954, when Castro was twenty-seven. "As have passed so many generations of men, soon each of us will pass as well. . . . God is the supreme idea of goodness and justice."

And while Castro tended to keep spiritual matters to himself, both his sister Juanita and their younger sibling, Agustina, are devoutly religious, in the tradition of their mother. His eldest brother, Ramón (Mongo), notwithstanding his fondness for women and rum, also attends church regularly. The Castros had enjoyed an extended private meeting with Pope John Paul II, which was exhaustively memorialized on video and in photographs for the family, but never disclosed to the media. All the Castro siblings, with the exception of Juanita, were present—including a suited-up Raúl. Even Emma, who lives in Mexico, flew in for the Pope's visit.

"They never left their Catholic roots," insists John Parke Wright IV, whose Tampa-based parents owned extensive ranching land in Cuba. "The family has always struck me as being Catholics of faith," said Wright, who regularly visits on U.S.-approved agribusiness matters. While in Havana, Wright attends Sunday mass in the city's magnificent cathedral, an eighteenth-century ode to the former supremacy of the Church. Wright is usually accompanied by Agustina, and often by Ramón Castro—the youngest and eldest, respectively, of the surviving Castro clan.

Fidel Castro arrived in the world with a surfeit of gifts: the discipline of a warrior, the intellect of a mathematician, and the endurance of an athlete. In equal parts, he was diminished by his flaws: blighted by the obsessions of the paranoid and the willfulness of a child. Yet he was either kissed by fate or blessed by the gods.

Rarely has a man been afforded such opportunity and the goodwill of so many. His endowments and nimble luck makes his legacy—a bankrupt country with one-tenth of its population having fled—all the more troubling.

Not surprisingly, Castro thought otherwise, that he would be triumphant after death. "Our enemies should not delude themselves," he told his appointed biographer. "I die tomorrow and my influence may actually increase. I may be carried around like El Cid. Even after he was dead, his men carried him around on his horse, winning battles."

PART TWO

THE FIDEL OBSESSION

"With Fidel, there is neither marriage nor divorce."
—Che Guevara

CHAPTER FIVE

The Pediatrician
and the Exterminator

Standing at the front door of his modest home in the early spring of 2006, Orlando Bosch Avila, Fidel Castro's most determined would-be assassin, offered his hand and a weak smile. Although Bosch was never a handsome man, age had softened his rough features. His huge brown eyes, hovering behind his trademark oversized black plastic eyeglasses, were almost childlike now.

Once upon a time, Bosch said, he spoke pretty good English, but those days were long gone. He was foggy too about some of the details of his life. In 1952 he began a two-year medical internship in Toledo, Ohio, followed by his residency "in the hospital where Martin Luther King died—but I can't remember the name." That was long ago—before he gave up pediatrics for terrorism, as the FBI and Justice Department have described his forty-five-year career as a paramilitary commando.

Bosch had another view of his career, suggesting to me that a book on his life be called *Orlando Bosch the Good*. "*Soy luchador y patriota*," he said. "I am a fighter and a patriot." Nor did he have second thoughts about the collateral damage he had inflicted. "The war [we] wage against the tyrant, you have to down planes, you have to sink ships," Bosch said on Miami television. "You have to be prepared to attack anything that is within your reach." When I asked whether he had regrets about the many civilian casualties resulting from his strikes, Bosch exhaled a long sigh. "We were at war with Castro," he explained. "And in war, everything is valid."

On August 18, 2009, Bosch will turn eighty-three, following in the footsteps of his college classmate and lifelong nemesis. "Fidel is only five days older than me," he noted glumly, holding up the fingers of his right hand. But Bosch's body was failing him and he fretted he would not live to see the demise of Fidel. His lower lip appeared bruised and droopy, the consequence of a series of strokes he had suffered in the previous year. There were heart problems as well and prostate cancer.

Bosch lives in a tidy, working class suburb on the western outskirts of Miami, a stone's throw from the roaring turnpike that slices through the Sunshine State. His paintings line nearly every wall, most simple pastorals of Las Villas, the verdant, graceful province in the midsection of Cuba where Bosch was born. Many were done while he was behind bars in Venezuela, Atlanta, and Miami, serving time, he said, for *la lucha* (the struggle). "Nineteen years in prison, all told," Bosch told me, speaking slowly.

At the time of my first meeting with Bosch, in 2006, his comrade-in-arms, Luis Posada Carriles, was two thousand miles away, in an immigration jail in El Paso, Texas. For two years, Posada would pace his small cell, far from friends and family in Miami. He had nothing but time to ponder his long career as an intelligence operative and failed assassin of Fidel Castro.

Meanwhile the Justice Department of George W. Bush dithered—trying to decide whether to prosecute its high-profile prey, set him free, or ship him off to a friendly Central American country. The Department's preference was for the latter move, but international pressure obviated that possibility. There had been another option: to detain him under the terms of the Patriot Act. The administration could have prosecuted Posada for crimes of terrorism or, if their knees buckled—as proved to be the case—merely charge him with illegal entry.

Posada and Bosch, conspirators for more than four decades, are a study in opposites: Posada is a cool customer. He is personable but not chatty, a confident man with a casual geniality. Bosch's raw fervor and boasts have been a constant for decades, surprising the most jaundiced investigators with his guileless disclosures and ideological zeal. Posada is more complex: a man of multiple agendas and employers.

At eighty-one in 2009, Posada was finally showing his age. His hair had turned a speckled white but he was sturdier than Bosch, notwithstanding an assassination attempt on him in 1990 that shattered his jaw and nearly severed his tongue, leaving him with a crushed, gravelly voice. Posada insisted that his assailants were Cuban agents—he said a Mossad agent had confirmed this for him, though he acknowledged that he has an array of enemies. One U.S. investigator maintains the attack had nothing to do with politics. "One of the women he was boffing was close to the Salvadoran army generals," he said. "It was revenge." Another theory, offered by a friend of Posada's, is that he was set up by an enemy in Venezuelan intelligence.

I first met Posada in June 1998 while working on an investigative series on exile militants for the *New York Times,* teamed with Larry Rohter. A former colleague from *Vanity Fair* had introduced me to a friend of the legendary militant. A week later, Posada left a message on my answering machine, suggesting that we meet in Aruba. He would pick me up at Aruba's small, low-key airport wearing Bermuda shorts and sandals, and a friendly smile. Posada bore little resemblance to the famous photo of him taken in 1976 showing a chiseled-featured, handsome man with a thatch of wavy black hair. His eyebrows, dense and unruly, slanted diagonally over his watery gray-blue eyes. He had the spryness of a much younger man, despite a creeping thickness around his middle.

Posada hauled my bags outside to a waiting van and drove us to a residential neighborhood: his safe house. The home, a tidy split-level, was hidden from view by a high stucco wall and a security gate and was on loan from trusted friends. Copies of his memoir, *Los caminos del guerrero* (The Ways of the Warrior), self-published in 1994, were on the bookshelf. Like Bosch, Posada is an amateur painter, who first took up the brush while in prison in Venezuela. Several of his canvases were displayed throughout the house. Posada served me some iced tea, while a maid busied herself in the kitchen.

Considering his fugitive status, Posada was remarkably breezy. I switched on my tape recorder and we talked for several hours. Barely a half hour into our first conversation, Posada lifted his shirt over his head, displaying a torso ribboned with scars from a 1990 attempt on his life in Guatemala. Both his arms were marked with holes where slugs had entered and exited, and there was a ten-inch gash across his heart. "One bullet entered here," he said, pointing to his jaw, "and it exited on the left side." After a long recovery process, Posada resumed his life's mission to take out Castro. "It's a war," he said. "A bad war."

Sometimes Posada would reach over and turn off my RadioShack tape recorder, allowing only notes taken by hand. (Back at our hotel, Rohter would transcribe tapes and collate notes as I continued on with Posada.) Posada explained that he had granted the unprecedented interview because he needed to generate publicity for his bombing campaign of Cuba's tourist industry, launched in 1997. Otherwise, he said, investors and tourists would continue flocking to Cuba, supplying an economic lifeline to Castro.

During our first session, Posada gave me a copy of his memoir and one of his larger canvases depicting the countryside near his native Cienfuegos, both warmly dedicated. But the attention he garnered from the *Times* series in 1998 was more than he had bargained for. Posada had agreed to meet with me because he wanted to publicize his efforts to topple Fidel Castro. I recorded as much as possible in the event that Posada developed some regrets, which he did—offering various, conflicting denials before admitting the interview took place.

Like many interview subjects, he was more candid and forthcoming during the intervals that he requested that the tape recorder be turned off. Nevertheless, over the three days I met with him, he revealed a good deal about his various bombing campaigns and his general philosophy. About six hours of our time together was taped.

His admissions of masterminding the bombing campaign—which killed an Italian tourist and caused extensive damage to several sites—generated international condemnation and handed Fidel Castro a propaganda bonanza. Worse, Posada had embarrassed his political supporters in South Florida, some of whom he named as providing him with financial support. Moreover, the FBI and the Justice Department were caught flat-footed by his confessions.

When I asked Posada in September 2005 his greatest regret, he instantly responded, "Speaking to the *New York Times*!" And then he laughed.

Like many Cuban stories, this one is rich in personal history and betrayal. At the center of it, not surprisingly, is Fidel Castro. In the 1940s, Luis Posada, Orlando Bosch, and Fidel Castro were schoolmates at the University of Havana. On campus, Castro was known for having his own apartment, brand-new cars, and a hefty allowance that his wealthy father showered on him. "I knew him very well," Bosch recalled, sitting in a rocking chair next to a photograph of himself from his university years. "We lived across the street from each other. He was intelligent, it's true. He studied law and I studied medicine. I was the president of the Medical School and Fidel was a delegate for the Law School. He could never win an election. I was also secretary general of the FEU [Federation of University Students] and he wanted to be president of that [the student union] as well, but he could never win."

The University of Havana's august law school was Cuba's launching pad for future politicians. It was also a hotbed of *gangsterismo*—a freewheeling world of political and criminal thuggery that characterized the university and Cuban politics. Some students, like the young Castro, carried firearms, and violent altercations were not uncommon.

Bosch had strongly opposed the dictatorship of Fulgencio Batista as a student leader, and later commanded Castro's rebel forces in Las Villas province. When Castro declared victory, Bosch was rewarded with the governorship of the province. But it wasn't long before Bosch accused Castro of betraying the Revolution. He abandoned his post and, for more than a year, led a deadly and effective guerrilla insurgency against the new government. In July 1960, he fled to Miami.

Luis Posada said he too remembers the intense law student from the backwoods of Birán. "He was three years ahead of me," Posada recalled. He pointed out that Castro was handsome but had a weak chin that was improved by a beard.

Unlike Bosch, Posada was not politically engaged during his student years. His family was upper middle class and ran a small printing press in Cienfuegos, a picturesque city on Cuba's southern coast. With a degree in chemistry, he began his career as a pest exterminator. In the mid-1950s, Posada secured a job with the Firestone Rubber and Tire Company, working at its plant in Havana before relocating to its headquarters in Akron, Ohio, where he mastered fluency in English.

Posada said that it was during the first months of Castro's reign—when revenge and retribution ran riot—that he became politicized. He was not alone in his dismay. Luis Ortega, the liberal-minded editor of Havana's most important newspaper, *La Prensa,* had returned to Cuba in January 1959 in solidarity with the Revolution. But he was so troubled by the random violence, arrests, and executions that he fled back to the States five months later. "It was a period of terror," he said. "Nobody was sure of anything then."

Sociologists speak of three waves of Cuban immigration to the U.S.: the first were those who never supported the Cuban Revolution; a second group who supported it but became disenchanted with Castro; and the last, who wanted better jobs and opportunities, not unlike economic refugees. The first wave of Cuban exiles that arrived soon after Castro took power were generally well off, better educated, white skinned, and virulently anti-Castro. This group would seize the political leadership of exile Miami—and never let go. Posada was part of the first wave, but he opted to stay in Cuba and fight for as long as possible.

He would turn not only against the new government, but his own family, who were dedicated *fidelistas.* One sister would rise to the rank of colonel in the Cuban Army and both brothers held good government jobs. From his earliest days as a neophyte counter-revolutionary, Posada allied himself with the CIA's efforts to sabotage the new government.

By 1960, Posada had made the acquaintance of the legendary master spook David Atlee Phillips, the CIA's Man in Havana, who was busy recruiting operatives to overthrow Castro. He would also likely have rubbed shoulders with Phillips's colleague, E. Howard Hunt, if not in Havana, in Miami. In 1961, the CIA set up what was then the largest substation in its history, called JM/WAVE. The station had one mandate and a single mission: to topple Fidel Castro.

Headquartered in a nondescript office building on a secluded, woodsy fifteen-hundred-acre tract on the University of Miami's south campus, JM/WAVE became one of the biggest employers in South Florida. Some four hundred full-time CIA staffers with a fifty-million-dollar annual budget at their disposal employed an estimated fifteen thousand Cuban exiles. A previous, much smaller incarnation of JM/WAVE had been run out of a fledgling CIA office in nearby Coral Gables.

According to Ted Shackley, the spymaster who oversaw the station, some four hundred "front" corporations hired thousands more. The station maintained its own private armory of cutting-edge weaponry and had a fleet of airplanes and hundreds of boats. Several grand mansions in Coral Gables along the water doubled as ports for JM/WAVE's armada of cruisers that made stealth hit-and-runs on Cuba. During its first years of operation, JM/WAVE orchestrated direct attacks against Cuba, then in 1963 switched to directing covert missions.

David Atlee Phillips and E. Howard Hunt had earned their stripes at the Agency by destabilizing left-wing governments and movements in Latin America. Their most notable feat was toppling the newly elected president of Guatemala, Jacobo Arbenz, in 1954 and installing a replacement more congenial to U.S. business interests. Guatemala never quite recovered; two hundred thousand people lost their lives in the ensuing civil war. Still, an eighty-eight-year-old Hunt told me in 2004 that he regarded the coup as a success. His only regret, he said, was allowing a young Argentine named Che Guevara to flee Guatemala.

One distinguished alumnus of JM/WAVE was Porter Goss, who had joined the CIA in 1960 straight out of Yale University with his friend and classmate William "Bucky" Bush, George H. W. Bush's younger brother. Goss worked closely with Cuban exiles before and during the Bay of Pigs invasion and the Cuban Missile Crisis and told the *Washington Post* that during this period he learned a lot about "small-boat handling" and had "some very interesting moments in the Florida Straits." (In September 2004, he was appointed CIA chief by George W. Bush, but stepped down after less than two years under charges that he had politicized intelligence gathering.)

It was at JM/WAVE that David Atlee Phillips set up what he called its "propaganda shop." Among Phillips's achievements was the establishment of Radio Swan, which beamed anti-Castro diatribes from Swan

Island off the coast of Honduras into Cuba. The late exile leader Jorge Mas Canosa was one of Phillips's most talented broadcasters, while Luis Posada was employed as a "training branch instructor" at the station until 1967.

In 1968, JM/WAVE was decommissioned, at which point the CIA had its first experience with a phenomenon called "blowback." The Agency had trained an army of assassins, then changed course concerning the target. But many exiles, as well as some of the station's senior staff, were having none of it. For them, the war against Castro would continue. The CIA had spawned a monster, a quasi-rogue agency, with staffers like Hunt and Phillips openly contemptuous of their superiors at Langley. In 1976, the CIA's controversial chief of intelligence, James Angleton, reflected on JM/WAVE with journalist Dick Russell. "It made sense to have a base in Miami," he said. "It was a novel idea, but it got out of hand. It became a power unto itself. And when people found there weren't jobs to be had, we had some problems."

Posada said he ran sabotage operations in Havana for nearly a year with CIA assistance. The Agency, he maintained, provided him with "time-bomb pencils, fuses, detonator cords, and everything necessary for acts of sabotage." Sometimes he would slip into Miami and return with "war materials."

But in January 1961, Posada's luck in Havana finally ran out. Following a close call after an operation went awry, he sought asylum at the Argentine Embassy. After a month's time, he was given a visa to Mexico. He arrived in Miami in time to sign up for the CIA-backed Bay of Pigs operation. Its failure—after President Kennedy refused to authorize air power for what he felt was a harebrained operation—deeply embittered Cuban exiles. Kennedy's subsequent deal with the Russians to end the Cuban Missile Crisis the following year—with a promise not to invade Cuba—deepened the wound for anti-Castro exiles and CIA veterans like Phillips and Hunt.

But in the detritus of the U.S. disaster and retreat, Posada found his calling, as well as a lucrative profession: he would be *"un guerrero,"* as he himself put it, a warrior.

Posada was one of 212 exiles chosen by the CIA to attend officer training school at Fort Benning, Georgia, where seminars in intelligence gathering, propaganda, and covert operations were taught. At Fort Benning, he made two crucial lifelong relationships: with Jorge Mas Canosa, who would become the exiles' most powerful lobbyist, and Félix Rodríguez, later famous for his role in the assassination of Che Guevara.

Posada graduated as a second lieutenant in the U.S. Army in August

1963. He had trained in guerrilla warfare, demolition, and spycraft. Posada was especially drawn to the world of espionage, in which he would become a master in propaganda and surveillance, as well as in the black arts of doctoring photos, forging documents, manufacturing and planting evidence, and creating exploding gimmickry. He delighted in confecting various noms de guerre for himself; he became Comisario Basilio, Bambi, Solo (for the spy in the 1960s TV series *The Man from U.N.C.L.E.*), and Lupo ("wolf" in Italian). There were dozens of bogus passports—fabricated as needed—from a host of countries, including the United States.

Posada was also a charmer: he was fluent in English and a dashing ladies' man, who could knock back half a bottle of Black Label scotch and not make a fool of himself. He was neither garrulous nor obsessed with politics: his only ideology was anticommunism. "There are no good communists," Posada told me. "All are bad." In short he was the perfect Cold War spook. In time, his talents would be sought by the CIA and various intelligence agencies in Latin America. Throughout the '60s, much of the '70s, and again in the mid-'80s during Iran-Contra, he was a paid asset of the CIA, a detail his defense attorneys have hammered home at every opportunity. David Atlee Phillips, who became CIA chief for Latin America, told congressional investigators (for the House Select Committee Hearings on Assassination in 1978) that Posada had worked with him on Chilean operations. (Presumably Track II, the CIA program to overthrow the government of President Salvador Allende in Chile in 1973, was among the operations.)

Posada always had a paycheck—even when pursuing his personal passion of eliminating Fidel Castro. Posada was "smart with money," Bosch told me, lamenting, "I'm the only one who didn't make money." At first he was sponsored by the CIA and other intelligence agencies in Latin America. Later he was subsidized in part by dedicated anti-Castro patrons like Jorge Mas Canosa and some of the members of Mas's powerful exile organization, the Cuban American National Foundation.

In his closest near miss at eliminating the Cuban president, Posada partnered with Antonio Veciana, a former banker who went on to found the anti-Castro paramilitary group Alpha 66, at the suggestion (and with the backing) of the CIA. The plan, conceived by Veciana's CIA handler, was to take out Castro at a summit in Santiago, Chile, in November 1971. Veciana hired two Venezuelans, both cohorts of Orlando Bosch, to pose as news reporters equipped with a 16-mm newsreel camera. But inside the camera, Posada planted a machine gun; it was a favored, old-fashioned CIA gadget.

A consummate professional, Posada thought of everything—even how to divert suspicion from the CIA should his assassins be killed. Planted on the men and in their hotel rooms were carefully crafted bogus documents that would lead police to two KGB agents living in Caracas. Veciana recalled that Posada was "an extraordinary shooter," who often practiced his marksmanship, mastering all manner of fire-arms—from pistols to automatic weapons. "As a young boy, Posada was fascinated with explosives and guns," Veciana told me. "He was a good shot even then."

According to Veciana, the assassins fixed the lethal camera on Castro but got cold feet after spotting Cuban security agents guarding the exits. Posada was furious. He had worked out the plan in minute detail, even devising a spin strategy for the hit. According to Fabian Escalante, former chief of Cuban Intelligence, the plot involved "a correspondent of the Soviet Tass news agency who was also a KGB officer [who] was in Caracas. Posada arranged to photograph his two agents while they were talking with the Russian, so that after the assassination of *El Comandante,* a media campaign would be unleashed showing the photos and accusing the Soviets of being the perpetrators. . . . Posada had fixed things with Eduardo Sepúlveda, colonel of the Chilean Mounted Police, responsible for security in the location where Fidel would give his press conference, so that instead of detaining the assassins, he would eliminate them and thus avert any indiscretion."

Though demoralized by the failure, Posada quickly regrouped with another collaborator, Osiel González, to plot another attempt to eliminate Castro—this time during an upcoming visit to Quito, Ecuador.

At one point, the men considered detonating a bomb "by planting explosives in the ashtrays at the airport," González recounted for me over *cortaditos* on Calle Ocho. But there were logistical problems. "In the airport in Quito there were no ashtrays," explained González, a dapper, handsome man in his seventies. "People throw the ashes on the floor and they stomp the butts on the floor. Second, the [security] who go ahead of Fidel are not stupid and they will search the place wherever possible—even a false ceiling. . . . [And] where were we going to get the explosives on such short notice? There was no time and we [had no place] to plant them. Well then, how are we going to do it? I called Luis [Posada] and told him."

Posada decided it had to be a hit, but this time he was not taking any chances: he would fire the weapon himself, using a state-of-the-art sniper rifle with a silencer. Posada positioned himself in an elevated hangar in Quito's airport just a few hundred feet away from where Castro would pass by after he deplaned. But at the last moment, the wily Cuban strongman switched his arrival to a nearby military base.

Later Posada dispatched yet another set of assassins with the killer camera to Caracas, but when Castro appeared, Posada's men were nowhere to be found.

Posada learned from such disheartening experiences, and developed a philosophy and modus operandi for future endeavors. Assassination attempts required dedicated anti-Castro Cuban exiles. Sabotage, bombings, and the like could be relegated to what he called "mercenaries," generally young, uneducated Central Americans who could carry out limited small tasks and be hired by intermediaries. "Compartmentalized," he explained to me in 1998. "I know who they are, but they don't know me."

Luis Posada wrote in his memoir that in September 1969, while sipping his usual prelunch daiquiri at El Centro Vasco, a popular Miami restaurant on Calle Ocho, he was approached by an "elegantly dressed" Venezuelan. The man was Erasto Fernández, Venezuela's DIGEPOL intelligence czar, and he had a tantalizing offer for the forty-year-old Cuban. Fernández had been impressed by Posada's track record at the CIA, and the Agency's recommendation of him. Fernández was also an admirer of Posada's freelance stints for Caracas intelligence over the years. Posada came on board as chief of security for DIGEPOL, which was soon rechristened as DISIP. By 1971, Posada was in the catbird seat at DISIP, having been promoted to its chief of counterintelligence.

In truth, Posada's relationship with the CIA had not been entirely smooth sailing. Agency memos in the late '60s questioned Posada's coziness with drug dealers and mobsters and a "tendency" to become involved in "clandestine sabotage activities," "gangster elements," and "thefts from [the] CIA, plus other items." A 1974 intelligence memo reported that "Posada may be involved in smuggling cocaine from Colombia through Venezuela to Miami, also in counterfeit U.S. money in Venezuela." Another noted that Posada was "seen with [a] known big-time drug trafficker," and a third referred to him as a "serious potential liability."

To what degree the profits of drug trafficking financed exile paramilitary strikes is unknown. Historians agree that Miami's renaissance as an American city owed much to the CIA's employment of thousands of Cubans in the early 1960s, followed by dizzying profits from the bustling cocaine trade in the '70s, estimated at $8 billion a year. Narcotics were a lucrative sideline for some militants whose motives were not entirely ideological.

Posada's move from Miami to Caracas suited the CIA, providing a degree of cover and deniability. In 1972, four anti-Castro militants had been caught alongside E. Howard Hunt trying to burglarize the Democratic Party's headquarters at the Watergate Hotel in Washington, DC. The ensuing scandal rattled the country to its core, and President Nixon was forced to resign. The CIA awkwardly sought to distance itself from the arrested burglars, its former employees. Prompted by reports of Agency excesses, several high-powered congressional hearings were launched to investigate the CIA's involvement in assassinations.

The CIA had been keen on Posada's alliance with DISIP for other reasons. Caracas had become the front line of the CIA's war against communism in the hemisphere. Castro's escalating involvement with Venezuela's leftist guerrillas had alarmed the Agency. The Cuban leader not only wanted to export his revolution, officials argued, but also had his eye on the country's vast oil reserves.

Soon after Castro's rise to power, Caracas became a hub of exile activity, sort of a sister city to Miami, with DISIP functioning almost as a satellite station of Langley. In an earlier variant of "rendition," some of the dirtier chores of the CIA were farmed out to DISIP. Roiling with guerrilla groups, wildcatters, and drug lords, Caracas was the Casablanca of the Caribbean. As such, it was the perfect home for Luis Posada Carriles.

At DISIP, Posada saw to it that all offices and businesses affiliated with the Cuban government were under continuous surveillance. Allied with the conservative Christian Democrats, he also poked into the private business of some in the opposition Adeco Party. One powerful Adeco politician, Carlos Andrés Pérez, didn't appreciate Posada's secret wiretaps of his conversations with his mistress. When Pérez was elected Venezuela's president in 1974, he promptly fired Posada.

Pérez, known as CAP, was a former spook himself and a consummate politician, deft at playing both sides of an issue. Although Pérez was a solid U.S. ally and suspicious of Castro, he was not looking for a showdown with the belligerent Cuban. He favored covert action, and to that end, provided CIA officers with government office space. While Minister of the Interior, CAP reportedly received ten thousand dollars a month from the CIA, according to journalist Don Bohning, who has chronicled the history of JM/WAVE.

Pérez continued the tradition of staffing DISIP with Cuban exiles. Because citizenship was a requirement at DISIP, the Cubans were rushed through a quickie nationalization process, then rewarded with key posts. Rafael Rivas-Vásquez had one of the longest tenures under Pérez

at DISIP. Born in New York City in 1937 to Cuban parents, he was educated in Havana. Like many university students, Rivas-Vásquez joined
the anti-Batista forces only to be transformed into an anti-Castro partisan. After receiving a master's degree in economics from the University
of Miami, he was hired by DISIP as an analyst in 1972. A large, rotund
man, he steadily climbed through DISIP's ranks and in 1974 was named
second in command. In 1989, during CAP's second term as president,
he became DISIP's chief.

But CAP's most crucial relationship was with a Bay of Pigs veteran
named Orlando García Vázquez. A U.S. Army vet and a CIA asset, García was responsible for CAP's personal security and served as his trusted
gatekeeper. García was bald, sported a goatee, and was partial to gold
jewelry, silk shirts, beautiful women, and booze. A shrewd player who
married at least five times, García kept his hand in both Cuban politics and the guerrilla wars raging throughout the hemisphere. He even
formed an acquaintanceship with Che Guevara in 1953 while living in
exile in Costa Rica. At this point both men were rebels—García having fought against Batista until it was too dangerous for him to remain
in Cuba.

García's loyalty to CAP was unflinching for forty years. The bonds of
their friendship were sealed when García got wise to a planned assassination attempt on CAP in Costa Rica. One oft-told version of the story
has it that García pretended to befriend the would-be assassins, drove
them on a bogus mission, then gunned them down while they stopped
by the road to urinate.

Salvador Romaní, an exile who led the anti-Castro organization Junta
Patriótica Cubana in Caracas for many years, remembered García as a
man of singular status. "Let me tell you that the influence Orlando García Vázquez had on Carlos Andrés Pérez was total," he began, speaking
between sips of a *cafecito*. "Every day, Orlando exercised with Carlos
Andrés Pérez in the exercise room in La Casona [the presidential resi-
dence] and most of the power players who made up the so-called CEN
[National Executive Committee] were jealous because Orlando García
was the most influential man." Romaní added that when García died
in Miami in 2005, Pérez attended his funeral despite "his bad physical
condition" following a debilitating stroke.

García's deputy, Ricardo "El Mono" (Monkey) Morales Navarette,
was even more colorful. Part James Bond, part Scarface, Morales was
a former agent in Castro's intelligence service who had reportedly been
recruited by David Atlee Phillips. A good-looking, dazzling talker, he
had met García through his brother. George Kiszynski, a veteran FBI

agent of thirty-four years, described Morales as "decadent, devious, brilliant, completely amoral, with an astonishing photographic memory." He was also a chameleon—politically and sexually. Unburdened by any ideology, Morales devolved into the CIA's Frankenstein.

Not infrequently, Morales operated as an informer for the FBI, DEA (Drug Enforcement Administration), CIA, Miami Police Department, and various Latin American agencies. In 1968, he provided most of the testimony that convicted Bosch and sent him to federal prison. Shortly before he joined DISIP, Morales barely cheated death when his car exploded in Little Havana, the barrio in southwest Miami where many Cuban exiles initially settled.

Both Morales and Orlando García, who remained on the CIA payroll, would play crucial roles in the 1976 Cubana de Aviación airline bombing investigation.

Ever resourceful, Posada quickly rebounded from his firing at DISIP, recycling his high-powered contacts into an even more profitable venture, a security and detective agency called ICICA. The firm, housed in a handsome building near DISIP, was an instant success and attracted clients like Chrysler and many of the hemisphere's most prestigious banks. It screened employees, handled theft investigations, and wired security systems. "It was the biggest in the country," Posada told me proudly.

Orlando Bosch arrived in Miami in July 1960 with his wife, Myriam, also a doctor, and their five young children. He soon found work as a pediatrician. While his day job was saving babies, his free time was devoted to eliminating his enemies.

Before fleeing Cuba, Bosch had founded the anti-Castro paramilitary MIRR (Insurrectional Revolutionary Recovery Movement). While in Miami, he redoubled his efforts for MIRR and initially accepted assistance from the CIA, which financed a training camp for him in Homestead, not far from the Everglades. But Bosch did not have the temperament to work with the CIA. Once he realized that there would not be a second Bay of Pigs, he wrote President Kennedy a rambling screed, shut down his camp, and went out on his own.

Bosch's new group, Cuban Power, was the most audacious of the anti-Castro groups, claiming credit for dozens of bombings and assassination attempts. Bosch referred to these as "justice actions." Any company, individual, or country seen as sympathetic to Cuba was regarded as fair game. By the mid-'60s, Bosch had been arrested half a dozen times in Miami for various bombings and violations of the 1939 U.S. Neutrality Act. In September 1968, he was arrested again, for firing a 57-mm bazooka into a Cuba-bound Polish ship docked at the Port of Miami. This time he was sentenced to ten years in federal prison in Marion, Illinois. In prison, Bosch reacquainted himself with Rolando Masferrer, who had run the most feared paramilitary group under Batista known as Los Tigres.

From his earliest days in Miami, some of Bosch's collaborators questioned his tactics—and his sanity. He was often described as "mad" and "crazy"—even *"esquizofrénico."* While some held him in the highest regard, others would roll their eyes. Still, Bosch had developed a cultlike following and began to attract powerful supporters. Governor Claude Kirk of Florida was among those who lobbied for his early parole after just four years. "When I think of free men seeking a free homeland," the governor explained, "I must necessarily think of Dr. Bosch." In 1972, Bosch walked out of federal prison in Atlanta.

One of Bosch's priorities was instilling discipline and obedience into the exile paramilitaries. On Good Friday 1974, exile leader José Elías de la Torriente was shot dead in his living room while watching television with his wife. Left outside his door was a piece of paper with a large zero drawn on it, with de la Torriente's initials. Missives were sent to the Miami media describing de la Torriente as a "traitor" and listing ten other exile leaders who would soon receive their own "zero." More than half would be murdered; others fled Miami.

Bosch disappeared in the wake of de la Torriente's murder, but emerged a few weeks later for an interview with the *Miami News.* "Nobody will dare raise a false flag here anymore, for fear for his own life," Bosch warned. "[Torriente's] slaying was a good lesson to the exile community, so that no one else will now come forth with phony theories to fool and rob the people." Miami became the crime capital of America, a city where bombs and killings had become virtually routine. "It's the old Chicago gangland style, nothing new," *Time* reporter Jay Mallin said in 1976. "Bosch is an extortionist, not a patriot. If you don't pay, he puts a bomb outside your office. There is no real militant patriotic activity anymore, it's been reduced to criminal."

The FBI suspected that Bosch played a key role in the carnage engulfing Miami. But before he could be arrested, Bosch left the country, violating the terms of his parole. Another casualty of his crusade was his marriage. "I'm going underground in a Latin American country to direct the internationalization of the war [against Castro]," he announced prior to leaving. "I know I will be a fugitive." In 2006, he told me, "I went to make sabotage against Castro," and eventually he joined forces with Luis Posada in Venezuela. In fact, Bosch had received the blessing of President Carlos Andrés Pérez, who instructed his Cuban-led security team of Orlando García, Rafael Rivas-Vásquez, and Mono Morales to attend to their fellow exile.

I asked Bosch how it was possible for him to work again with Morales, after Morales turned state's evidence against him. "El Mono greeted me with *un gran abrazo,*" Bosch explained, demonstrating the attempted embrace. "But I stepped back and only shook his hand. I told him I would forgive, but not forget." Nevertheless, as was often the case with Bosch, things did not go smoothly.

On October 10, 1974, the anniversary of Cuban independence, Bosch set off bombs at Panama's Venezuelan embassy and at a cultural center in Caracas, shortly before Cuban officials were to arrive. True to his modus operandi, Bosch boasted about his handiwork, embarrassing the Venezuelans and provoking his arrest a month later. Eager to unload Bosch, Venezuela contacted the U.S. To their surprise, officials learned that the Justice Department did not want him back, regardless of his fugitive status.

Bosch said he won his release after negotiating an unusual deal with DISIP. He would no longer bomb targets in Caracas. In exchange he was promised that no upper-echelon Cuban officials would be allowed to visit Venezuela.

Bosch then headed to Curaçao, using a false passport in the name of Pedro Peña, and linked up with his collaborator Guillermo Novo. The two men flew south to Santiago, Chile, where they found a generous and accommodating host in General Pinochet for the next year. President Augusto Pinochet and his intelligence organ, DINA, allowed Bosch to strike his targets with impunity—leading to his bombing the Cuban embassy in Mexico and kidnapping Cuban diplomats in Argentina. But there was a price. The Chilean junta informed Bosch that they had some pests of their own they wanted eliminated—such as former Ambassador Orlando Letelier. "Pinochet's people were always telling us that they wanted Letelier killed," Bosch said.

Like Posada, Bosch would float about the hemisphere pursuing his targets—even slipping into the U.S. when needed. "With our group of guerrillas we planted bombs," Bosch told me. Then he shrugged and raised his hands palms-up in a gesture of mock helplessness. "We did everything that was possible to be done," he told a reporter at the time.

While in Santiago, Bosch fell in love with a lushly beautiful *chilena,* Adriana Delgado, twenty years his junior. The two married in February 1975 and had a daughter, Karen, not long after.

Bosch was a fugitive from U.S. justice when he founded CORU

(Coordination of United Revolutionary Organizations) in the Dominican Republic, a country hospitable to Cuban exile paramilitaries as well as legitimate exile business interests. The creation of CORU, with its master plan to bring down Castro, established Bosch as the Godfather of exile militants. CORU's inaugural two-day meeting on June 6 and 7, 1976, was held at a secluded mountaintop retreat near Bonao. Twenty exiles attended, representing the major militant groups, including Posada, Frank Castro, Ignacio and Guillermo Novo, and José Dionisio Suárez Esquivel. "Everything we did was planned there," Bosch told me, noting that the attendees included "all the major military and political leaders. It was a truly great meeting." CORU's mission was simple, he said: "to fight Castro's friends and minions." Subsequently CORU took responsibility for hundreds of bombings, kidnappings, and killings in Latin America, Cuba, and the U.S.

One of CORU's priorities was to bring down a Cuban airliner. The group reasoned that such an audacious act would demonstrate their might, terrify the Cuban government, and focus the world's attention to their cause. "Several informers infiltrated, of course," Adriana Bosch interjected, with a roll of her eyes. "It never fails." One such informer notified the CIA that the meeting had taken place at the "home of former senator of Batista govt.," according to an Agency memo, and noted that "Orlando Bosch and others discussed terrorist acts such as placing bombs on Cuban aircraft."

In early 1975, the intelligence services of Chile's General Pinochet, Argentina's General Jorge Rafael Videla and Paraguay's dictator General Alfredo Stroessner devised a secret plan to hunt down and assassinate political opponents and leftists throughout the hemisphere. The plan was called Operation Condor and functioned as the international operations of the Dirty War, as the internal purging of opponents was known. DISIP's Orlando García told author John Dinges in an interview in 2002 that General Juan Manuel Contreras, Pinochet's right-hand man who ran DINA, had visited his office in Caracas. "Contreras wanted us to capture Chilean exiles and turn them over to Chile with no legalities," García recalled. "He wanted us to put them on a plane, and Chile would pay the fare. He said, 'We have to eliminate the enemies.' I knew that meant only one thing—we knew the people he captured would be tortured and killed." García said that Carlos Andrés Pérez kiboshed the proposal.

But Contreras had more success recruiting CORU members to do Condor's bidding, and was confident that their rabid anticommunism would inoculate them from sentimentality. According to Cuba's master spook, Fabian Escalante, who alleges CIA complicity in the attacks, "Bosch was going to offer himself to Pinochet, along with this group of terrorists of Cuban origin, who would become killers within Operation Condor." He met up with General Contreras, made contact with American-born DINA agent–hit man Michael Townley, and soon organized the kidnapping and murder of two Cuban officials in Argentina.

Bosch did not dispute Escalante's account. "We did all we could," he told me. "And we ended up doing an attack against the Cuban ambassador in Buenos Aires," he said, referring to two officials in the Cuban embassy who had disappeared.

Around the same time, bombs began to go off in Miami—sometimes daily. On the night of December 3, 1975, and into the next day, thirteen bombs went off, striking at the very lifeline of the city: the airport, the police department, the State Attorney's Office, the Social Security building, the post office, and the FBI's main office.

Before the bombs went off, there would usually be a phone call. The caller would not speak but would play the first haunting strains of the lute-driven melody of a 1970 Simon and Garfunkel hit: *"I'd rather be a hammer than a nail. Yes I would, if I only could, I surely would. Hmmmm."*

It had originally been a Peruvian folk song, also called "El Condor Pasa." The song's title was a crucial clue that would lead investigators to the bomber Rolando Otero, a hyper-intense young Cuban with a Brillo-like goatee, who worked closely with Mono Morales and Orlando Bosch. Otero even called himself El Condor after the fearsome vulture of the Andes, renowned for its wingspread and radarlike vision. It was not lost on investigators that Condor was the name of the foreign operations of the Dirty War as well.

The message was clear: the U.S. was not off-limits in the war against Castro.

CHAPTER SIX

Murder in the Sky

In the summer of 1976, Orlando Bosch received an invitation that he could not refuse. The president of Venezuela, Carlos Andrés Pérez, a staunch anticommunist during his tenure as Minister of the Interior, had extended an olive branch welcoming him back to Caracas. According to Bosch, he had been contacted three times by DISIP's Orlando García, who even mailed him a visa to encourage his return. On September 8, 1976, García and his deputy, Ricardo "El Mono" Morales, greeted Bosch at the airport.

This time a pact was agreed upon: Bosch would be allowed to base himself in Caracas as long as his targets did not include Venezuela, Costa Rica, or the Dominican Republic. In return Bosch was given a Venezuelan passport, bodyguards, a DISIP identity card in the name of Carlos Sucre, and a deluxe suite at the swank Anauco Hilton, where García and Morales also lived.

But his Venezuelan hosts came to the quick and grim realization that they would not be able to control their guest. Soon after his arrival in Caracas, a fund-raising dinner was given in his honor at the home of a wealthy Cuban doctor. All of DISIP's top exile spooks, Posada, Mono Morales, and Orlando García, attended. According to a CIA memo dated October 14, 1976, during the dinner, Bosch sought to extort "a substantial cash contribution to [Bosch's] organization" from the Venezuelan government in exchange for a promise to abstain from attacks in the U.S. during President Carlos Andrés Pérez's upcoming trip to the United Nations. Bosch was given five hundred dollars. Evidently it was not enough.

On September 21, Orlando Letelier, Chile's former ambassador to the United States and an outspoken critic of the Pinochet junta, was assassinated when a bomb placed under his car exploded as the vehicle approached his office on Washington's Embassy Row. Also killed in the blast was twenty-five-year-old Ronni Moffitt, the American wife of Letelier's assistant, Michael Moffitt, who was sitting in the backseat and miraculously survived.

The murders, six weeks before the presidential election, stunned the world. The FBI immediately suspected that Cuban militants, in cahoots with the Chilean secret police, were responsible. Several militants were known to be as garrulous as they were daring, informing the FBI that CORU members José Dionisio Suárez, Virgilio Paz Romero, and the Novo brothers—Guillermo and Ignacio—had carried out the car bombing on orders from Chile's General Manuel Contreras. "These guys talked like a bunch of old washerwomen," said E. Lawrence Barcella, the assistant U.S. attorney whose office eventually solved the case. "We learned about Guillermo Novo from Bosch, and Novo bragged about being supported by the Chilean junta." CORU had mastered the new art of exquisitely timed car bombings, which became its signature. A Washington map delineating Letelier's daily route to work was later found in Posada's home.

Only after the assassination of Letelier did CIA officials take seriously their problematic relationship with militant groups and the threat to public officials. A few weeks after the Letelier hit, CIA director George H. W. Bush picked up the phone in his Langley office and called Congressman Ed Koch, the future mayor of New York, to warn him that he was a possible target, based on intelligence received in July. Bush told Koch that his proposed legislation to cut off U.S. military assistance to the repressive government of Uruguay had prompted a paramilitary affiliated with Operation Condor "to put a contract out for you."

George H. W. Bush at the CIA had been given similar warnings concerning Orlando Letelier and another stating that a Cuban airliner was a desired target. But neither of these looming tragedies warranted the intervention of the CIA.

An October 14 CIA memo stated that its informant had overheard Bosch boasting that "now that our organization has come out of the Letelier job looking good, we are going to try something else." It noted that plans were solidified soon after. A few days following the fundraising dinner, the memo continued, Posada was reported to have said: "We are going to hit a Cuban airplane . . . Orlando has the details."

As it happened, the CIA had been warned that Orlando Bosch had chosen a Cuban airliner as a priority target four months earlier. A June 1976 memo entitled "Possible Plans of Cuban Exile Extremists to Blow up a Cubana Airliner" informed the Agency that a group led by Orlando Bosch "plan to place a bomb on a Cubana airline flight traveling between Panama and Havana," citing a specific flight on June 21.

Its source was described as a "usually reliable businessman with close ties to the Cuban exile community."

Lázaro Serrano Mérida was suavely handsome with a smile that made his cheeks dimple. At thirty-two, he juggled two jobs, one as a Cubana Airlines flight attendant that paid the bills. But it was his career as a songwriter and singer that consumed most of his waking moments. Onstage at the Tropicana, Havana's famous nightclub, Serrano was known as Channy Chelacy. Although not yet a famous crooner, he was well regarded in music circles and had written songs and arrangements for the Quartet Aida, the hottest girl group in Cuban history.

In fact, Serrano's girlfriend was Moraima Secada, the silky voice of the Quartet Aida, whose nephew Jon Secada would make his own name years later in Miami. The other voices of the quartet were Haydée Portuondo, the dazzling Elena Burke, and Haydée's younger sister, Omara Portuondo, the gifted bolero singer who would have a stunning comeback with the Buena Vista Social Club. In the 1970s, the four stars had solo careers but continued to sing together at the demand of their fans at sold-out venues.

On October 6, 1976, Serrano was working a Caribbean milk run for the airline. He was anxious to get back to Havana and work on his new show with Moraima. There was also his impending wedding, an event that Moraima decreed would be the party of the year.

Cubana flight #455 left Guyana at 10:57 a.m. The first stop was Trinidad, then Barbados, with a final stop in Kingston, Jamaica, before its scheduled landing in Havana at the end of the day.

In Trinidad, twenty-four members of Cuba's national fencing team boarded the plane. Dangling around their necks were gold and silver medals that they had won at the international youth fencing championship in Caracas. Although exhausted, the group—many of whom were teenagers—was elated. They had celebrated by dancing the night away with Los Van Van, Cuba's veteran rock 'n' roll band, who happened to be performing in Venezuela. The team had flown in on a Pan Am flight from Caracas and had arrived ten hours earlier.

The first two short hops of the journey were uneventful, but just eight minutes after taking off from Barbados, a bomb exploded in the rear restroom of the plane. "We have an explosion on board," the pilot, Wilfredo Pérez, radioed the control tower at 1:24. "We're descending fast. We have a fire on board." Then came a second, deafening blast. Minutes later, horrified sunbathers at the Paradise Hotel watched the DC-8 jet nosedive into the sea.

All seventy-three passengers and crew aboard were killed: fifty-seven Cubans, six teenage exchange students from Guyana, a young Guyanese family of five, and five North Koreans.

Moraima Secada's records continued to sell. But she never recovered from her fiancé's death. The virtuoso singer rapidly spiraled downward into depression and booze and died ten years later. "Her liver gave out," said her friend Rosario Moreno, "but really it was her heart."

The downing of Cubana flight #455 was the worst act of airline terrorism in the hemisphere prior to 9/11. The targeting of a civilian aircraft has prompted three decades of court trials, charges, and countercharges, and not a few conspiracy theories. But certain facts are not in dispute.

Two young Venezuelans, Hernán Ricardo Lozano and Freddy Lugo, boarded the Cubana plane in Trinidad shortly after 11 a.m. Each had checked a bag. Although Ricardo was only twenty, he had been working for Luis Posada Carriles in Caracas for almost five years. Eager and ambitious, Ricardo did all manner of odd jobs at Posada's detective and security agency, ranging from photography to surveillance. He had recently recruited his friend Freddy Lugo, twenty-seven, to assist him. Lugo walked onto the plane with two cameras, one around his neck and the other in a handsome alligator shoulder satchel.

Hernán Ricardo was traveling with a Venezuelan passport in the name of José Vásquez García. Two other passports, including a U.S. document with a bogus name, as well as his own genuine Venezuelan passport, were in his valise. Prior to boarding the flight, Ricardo had stuffed C-4 plastic explosives into one of the cameras and into an empty tube of Colgate toothpaste. Lugo recalled his friend "playing with something that looked like dough of a whitish or beige color; he was softening it."

About twenty minutes into the flight, he pushed the camera under a seat in the midsection of the plane and stashed the toothpaste tube in the rear bathroom. But in his nervousness he jammed the restroom door. Stuck inside, he banged on the door for assistance, according to a passenger who disembarked in Barbados. A stewardess tried to open the door. Unsuccessful, she recruited the plane's co-captain to kick the door loose and rescue the young assassin.

At the airport in Barbados, the two men hailed a taxi to take them to the Holiday Inn in Bridgetown, where they checked into room 103 under fictitious names. En route, Ricardo asked the driver to stop the cab so that he could get out for a few moments and watch an airplane passing over. At the hotel, Ricardo immediately placed a call through the front desk to Luis Posada's detective agency and left a message with his secretary asking that he call back immediately. He then called his girlfriend, Marines Vega, who worked at the agency, and asked her to relay an urgent message to Posada: "We are in a desperate situation and need help. . . . The bus was fully loaded with dogs," he told her, using a crude code of "bus" for "plane" and "dogs" for "passengers."

Ricardo next placed a call to a "Señor Paniagua," the nom de guerre of Orlando Bosch, or "Señor Pan y Agua"—Mr. Bread and Water—as Freddy Lugo pronounced the name. "I asked him who Mr. Pan y Agua was because I found it amusing that someone would have that name," Lugo wrote in his subsequent confession, "and he told me that it was a dear friend of his named Orlando Bosch." At the time, Bosch was living in Caracas at the home of an exile comrade. One of Ricardo's more recent jobs was driving Bosch around and acting as his all-around aide-de-camp. Ricardo did not make contact initially, as the phone number he gave the operator had one wrong digit.

Hoping to bury their tracks, the two men changed hotels and checked into the Village Beach Hotel, room 61, where Ricardo continued trying to contact Posada and Bosch. Ricardo also tried making contact with his mother, telling her, according to Lugo, "to give the telephone number of the Village Beach Hotel in Barbados to Mr. Luis Posada so that he could call and to tell him that there was a problem." As Ricardo was frantically placing calls, he imagined that a Cuban intelligence agent was in the lobby.

Visibly agitated, the young men opted to take a walk, hoping to calm their nerves. But as word of the tragedy buzzed among the locals, the panic-stricken Venezuelans decided they had to leave Barbados immediately. They fled to the airport in such a hurry that they left their luggage in their hotel room.

Arriving back in Trinidad's capital, Port of Spain, they took a taxi to the Holiday Inn, checked in under assumed names, and continued to try to reach Posada. Finally, Ricardo made phone contact with Orlando Bosch, who expressed some dissatisfaction with their handiwork: "My friend, we have problems here in Caracas," Bosch told Ricardo. "You never blow up a plane while it is in the air," he said, seeming to suggest that the plane should have been on the ground for the attack.

The taxi driver, Kenneth Dennis, who had heard the news about the bombing on the radio, found the behavior of his two high-strung passengers suspicious. So did the hotel's reception clerk. Both notified the Trinidad police, who promptly swooped in and arrested Ricardo and Lugo.

Trinidad's deputy police commissioner, Dennis Ramdwar, forty-nine years old and a police veteran of more than two decades, understood the gravity of the crime and its implications. "I followed our normal procedures," he told me in 2006, speaking with a faint Caribbean lilt, explaining that he ordered that the men be questioned separately. A careful man, he arranged that several officers witness and participate in the interrogations. He also summoned two Spanish speakers to serve as interpreters.

Ramdwar zeroed in first on Hernán Ricardo, who was more talkative, and whose name did not match the one he had used to check into the Holiday Inn. The following day, he and his team interviewed Freddy Lugo. Both men initially denied knowledge of the crash.

On Sunday, October 10, Ramdwar visited Hernán Ricardo and showed him several plane tickets, a notebook, and a diary. "He told me the tickets were his and the notebook and diary were also his," Ramdwar wrote in his report. Ramdwar then questioned him about several names and phone numbers of interest to him. One notation read, "Orlando 713916." At which point Ricardo said he would give a formal statement.

Ricardo's testimony to Ramdwar came in fits and starts over the next two weeks. By the end of the second interview, Ramdwar realized he was investigating the crime of his career, if not one of the hemisphere's most horrific crimes.

At eight the next morning, Ramdwar flew to Caracas for meetings with officials in Venezuela's foreign ministry and the top brass at DISIP and the Ministry of the Interior. By the end of the sessions, it was clear to those present that the two young men in Trinidad's jail had not acted alone.

Ramdwar returned to Trinidad and visited Freddy Lugo in his cell. Lugo began to recall some details, such as Ricardo using a bogus passport. By the end of the day, Lugo asked to see him again. Lugo said that he now recalled that Hernán Ricardo had told him on their return flight to Trinidad that "Orlando Bosch and Luis Posada must be worried about him." He also said that about twenty minutes after the Cubana plane left Trinidad, his friend "became very nervous [and] was sweating, and went to the bathroom." When Ricardo returned to his seat, Lugo said, he was "even more nervous and sweating heavily."

The following afternoon, Lugo asked to see Ramdwar and his team in the commissioner's office. "He told me that he had thought the whole matter over and wished to tell me the truth," Ramdwar wrote in his report. He informed Lugo of his rights and that his comments could be used against him in a court of law. Lugo assented and unburdened himself, telling the group of investigators that he "was convinced that Hernán Ricardo was the one who placed the bomb on the aircraft," On their flight to Trinidad, Lugo said, his friend had told him he was going to blow up a Cubana aircraft."

The next day at 6:30 p.m., Hernán Ricardo requested to see Ramdwar alone with just the interpreters present. Ramdwar assented, and Ricardo began his remarkable account. Young Ricardo struck the investigators as being worldly beyond his years, especially when he told them that his collaborator, Orlando Bosch, headed a paramilitary umbrella organization called "El CORU," which he also called "El Condor." Seeking to impress the police commissioner, he drew a chart of the organization's hierarchy and pointed out that Luis Posada had been a powerful person in Venezuela's intelligence apparatus.

Ricardo also mentioned that he and Lugo had been in Barbados on July 10, the very day a British West Indies Airways ticket office was blown up. He noted, somewhat self-importantly, that he knew quite a bit about that bombing as well as another bombing at the Guyana Consulate in Trinidad.

By the evening of October 19, Ricardo had more to say to Ramdwar and his team of investigators. He said he was speaking "in the greatest confidence" and asserted that he and Freddy Lugo were "members of the CIA in Venezuela," although Lugo was only a "Grade D" while he was in a superior category of "Grade B-1." Ricardo said he had been recruited in "1970 or 1971" and had been trained in counterintelligence in Panama and Venezuela. He also said that he knew who had blown up the plane and identified them as Venezuelans who were still in Trinidad.

Ramdwar again cautioned the young man that his testimony could be used against him. Ricardo responded by saying that if Ramdwar "used his police brain it would be clear who bombed the plane." When Ramdwar informed him that he was quite certain who had committed the crime, Ricardo became very quiet. Then he proceeded to make a full confession: "I want to tell you in the utmost confidence that Lugo and I blew up the plane," he told his questioners, and asked for pen and paper. Drawing an elaborate sketch of the bomb, timer, and detonator, Ricardo explained to Ramdwar how he detonated the explosives using a pencil-size timer—that he had stored in a tube of toothpaste—minutes after the jet soared into the sky above Barbados.

He then went on to describe a nefarious plot, one that was hatched, he said, by his employer, Luis Posada, and his close collaborator, Orlando

Bosch. "He told me that Bosch was conscious of all his activities and that he always informed his immediate superior, Posada, or Orlando Bosch personally," Ramdwar wrote in his report. "Ricardo told me that he had made a call to Bosch and had informed him by telephone of the results of the operation, and said that Posada also was informed." The night before the bombing, Ricardo, who had been paid $25,000 for his services, had a final meeting with Bosch and Posada in the lobby of the Anauco Hilton.

Freddy Lugo told Trinidad's investigators that Ricardo had compared his exploits to those of Carlos the Jackal, the Venezuelan terrorist then at the height of his fame. *"Coño, 73! Más que el Chacal,"* he boasted to Lugo. "Damn it, 73! More than the Jackal!" On the short plane hop back to Trinidad, Lugo said, Ricardo had alternated between euphoria, panic, and tears while he downed shots of whiskey. "The Jackal can have his history as a great terrorist, but I already beat him, and the Palestinians too, in terrorism," Lugo recalled. At one point, Ricardo said he had trumped the notorious Jackal. "Now I am the one who has the record because I am the one who blew up that thing." Later he broke down, saying: "Damn it, Lugo, I'm desperate and feel like crying. I've never killed anyone before."

The plan had been for Hernán Ricardo to continue to the U.S. after the bombing. To do this, he needed a U.S. visa from the FBI's legal attaché in Caracas, Joseph Leo, who explained to Ricardo that he needed a letter of employment in order to qualify. On October 1, 1976, Ricardo returned to Leo's office with a letter signed by Posada on his ICICA business stationery attesting that Ricardo was his employee.

Leo said later that a few things about the smooth-talking Hernán Ricardo unsettled him, though not enough to deny him a visa. Two days after the bombing, Leo wrote a detailed seven-page memo to the FBI in which he admitted that he had met Ricardo on several occasions and described him as a photojournalist "in the personal service of Luis Posada." Luis Posada, however, saw matters differently. "Ricardo was a friend of Joseph Leo," he said.

On a previous occasion, Ricardo had sought Leo's cooperation in one of his missions. In fact, he had asked for Leo's advice and "suggestions regarding courses of action that might be taken against the Cuban Embassy in Caracas by an anti-Castro group" that Ricardo had founded. Ricardo returned to see Leo at the end of September and asked for an expedited U.S. visa. Leo noted that Ricardo had been in Trinidad on September 1, "the very day the Guyanese consulate there had been bombed." Guyana's cordial relations with Cuba infuriated militant exiles, who wanted an international embargo against Cuba. Leo wrote in his memo that he wondered whether, "in view of Ricardo's association with Posada, his presence there during that period was coincidence." Leo also noted that Ricardo "might also be visiting Barbados" on his upcoming October 6 trip.

On October 20, two weeks after the bombing, Hernán Ricardo signed his confession. Then he returned to his cell and slit his left wrist. A doctor attended to him and he quickly recovered.

The day after the Cubana bombing, the CIA made what its records termed "unsuccessful attempts" to reach Luis Posada. But another memo stamped SECRET clearly indicates that the CIA had strong suspicions right away. "Posada suspected of working with Orlando Bosch and others in plot," it reads. "Also mentioned: Ricardo [Mono] Morales Navarette, Hernán Ricardo Lozano, etc. Persons suspected in Letelier killing also mentioned. CIA did trace on them for FBI."

According to an FBI memo written the same day, a confidential source "all but admitted that Posada and Bosch had engineered the bombing of the airline." A subsequent search of Posada's detective agency turned up a schedule of Cubana flights. Two weeks later, in a second FBI document, a CORU informant took credit for the bombing, justifying it as an action of war, though he noted that some in the group had expressed misgivings.

Two days after the downing of the Cuban jet, a statement was released by CORU members in Miami claiming responsibility for the bombing and detailing the method of its execution. The missive sought to justify the attack by claiming that the craft was "a military plane camouflaged as a civilian DC-8 aircraft" and dismissed the plane's passengers as "57 Cuban Communists [and] five North Korean Communists."

There was no doubting the statement's authenticity, which was corroborated by CORU members who also phoned reporters at the *Trinidad Express*. The declaration was signed *"Independencia o Muerte"*—"Independence or Death"—a venerated Cuban chant. It was dated October 10—the date marking the beginning of Cuba's Ten-Year War for independence from Spain begun in 1868, known as *El Grito de Yara* (The Cry of Yara).

Bosch said he was scheduled to meet with President Pérez, but the brouhaha following the bombing chilled their relationship. "I was supposed to meet with President Pérez on October 10, but then the plane blew up on the sixth and all the trouble started," he told a reporter. "I had a lot of conversations with [Orlando] García," Bosch continued. "I asked him what I should do and he said, 'Nothing is going to happen. Just stay quiet. Don't worry: everything is going to be nice.'"

But the following day, Orlando García attended the briefing by Trinidad's police chief, Dennis Ramdwar, about his interrogation of Lugo and Ricardo. By the end of the meeting, it was clear to García that the young Venezuelans in custody in Trinidad would implicate Bosch and Posada—and maybe others.

Miami attorney Alfredo Durán, who would later represent Orlando García, recalled landing in Caracas soon after the airliner was blown up. Because of the attack, all arriving Cuban-Americans were being thoroughly scrutinized and vetted. "There had been a lot of tolerance for anti-Castro activity," recalled Durán, a Bay of Pigs veteran, "but when the bombing of the plane happened, the welcome mat was pulled. It was all over." For the next few months, all Cuban exiles were detained at the airport, taken to DISIP, and their passports held. "That's how much bad 'odor' there was," said Durán.

On October 13, Venezuelan police picked up Luis Posada and Orlando Bosch in Caracas. Posada writes in his memoir that he was told initially he was being held at DISIP's offices "for a few days for my own protection." The two were accorded red carpet treatment and allowed to order dinner from their favorite restaurants, along with the finest whiskey.

Two days later, Bosch was led into Mono Morales's DISIP office for a secret meeting with Orlando García and Morales. At the end of the meeting, Morales handed Bosch an envelope full of cash and said, "Here's some money for you to get out of the country." Bosch asked what would happen to his comrade. "Posada is staying," García replied. "There is no alternative." Mono Morales urged him to leave. "Better you get out first, and later we'll see what we can do for Posada," Morales told him. Bosch told me that he responded without hesitation. "Either we both leave," he said. "Or I stay with him."

I asked Bosch why he did not leap at this offer of immediate freedom. "Because he was my friend," he said. "And I could not go and leave him in prison." Then he added, "And I was responsible for all of that."

In 2006, Bosch was on a Miami television program and offered some justifications for bringing down the airliner. "Who was on board that plane?" Bosch parried with the show's host. "Members of the Communist Party, *chico*! Our enemies . . . I was in Caracas. I saw the young girls [Cuban fencers] on television. After the end of the competition, the leader . . . gave a speech filled with praise for the tyrant."

When I asked Bosch if he was responsible for the bombing of the Cubana airliner, he paused as he collected his thoughts. "I have to tell you no. If I tell you I did it, I'm incriminating myself," he said. "If I tell you I didn't, you won't believe me."

Nine days after the bombing, more than a million Cubans massed in Havana's Plaza of the Revolution for a memorial to those who had died on the plane. Fidel Castro gave a thunderous speech brimming with fury: "We can say that the pain is not divided among us. It is multiplied among us," Castro intoned. He went on to accuse the CIA of complicity in the attack. "At the beginning we had doubts as to whether the CIA had directly organized the sabotage or had carefully elaborated it through its cover organizations made up of Cuban counter-revolutionaries," Castro told the crowd. "We are now decidedly inclined toward the first theory. The CIA participated directly in the [detonation] of the Cubana Airlines plane in Barbados."

Each subsequent October 6 until 2006, Castro marked the anniversary with a fiery speech and repeated his charge that the CIA had a hand in the bombing. In fact, there is no evidence that the CIA was directly complicit in the attack. Negligent in not warning Cuba of the imminent danger of the attack—certainly yes. Additionally, the United States has refused to declassify hundreds of pages of known documents pertaining to the airline bombing, Posada, and Bosch. This refusal has fueled conspiracy theories and leaves unanswered questions about an act that has come to stand as an iconic symbol of America's insidious maneuvers in Latin America. Why did the Reagan-Bush administration later hire Posada in the Iran-Contra operation? And why was Bosch granted U.S. residency when the CIA and FBI had concluded that the two men had blown up the Cubana plane?

Peter Kornbluh of the independently funded National Security Archive, which released many of the CIA's and FBI's memos, questioned why Joseph Leo and other intelligence officials never raised alarms prior to the downing of the plane. "There was concrete intelligence that they planned to blow up a plane," says Kornbluh. "How could they not notify the Cubans?"

On the twenty-fifth anniversary of the tragedy, just weeks after the 9/11 attacks, Fidel Castro reminded his audience that Cuba was the first to know airline terrorism in the hemisphere: "On a day like today, we have the right to ask what will be done about Posada Carriles and Orlando Bosch, the perpetrators of that monstrous, terrorist act."

After Castro's health precipitously declined in the summer of 2006, Venezuela's Hugo Chávez stepped in for his friend to serve as the point man and aggrieved memory keeper of the airline bombing. Rarely has he missed an opportunity to remind the world that both Posada and Bosch reside in Miami, and to chastise the U.S. for its "double standard on terrorism."

There had been a brief moment in history, however, when Chávez and Luis Posada were fighting on the same side, hunting down Castro-backed leftist guerrillas challenging the government. Chávez first stepped into the conflict in the late '60s when he began his military service and again in the mid-'70s, when he was a member of the Venezuelan army's counter-insurgency unit, a battalion known for its scorched-earth campaign against the guerrillas.

Posada told me that he pursued his targets remorselessly: "I persecuted them very hard," he admitted. "Many, many people got killed." Posada's good friend Paco Pimentel related one episode to me: "Luis hunted down a guerrilla and put a grenade on his chest and tied the guy to himself. He told him, 'You better show me all the hiding places. And if you trick me and take me into an ambush, we will both die together.'"

Likewise, Chávez was an ambitious soldier who rose through the ranks to become a lieutenant colonel. But while hunting guerrillas, Chávez underwent what he has described as an epiphany. One night, as he heard the groans of a guerrilla being tortured, he began to question his role in the operation—and his politics.

In 1989, Carlos Andrés Pérez won a second term as Venezuela's president, but his tenure was marred by mass protests against government corruption. At the time, Hugo Chávez was a rising star in the army. Three years later, Chávez led a coup against Pérez. Although the coup failed, Chávez's fearless speeches on national television transformed him into a hero. Chávez went to prison but Carlos Andrés Pérez never recovered his standing and was impeached the following year. His successor, Rafael Caldera Rodríguez, responding to the public clamor for his release, pardoned Chávez in 1994.

Just four years later, Chávez, who tempered his military pedigree with an eccentric, folksy charisma, swept into the presidency on a wave of populism and nationalism. Once installed in Miraflores Palace, he fashioned himself as the new Juan Perón. He didn't have a lush Evita by his side, but he had oil. Almost immediately, Chávez forged a mentor-protégé relationship with the region's preeminent maverick, Fidel Castro. Their enduring and curious alliance was based on common interests and common enemies, one of whom was Luis Posada Carriles.

On his weekly radio program *Aló Presidente* in 2005, Chávez played the audiotape of the desperate pilot of the Cubana plane radioing for help, followed by an excerpt of a speech by Castro reacting to the downing. "If the United States does not extradite Luis Posada Carriles, we will be forced to reconsider our diplomatic ties," Chávez warned. Then he offered his own conspiracy theory. "George Bush, the father, was director of the CIA at the time of the bombing," he intoned ominously. "That's the truth. So, maybe now they fear that [Posada] will talk, and that's why they protect him."

In April 2005, a nurse living in New York City named Roseanne Persaud Nenninger phoned me, having read a *Washington Post* article of mine about the recent entry into the U.S. of Luis Posada. Nenninger, born and raised in Guyana, said she wanted to speak about her brother, nineteen-year-old Raymond, who had died on the doomed Cubana flight.

Raymond Persaud had wanted to be a doctor, but his father could not afford to send him to medical school in the U.S. When he was offered a full scholarship to study in Havana, Raymond leapt at the opportunity.

Charles Persaud moved his family to the United States in 1979 and for years obsessively gathered boxes of information on the bombing. In 2002, he passed away after a heart attack. "He died of a broken heart because he never recovered from my brother's death," said Roseanne.

Roseanne was not the first person to tell me how the Cubana downing had devastated her life. Years earlier, I was having a manicure in a Miami *peluquería* run by María González, who told me she had good reason to be fatalistic about life. As a young girl growing up in Havana, she had been a talented fencer who had made the national team that would compete at the Caribbean Youth Fencing Championship in Caracas in October 1976.

But just before boarding the Cubana plane at José Martí Airport, one of the team's coaches broke the news that they had just discovered in her passport that she was only twelve—not the required age of at least thirteen.

María burst into sobs as she was led inside the terminal. Nancy Uranga, twenty-two and pregnant, was summoned to the airport to replace her. For María, it was a crushing disappointment. Athletes in Cuba are accorded the respect—even adulation—of movie stars. At home in her family's cramped apartment in La Vibora in central Havana, she curled up on her narrow bed and wept. "For three days," she said, "I cried all day and all night."

On the evening of October 6, María's father came into her room, and quietly told her she would not be seeing Nancy or her teammates—ever again.

Because the Cubana plane had been on a Caribbean island hop, several countries initiated investigations, and a tussle ensued over who would get jurisdiction. The Cubans argued they should because it was their airliner and because fifty-seven Cubans had perished. Guyanan officials pointed out that they lost twelve citizens, and Barbados noted that the crime had been committed in its airspace. Trinidad had two suspects in custody and had obtained detailed confessions.

Jurisdiction was awarded to Venezuela, in part because two of the suspects, Ricardo and Lugo, were Venezuelan. Additionally, Posada had become a Venezuelan citizen, and both he and Bosch were based in Caracas. Barbados and Trinidad also voiced concerns that Cuba might mete out the death penalty, outlawed in Venezuela. Moreover, President Carlos Andrés Pérez, infuriated by the attack, had a secret meeting with Fidel Castro in which he pledged to improve relations between their countries and promised an aggressive prosecution.

Over the next decade, there would be numerous trials, confessions, and retractions in the Cubana bombing tragedy. It was a case fraught with peril for its prosecutors, witnesses, and judges, prompting unprecedented government interference and judicial dithering.

Throughout the proceedings, the four men were held in prison, which incensed their supporters. In protest, during the nine-month period following their arrest, Bosch and Posada's comrades in CORU set off bombs at five Venezuelan government businesses, including the Viasá airlines ticket offices in San Juan, Puerto Rico, and Miami, the country's mission to the UN in New York City, and the Venezuelan Consulate in San Juan. Bosch referred to the bombings as "messages," warning that "there will be a couple messages more."

Frank Castro, a trusted confederate of Posada and Bosch, going back to the founding of CORU, stepped into the leadership role in their absence. A 1978 CIA memo referred to Frank Castro as the new "behind the scenes leader of CORU" and noted that he had approached Venezuelan authorities with a chilling offer: "In return for the release of Posada, and perhaps Bosch, there will be no more terrorist acts in Venezuela or against Venezuelan properties." The memo pointed out that in the previous year a Venezuelan DC-9 plane had been bombed on the ground at Miami International Airport "in protest against Posada's and Bosch's imprisonment."

At the same time, the trial became a cause célèbre among the exile political leadership. Miami's mayor and city commissioners vowed to free the two and organized fund-raisers to pay for lawyers and lobbyists. Miami's mayor, Maurice Ferré, visited Bosch in prison while the city commissioners declared an official "Orlando Bosch Day." The impact of the campaign on Caracas's justice system, long susceptible to political pressure and *mordidas* (bribes), would be significant.

The Venezuelan government had two conflicting goals: to avoid a showdown with Cuban militants and to demonstrate to the world—and to Castro—that it was serious about prosecuting the case. The country had a third goal: to divert attention from the involvement of its own intelligence agency, DISIP. Recently declassified State Department cables reveal that the United States asked Venezuela to extradite Bosch immediately after the attack. Instead Venezuelan intelligence initially tried to smuggle him out of the country. It was far more expedient to focus attention on Posada, a former CIA agent, than on Bosch, who had so recently been welcomed into the country by CAP's chief of security.

Several judges and prosecutors received death threats. Judge Delia Estava Moreno, who had issued the four arrest warrants, received more than one. Fearing for her life, she resigned from the case, but not before referring it to a military tribunal in August 1977. When the tribunal's presiding judge, General Elio García Barrios, indicated publicly that he found the evidence against the four men compelling, he too began to receive death threats.

Fearing more bombings and assassinations, the Venezuelan government began to pressure the tribunal's panel of judges to absolve Posada and Bosch. "It would be inconceivable to allow them to go free," General García told Venezuelan reporter Alexis Rosas, "but we are being strongly pressured. . . . Whatever the government wants is what will get done." The judge's son and driver were later slain in a drive-by hit, a killing the judge described as a hit by the "Cuban mafia."

In September 1980, the military tribunal announced that there was insufficient evidence to try the four men and ordered their release. The following day, in protest, Fidel Castro ordered all Cuban diplomats out of Venezuela. President Pérez developed second thoughts about the ruling and the court amended its decision. Prosecutors appealed and the government simply ruled that the military lacked proper authority to try the case. Two causes were cited: the men were not military personnel and the crime of aggravated homicide could not be adjudicated by a military tribunal. The Military Court of Appeals agreed and surrendered jurisdiction. The trial was then kicked back to a civil court while the suspects were kept behind bars.

Meanwhile, politicians in Miami urged the Reagan-Bush administration to press for the release of Bosch and Posada. The administration, however, was well aware that the CIA and FBI believed that both men were guilty. After all, Mono Morales was an FBI informant. Just three weeks after the plane's downing, he had told the FBI that the bombing had been brainstormed at two meetings at the Anauco Hilton in Caracas, one in his own residential suite. Both meetings, he said, were attended by Posada, confirming what Hernán Ricardo had told DISIP's operations chief. However, Morales, who signed the arrest warrants for Posada and Bosch, had a pointed warning for the FBI. "Some people in the Venezuelan government are involved in this airplane bombing," he said, according to a memo released by the National Security Agency (NSA). "And if Posada Carriles talks, he and others in the government will 'go down the tubes.'" Morales concluded that if people started talking, "we'll have our own Watergate."

DISIP's deputy chief, Rafael Rivas-Vásquez, early on informed U.S. authorities that the Cubana bombing had been planned at CORU's kickoff meeting in the Dominican Republic. How did he know? His predecessor, Luis Posada, had told him. Orlando García also forwarded to the CIA his investigation, which concluded that all four men were part of the conspiracy. But the U.S. expressed scant interest in the case, he told his friends. "My father said they were all guilty," said Rolando García, one of García's three sons who later worked with him at DISIP. The CIA's laissez-faire response affected his father's view of George H. W. Bush, who was then CIA director. "He had a very low opinion of George Bush," said Osvaldo García, the youngest of García's sons, "going back to how he handled things when he was at the CIA."

By 1981, Reagan-Bush administration officials had other considerations: they knew that they would soon need the backing of exile militants for a secret arms-for-hostages operation in El Salvador.

For Orlando Bosch and Luis Posada, prison life at Venezuela's San Juan de los Moros was not unlike summer camp. In their wing, there were sunny courtyards and pleasant common rooms to accommodate their steady stream of visitors—including a number of Miami's most influential politicians and powerbrokers. Bosch and Posada's cell, while small, had a television and pretty wallpaper that Adriana Bosch had picked out. There were even conjugal visits. Adriana frequently visited her husband while Posada's love life continued at its usual brisk pace, with various attractive women regularly visiting him.

The men, however, were confined alongside some of their leftist guerrilla enemies. When the two sides crossed each other's path, there was palpable tension and no small amount of name-calling. One shouting match concluded with the hotheaded Hernán Ricardo baiting his foes by hollering out, *"Sí, pusimos la bomba! Y qué!"*—"Yes, we planted the bomb! . . . And so what!" Ricardo's boast would become the title of a book by journalist Alicia Herrera, a childhood friend of Freddy Lugo, who happened to be visiting at the time. "You can imagine how much damage that wretch has done to us," Lugo despaired to Herrera. "Bosch and I look[ed] the other way. . . . He did the same thing in Trinidad; he went mad. I don't know why: he started confessing everything."

In late March 1977, a reporter named Blake Fleetwood, writing for the magazine *New Times,* took a chance and stopped by the prison one morning. He had disregarded Venezuelan authorities, who were doing their utmost to keep reporters away from the detained men. He was well rewarded for his efforts and spent six hours with the two famed militants. After Fleetwood chatted with Bosch in the courtyard, Bosch brought him to his cell and introduced him to Posada. Offering the young journalist a French liqueur and a Cuban cigar, Posada jested that "America may have an embargo against Cuban cigars—but we don't."

While the reporter found Posada a cagey customer, Bosch was forthright, garrulous, and furious about his perceived betrayal by Venezuelan authorities. Both men expected to be found guilty of the crime, owing to the confessions of Lugo and Ricardo, but anticipated some form of political intercession on their behalf. Neither denied his involvement in the bombing of the plane, said Fleetwood. "They said they did the Cubana bombing," he recalled. "Their defense was that their activities were known to the Venezuelan government, whom they claimed 'gave us IDs, weapons.'" There was just one misgiving, according to Fleetwood: "The bombs were supposed to go off when the plane was on the ground." Presumably, such an action would have generated less bad publicity than a blazing airliner nosediving into the sea.

Bosch claimed that Orlando García had promised to release him "as soon as the publicity blows over." Although Bosch said he was initially inclined to protect his Venezuelan hosts, all bets were now off. "If they want to put me on trial," he warned, "they will also have to accuse the

Minister of the Interior, the DISIP director, and the president. These people conspired with me. They should be put in jail as well."

Posada invoked his tenuous ties to the CIA whenever possible. "In Miami, I was on a CIA draw of three hundred dollars [a month] plus all expenses," he told Fleetwood. "Later the CIA helped me set up my detective agency from which we planned *actions,*" the euphemism for attacks or bombings.

Fleetwood learned he was lucky to leave Venezuela with his tapes as well as his life. The following day, he submitted questions to CAP's office, seeking to confirm Bosch and Posada's accounts. They were never answered. Instead, Venezuelan authorities phoned the U.S. ambassador in Caracas, Peter Vaky, to voice their displeasure. Author Taylor Branch and Eugene Propper, then the U.S. sttorney charged with investigating the Letelier assassination, recalled the incident in their book *Labyrinth:* "The [ambassador] was unhappy because President Pérez was unhappy—and nearly to the same degree." So distressed that "President Pérez had ordered DISIP to arrest Fleetwood . . . [and] Ambassador Vaky was demanding an explanation." Warned by Propper's office, the young journalist was able to slip out of Caracas under another name and eventually out of the country. Upon his arrival back in New York, he turned over copies of his tapes to Propper's office.

In June 1978, the imprisoned militants had another visit: this time from two investigators dispatched from the House Select Committee on Assassinations. The two investigators, Gaeton Fonzi and former Miami police detective Al Gonzales, found Bosch and Posada diametric opposites: Bosch, they noted, was "a true ideologue and quite proud of it" who guilelessly extolled his determination to bring down Castro, while Posada appeared smug, almost slick, in his certainty that powerful people would be looking after him. "He strolled into the room casually self-assured, a good-looking guy in his late forties, tanned and tall with no hint of prison pallor," Fonzi later wrote. "His brown hair was trimmed and styled, his shirt tailored, his trousers sharply creased. Posada put his feet up on the desk, smiled, and admitted to very little." At one point, when asked about his ties to the CIA, he smiled and said, "All Cubans work for the CIA."

Bosch had resigned himself to prison for the immediate future and busied himself painting and writing. Moreover, he was able to continue his career as anti-Castro militant, regularly meeting with his confederates at the prison and plotting ongoing attacks against Fidel Castro, Cuba, and its allies.

Posada was less sanguine about his chances of ever beating the charges once his case went to court. After several appeals and endless legal wrangling, Posada decided to take matters into his hands when his case again went to trial, and he was charged with first-degree murder. In 1985, while awaiting the verdict in his trial, he escaped from prison by bribing the warden. The fifty thousand dollars of bribe money had been raised by Jorge Mas Canosa, according to Mas's brother, Ricardo, who said he handled parts of the transaction.

It was Posada's third attempt: two previous attempted escapes undertaken with Hernán Ricardo had failed. In August 1982, the escapees had made it to the Chilean embassy, where they were hospitably hosted for three days. But after much haggling between Chilean and Venezuelan authorities, they were denied asylum. Even a stalwart ally like General Pinochet was unwilling to expend the political capital needed for such a damaging case. Posada however did not carry a grudge. In 1998, he told me that "Pinochet was the best dictator Latin America ever had."

Following his 1985 escape, a shrimp boat owned by a Miami supporter ferried Posada to El Salvador, where he was met by Félix Rodríguez, his former comrade from Bay of Pigs. Rodríguez had an unusual employment opportunity for Posada: to be his deputy in a covert operation directed by Lieutenant Colonel Oliver L. North of the National Security Council to assist the Contras fighting to dislodge the Nicaraguan government. Rodríguez had been solicited for the assignment by an old CIA friend from Vietnam, Donald Gregg, Vice President George Bush's national security adviser.

Almost overnight, Posada underwent a spectacular reversal of fortune—from a prisoner charged with the heinous act of air terrorism to a man running a secret operation directed from the White House. Posada was not only back in favor—he was on the government payroll.

Posada was given a Salvadoran passport and driver's license in the name of Ramón Medina Rodríguez. He was put in charge of organizing the flights that ferried supplies for the Contras from the Salvadoran air base at Ilopango to the battlefront in Nicaragua. Among his duties was coordinating the efforts of the Contras, the secret American advisers, and U.S. Army pilots with their allies in the Salvadoran right-wing military, where Posada had cultivated useful friendships. With his command of English, he doubled as a translator for the operation.

When the Iran-Contra scandal burst onto the front pages of newspapers in 1986, Posada said he earned every penny of his U.S.-taxpayer-financed salary of roughly ten thousand dollars a month. He told me that in a matter of hours he had dashed to all the U.S. safe houses in El

Salvador, ferried American "advisers" out of the country, and disposed of incriminating materials that would have proven troublesome to the White House.

Félix Rodríguez met with George Bush at the White House in January 1985 to discuss the secret operation. It was a frustrating meeting, according to Posada, with Rodríguez doing all the talking. The vice president nodded his head congenially and smiled, but said little. When I pressed Posada in 1998 about whether the White House knew about the illegal arms supply operation, he laughed heartily and said, "Everyone knew."

With Posada safely out of the picture, the Venezuelan judiciary moved forward with the trials of his co-defendants. But the government remained troubled by the case and its potential for political blowback and worse. Its misgivings were evident when the court inexplicably barred the Lugo-Ricardo confessions along with the entire case file meticulously compiled by police investigators in Trinidad and Barbados. Instead, the court arrived at the spurious decision that all the reports were inadmissible because they were in English.

Nevertheless, in July 1986, Hernán Ricardo and Freddy Lugo were convicted of homicide for having planted the bombs on the plane. For the murder of seventy-three civilians, they were sentenced to twenty years in prison, the minimum allowed under Venezuelan law. They were released in 1993, after serving just sixteen years.

Orlando Bosch was even luckier—he was flat out acquitted. The verdict was not surprising as virtually all the evidence and case files against him had been mysteriously ruled inadmissible by the presiding judge. He was allowed to leave prison a year later. On February 16, 1988, a supremely confident Bosch flew to Miami, despite the fact he had been denied a U.S. visa. Upon his arrival in the U.S., he was detained for his prior parole violation and for illegal entry.

The powerful exile leader Jorge Mas Canosa arranged for his lawyers, Hank Adorno and Raoul Cantero, to represent Bosch. The attorneys attended to the case with dispatch and gusto. On Miami radio, Cantero, who happens to be the grandson of Fulgencio Batista, described his client as "a great Cuban patriot."

Cantero's view was not shared by Secretary of State Henry Kissinger, who authored a classified memo entitled "U.S. Position on Investigation of Cubana Airline Crash." "U.S. government had been planning to recommend Bosch's deportation before Cubana Airlines crash took place for his suspected involvement in terrorist acts and violation of his parole," Kissinger wrote. "Suspicion that Bosch involved in planning of Cubana Airlines crash [leads] us to suggest his deportation urgently."

While the Justice Department reviewed his case, bomb threats were made against the Miami office of the Immigration and Naturalization Service (INS). "My colleagues and I conducted exhaustive investigations of Bosch from the time of his arrival," FBI agent George Davis wrote in a memo to Secretary of State George Shultz in 1989. "He was regarded by the FBI and other law enforcement agencies as Miami's number one terrorist." Attorney General Richard Thornburgh described Bosch as an "unreformed terrorist," and recommended that he be immediately deported.

But there were political considerations in Miami. In 1989, securing the release of Orlando Bosch became the cornerstone of the congressional campaign of Cuban exile Ileana Ros-Lehtinen. Ros-Lehtinen lauded Bosch as a hero and a patriot on exile radio stations, and raised $265,000 for his legal fund. Her father, Enrique Ros, a devoted ally of Bosch, was her political mentor. She was also ably assisted by her campaign manager—a political neophyte, but one who had the ear of the White House. His name was Jeb Bush.

After the INS classified Bosch as an "excludable alien," Jeb Bush visited with Bosch's supporters, who were leading a limited hunger strike. On August 17, 1989, Jeb Bush attended a meeting he had arranged for Ros-Lehtinen with his father to discuss the Bosch matter. The following July, in an unprecedented intercession, President George H. W. Bush rejected his own Justice Department's recommendation and authorized the release of Bosch. Two years later, Bush granted Bosch U.S. residency, conditional on his renouncing violence.

Not long after his release, Bosch announced that he was ready to "rejoin the struggle" and called the agreement he had signed forswearing violence "a farce." The FBI shared his view, noting that Bosch promptly renewed his militant activities with impunity. Robert Gelbard, a senior State Department official, said that when he filed complaints about Bosch, requesting his arrest for violating his parole conditions, Bosch didn't stay in jail long. Bosch seemed to know that someone was looking after him. Invariably, he would soon be released and plotting his next strike against Castro. Gelbard said it was explained to him that "Jeb Bush would get on the horn with his father and Bosch would be right back on the streets again."

Nevertheless, Bosch's defiance would be an ongoing source of embarrassment for the Bush family. "I said he should have never been allowed to stay in the U.S.," Thornburgh, the former attorney general, told me in

2007. "They knew but they didn't listen." When Bill Clinton was questioned by a *Newsweek* reporter about his pardon of fugitive financier Marc Rich, he snapped, "I swore I wouldn't answer questions about Marc Rich until Bush answered about Orlando Bosch." Few Republicans raised the issue again. Bosch seemed unconcerned about the political costs or any limit on his freedom. "They bought the chain," he boasted to a *Miami Herald* reporter, citing a Cuban adage, "but they don't have the monkey."

CHAPTER SEVEN

Miami Vice

They were an odd trio linked by a single passion. Diosdado Diaz, Luis Rodriguez, and George Kiszynski had more than seventy-five years of pooled experience investigating exile militant groups. Before they retired or moved on to other assignments, the three were long-term members of the South Florida Joint Terrorism Task Force (JTTF)—an investigative team with representatives from the State Attorney's Office, the FBI, and the police departments of both the City of Miami and Miami-Dade County. The Task Force is hosted by the FBI's Miami bureau, working out of the Bureau's offices on NW 2nd Avenue, and is the first line of defense for criminal conspiracies and terrorism for the Sunshine State. Of course, not all matters concern exile paramilitaries. After 9/11, one task involved interviewing Osama bin Laden's sister, when she was a student at the University of Miami.

Diaz, who is known as D.C., retired from the City of Miami's Police Department in 1999 after twenty-seven years and went to work as a trainer for a Department of Defense contractor. Diaz has a shaved head and aqua-blue eyes and is invariably decked out in sneakers and shades—with a gun and holster tucked under his blue jeans above his ankle. Partial to jokes and profane epithets, he could not be more different from the soft-spoken Kiszynski.

A career FBI man who logged thirty-four years before retiring in 2005, George Kiszynski has a trim white mustache and neatly parted hair. Gold wire-rimmed glasses frame his pale eyes. A cautious, measured man, Kiszynski was raised in Buenos Aires by an Italian mother and Polish father. Known as Jorge to most of his informants, he is the only U.S. investigator who has conducted two formal interviews with Luis Posada.

Luis Rodriguez is the youngest of the three, though he has clocked more than two decades working for the Miami-Dade Police Department. Dark and intense, he is a "soccer dad" who bears a resemblance to the movie star Andy Garcia. From 1992 to 2002, he was a member of the Joint Terrorism Task Force.

The three did not agree on all police matters but shared several points of consensus. First was that Cuban intelligence had long ago infiltrated most of the exile groups, sometimes setting up sting operations. Second was that some militants invoked the cause of freedom in Cuba to shroud less noble motives—such as drug dealing, arms trafficking, or illegal gambling. Third was the reluctance of Miami prosecutors to take on the paramilitaries and their members. Indeed, it seemed that anyone who claimed to be a soldier in the War Against Castro was admitted to a parallel justice system with unusual privileges.

In 1982, D. C. Diaz developed a relationship with Ricardo "El Mono" Morales. The former DISIP official had been in Miami, testifying as a police informer in a major narcotics investigation known as Tick Tock. Following an exhaustive deposition by defense lawyers, a shaken Morales asked Diaz to join him for a drink at the Marriott hotel bar on Le Jeune Road, near the airport.

During a long, rambling conversation, Morales admitted his guilt in the Cubana bombing but maintained that the plane had been a military craft. Moreover, he insisted by way of justification that the passengers were Cuban intelligence officers. "El Mono said that Posada made the bombs," recounted Diaz, "and that there were two bombs: the bomb inside the camera and another stashed in the cargo hold of the plane in Barbados, which was the one that brought the plane down." The explosives had been placed inside the cargo hold—close to one of the wings—by an airport employee in Barbados, according to Morales. However, "Lugo and Ricardo didn't know there was a second device because they never told them." Diaz said he found Morales, on this occasion, to be compelling, candid, and credible.

When the plane exploded, Morales told Diaz, he was in his (DISIP) office chatting with Posada. "And they heard the screeching of tires and looked out the window, and he said he sees two Scotland Yard officers [Barbados being part of the British Commonwealth] getting out of the car. So El Mono looks at Posada and says, 'We've got problems.'"

Because of Bosch's excessive drinking, Diaz believes that he played a minor, if any, role in the Cubana bombing. "When he was here in Miami, the extreme militants didn't trust him because he was a drunk and he'd blab about anything," said Diaz. "He could not keep a secret." In Caracas, his behavior was even more erratic. "He was an embarrassment to the government, drinking every night, raising hell," recounted

Diaz. On the day of the bombing, Morales told Diaz, Bosch came to his office and said, "You know there's been a bombing. I'm going to take credit for it." Morales also claimed that "the CIA knew about it because those were the Cold War years," suggesting there were few secrets between Langley and DISIP.

Kiszynski said he was always wary with Morales, adding, "You wouldn't want to be on his wrong side." Kiszynski and Rodriguez listed the same suspects for the Cubana bombing: Posada, Bosch, Hernán Ricardo, Lugo, Morales, and Frank Castro, who got off scot-free and settled down in the Dominican Republic. Kiszynski pointed out that Freddy Lugo and Hernán Ricardo "are just the kind of types that Posada would use for an attack," considering Posada's history of employing young, uneducated Central Americans to do the grunt work.

Kiszynski and Rodriguez also believed that García played some kind of role. "I went to interview him on another matter," said Kiszynski. "He was a heavy smoker, very smart, very Machiavellian. If Orlando García wanted to solve the Cubana case, he could have. He would have known exactly what happened." Rodriguez was not as sure. "Possibly Orlando García knew about it," he said, agreeing with Diaz. "But I don't think he was a conspirator."

Later in 1982, Posada's attorney, the flamboyant Raymond Aguiar, known as the Clarence Darrow of Caracas, flew to Miami in his private plane for a date with El Mono. At the time, Morales had plans to resettle in Miami and hoped his "confession" would ease relations between him and exile militant leaders who no longer trusted him. In a videotaped confession, Morales took responsibility for the bombing, and asserted that Bosch and Posada were completely innocent. He also railed against President Carlos Andrés Pérez, and insisted that Hernán Ricardo and Freddy Lugo had been working solely for him, not Posada and Bosch, a statement that was verifiably untrue.

Orlando García told his son Rolando, who worked with him at DISIP from 1989 to 1999, that he was not surprised. "My father told me El Mono would say whatever people paid him to say," recalled Rolando. When I asked Bosch about Morales's "confession," he smiled faintly and waved his hand by his head, Cuban style. "El Mono said he did it," Bosch said with a shrug. "So he did it."

Evidently, El Mono's reversal and dramatic appeal on behalf of his comrades was not enough to satisfy all his critics. Not long after his taped confession, Morales was shot dead in a Key Biscayne bar by a drug thug named Orlando Torres. Pleading self-defense, Torres got off, but later did time for arms smuggling after being busted by none other than D. C. Diaz. In a surreal film noir twist, Posada's high-flying attorney was murdered a year later, in a matter not related to the case.

In 1985, an informer, "a walk-in," showed up at the Miami FBI office and asked to speak with D. C. Diaz about an arms operation being run from Miami to El Salvador. Diaz said he soon suspected that he was dealing with a low-level Cuban agent—what the FBI refers to as "a dangle," an informer who may have multiple allegiances and motives. Typically, "dangles" demonstrate their anti-Castro bona fides by working the longest hours within a militant group. Sometimes a dangle will notify the FBI before a strike occurs, sometimes after. If the information is solid, agents will glean what they can get, then continue to keep an eye on the informer. On this occasion, Diaz's suspected dangle was having an affair with the wife of a Bay of Pigs vet and anti-Castro militant who was moving weapons to El Salvador. "We were able to intercept several large loads of weapons," recalled Diaz. "And one thing led to the other."

But when the FBI queried the CIA about the mysterious arms shipments, the Agency claimed to be clueless. "We had penetrated a CIA operation. The funny thing about it was that Mr. Posada, the great Cuban hero, was making long distance calls to all his friends in Miami from a safe house," said Diaz, enjoying a moment of rich sarcasm, "run and paid for by the CIA." Transcripts of Posada's phone records later subpoenaed by the Senate committee investigating Iran-Contra confirmed the calls. "In other words, the CIA was lying to us the whole time," said Diaz.

Growing up in Havana in the 1950s, D. C. Diaz had heard tales about Orlando Bosch as a hard-drinking, hard-driving man. That impression was reconfirmed in 1974. "I stopped this car that was weaving all over Calle Ocho," recalled Diaz. "And the guy jumps out and this woman in the car slides over to the driver's seat. It's Bosch and he's so drunk, he couldn't even walk." Diaz let Bosch off with a warning not to take the wheel again, and let his female friend drive him away.

Booze is a touchstone referenced in virtually every conversation about the exile paramilitaries during the 1970s—the elixir that made so much possible. There is Bosch's bottomless drinking, Posada's passion for Black Label scotch, and El Mono's constant inebriation. *El Mono fue borracho y un perdido y un chivato*," Bosch told me about Morales. "He was a drunk, a lost soul, and a snitch." At DISIP, Orlando García rarely went to work without a grim hangover. Did García know about the Cubana bombing, as some maintain? Or would he have remembered, even if told? "It depended on his mood," explained Salvador Romaní. "If he wasn't drunk, he was very cordial. But very dangerous when he drank—and he always drank."

The three former investigators concurred that Orlando Bosch never retired from the sabotage business. For years, they sought permission to wiretap him but were denied. Some agents on the JTTF concluded that Hector Pesquera, the FBI special agent in charge of the Miami bureau from 1999 to December 2003, was especially pliant to local political pressure.

Any potentially sensitive prosecutions—including all exile cases— were run by the political leadership of Tallahassee, the state capital, and Miami. For years, this meant that Governor Jeb Bush, who owed a good deal of his support to exile hardliners, and Miami's congressional representatives, weighed in on investigations, commutations, and pardons. The State Attorney's Office and the U.S. Attorney's Office in Miami have long been regarded as among the most politicized in the country.

Still, in the summer of 2001, the Joint Terrorism Task Force almost nailed Bosch, even without a wiretap. Investigators had apprehended Andrés Nazario Sargén, the leader of Alpha 66, the militant exile group. Sargén had scooted into his local Miami post office to pick up a box of detonators and C-4 plastic explosives. "We took Sargén to a motel room and he spilled the beans," recalled Rodriguez. "We confronted him with all the evidence we had, including a boat docked on the Miami River that we had under surveillance. Sargén told us that their plan was to sail into Caibarién, on the northern coast of Cuba, and blow up the oil refineries there, because they have this fetish about Cuba's oil business."

Sargén agreed to turn state's evidence against Bosch—even agreeing to wear a wire. "No one else but Bosch would have had those detonators," said Rodriguez. "Then Sargén got cold feet and refused to name Bosch, who was like a guru to all of them. If he had, we would have had Bosch—even without a wiretap. And he would have gone away for a long time, because he was a convicted felon and parole violator." Sargén died in 2004 at the age of eighty-eight.

Miami's exile leadership rejoiced at the arrival of George W. Bush in the White House in January 2001. Finally, said exile hardliners, there was someone in the Oval Office who understood that regime change was the only way to deal with Fidel Castro. Almost immediately, the Bush administration set about enacting a sea change in U.S.-Cuba policy—shutting down nascent diplomatic forays, ramping up hostility, and imposing onerous restrictions on travel and remittances sent to the island. Investigators in the FBI's Miami office were instructed to shutter outstanding cases on exile plots against Cuba and to concentrate solely on finding Cuban spies lurking in South Florida.

In August 2001, José Dionisio Suárez and Virgilio Paz, both convicted for their roles in the murder of Ambassador Orlando Letelier and his young American companion, were released from prison, at the behest of Miami's congressional representatives. A month earlier, militant Hector Cornillot Llano had been discharged after serving thirteen years. The releases followed a U.S. Supreme Court ruling in June 2001 (in a case brought principally on behalf of imprisoned exiles) that indefinite detention of alien felons who have served prison time and are liable for deportation, but for whom no country can be found, is unconstitutional. However, instead of being deported like other noncitizen criminals, convicted exile militants were allowed to settle into the good life in Miami. Moreover, no attempt to find an alternative country to Cuba was even considered.

After the tragedy of September 11, 2001, it was assumed that the policy of releasing convicted assassins would stop. President Bush famously told the world that the choice was black and white: "We've got to say to people who are willing to harbor a terrorist or feed a terrorist," Bush proclaimed, "that they are just as guilty as the terrorists."

Soon there emerged what would be called the Castro Exception. Anyone able to wrap himself in the banner of *Viva Cuba Libre* seemed eligible for a pass. Even a serial killer such as Valentín Hernández could walk out of jail post-9/11 and resettle with his family in Fort Myers, Florida. Hernández had gunned down Luciano Nieves, a supporter of dialogue with Cuba, in 1975 by ambushing him in the parking lot of a Miami hospital. Nieves had just come from visiting his ailing eleven-year-old son. Two years earlier, Hernández had been charged with aggravated assault for attacking Nieves with a restaurant stool. During his trial, Hernández escaped by slipping through a bathroom window during a break. He was a fugitive when he killed Nieves, and remained one for two years after Nieves's murder, protected by sympathetic or intimidated exiles. Less than a year later, Hernández and his accomplice Lazo murdered a former president of the Bay of Pigs Association, Juan José Peruyero, in an internecine power struggle. Hernández was finally captured in Puerto Rico in July 1977 and sentenced to life in prison. His accomplice, the anti-Castro zealot Lazo, has never been brought to justice.

Luis Posada made his last attempt to eliminate Fidel Castro at the

Ibero-American Summit in Panama in November 2000. But Posada and his three veteran collaborators, Gaspar Jiménez, Guillermo Novo, and Pedro Remón, were outwitted by a clever sting operation by Cuban intelligence agents, who won the confidence of the would-be assassins. Fidel Castro celebrated by holding a ballyhooed press conference, proclaiming their capture, along with a small arsenal of weapons and explosives. The foursome were charged in Panama with the attempted assassination of Castro.

After the men's trial and conviction in 2004 (reduced to several lesser felonies such as "posing a danger to society," possession of thirty-three pounds of C-4 explosives, and document fraud), Miami's exile leadership led a spirited campaign to free the four veteran militants. South Florida's three Cuban-American members of Congress, Lincoln Díaz-Balart, Mario Díaz-Balart, and Ileana Ros-Lehtinen, wrote letters on official U.S. Congress stationery to Panamanian president Mireya Moscoso, seeking their release. Cuban exile militants had another potent political ally: Senator Joe Lieberman, chairman of the powerful Senate Homeland Security Committee, had long given them a sympathetic hearing. Lieberman had been elected to represent Connecticut in 1988 in large part through the contributions of the late Jorge Mas Canosa, which immeasurably helped Lieberman oust Lowell Weicker, who favored lifting the embargo on Cuba.

Two prominent Miami lawyer/power players spearheaded the campaign to secure the release of Posada and his cohorts: Simon Ferro, former ambassador to Panama, and Herminio San Roman, former director of Radio Martí, the Miami-based station that broadcast into Cuba, began quiet negotiations with Moscoso, who maintained a home in Miami's Key Biscayne. They also met with members of the Miami Joint Terrorism Task Force to convey their disapproval of the ongoing investigations of the jailed men. Any efforts on the part of the Task Force that could be perceived as undermining the release campaign, the agents were told, would not be appreciated.

On August 24, 2004, Posada and his fellow conspirators—all with colorful rap sheets—received a last-minute pardon from the outgoing Moscoso. Rumors floated about Miami that a significant sum of money had been paid to secure their freedom—reports never confirmed. Ahead of the pardons, quiet inquiries were made and backdoor deals considered by the Bush administration, which had been shopping for a country to grant Posada asylum to keep him out of sight and out of the news.

While his comrades flew directly to Miami for a rousing welcome, Posada found his case was trickier: he was, after all, a fugitive wanted in Venezuela. Initially, he was flown in a private plane to Pedro San Sula, Honduras, traveling with a bogus American passport in the name of "Melvin Clyde Thompson." In Honduras, he was met by one of his patrons, Rafael Hernández Nodarse, a Bay of Pigs veteran and wealthy media mogul, described by the *Miami Herald* as "a brash, contentious cross between William Randolph Hearst and the fictional Scarface character Tony Montana." Nodarse's first radio station in Honduras was named Radio Swan, in homage to the famed CIA anti-Castro propaganda station. There would be a celebratory dinner for Posada and a red carpet stay at one of Nodarse's hotels.

For the next several months, Posada vacationed and received medical care, compliments of Nodarse. Still, he remained hopeful he could rejoin his friends and family in Miami. Over time, he was given reasonable assurances from his allies that he would be welcome there without interference from law enforcement. After all, Orlando Bosch, who remained openly boastful about his operations against Castro, was leading a comfortable life in the Sunshine State.

I remembered Posada's wink of a smile when he told me that he had quite a few passports from different countries under fictitious names, including an American one. When I asked when he last visited the United States, he chortled with amusement. "Officially or unofficially? I have a lot of passports," Posada said. "If I want to go to Miami, I have different ways to go. No problem."

But when Posada danced into Miami in March 2005, the administration cringed. How was it possible that a self-described "warrior" and "*militante*"—long a fixture on the U.S. immigration authorities' watch list—had crossed into the United States with a bogus passport and visa? And was it conceivable that the Bush administration, notwithstanding its purported commitment to the war on terrorism (rule 1 of U.S. counterterrorism policy: "make no concessions to terrorists and strike no deals"), would consider residency for a notorious fugitive?

In any other American city, Posada would have been met by a SWAT team, arrested, and deported. But in the peculiar ecosystem of Miami, where hardline anti-Castro politicians controlled Spanish-language radio stations and the ballot boxes, the definition of terrorism remained a pliable one. His lawyer made the tortured argument that those who planted bombs in Havana could not be held responsible for innocent victims unless it could be proven that those victims were, in fact, intended targets.

By 2005, such double standards on terrorism were a hard sell. Moreover, polls in South Florida revealed a new reality: only a narrow segment of older exiles regarded militants like Bosch and Posada as heroes. Younger exiles were focused primarily on their homes, jobs, and taxes— not bringing down Fidel Castro.

On May 17, 2005, Posada held an ill-advised, bizarre press conference in Miami. Although the U.S. government was not seeking to arrest him, he said, he was abandoning his asylum petition. Not wanting to make any further problems, he said, he had decided to leave the country. But his public airing of his legal problems was too much, even for his allies in the Bush administration. Posada was arrested immediately after the press conference. Still, he was taken away in style: he was not handcuffed but escorted to a golf cart, which ferried him to a helicopter nearby. He was then whisked off to an immigration facility in El Paso, Texas, far from his friends and allies.

Posada's camp suffered another blow in November 2005, when Osvaldo Mitat along with Santiago Alvarez, Posada's longtime patron and cohort, were arrested and charged with illegal possession of false passports and hundreds of firearms, including AK-47s. When captured, Mitat told agents, "Unfortunately, you guys are doing your jobs and we got caught with a bunch of guns," adding, "I love the United States."

Investigators believed that Alvarez had assisted Posada with his Panamanian pardon and his return to the U.S. Alvarez had his own track record and close calls. "Alvarez was the one who gave the order to fire on the *Sierra Aranzazu* as it sailed toward Havana on September 13, 1964," said journalist Don Bohning. "He had mistaken the Spanish vessel for the *Sierra Maestra,* a Cuban ship that was to be leaving Havana for Japan about the same time. It caused a major diplomatic flap."

Central to the government's case against Alvarez and Mitat was the testimony of a confidant of theirs, Gilberto Abascal, who had led FBI agents to the weapons stash. It was Abascal who informed U.S. and Cuban authorities that contrary to Posada's claim to have crossed the U.S. border by bus into Texas, the storied militant had arrived in Miami on a boat. The vessel, the *Santrina,* owned by Alvarez, had stopped in Isla Mujeres, off the coast of Cancún, Mexico, for repairs before sailing on to Miami. Prosecutors verified Abascal's account and charged Posada with illegal entry and for lying to federal officials that he had come through the border in Texas.

The arrests of Posada, Alvarez, and other militants infuriated their supporters, who argued that such militants had been nurtured and bred at the knee of the CIA. Lawyers for the two men threatened to turn the tables and put the U.S. government on trial.

Held without bail and facing thirty years, the wealthy Santiago Alvarez retained an A-list defense team, including former U.S. Attorney Kendall Coffey and Arturo Hernandez. The lawyers cast Gilberto Abascal as the villain—alleging that he was not only an FBI informer, but also a Cuban agent who had set up their clients in a sting. The lawyers vowed to blow the lid on the FBI's use of "dangles." In April 2001, Abascal had warned the FBI about another attack organized by Alvarez. But in that case, he did not make contact until after the three commandos were captured in Cuba. In response to charges by the attorneys, Abascal issued a vehement denial. "This case will be huge in its impact," Hernandez told reporters. "It will be a big as Elián—transcendental in what it reveals." Once again, a crime story had evolved into a parable on the marathon anti-Castro wars.

The attorneys' gambit had its intended impact: prosecutors acceded to an unusual plea agreement as the trial was to begin. Instead of serving up to fifty years if convicted on all charges, Alvarez secured a sentence of just forty-seven months, and Osvaldo Mitat thirty-seven months. In 2007, their sentences were further reduced by more than a year when they agreed to turn over yet another massive arms cache, including more than fourteen pounds of plastic explosives, two hundred pounds of dynamite, thirty semiautomatic and automatic weapons, one grenade launcher, and two handmade grenades, as reported in the *Miami Herald*. "These would have been a treasure trove for our nation's worst enemies," said attorney Coffey, who went on to suggest that his clients were protecting the country from Islamic militants. "What would have been a treasure chest for Al Qaeda is a godsend for our community."

It seemed for a brief time in 2005 that it would not be business as usual. Two grand juries had been convened to look into Posada's activities. Complicating matters was a very public and sensational feud: José Antonio Llama, a former director of the Cuban American National Foundation, had charged the exile group with having orchestrated attacks on Castro and tourist targets inside Cuba.

José Antonio Llama, known as Toñín, had been a close collaborator of the late Jorge Mas Canosa. In 1998 he went on trial—with four other exiles—for a failed assassination attempt on Fidel Castro. This one was planned for the Ibero-American Summit on Isla Margarita, Venezuela, in 1997. The hopeful assassins intended to shoot down Castro's plane from their cabin cruiser as it landed. The boat, *La Esperanza*, had been purchased by Llama for the mission.

According to the FBI, Posada was a crucial player in this seemingly harebrained attempt on Castro, having booked the assassins' rooms in Isla Margarita. The men were ultimately acquitted in a trial held in San Juan, Puerto Rico, after the judge, quite inexplicably, tossed out a key confessional statement.

But in June 2006, an embittered and frustrated Llama admitted that federal prosecutors had been right. According to Llama, he had loaned $1.4 million to the CANF to buy materials intended to attack Cuban targets. Despite years of entreaties, Llama claimed, the group had never paid him back. Among his purchases were a cargo helicopter, seven vessels, including the boat, and a large cache of explosives. Of great interest to investigators was the purchase of ten small remote-control planes, known as ultralights, for $210,000.

To bolster his allegations, Llama disseminated a press release which detailed the creation of El Grupo Bélico—or The War Group—at CANF's annual meeting in Naples, Florida, in 1993. The group's mandate was singular, wrote Llama in his statement: "destabilizing the Communist government of Castro. . . . Mas Canosa requested that the proposal be discussed behind closed doors by the executive committee and not openly in the meeting hall of the Foundation. . . . Pepe Hernandez was selected by Mas Canosa to lead this new group. . . . Pepe is a veteran of the Brigade 2506, ex-captain of the special forces of the U.S. Marines and had the qualifications for this job. He was the logical candidate."

Francisco "Pepe" Hernandez had purchased one of the long-range rifles that had been captured in the *Esperanza* caper. It was later widely expected that he would be indicted with the four other men. "We had him brought in, fingerprinted him, the whole deal, but Janet Reno made the final decision and she would not indict him," said one FBI agent, who pointed out that U.S. Attorney General Reno had seemed loath to prosecute exile paramilitants when she was state attorney in Miami in the late '70s into the '90s.

Luis Posada's close confederates, the late Arnaldo Monzón Plasencia and Ángel Alfonso Alemán, were other key players, according to Llama. "[Posada] had a plan, the bombs in the hotel in Cuba. . . . The War Group was involved in obtaining democracy in Cuba by whatever means." Other members were Elpidio Núñez, Horacio García, and Luis Zúñiga, who left CANF in 2001 to create the more militant exile lobby, the Cuban Liberty Council. On the other hand, Pepe Hernandez had renounced paramilitary strikes and had steered CANF away from its hardline path.

Llama told *El Nuevo Herald*'s Wilfredo Cancio Isla that he was writing his memoirs, to be entitled *De la fundación a la fundición: historia de una gran estafa* (From the Foundation to Meltdown: Story of a Big Swindle).

While CANF members fought back, calling Llama's charges "an extortion and defamation attempt," two FBI sources said otherwise. "It's all true," said one agent, who had seen the ultralight planes parked in Miami. "The idea was they could fly into Cuba, unmanned, and drop bombs. So when Castro was giving a speech in the Plaza de la Revolución, they could send one of these ultralights into Havana and take out Castro without losing a pilot." Of course, there would be significant collateral damage. "And no doubt Castro knew about the ultralights because he had Juan Pablo Roque," he added, referring to the infamous sleeper agent inside the Brothers to the Rescue.

In February 1996, the Brothers to the Rescue had flown three Cessnas near Havana, two of which were shot down by Cuban MiGs. A day earlier, the movie-star handsome and equally amoral Roque had disappeared from his Miami home and exile "wife" and fled back to Cuba.

The Brothers' flights were intended to rescue fleeing Cubans lost in the Florida Straits, though sometimes they provocatively strayed into Cuban airspace. The shootdown, despite repeated warnings to the group to desist from the flights, fomented sufficient outrage for Congress to muster the votes to pass the Helms-Burton Act, formerly known as the Cuban Liberty and Democratic Solidarity Act, which had been shelved for lack of consensus. The legislation, signed into law by President Bill Clinton, dramatically tightened the embargo, codifying it into law and thus making it reversible only by Congress—not the president.

Many Castro watchers speculated that the Cuban leader got what he wanted: a halt to the quasi-détente that U.S. policy had been sliding toward. One FBI agent who worked on the investigation said it was also possible that Castro initially believed the planes were not Cessnas but the potentially lethal ultralights. "Castro may have believed they were going to drop bombs, not leaflets, " he theorized.

Posada's lawyer at the time, Eduardo Soto, had no comment on Tony Llama's allegations but said he was primed to play hardball. Soto's father, a friend of Posada's going back to their youth in Cienfuegos, had arranged for his son to represent Posada pro bono. Soto Jr. devoted much of his website to his celebrity client: in one collage there was a photo of Posada next to a photo of former president George H. W. Bush, bordered by a snapshot of Oliver North. Leaving nothing to the imagination, the final image was of the famed marble-floor insignia at Langley reading "Central Intelligence Agency."

"Not only is Louie not a threat to national security," argued David

Sebastian, who was the point man on Posada in Soto's office, "*he was national security.* He was part of Operation Southern Front, which is what they called it before Iran-Contra, and he worked for the Hammer," Sebastian said, referring to Oliver North's code name. "Everyone knew that Ramón Medina was Luis Posada, and that he was a very important person. From 1967 to 1986, Luis was a compensated agent of the CIA. And George Bush, the vice president, knew what he was doing."

Justice and the FBI were not convinced. "The FBI is unable to rule out the possibility that Posada Carriles poses a threat to the national security of the United States," wrote FBI agent Thomas Rice a month after Posada's arrest in Miami.

Posada would be kept segregated from the general inmate population for the next twenty-one months. When he left his cell, he wore a bulky bulletproof vest. Although he had few visitors, he was often on the phone speaking to his family and supporters in Miami, many of whom signed petitions asking the U.S. to release him. "I am an optimist," Posada wrote me the day after his August 2005 arraignment. "I continue to be and always will be. I believe in God."

But Posada was not on speaking terms with everyone. For instance, he and his old Iran-Contra comrade Félix Rodríguez had been publicly feuding for years. FBI veteran George Kiszynski said their split stemmed from their different methodologies. "Félix does things in a more traditional way," Kiszynski said, with a smile. "Posada is more unorthodox. Sort of anything goes."

Posada had a similar view regarding marriage. Despite decades of estrangement and an outsized-Lothario reputation, his wife, Nieves, the mother of his two grown children, never divorced him. During Posada's incarceration in El Paso, Nieves reappeared as his advocate—lobbying with his lawyers and fussing about his health—just as she had when he was imprisoned in Caracas. She said she was bewildered why authorities were detaining her husband. "I don't understand how come Orlando [Bosch] got out and Luis's case is taking so long," one of her husband's attorneys recounted her saying, adding, sotto voce, "I think Nieves is still in love with him."

Homeland Security learned that Nieves could be as fierce as her husband when agents visited her in West Kendall, Miami. Agents peppered her with questions about her husband's friends and sources of money, and how she came to buy her attractive apartment duplex. Nieves had nothing to say, said one of Posada's attorneys.

On August 30, 2005, a few dozen reporters crammed an El Paso courtroom to observe Luis Posada's trial for illegal entry into the U.S. We were surprised to learn, however, that other than Posada's own witnesses, there would not be much to watch.

That morning, the court addressed Venezuela's request for Posada's deportation to stand trial in the Cubana bombing of October 1976. Posada's former business partner and attorney, Joaquín Chaffardet, testified that should the U.S. deport Posada to Venezuela he would likely be tortured. Curiously, prosecutors offered no rebuttal, questions, or witnesses, nor did they question Chaffardet's personal and business ties with Posada going back forty years. Indeed, they seemed to be sleepwalking through the proceedings—marching toward a preordained verdict. Evidently not authorized to make decisions, prosecutors delayed proceedings several times to phone their superiors in Washington.

In the afternoon, Posada took the stand in his orange jumpsuit, and the government's lead lawyer, Gina Garrett-Jackson, began to question him. There were no questions about his long paramilitary career, only what he had told the *New York Times,* in its series, published over the summer of 1998, that I co-authored. While it was true that the exclusive interview that Posada gave to the *New York Times* had galvanized national attention, the government had its *own* files—material meticulously collected by law enforcement over forty-five years that was quantifiably more damning.

At one point, baited by the prosecution, Posada began to swipe at the *Times.* He demurred about his previous admissions, then complained that he had not known that I had a tape recorder nor even a notepad during the interview. He even claimed that he did not understand English, notwithstanding his work as a translator with the U.S. Army. In fact, the tape recorder was directly in front of Posada, who flipped it off when he did not want something recorded, permitting only notes by hand.

During the recess, two government lawyers ambushed me in the restroom and asked if I didn't feel it necessary to take the stand to defend the *Times.* To their consternation, I said that the news stories spoke for themselves and I would not willingly make their case for them. I was a reporter, not a prosecutor. Indeed, if I were compelled to testify, the First Amendment protections of the press would become little more than cosmetic. I did, however, respond to Posada's flimsy assertions to a lively swarm of reporters outside the courtroom.

Ironically, while I was trying to avoid being entangled in Posada's arraignment, Blake Fleetwood, the journalist who had interviewed

Bosch and Posada in prison in 1977, was waiting for a subpoena that never arrived. Fleetwood had been in contact with DHS/DOJ officials and had told them he would be willing to testify at Posada's arraignment and make his notes and tapes available to them. In fact, the government had had Fleetwood's material in their custody since 1977, as Fleetwood had cooperated with U.S. Attorney Eugene Propper during the Letelier trial.

The next day, when I took my seat in court before the judge arrived, Posada caught my eye and waved. He held up the copy of my book, *Cuba Confidential,* that I had given his attorney and said in a stage whisper *"Que bueno!"*—"very good."

Later that day, I arranged, through his lawyer, to see him for an interview. But Posada was weary from the court proceedings—and perhaps wary from our last interview. He asked that I write up some questions and give them to him, which I did straightaway. He wrote me back promptly—both of us writing in Spanish:

Dear Ann,
    An affectionate greeting with my best wishes for you and your family. By now I have read 55 pages of your book and I thought it excellent. When I read it completely I will have a better-informed commentary. I hope to soon get out of this problem with the help of God. When I obtain my freedom or maybe after the trial we can have an interview (without the hidden tape recorder). You can write me here at the Detention Center.
                                     May God bless you,
                                     Luis Posada
                                     Detention Center of El Paso—Sept 1, 2005

It was evident to courtroom observers that the government had no appetite for prosecuting Posada. Forced to act, the Bush administration had decided to shuffle the paperwork for as long as possible, but leave as few fingerprints as possible. If the media could not make the government's case against Posada, there would be none, leaving the judge no option but to rule for the defense.

The charade was apparent to reporters and attorneys alike. Posada's lawyers said they had been privately assured by the DOJ that Posada would not be deported. "For political reasons, they didn't want to come right out and say that they will go for deferral [Posada remaining in detention in the U.S.]," one of Posada's attorneys explained at the time. "They wanted the judge to decide." And he did. To no one's surprise,

Immigration Judge William Abbott ruled in Posada's favor, eliminating Venezuela as an option for deportation.

Following Posada's arraignment, I interviewed his witness and good friend Joaquín Chaffardet. An urbane, dapper attorney partial to Marlboro cigarettes, Chaffardet had been the former secretary general of DISIP and Posada's partner in his detective agency. Chaffardet had also been indicted, but not convicted, for organizing Posada's prison escape in 1985. "I absolutely justify that decision," he told the *Washington Post*. "It is not justice to have someone waiting nine years for a trial after being already acquitted."

Chaffardet told me that although Posada would never say so publicly, his friend always harbored misgivings about Bosch. "You know that Bosch is crazy, don't you?" he said, arching one eyebrow. "He's always been crazy. Luis never trusted Bosch, because he said there was nothing he wouldn't do." According to Chaffardet, Posada often fretted that Bosch was dangerously out of control. So concerned was Posada, his friend said, that he alerted authorities in Caracas and in the U.S.

In September 1976, Posada asked Chaffardet to accompany him to see Martinez Granados, DISIP's chief of investigations. During their meeting, Posada said that Bosch was in Caracas and plotting unthinkable violence. "He told Martínez that Bosch was 'crazy, a killer, a terrorist; that there was nothing he would not do because of his schizophrenic personality,'" said Chaffardet, who noted that the meeting lasted longer than an hour.

It was also true that, unlike Bosch, Posada described the Cubana bombing as "a tragedy" in his memoir. Others are more cynical. Bernardo Álvarez Herrera, Venezuela's ambassador to the U.S., viewed Posada's words as a ploy: "Of course," he told me in his Washington office. "Posada is a professional."

Chaffardet went on to say that he had "no doubt" that Posada was the source of a June 1976 CIA memo entitled "Possible Plans of Cuban Exile Extremists to Blow Up a Cubana Airliner." Among the most damning documents found in the Agency's files, the memo was attributed to a "usually reliable businessman with close ties to the Cuban exile community." At the time, Posada was a successful entrepreneur running ICICA, his private-eye firm, with Chaffardet. The memo warned the Agency that a group led by Orlando Bosch "plan to place a bomb on a Cubana airline flight traveling between Panama and Havana," and specifically named Cubana flight #467 on June 21, 1976, as a target. As it turned out, Posada had been providing information to the CIA and DISIP for years. According to both Rafael Rivas-Vásquez and Orlando García, men who served as DISIP's directors for twenty-five years, Posada was their informant at the initial CORU meeting.

Chaffardet conceded that his old friend was between the proverbial rock and a hard place. If Posada came forward with his record of informing on Bosch, it would tarnish his reputation and alienate Bosch's powerful political allies in Miami, the very same politicians that had stood by him as well.

When I asked Posada about his feelings toward Bosch, he said only that he was *"un patriota,* who has given everything for the cause of liberty." For his part, Bosch was willing to put *la causa* of eliminating Fidel Castro before all else. In May 2006, I asked him his response to the CIA memos that established that Posada had informed on him. Waving his hand dismissively, he said the memos were the hand of "Castro's people." He added that Posada called him often from jail, but indicated that there was not a close bond. "Every week, I speak with him," he said. Then he added a qualifier. "He's not my friend. He's my brother in the struggle."

However, in several CIA memos released by the National Security Archive, Posada left no doubt that he felt that Bosch was capable of unimaginable violence—far outside the borders of the anti-Castro war. In February 1976, Posada warned the CIA that Bosch and another exile, Rolando Otero, were plotting to kill the nephew of former Chilean president Salvador Allende, Andrés Pascal Allende, in Costa Rica; Posada's information resulted in their arrest the following month. He also informed on a plot by Bosch to assassinate Henry Kissinger, conceivably in retaliation for the secretary of state's backdoor diplomacy with the Cuban government. "Attempt against Kissinger allegedly planned for Costa Rica," the memo states. He was equally worried that his informant status might become known to Bosch. "Posada informing agency that he must go through with attempt to contact Bosch as though he did not know that Bosch had been arrested," the 1976 memo reads. "Posada concerned that Bosch will blame him for leak of plans."

Posada's motives, certainly, were not entirely altruistic. Seeking to reingratiate himself with the CIA, in the hopes of obtaining American visas for himself and his family, he had stepped up his informer activities. And there was one other possible explanation for Posada's extensive informing: he was setting up his own alibi.

During my 1998 interview with Posada, I showed him a fax signed by him and sent to his collaborators in Union City, New Jersey, about a nettlesome problem: the reluctance of American news organizations to take seriously his claims that bombs were indeed going off in Cuba. "If there is no publicity, the job is useless," he wrote them. "The American newspapers publish nothing that has not been confirmed. I need all the data from the [bombing of the] discotheque in order to try to confirm it. If there is no publicity, there is no payment." The fax also discussed payments, saying that money would be "sent by Western Union from New Jersey" to "liquidate the account for the hotel." At the bottom of the fax was his distinctive handwriting and nom de guerre, "Solo."

I had received a copy of the fax from a Venezuelan source. The original had been given to the FBI by Antonio (Tony) Alvarez, a Cuban-American businessman who shared an office in Guatemala City with a confederate of Posada. Alvarez became alarmed when he learned about some of Posada's activities being run out of his office. Upon receiving the fax, the FBI sent agents to Guatemala to interview Alvarez, who related precisely how Posada's bomb factory worked and its intended targets in Havana. "We found Tony Alvarez entirely credible," said Luis Rodriguez of the Joint Terrorism Task Force.

When no action was taken by the FBI, Tony Alvarez turned to the *New York Times*.

Posada asked me whether I thought the fax would cause him problems, but he seemed to know the answer. His aspect darkened and he told me, "They are going to put the finger on me." Actually, he need not have worried.

"We thought it would be a slam dunk," said one JTTF agent in 2005. "We'd charge and arrest Posada. Then we had a meeting and the chief said, 'Hey, wait a minute. Lots of folks around here think Posada is a freedom fighter.' We were in shock. There are two guilty parties that prevented that investigation from going forward. The Cuban government blocked access to the witness and evidence. Here in Miami, [Hector] Pesquera did his part. And don't forget you have the three congressmen going to bat for a guy who likely blew up a plane and killed seventy-three innocent people and later the Italian tourist in 1997. It was a huge miscarriage of justice. Then Posada showed up with his gang in Panama and tried to take out Castro."

The agent paused and shook his head. "By then they had shut down every investigation involving these guys."

CHAPTER EIGHT

Requiem for a Would-be Assassin

As a rule, I don't believe in conspiracy theories. They tend to be tidy and selective, whereas life is messy and veers toward the random. But the case of Luis Posada Carriles has tested those convictions.

After Homeland Security officials finally got around to arresting Posada in April 2005 and charging him with illegal entry, I assumed that the Justice Department would act on his self-admitted history of paramilitary attacks and deport him somewhere. And I would continue to cover his case. Instead, the government dithered for two years while Posada languished in an immigration jail in Texas. And I found myself an unwitting player in the tangled drama of the *United States v. Luis Posada Carriles.*

Not long after Posada's arrest in Miami, FBI and Homeland Security agents began to phone me, seeking information about the *New York Times* series. One agent came straight out and asked if I would share some of my research materials—as well as my copies of FBI and CIA files on Posada. "Do us a favor," he said. "We can't find ours." I laughed politely, assuming it was a strained attempt at humor. But he wasn't kidding.

A few weeks later, my husband phoned me at the hair salon to tell me that two Department of Homeland Security (DHS) agents had arrived at our home in Santa Barbara, California, to serve me with a subpoena. I told him to ask the agents to leave and refer their inquiries to the *New York Times.* Eventually, the Department of Justice served the *Times,* and over the next year, an elaborate dance played out in the U.S. District Court for the Southern District of Florida. In the first round, the *Times* filed a motion to quash the subpoena, leading the Justice Department and DHS to withdraw it in August 2005.

It turned out that the Bush administration was of two minds. The politicos wanted to appease exile hardliners and allow Posada a life of quiet retirement, preferably out of the U.S. At the same time, career law enforcement officials hungered to bring him to justice. In August 2008, Honduran president José Manuel Zelaya Rosales made a jaw-dropping revelation. He said that the U.S. ambassador to Honduras, Charles Ford, had solicited him to grant political asylum to Posada. In an interview with the Tegucigalpa newspaper *Tiempo,* the Honduran president said that he had rejected Ford's request because he was convinced Posada was a terrorist. Ambassador Ford did not respond to the newspaper's request for comment, but a Justice Department prosecutor confirmed to me that the query to Honduras had been made.

While the administration was looking for a cozy retreat for Posada, the *Times* was battling with the Justice Department over "reporter privilege," which protects journalists from being dragged into judicial proceedings. On September 11, 2006, the Justice Department whirled into action (perhaps emboldened by the symbolism of the date) and notified the *Times'* lawyer, Tom Julin of Hunton & Williams, that the government would issue yet another subpoena.

On the same day, the DOJ struck a plea deal with Posada's comrades Santiago Alvarez and Osvaldo Mitat. The two men agreed to two years in prison, thus avoiding a trial and a pesky news story. (Alvarez was still in prison when, in May 2008, a Cuban television news special revealed that a company run by him, Judicial Rescue Foundation, had been providing cash to dissidents in Cuba. The money had been passed along via the chief of the U.S. Interests Section in Havana—a revelation that caused embarrassment to all parties concerned.)

A month later, another trio of Posada confederates resolved their pending prosecutions, eliminating another headline story. Ernesto Abreu, Rubén Darío López-Castro, and José Pujol pled guilty to a charge of obstruction of justice for refusing to testify (against Posada) to a federal grand jury, despite grants of immunity.

Also on September 11, a magistrate in El Paso recommended that Posada be released, pointing out that the Justice Department had yet to file charges. But contrary to the fulminations of Fidel Castro and Hugo Chávez, Judge Norbert Garney's ruling was not a case of judicial bias; rather it stemmed from the simple fact that the U.S. government never mounted a case to justify Posada's continued detention.

Evidently the Bush Justice Department had found another prey. Instead of drawing upon forty-five years of voluminous CIA and FBI files on Posada, or detaining him under the terms of the Patriot Act, the Justice Department went after me and the *New York Times,* claiming our cooperation was necessary for them to proceed. The ironies were rich.

After all, if I hadn't written about Posada, as one government prosecutor told me, there would have been no scandal or embarrassment for the Bush administration. By going after the *Times'* series, the administration achieved three goals: putting off action on Posada for as long as possible, somewhat neutralizing the lead reporter on the case, and punishing its least favorite newspaper, the *New York Times,* with onerous legal work and expense.

On October 6, 2006, the thirtieth anniversary of the bombing of the Cubana plane (one had to give the DOJ its due for exquisite timing), I received a new subpoena for the tapes of my interview with Posada. This one, issued by a federal grand jury in Newark, New Jersey, was signed by the country's top crime-fighter, Attorney General Alberto Gonzales. While the Justice Department had become a lightning field for criticism about its handling of the war on terrorism, no one could question its dedication to its war against the Fourth Estate. Once Gonzales was installed at Justice, a veritable rain of subpoenas poured down on the media, unprecedented in U.S. history. For my part, it raised a peculiar pickle: contemplating how far one should go to protect the civil liberties of an accused terrorist.

For the *Times* 1998 series, my co-author, Larry Rohter, the paper's editors, and I picked out the strongest and most compelling parts of the transcripts and notes. Contrary to what the great minds at Justice seemed to think, we didn't hold back the best bits—we published them. Moreover, in October 2006 the *Atlantic* magazine published a ten-thousand-word article by me on the Cubana bombing, along with Posada's handwritten notes from 1998 in which he offered editorial guidance to me: "He does not admit the bombs in the hotels, but he does not deny [them] either," he wrote. The magazine's website also linked to a handwritten Q&A I did with him in 2005.

My case, thankfully, did not involve confidential sources. On the contrary, Posada had been seeking publicity and had never asked for confidentiality. The law, according to the U.S. Court of Appeals for the Third Circuit, where the case was filed, and the Justice Department's own guidelines, seemed quite clear: Prosecutors cannot compel reporters to turn over information that they can obtain through other means. Only after other avenues have been pursued should the government turn to the media to build a prosecution.

Perhaps I am a strict constructionist, but it seemed to me that the Founding Fathers of the Constitution were quite clear that they did not intend for the government to be allowed to raid the news media for their work files. Most especially after they had bungled a case and destroyed crucial evidence. And that is exactly what happened in the case of Luis Posada.

The summer of 2003 seemed to Posada's allies, a deep bench of Miami politicos, an auspicious time to dispose of the evidence files in his case. But this needed to be done quietly. By then, some of best and most dedicated agents in the Miami FBI, defeated by office politics or low morale, had retired or asked to be transferred out of exile militant cases. However, prior to their departures, five boxes of files and crucial evidence against Posada had been carefully collected and stowed in the evidence room known as "The Bulky." The most important Posada documents had been set aside in an oversized envelope labeled in bold letters "Important Evidence." Inside were the original Western Union cables and money transfers sent to Posada from his co-conspirators in Union City, New Jersey. Meticulously collected over five years, the material made a criminal conviction quite likely.

However, if Posada's case was closed, all the thorny evidence in this politically tricky matter could disappear. And so it went, in August 2003, when the Miami bureau of the FBI made the stunning decision to close its case on Posada, thus green-lighting the destruction of all its evidence and a healthy chunk of its files.

It was a major decision and thus required the assent of the Miami FBI's bureau chief, Hector Pesquera, or the bureau's supervisor—though former agents say likely both. But it also necessitated the signature of the U.S. Attorney for the Southern District of Florida, Marcos D. Jiménez. The politically adroit Jiménez, whose brother Frank was Jeb Bush's deputy chief of staff, had been installed by the Bush administration, replacing the well-regarded Guy Lewis. Both Jiménez brothers had worked on the 2000 recount battle for the Bush-Cheney ticket.

To the surprise and dismay of JTTF veterans, Hector Pesquera had put his son, Ed Pesquera, in charge of the Posada investigation, despite his having little knowledge of the case. According to an FBI spokesperson, the destruction was done with a shredder. Among the most high-value documents was the FBI's copy of the original signed fax that Posada had sent to collaborators in Guatemala in 1997 with his Salvador phone number printed at the top. It was the same fax in which Posada had complained of the U.S. media's reluctance to believe reports about the bombings in Cuba, a lament that directly tied him to the attacks. One agent involved in the Posada investigation described the destruction as "devastating" in its impact on trying the case in the future. It also sent an unvarnished message to agents working in the Miami bureau that Posada was off-limits.

I learned about the evidence purge two years after the fact. In 2006, while working on my *Atlantic* article, I called the FBI's Miami spokeswoman, Judy Orihuela, for confirmation. She was clearly taken aback by my query but promised to call back shortly. She did, confirming that the destruction had taken place but explaining it as a consequence of a "routine cleaning" of the evidence room. Once a case is closed, she said, its materials are greenlighted for destruction in order to free up space in The Bulky. She also confirmed that "the supervisory agent in charge and someone from the U.S. Attorney's Office would have had to sign off" before evidence was removed and destroyed. Striving for the best possible spin under the circumstances, Orihuela said that the bureau believed that Posada had disappeared from sight and was out of action, with his location unknown. Therefore, the reasoning went, keeping his case file open was no longer warranted.

Posada's precise location and recent activities, however, had been front-page news. He and his three comrades were sojourning in a Panamanian prison for their attempted assassination of Fidel Castro since November 2000.

Arguably more astonishing than the FBI tossing out the Posada evidence was the reaction—or more precisely lack of reaction—of the media in Miami. No one questioned, either in the news or editorial pages, the motives of wiping out the evidence in the most politically charged case in South Florida. No one asked if, perhaps, old case files of carjackings and nickel-and-dime robberies might have been more appropriate for the shredder, if space was so urgently needed. Once again, only the passing searchlight of the national media—in this case my articles in the *Washington Post* and the *Atlantic,* followed by a spate of stories on the internet—spurred the Miami media to even report what had happened. And not because of a dearth of capable reporters, but rather paralysis, fear, and a sprinkling of turf jealousy in the head offices.

Curiously, preserving case files and evidence against Posada has proven challenging in several countries. As far back as 1988, Venezuelan president Carlos Andrés Pérez asserted that "the [Cubana bombing] file had been tampered with," noting that "I am knowledgeable about this monstrous crime because the initial responsibility was mine." His successor, Hugo Chávez, likewise complained that in the days before he assumed the presidency in 1998, many sensitive DISIP files were destroyed, including Cubana case records.

In 1992, a fire at the police station in Port of Spain, the capital of Trinidad and Tobago, destroyed many of the files in the Cubana bombing. When I called Dennis Ramdwar, Trinidad's former police commissioner, who had interviewed the Cubana bombers, Hernán Ricardo and Freddy Lugo, he was initially helpful. But during subsequent calls, Ramdwar, now eighty-four, said, "I don't want to talk about it and get in between Chávez and the U.S." Nor did he want to comment on his files on Bosch and Posada. "They have powerful friends who protect them," he said. "They did then and they do now."

There were other dicey details surrounding the investigation. The Miami-Dade Police Department's liaison to the Joint Terrorism Task Force was a detective named Luis Crespo Jr. Although personable, he is the son of Luis Crespo, one of the most famous anti-Castro militants, known as El Gancho, or The Hook, because of the hand he lost to an ill-timed bomb.

Working alongside Crespo Jr. was detective Héctor Alfonso, whose father is another legendary anti-Castro militant, Héctor Fabian, who hosts a Spanish-language talk radio show in Miami. Assigned to the MDPD intelligence unit, Alfonso had access to highly sensitive information on homeland defense, including materials on Cuban exile militants. "Say you had a tip for the FBI about a bombing," mused D. C. Diaz, who spent almost three decades in the MDPD. "Would you want to give it to a guy whose father is Luis Crespo?"

In fact, Posada had many influential allies. One of his attorneys told me that he had been assured that Posada's case was "being handled at the highest levels" of the Justice Department. "All they have to do to detain Posada indefinitely," he explained, "was to have [Attorney General Alberto] Gonzales certify him as a national security threat. But they're not going to do that," he added. "That would create problems for the Bush people with their base in Miami." In other words, the government did not want to mount its own case and risk alienating Cuban-American supporters. Better to have journalists build their case and then let Posada's lawyers rough up the reporters in deposition or trial.

Former attorney general Gonzales more or less confirmed this strategy when confronted by Rep. William Delahunt at a congressional hearing in 2007: "The designation by yourself of Luis Posada Carriles as a terrorist under the Patriot Act, an act which you have supported and this administration has advocated, does not require any judicial review. Is that a fair statement?" Gonzales agreed. "I think that is a fair statement, Congressman," he said. "But again, with respect to your specific question as to why hasn't this happened, I need more information." Delahunt cut him off. "With all due respect, Mr. Attorney General, as my colleague from California said, the buck stops with you on this one." Gonzales seemed to concede the point and responded, "I understand."

In the summer of 1998, in the wake of the *New York Times* series, there was a rare respite from the steely tensions between Cuba and the U.S. In July 1998, a small group from the Justice Department and the FBI visited their counterparts in Havana. The purpose was to gather information on the tourist bombings a year earlier in Cuba directed by Posada in violation of the U.S. Neutrality Act.

The Cuban team of investigators, led by Lt. Colonel Roberto Hernández Cabellero, were hospitable hosts but there were limits to their cooperation. The American team was not allowed to directly interview witnesses or examine evidence. After requests were made for direct examination, the delegation was told by the Cubans that "'We'll take it up with our superiors,'" said one member. "'We'll see,' and we never heard from them."

However, the Cubans screened a surveillance video for their guests, showing Posada, Santiago Alvarez, and another collaborator coming and going from the swank Camino Real Hotel in San Salvador and driving around town. Upon their return to the U.S., the investigators discussed the video for days. They concluded that the Cubans could have easily rid themselves of Posada. Instead, they opted to do surveillance, leading them to deduce that Posada's value as propaganda fodder outweighed his threat potential.

Cuban intelligence also turned over to their visitors from Miami extensive information on militant groups operating in South Florida. The data had been mined by their infiltration teams, assigned to monitor exile leaders and paramilitary groups. Two months later, to the shock of the Cubans, the Miami FBI arrested and charged five of their agents, who became known as La Red Avispa, the Wasp Network, in the U.S. and as the Five Heroes in Havana. Others were rounded up and deported.

The spy team's ringleader, Gerardo Hernández, who is serving a life sentence, offered details on their operations during the making of a documentary by Saul Landau in 2009. "I compiled information the other agents delivered to me, those who had maintained their own identities, like René González. He kept his own name. He stole an airplane from

Cuba. Someone like that can count on gaining [their] trust and can approach an organization. Not so in my case, since I didn't even have a real story. So my mission was to compile information the others gave me, and send it to Cuba."

The Cuban agents seamlessly made the transition to Miami exile life and were fully embraced by the community. The arrests of the five, who had been running operations for more than two years, stunned their neighbors, friends, and trusted cohorts in exile militant groups. The spy quintet, however, were cool-headed when detained, having been well schooled by Cuban intelligence. "We were put in separate offices, each one of us. They handcuffed me to the wall," said Hernández. "I had the 'honor' that Hector Pesquera came to see me. He was the director of the South Florida branch of the FBI, and he was Puerto Rican," the former spy said, recounting his interrogation. "And my assumed identity, Manuel Viramonte, was Puerto Rican, too. I told him I was from Puerto Rico and so he started asking me questions about Puerto Rico. All kinds of questions. Who was the governor in such and such a year? Where did you live? What bus did you take to get to school? What route did you take? And when he saw I was able to answer these questions he got really upset. He slammed his fist into the table and said, 'I know you are Cuban and you are going to rot in prison because Cuba isn't going to do anything for you.'"

Pesquera's assertion about Cuba's reaction proved not to be the case. Indeed, an apoplectic Fidel Castro brainstormed a relentless public relations campaign, one not seen since his battle over Elián González. Soon posters appeared all over the island, demanding justice for *Los Cinco Héroes,* the Five Heroes. In June 2001, the five were convicted in a Miami courtroom on twenty-six counts—ranging from espionage to conspiracy to commit murder (in the deaths of two passengers and two pilots flying in two Brothers to the Rescue planes shot down in 1996)—and sentenced to lengthy prison terms.

Privately, several FBI agents expressed surprise about the arrests. "These were low-level guys," said one agent. "It was a political decision to make a federal case and example out of them, and it cost millions. They should have been deported or traded for something we want from the Cubans. Like some of our fugitives living in Havana."

In the fall of 2006, the newly constituted Posada team investigators met again in Havana with their counterparts. Posada's file was still in the stacks as FBI files are never eliminated. However, the crucial evidence and supporting materials that had been put through the shredder in 2003 had to be replaced to rebuild the case.

The South Florida congressional delegation was notified of the trip in advance and Rep. Lincoln Díaz-Balart was not pleased. His chief of staff, Ana Carbonell, called U.S. Attorney Alex Acosta in Miami "to vent" that the case was even being investigated, and warned that "the Miami community [would] not be happy about such cooperation." Carbonell denied making the call, but a source close to Acosta said that the U.S. attorney had informed her "that the matter was above his pay grade." Authorization had come from the Department of Justice in Washington, which had seized control of the Posada investigation.

There was activity on all fronts, re-interviewing witnesses from 1997 and ferreting out whistle-blowers.

But just days before Posada's immigration trial was to begin in El Paso, U.S. District Judge Kathleen Cardone dismissed the sole charge against Luis Posada for illegally entering the country. In a withering opinion, she chastised prosecutors for "fraud, deceit, and trickery," for attempting to shoehorn a terrorism case into an immigration proceeding. Even critics of her decision conceded that the judge had made a few solid points. "The government's tactics in this case are so grossly shocking and so outrageous as to violate the universal sense of justice," Cardone ruled.

Posada's lawyers had made much of a woeful interpreter who had conducted an interview with Posada about his career as a militant. Citing several errors in translation, they won the judge's ire. "This is not an acceptable practice in interpretation, and it caused severe confusion during the interview," Cardone wrote in her opinion.

However, none of the government attorneys pointed out that Posada had learned English as a young man and did not need a translator or that he had served as a translator during Iran-Contra for American servicemen. I had interviewed him mostly in English, as had Blake Fleetwood, and at no time did Posada indicate he did not understand anything. His attorney, Matthew Archambleault, who handled his El Paso arraignment, spoke to him only in English.

With all immigration charges against him dropped, Luis Posada walked out of jail on May 8, 2007, a free man—albeit one branded by the U.S. Justice Department as "a dangerous criminal and an admitted mastermind of terrorist plots." Because he was on the no-fly list, Posada was driven back to Miami from El Paso. It was a long, humid car trip, but he had no complaints.

One year later, on August 14, 2008, the U.S. Court of Appeals for the Fifth Circuit in New Orleans reversed Judge Cardone's ruling and reinstated the indictment against Posada for having lied under oath about his entry into the States. The court ruled that regardless of some minor errors in translation, Posada understood the crucial question at the heart of the charges against him. "And when you came to the United States on March 17th or 18th, where did you enter?" Posada had answered: "Matamoros," the Mexican side of the border and Rio Grande across from Brownsville, Texas. Because investigators knew from an informant that Posada had arrived by boat via Isla Mujeres, his response constituted perjury.

Cuba, however, regarded the court ruling with characteristic suspicion. *Granma* noted that it came just three days after Samuel Lewis Navarro, Panama's vice president, indicated that he would be seeking Posada's extradition to stand trial on far more serious charges.

The release of Posada added pressure on U.S. Attorney General Alberto Gonzales to declare him a security threat and arrest him under the Patriot Act, legislation he had crafted. But Gonzales steadfastly refused, which prompted questions about the U.S. having a double standard on terrorism. José Pertierra, the attorney retained by Venezuela in the matter, chided the Bush administration's inaction as an "a la carte war on terror: a war that distinguishes between 'good terrorists' and 'bad terrorists.'"

Cuba responded by erecting a billboard outside Havana's José Martí International Airport, showing a poker hand of cards, with George W. Bush half smirking, half frowning as the ace of spades. Adolf Hitler was the ace of hearts. Two more aces featured Luis Posada Carriles and Orlando Bosch. A play on the Spanish word for "aces" spelled out "Full of Murderers."

Cuban intelligence seemed to be of two minds about Posada. Sometimes he was the nefarious mastermind behind decades of attacks against Cuba. Other times he would be dismissed as a hired gun. In a July 2007 interview in *Granma,* Fabian Escalante, Cuba's former chief of intelligence, opted for the latter. "Posada was never the leader of anything. Posada is a hired assassin, a paid terrorist. He is a killer, an assassin like those in U.S. movies, who would murder anyone without a trace of emotion, just for money, out of self-interest." Then he suggested Posada was a figure of keen importance. "But he is a very, very dangerous witness. . . . [He] knows too much and constitutes a real danger for those who used him for more than forty years."

With Fidel Castro incapacitated by his devolving health, Hugo Chávez took the lead, gleefully ripping the Bush administration's handling of the matter and denouncing Posada as "the father of this continent's terrorists." Moreover, Venezuela would commit a million dollars for a movie based on the life of Posada, and Chávez himself was launching a star search among Latin American actors to play the lead villain role.

From his sickbed, Castro seconded Chávez, spewing scorn, indignation, and occasional delight. *Granma* hammered the U.S., charging that the release of Posada was part of a devious Bush administration plot. Repeating earlier allegations, Havana linked Posada's activities with former President George H. W. Bush, the president's father, and his career at the CIA, pointing out that Bush's tenure as its director neatly overlapped with Posada's and Bosch's glory days as militants.

A week after Posada's release, the Cuban government's Union of Young Communists staged its own mock trial—which naturally concluded with a resounding verdict of guilty. The verdict was announced on the José Martí Anti-Imperialist Platform, directly across from the U.S. Interests Section in Havana. The massive concrete stage with its state-of-the-art sound and lighting, flanked on one side by metallic palm trees, had been built in 2000 during the Elián González saga. Locals refer to it as the *Protestódromo* or Protestodrome.

A month later, Cuba cranked up the drama—hurling a flamethrower at Washington. On May 11, 2007, *Granma* published what it claimed were the exact conversations from fourteen telephone calls between Luis Posada and his friend, Francisco "Paco" Pimentel, between February 21 and September 9, 1997, when both men were living in Venezuela.

Excerpts from the calls, but not the full transcripts, were published in the government daily and later in the *Miami Herald*. Cuba claimed that they had given the incriminating phone chronicles to the FBI when JTTF agents visited Havana in 1998 and again in 2006. One startling snippet had Posada telling Pimentel in April of 1997 that "the first one has already gone off at the Meliá Cohiba Hotel and they don't dare say so." On August 11, Posada called his friend and told him, "Paco, and now two [bombs] more, one we put in the Sol Palmeras de Varadero Hotel, one of those new ones of the Spanish, and another one in a discothèque in the center of Havana." Another call from Pimentel to Posada reportedly suggested that they retaliate against foreign businessmen with ties to Cuba, such as "that homosexual . . . Oscar de la Renta."

The phone transcripts named Posada's confederates as: Dr. Alberto Hernandez, who briefly succeeded Mas Canosa as chairman of the Cuban American National Foundation (CANF) before abandoning the organization for the Cuban Liberty Council; the late Arnaldo Monzón Plasencia, who had run CANF in New Jersey and who died in 2000; Nelly Rojas, an activist and friend of Posada, who helped him in his escape from prison; and Luis Orlando Rodriguez, a former U.S. Army colonel; and there were others.

On another call Posada informed Pimentel about a doctor, the boss of Gasparito [Gaspar Jiménez, who was captured with Posada in Panama in 2000], who is fully in it and has been key in this. . . . These actions have to do with me and now I assure you that I am supported by a lot of cash." The doctor was identified in the *Granma* article as Alberto Hernandez, whose office was said to be the place where the money was sent for the operation. (Both Hernandez and Monzón were trusted friends of the late Mas Canosa.) These funds financed fourteen bombs, claimed the article, eight of which exploded, while four were deactivated and two were disarmed at José Martí International Airport.

The incendiary phone transcripts transfixed exiles, Washington, and Cubaphiles. They were indisputably damning and had a certain logic connecting likely players with the bombing operation. But they posed as many questions as they answered. If Cuban intelligence had been able to wiretap the two conspirators, presumably knowing their location, why did they not retain the men or prevent future attacks? And why did they release only edited transcripts and not the full audio?

Posada, it turned out, was worth more to Fidel Castro alive than dead. "They'll never get better propaganda than Luis Posada," said FBI veteran George Kiszynski. "He's as good as it gets."

When the first wave of exiles arrived in Miami in 1959, there was a profound sense of loss: of country, institutions, and social standing. To remedy the latter, thriving exiles built an elegant, private watering hole for their own on SW 92nd Avenue. A monument of nostalgia, the venue was named the Big Five Club in tribute to the five major social clubs of pre-Revolution Havana (the Miramar Yacht Club, Vedado Tennis Club, Casino Español, the Biltmore Yacht and Country Club, and the Havana Yacht Club). Over the years, the venue became the site of countless galas and political fund-raisers for Miami's exile leadership.

In November 2007, the Big Five Club hosted an art show/fund-raiser to benefit Posada and his comrade in arms, José Dionisio Suárez, whose nickname spoke volumes: *"Charco de Sangre,"* or "Pool of Blood." The event chilled the hearts of law enforcement. Not only was Posada's public emergence humiliating, Suárez was the convicted killer of Orlando Letelier and Ronni Moffitt. He had served just ten years in prison when

Representative Lincoln Díaz-Balart successfully lobbied for his release in 2001. The gala of "assassin art" featured forty canvases painted by the two anti-Castro career militants.

Exiles in Union City, New Jersey, the second-largest population of Cubans in the U.S., also rallied to the cause. A show of Posada's paintings went on display in December 2007 at Hudson Hall, a tax-supported community center in West New York, New Jersey, bordering Union City. The event was also a fund-raiser to help pay Posada's mounting legal bills and was duly featured in the local Cuban-owned newspaper, *Avance,* with photos of Posada with his paintings and fans.

But all was not rosy for Posada's team—and he knew it. Not far from his Jersey fund-raiser, federal prosecutors were plotting his arrest, trial, and imprisonment from the bleak, fluorescent-lit rooms of the U.S. Attorney's Office on Broad Street in downtown Newark, New Jersey.

The Justice Department's Posada team was led by two career prosecutors from its National Security Division, John Van Lonkhuyzen, a caustic man in his fifties, and his swing opposite, a soft-spoken attorney named Paul Ahern. They were a duo well suited to play good cop/ bad cop. Assisting them were two investigators relatively new to the JTTF, Omar Vega of the FBI and Jorge González of Miami-Dade Police Department, both Cuban born.

In January 2006, the DOJ had convened a grand jury in Newark to look into the roles of Posada and his collaborators in the 1997 bombings in Cuba. FBI investigators concluded that Posada had smuggled plastic explosives into Cuba inside Prell shampoo bottles and the soles of shoes. An Italian tourist was killed by one such bomb on September 4, 1997, at the Copacabana Hotel.

In late 2006, when the DOJ's investigation was handled by Ed Nucci and later by David Deitch, the Justice Department offered Posada a deal: plead guilty to financing the 1997 bombings in Havana and serve less than five years in prison. If he accepted the deal, his five confederates in Union City (Rubén and José Gonzalo, Ángel Alfonso, Abel Hernandez, and an accountant named Oscar Rojas) would be spared indictment. According to Gilberto García, who represented the men (most were named on Posada's infamous fax), the deal was a good one for everyone all around.

In Union City, the feeling was that Posada could spare the men and their families a good deal of grief, do a small amount of time in prison, and be seen as a hero. But when their attorney, García, flew to Miami and presented the deal to Posada's legal team in September, he was stung by the reaction. According to García, there was "zero interest" in any deal under which Posada received jail time. "I was told to 'butt out'—those words exactly—by Eduardo Soto," said García, referring to the father of Posada's attorney, Soto Jr. It was the father, he said, who had known Posada since Cuba, who was "calling the shots."

For a time, rejecting the deal seemed a decision that Posada would likely regret. On September 19 and 20, 2007, three high-value witnesses were called to the Newark grand jury to testify about the flow of money from U.S. exiles to Posada to support militant strikes. The government had put the squeeze on knowledgeable players, said a Posada attorney, compelling them to provide damning testimony. One witness, who worked for Abel Hernandez at his popular restaurant Mi Bandera, testified that some twenty exiles in Union City had wired money to Posada in 1997. According to Gilberto García, her testimony was corroborated by her friend, who owned the Western Union in Union City, from which the monies were sent to Posada. (In February 1998, the Western Union was sold to Abel Hernandez, one of the men named on the fax.)

The prosecutors were particularly keen on the role of the CANF and its officers. This was an especially rich irony: CANF had morphed into a moderate exile group by 2000. It had veered so close to the center that it was vanquished from the Bush White House for having gone "soft." Most of the group's hardliners who were tied to Posada had joined the Cuban Liberty Council, which had established itself as the Bush administration's pet exile group.

I, too, was under considerable pressure. The judge assigned to hear our case did not have a record favorable to First Amendment cases. In fact, he had no record. Judge Peter Sheridan had been a lobbyist and attorney for the New Jersey Republican Party until a year earlier. Among the party faithful, he was known as conservative in a state where the GOP steers a center-moderate path. Both he and his brother had been outstanding fund-raisers for the state GOP.

It was an appointment that did not bode well for the *New York Times* and myself. To our surprise, Judge Sheridan did, however, recognize "limited reporter privilege"—an important hurdle for us. The operative word, however, was *limited,* as in other matters he fairly consistently ruled for the Justice Department. *Times* attorney Tom Julin and George Freeman, in-house legal counsel for the paper, pondered an appeal to the Third Circuit. After some debate, they concluded it was unlikely they could prevail, as the judge's decision had been written narrowly enough—with recognition of reporter privilege—to avoid being overturned. Another deterrent against appeal was that it was conceivable that the Third Circuit (due to some recent appointees) might use the case to rule against reporter privilege and thus damage this crucial protection for all journalists and media.

The best we could do was procrastinate and hope the government, bowing to political pressure from Miami, dropped the case. But throughout 2006 and 2007, the DOJ was relentless—quick to issue threats and deadlines. If I did not turn over the tapes by July 11, 2007, I would be found in contempt and possibly sent to jail. It didn't end there. On July 23, 2007, I was instructed to appear before the Newark grand jury. To be dragged into a criminal prosecution was a reporter's nightmare. For the next six months, Julin battled with the DOJ to prevent such an outcome. There was another issue. In my view, professional journalistic ethics required that I publicly disclose such an appearance. Making matters even more tricky was the fact that the DOJ was claiming that its dealings with me were confidential and under a "gag," hence prohibiting any disclosure. The point eventually ended in a draw when the *Times* rejected the gag and prosecutors declined to seek a court ruling to back their claim.

At the same time, Congress waded into the Posada waters. On November 15, 2007, the House of Representatives held an all-day hearing on Posada convened by Rep. William Delahunt, who chairs the House Foreign Affairs Subcommittee on International Organizations, Human Rights, and Oversight. In his opening statement, Delahunt said there was "compelling evidence" that Posada was responsible for the Cubana plane bombing in 1976, along with the hotel bombings in 1997, adding that he was "bewildered" by the administration's reluctance to prosecute him.

One of Posada's attorneys, Arturo Hernandez, challenged the characterization of his client. "Mr. Posada Carriles is not and has never been a terrorist," he said. "His lifelong ambition has been to bring democracy and freedom to his place of birth." Hernandez went on to dismiss five decades of evidence as "based on dubious double hearsay from unidentified sources."

In his testimony, freelance writer Blake Fleetwood said that during his interviews with Posada and Bosch, both men "proudly bragged of their complicity in hundreds of murders, bombings, and assassinations." Fleetwood was soon confronted by the ranking Republican on the subcommittee, Rep. Dana Rohrabacher, who wrangled a concession out of Fleetwood that the two militants had not confessed to having been "personally involved" in the intentional killings of innocent civilians. Rohrabacher, who evidently was sitting in for Ileana Ros-Lehtinen who did not attend, insistently referred to the murdered Letelier as "a

Castro agent." When challenged to back up his assertion, he cited an item by the conservative columnist Robert Novak that stated—erroneously, as it turned out—that Letelier had been a Cuban asset.

Peter Kornbluh of the National Security Archive ran a slide show of CIA and FBI memoranda that left no doubt that Posada was a key conspirator in the Cubana bombing. The most moving witness was Roseanne Nenninger, who spoke emotionally of losing her nineteen-year-old brother on the doomed jetliner.

The committee asked me to testify as its "historian," walking them through Posada's history from 1959 to the present and providing background on the 1998 *Times* series. I disclosed I had been fighting a subpoena by a federal grand jury investigating Posada's involvement in the Havana bombings in 1997, and noted that "if the government had been serious about criminally prosecuting Mr. Posada . . . it could have done so long ago." Indeed, the government had reams of material if it wanted to put him on trial—without tampering with the First Amendment protections of the press.

Meanwhile, the *Times* attorney, Julin, sought to negotiate to keep me out of the grand jury and out of jail: I would not be compelled to testify before the grand jury if I met privately with the DOJ and confirmed the circumstances of my interview with Posada and the material on the tapes. It was not my first choice for a resolution, but it was the best available. On November 26 and 27, 2007, I did just that, meeting with the two prosecutors and two JTTF agents on a mirthless, rainy day on the eleventh floor of the U.S. Attorney's Office in Newark.

The subpoena and the possibility of being compelled to testify motivated us to locate and recheck the old tapes. To this end, we retained a Cuban-American certified translator-transcriber to review them, a process that unearthed various words and the odd phrase that had been inaudible to transcribers at the *Times*. Posada's comments regarding the hotel bombing turned out to be even more damning than we had thought.

Two months earlier, a new grand jury had been seated in Newark, New Jersey. The previous one had spent eighteen months on Posada's case, and by all reports had heard from scores of witnesses who tied Posada to the bombings in Cuba. "They have more than enough to prosecute the case," said Gilberto García, the attorney representing the Union City men, all of whom had received target letters. "They've had enough all along and they don't need any more." Although he was on the other side, he said he found the depth of the government's case "breathtaking." Still, his clients were not talking. "You've got to take your hat off to my guys—they are ready to hang tough," said García. "We were sure they were going to indict last year. Omar Vega [JTTF agent] told us in December [2007], 'It's their last chance to come and save themselves,'"referring to plea deals offered the men. "My guys are fearless, whatever you think of them. They told them, 'Fuck you!'"

By year's end, García said he had changed his mind and was breathing easier. After months of anticipating imminent indictments, he now said, "They have what they want but it's not going to happen before the election [in November 2008], if ever. I think someone upstairs has told them to not do it."

In late May 2008, attorney Tom Julin received a call from John Van Lonkhuyzen of the DOJ, who informed him of an extradition request from Italy. "I have in my hands a copy of a request from the public prosecutor in the court of Rome under Mutual Legal Assistance Treaty," Julin recounted from his notes of the conversation. He went on to add that the DOJ had been asked "to arrange an examination of Ann Louise Bardach before Roman prosecutors" concerning the *New York Times* articles published about Posada. He noted that because an Italian national, Fabio di Celmo, had been killed in one of the hotel bombings orchestrated by Posada, Italy was conducting their own investigation.

The Department of Justice attaché in Rome had asked Van Lonkhuyzen to advise me that the request for judicial assistance would be coming. Under the Mutual Legal Assistance Treaty with Italy, once a request is made, the U.S. courts can issue subpoenas to compel a witness to testify. Van Lonkhuyzen warned that if I did not cooperate, a legal proceeding would commence in the U.S. District Court for the Central District of California and yet another subpoena would be issued to compel my testimony.

Several things surprised me about the call—but not the fact that there was an Italian inquiry. Cuban officials had lobbied Italy to investigate the murder of di Celmo—and they had some leverage. Italy is among the largest investors in Cuban tourism. Raúl Castro's daughter Mariela is married to an Italian with business interests, and relations between the two countries have long been amicable. Cayo Largo, a bejeweled slip of an island off the southern belly of Cuba, has several hotels that are jointly owned by Italian companies. At one point, the island's postage-stamp-sized airport offered daily flights to and from Milan, which happens to be the hometown of tycoon-politician Silvio Berlusconi.

Members of the JTTF back in the late 1990s had proposed having the Italians take the lead on the investigation, thus limiting the politi-

cal collateral damage a Posada trial could inflict on the U.S. Most curious, however, was the fact that the DOJ had been notified by the Italian
attaché more than six months earlier on December 14, 2007, but had
shuffled the paperwork for half a year before passing on the message.
Also interesting was the timing of the Italian intervention, arguably a
deus ex machina for the Bush administration.

Evidently, Attorney General Michael Mukasey had decided he would
not indict before November 2008, if ever. Never mind that the Justice
Department had spent millions on its investigation of Posada, exhausted
multiple grand juries, and sent target letters to Posada and his confederates. Mukasey proved as stubborn as his predecessor in his resolve not
to file indictments. A tea-leaf reader was not required to figure out that
2008 was an election year. Additionally, the three Miami GOP congressional representatives were facing challengers of some note and heft.
And all three had been stalwart backers of Luis Posada and Orlando
Bosch.

However, if the attorney general's hand was forced, he could dump
the case on the Italians and spare Republicans a good deal of embarrassment. By 2008, George W. Bush had basement-low poll numbers
and a diminishing pool of friends. One of the remaining was the controversial Berlusconi, who as luck would have it had slipped back into
the prime minister's seat in Rome.

The climate and players in the Posada drama would change dramatically in the wake of the 2008 presidential election. No longer could the
aging militant count upon the good graces of the Bush administration.

In February 2009, Tom Julin again heard from Van Lonkhuyzen at
the Justice Department. His colleague Paul Ahern was no longer on
the case, becoming the third prosecutor to drop out of the investigation since 2006. It was unclear whether the resignations stemmed
from burnout or boredom with running grand juries for three years to
no avail. Ahern's replacement was Rebekah Sittner, who presumably
would play "the good cop" to Van Lonkhuyzen's brash guy.

This time Van Lonkhuyzen told Julin he was determined to facilitate
the Italian request and had already sought a judge's order. He added
that he did not believe that Posada could successfully resist deportation to Italy.

The arrangement had another side benefit for him. With the Roman
prosecutor operating as the front man, the DOJ was getting another
round with me, sort of an end run around the strict limitations imposed
on our 2007 meeting. The *Times* pondered an appeal but concluded

that the chance of a successful outcome was remote as Posada had not been a confidential source.

Giancarlo Capaldo, the chief prosecutor of Italy, sometimes referred to as the Italian attorney general, is a man of significant judicial achievement. He has been likened to Spain's Baltasar Garzón, the judge who issued the arrest order for Augusto Pinochet when the Chilean dictator was visiting London in 1999. A year earlier, Capaldo began investigating the twenty-five murders committed in Latin America during the so-called Dirty War. All the victims held dual citizenship with Italy. After a six-year investigation, Capaldo had obtained indictments and filed extradition orders for Argentina's former junta leader Jorge Videla, Uruguay's former dictator Juan Bordaberry, General Enrique Morales Bermúdez of Peru, and 135 other military officers.

Van Lonkhuyzen was also assigned to reinvestigate the murder of Orlando Letelier around the same time as Capaldo. That inquiry limped along until Pinochet's death in 2006 and no indictments were ever made. It appeared that his investigation of Posada was following a similar path, although it is likely that the Bush administration would have blocked prosecution against the right-wing junta leaders.

The meeting with Capaldo, his deputy, and an interpreter took place on April 1, 2009, in downtown Los Angeles at the U.S. Attorney's Office. During the two-hour session, Van Lonkhuyzen, accompanied by his team, played four short excerpts from the tapes that had been cleaned up and enhanced in clarity by the FBI's lab. One snippet was of a question I repeated to Posada regarding his bombing campaign: "So you don't have any problems with admitting your part in that because you regard that as a legitimate war action in Cuba—the hotel bombings?"

While I, Larry Rohter, and editors at the *Times* had been unable to make out his response from this particular utterance, the FBI lab had been able to do so. I listened carefully as the tape was played for me. Posada's reply was now discernible—and was just one word: *"Sí"*— "Yes."

Three months into the Obama administration, the wheels of justice began to roll in the case of Luis Posada Carriles. On April 8, 2009, the eighty-one-year-old anti-Castro warrior, who some said was now exhibiting signs of forgetfulness, was indicted by the Justice Department. The charges, however, were not for committing acts of terrorism but for far lesser crimes such as perjury and making false statements during his immigration proceeding. One count was for lying about how he entered the U.S. in 2005.

Another count was for perjury for what Posada told the court regarding his assertions to the *New York Times*. "[Posada] had been involved in soliciting other individuals to carry out said bombings in Cuba," read the indictment, "as he himself had told a reporter whose identity is known to the grand jury and as was written in said *New York Times* article." In fact, I had never appeared before the grand jury but clearly my interview with Posada had been cited by prosecutors. However, having been referred to in the indictment meant I would (most regrettably) be subpoenaed again when his case went to trial, scheduled for March 2010.

Hence, another motion filed by attorney Tom Julin was needed to obviate that possibility. As for Posada, were he ever to face serious criminal charges, they would likely be in Rome, not Miami. After four decades of shuffling and waffling, it appeared that Washington had finally disposed of the messy matter of Luis Posada Carriles.

In 1987, the late, great Cuban director Néstor Almendros released his critically acclaimed film about political prisoners in his homeland, a documentary entitled *Nobody Listened,* which shattered whatever was left of the utopian view of Cuba. The title would also work well for a sequel set in Miami and dispel any lingering illusions about the nature of Cuban exile politics. In the sequel, Luis Posada and Orlando Bosch would be the antiheroes.

Orlando Bosch takes a long nap every afternoon and rarely has a Scotch anymore. But he remains a man who needs a crusade, an enemy, and a drink. "I would kill him," he told me emotionally in 2006— "him" being, of course, Fidel Castro. "Who wants to more than I?" he said plaintively. "But I can't do any more. I have given it 100 percent." Bosch was cordial but cool on the topic of Posada and the Cubana bombing. "One day after I'm gone, the world will find out exactly what happened to that plane," he said slyly.

During our first talk, Bosch's wife, Adriana, an attractive woman with glossy auburn hair, arrived home from errands and joined our conversation. Their daughter Karen and her two toddlers, were living with them at the time, while Bosch's four older children from his first marriage lived nearby. Sometimes Adriana would prompt her husband when he spoke. "If he speaks too long, he gets stuck," she explained. "The therapy for his stroke is not complete."

Life with Bosch was never easy—while he was in prison or at home. Always an uncompromising man, he had moods that had grown more mercurial, intense, even paranoid, in the previous year. Karen Bosch told me she has a half-brother who suffers from schizophrenia. "It gets passed on in a family," she explained, as her mother nodded glumly. "My father has it, but not so bad." Her father's physical decline had only worsened his manic swings. "After his stroke," she said, "we learned he had had ten smaller strokes before."

Adriana seemed exhausted and teary-eyed during my second visit. Bosch had been phoning friends, questioning the loyalty of his wife and daughter. "He was better before because his [anti-Castro] activities fulfilled him," she said wearily. "*Fue su obsesión*," she says. "It was his obsession. So he was okay. Now it is very difficult." Bosch was a man without a war. His raison d'être and lifelong foe, Fidel Castro, was equally infirm—leaving Bosch with only his devoted family to rail against. "It's a competition to see who dies first," Adriana said wearily.

For the elite *guerrilleros* of the Anti-Castro War, or Cuban Iliad, it was not the battlefield that delivered the cruelest indignities, but survival and time. In July 2005, former DISIP chief Orlando García died in Miami at the age of seventy-eight. In 1991, García had seen his fortunes plummet in Caracas after he was charged in an arms-dealing corruption scandal that prompted a breach between him and Carlos Andrés Pérez. García returned to Miami, and by 2002 his health was shot. A lifetime of chain-smoking had left him with crippling pulmonary fibrosis.

Although he was a U.S. citizen and Korean War vet, García was denied veterans' benefits. Alfredo Durán successfully represented García pro bono in his suit against the Veterans Administration. "Everybody thought García and CAP were so corrupt that they had billions," said Durán, "but the truth was Orlando was destitute, he had nothing." Not even his trove of photos, diaries, and memorabilia that he entrusted with his brother Wilfredo survived. His son Osvaldo recalled his father telling their uncle to "hold on to these files; if I ever write a book, these are my most important files." But in the shuffle following his brother's death, the box of García's papers, including irreplaceable DISIP files, was thrown out.

His widow, Lucy Querales-García, told *El Nuevo Herald* that her husband "knew everything [about the Cubana bombing] and was aware until his last moments about the reports on the newscasts. He murmured about what was true and what was false, but he didn't have the energy to join a public debate." Orlando García said that he intended to take his secrets to the grave, and for the most part, he did. Although he skillfully dodged the press, García confided to trusted friends who came to pay their final respects that Posada had been the mastermind of the bombing. "I am going to die in three or four months," he told Antonio Veciana during one visit. "What do I need this trouble for? Why say anything now and damage him?"

Carlos Andrés Pérez moved to Miami Beach in 2000, where, following a series of strokes, he was confined to a wheelchair. He was deeply embittered by Chávez's rise to power and equally displeased by the U.S. government's tortoise pace in responding to his request for political asylum. CAP's own history with Castro was rife with feuds, truces, betrayals, and enmity. In 1989, during one truce, Castro attended CAP's second inauguration in Caracas. Orlando García, according to his sons, hand-delivered the invitation to Castro in Havana, after spending four days in a protocol house in Miramar. Soon after, García, CAP, and Castro held several private meetings and had reached a convivial rapprochement—one that was shattered by the rise of Chávez.

In November 2000, Rafael Rivas-Vásquez, a man who kept many secrets during his years at DISIP from 1972 until 1994, passed away. He was only sixty-two when he succumbed to pancreatic cancer at his home in Miami. Before he left Caracas, he reportedly passed on to two Venezuelan journalists a cache of files that implicated Posada and Bosch in the Cubana bombing, including his own interview notes with Hernán Ricardo. The writers, Alexis Rosas and Ernesto Villegas, avowed leftists, published a book based on those files in 2005.

Other players from the Cubana airliner tragedy resumed their lives without too much trouble. Freddy Lugo drives a cab and lives in the working-class neighborhood of Catia in Caracas. He maintains his innocence and says that he was duped into going along on the Cubana flight by Hernán Ricardo, who promised him a new camera. Ricardo evidently landed on his feet after serving ten years in prison for planting the bombs on the aircraft. According to the *Miami Herald,* he was working for the DEA at one point.

Some Bosch-Posada veterans are thriving. In 2002, then-governor Jeb Bush appointed Raoul Cantero III, Mas Canosa, and Orlando Bosch's attorney, to the Florida Supreme Court, notwithstanding Cantero having no experience as a judge. Later, Bush lobbied for a U.S. Supreme Court appointment for Cantero. In August 2008, Cantero stepped down from the court to resume a lucrative private practice in Miami.

The former chief of the Miami FBI, Hector Pesquera, landed a tony sinecure as coordinator of homeland security for Broward County after leaving the bureau in 2003. In November 2008, he stepped down (when Broward's sheriff was voted out of office) and took a similar job with the Port of Miami. His son Ed Pesquera remains in the Miami bureau but was dropped from the Joint Terrorism Task Force's Posada investigation when it was reconstituted in 2005.

In April 2007, Venezuelan police raided the Caracas home of Posada's former business partner and attorney Joaquín Chaffardet, who fortuitously was out of the country. They claimed to have discovered weapons and documents, but Chaffardet's wife said the agents planted C-4 explosives and compromising materials during their five-hour search. Venezuela charged that Chaffardet was an "accomplice" of Posada and challenged his testimony at Posada's El Paso hearing. He was present for Posada's triumphant return to Miami, where the two toasted their freedom.

Orlando Bosch also had a reunion with his old comrade. The two battle horses of the Cuba Wars celebrated by dining at Miami's Big Five Club. Luis Posada and Orlando Bosch were old and infirm, but they were free.

Throughout 2008, Posada sightings became almost commonplace as he popped up at galas, memorials, and fund-raisers. On February 15, 2008, Posada celebrated his eightieth birthday with friends and family. He was upbeat and optimistic notwithstanding a raucous demonstration in Miami by the antiwar group CodePink, demanding his arrest. Nor did he seem unduly perturbed by the news that Panama's Supreme Court had overturned the pardon granted him and his confederates and had reopened its case against him. There was also a "target letter," warning him of possible indictment by the DOJ for his role in the Cuban hotel bombing attacks.

In March, he attended the memorial service for the virtuoso Cuban bassist and composer Cachao, mingling with the who's who of Miami. The same month he showed up at a tribute for Dr. Oscar Elías Biscet, the imprisoned Cuban dissident. There was solemnity at the event but also laughter. Across the room from Luis Posada, amid the ding of clinking glasses, were two of his patrons: Representatives Lincoln Díaz-Balart and Ileana Ros-Lehtinen.

On May 2, 2008, Los Municipios de Cuba en el Exilio (the Cuban Municipalities in Exile) and the Junta Patriótica Cubana held a gala fund-raiser in Posada's honor at the Big Five Club. The three Miami congressional representatives were invited but, perhaps mindful of the media's interest, they stayed clear of the festivities. However, some five hundred exiles came to pay tribute to Posada at a candlelit banquet that raised thousands for his legal bills.

There would be other fund-raisers throughout 2008 and 2009, but the evening at the Big Five Club was among the most memorable. Posada was in top form in a snappy dark blue suit, shaking hands and blowing kisses. "He had some facial surgery and he looked very different, much better," said Carol Williams of the *Los Angeles Times*. "The scars on his lower face were gone and his chin and lower jaw appeared to have been smoothed out."

"We must not wait for Fidel Castro to die," Posada told the crowd, "[or] for Raúl to make mistakes . . . liberty is not something we must beg for. It is conquered with the sharp edge of the machete. We ask God to sharpen our machetes because difficult times are arriving."

On April 24, 2009, two weeks after the DOJ indictment came down for perjury and illegal entry, Posada was again being feted in Miami. It was a lazy Sunday afternoon, when many might have preferred quiet family time or watching a baseball or soccer game. Nevertheless, more than three hundred supporters filled the Big Five Club for another fund-raiser for the unrepentant militant.

"The people have responded in an extraordinary manner," Nelly Rojas, of the Committee to Aid Luis Posada Carriles (CALPC), told *El Nuevo Herald,* "because Posada is a true patriot." Attendees paid forty dollars to attend the luncheon and many were writing far larger checks to contribute to his mounting legal bills.

Osiel González, Posada's longtime compatriot from the paramilitary group Alpha 66, maintained that "although he has been accused of many things, never have they proven anything." Posada's sole crime, he said, was being *un luchador anticomunista*—an anticommunist soldier.

Posada was duly summoned to the stage, and the crowd, bedecked in their Sunday best, rose to their feet and applauded. When he spoke it was clear that neither age, infirmity, nor prison had diminished his belief in armed struggle.

The assembled leaped to their feet, cheering until he raised his hand in modest acceptance. All was well.

PART THREE

RAÚL'S REIGN

"Accept help from anyone, but remember—trust no one."
—Fidel Castro, April 17, 1954,
prison letter to comrade

CHAPTER NINE

El Relevo—The Relief Pitcher

As political brother acts go, the most dazzling and famous of the twentieth century were the Kennedys, Jack and Bobby. The more enduring and successful, however, have been the Castro brothers, Fidel and Raúl. They took on the Kennedy boys after Eisenhower, then went on to torment another nine American presidents—as they glided into the twenty-first century. And they didn't stop until they implemented their post-Fidel succession plan, moving Raúl into the top slot in January 2008. Along the way, they created a brand synonymous with revolution.

Contrary to the naysayers in Miami and Washington who predicted that Cuba would implode without Fidel standing front and center, Raúl's ascension was notable only for its silent efficiency. The quiet changing of the guard surprised the world, but not the Castros. In the previous decade, they had fine-tuned the most arcane details of the succession.

While reams and tomes have been written about Cuba's Maximum Leader, far less is known about Raúl who, five years his junior, dodged the limelight with the same zeal with which his sibling pursued it. In January 1994, I had an unusual encounter with the younger Castro. Minutes into an interview with Fidel Castro at the Palace of the Revolution, Raúl came bounding over to us. Given his reputation at the time as a steely apparatchik, it took me a few moments to realize who he was. A small, trim man, Raúl was ebullient and garrulous. He quickly hugged me, his face to each cheek, Cuban-style, while needling his brother (he and the top members of the Politburo were impatiently waiting to meet with him while he entertained an American reporter). Fidel neither budged nor uttered a word but fixed his eyes on his brother like a cobra. Fearlessly, Raúl offered another jest, chuckled at his offering, then bolted back across the room.

I had learned a crucial lesson about Cuban politics: Raúl Castro shared the throne with his brother. That is not to say that the brothers did not have their feuds, resentments, or grievously wounding disputes.

But theirs was a potent, symbiotic alliance of lifelong partners. Though they could not have been more different—in personality, appearance, or disposition—their striking contrasts provided a useful counterpoint. For nearly five decades, they have been a formidable, unvanquished duo.

In 1964, journalist Lee Lockwood challenged Fidel about Raúl Castro's bona fides. "He was known as your brother and as a brave soldier," Lockwood pointed out, "but not particularly as a revolutionary leader." Castro's response spoke to the schizoid nature of their relationship, as he alternately championed, then diminished his brother: "When I speak to you of Raúl, I forget completely that he is my brother," he told the American photojournalist. ". . . I have the privilege of knowing him better than anybody else. Though *unquestionably my presence pretty much overshadows him,* I can tell you that Raúl, from the political point of view, possesses magnificent aptitudes. But, what happens? He does not make decisions, because he knows it is not his right to do so. He is extraordinarily respectful. He always consults with me about all the important questions. . . . I myself wasn't even capable then of understanding all his worth." It was Castro's final comment that was the most telling: "Of course, under the present circumstances, *the constant presence of one outstanding leader tends a little to obscure the rest.*"

From the start of Fidel's reign, the younger Castro wielded immense power. He was, after all, the Commander in Chief of Cuba's Armed Forces, the backbone of the Cuban Revolution, and he held an array of other lofty sinecures, from being the First Vice President of the country to Second Secretary of the Communist Party. Because of his special familial status, he was the only member of the ruling cadre who could opt out of state receptions, Politburo meetings, or his brother's interminable speeches. Such privileges, along with a vigilantly guarded personal life, have made Raúl the mystery man of Cuba.

In December 2006, with his brother in declining and fragile health, Raúl Castro addressed the University of Havana Students' Federation, and regaled his audience with some personal reminiscences. The younger Castro was uncharacteristically relaxed for being in a public arena, and revealed a side long known to family and friends, but rarely glimpsed by the outside world.

At the age of four, he said, he had accompanied his mother on a trip from their family estate in rustic Birán to visit La Salle Academy, a school run by the Christian Brothers in Santiago. Raúl's two older brothers, Fidel, age nine, and Ramón, age eleven, attended the school. Playing in the courtyard with his siblings and other boys, young Raúl decided he did not want to return home. "It was like paradise," he recounted. Despite the fact that he was too young to be a pupil at the school, he convinced his mother and the principal to allow him to stay with his brothers. "There was no classroom for me, [so] I did whatever I wanted," he told the rapt, televised audience. However, as night fell, young Raúl became homesick—missing not only his mother, he said, but his "bottle." Without a trace of discomfort, Raúl continued: "I had to have one [bottle] every night to go to bed. One of the teachers had to go to the pharmacy and buy me my bottle."

Raúl went on to recall his first attempt to ride bareback, after watching a friend who had done so: "I ended up with all my bones on the ground. There was this little old farmer that helped me get to my feet and who told me, 'You see, he who imitates, fails.'" The object and meaning of Raúl's parable was evident: he was not Fidel—in personality or style. It was a message he would continue to issue for the next three years to his countrymen and the world at large: adjust your expectations. There would be an indisputable charisma deficit—but for many, that was a blessed relief. Raúl would be his own man, yet deferential to the supremacy and legacy of his brother. "Fidel is irreplaceable," Raúl said, adding for emphasis, "I know so—because I've known him forever."

Raúl then sent an unmistakable signal that he had a different operating approach than his brother. "Sometimes people fear the word *disagree,* but I say the more debate and more disagreement you have, the better the decisions will be," he told the astonished students. It would be one of several comments over the next three years in which Raúl Castro signaled he had come into his own, and was a very different man from his brother.

In 2005, following his two public falls, Fidel Castro laid out the grand plan in the event of his sudden death or incapacitation. "If anything happens to me tomorrow," he told his co-biographer, Ignacio Ramonet, "the National Assembly will surely meet and elect [Raúl]. Have no doubt. The Politburo will meet, and they will elect him."

The legacy issue had long been on Fidel's mind. In 2000, a relative of a senior Party official told me there was a contingency plan in the event of a catastrophe involving Fidel Castro. If he were to die or become stricken with a debilitating illness, members of the Politburo were to await contact from Raúl Castro instructing them what to do and where to go. The plan, he said, was intended to dampen any improvisatory spirit that might lead to a coup.

Castro said that one reason he selected Raúl as his successor was to scare off factions of would-be reformers in the government. "Because

Raúl had been in the Communist Youth, they saw him as more radical," he said. "I knew they were afraid, they were worried. That was one factor." The deciding factor, of course, was that Raúl was the man he most trusted in the world: his unflinchingly loyal right hand since childhood.

While Fidel first announced his appointment of Raúl as his successor in 2002, he had made up his mind by the late '60s. Indeed, he invoked the same baseball idiom and talking points when speaking about his brother for forty-plus years. One Cuban poster of 1968 featured a new-realism portrait of a young Raúl in a *campesino*'s straw hat with a legend across the top assuring him that *his* relief team of young sugarcane cutters would not let him down. In bold chartreuse letters set against a mandarin-red background, the poster read, "*Comandante Raúl: El Relevo no fallo!*" or "Commander Raúl: The relief team will not fail [you]." The poster underscored the co-rulership of the brothers along with the implicit warning that fidelity toward Raúl must also be unwavering.

Fidel's 2002 announcement of his successor was codified on July 31, 2006, when Raúl "temporarily" assumed the roles of his direly ill brother. Critics promptly denounced the transfer of power between the siblings, citing it as exhibit A proof that the Castros were hell-bent on foisting a monarchy on Cuba.

For the previous decade, Raúl's control of the Armed Forces had never been in doubt. A military coup, insistently cited as a probability by hopeful exile hardliners (and the CIA of the 1990s), was never in the cards. After 1989, following a scandal in the Interior Ministry and the defection of several senior officers, the Castros meticulously weeded out suspected dissident elements within the Ministry of the Revolutionary Armed Forces (MINFAR), the government behemoth that runs the FAR, or the Army. By the time of the Soviet pullout from Cuba in 1990, Raúl had solidified and broadened his power base. More significantly, he saw to it that the Ministry of the Interior (MININT), which he regarded as having become rogue and corrupt in the 1980s, was answerable directly to him. The purging of MININT culminated with the installation of Raúl's trusted friend and ally, General Abelardo Colomé Ibarra, as its chief.

Inside the Armed Forces, Raúl retired several nettlesome, aging *históricas*—hardliners—while shoring up the FAR's role as the central organ and decision maker of the government. By 2005, all the first, second, and third tier of commanders in the FAR were committed *raulistas*. Any doubters or dissenters had been retired from the Army or pushed to the sidelines. Those left in command were well positioned and willing to use force, if needed.

Today, Raúl's Army controls at least 60 percent of the Cuban economy, according to a 2008 analysis by economists at Florida International University. The FAR's sub-companies, like GAESA (Grupo Administración Empresarial, or Business Administration Group) and its subsidiary, Gaviota, are the country's main players in Cuba's ever-growing tourism business. The *RUSI Journal,* the defense publication of Britain's Royal United Services Institute, has judged the Cuban Armed Forces to be "the most stable, best managed, and economically influential institution in Cuba."

While Fidel recognized the talents and advantages of his brother, he pointed out one notable limitation. "He is close to my age; the years are passing," he fretted to Ramonet. "It's a rather generational problem."

Such wisdom, however, seemed to vaporize when the National Assembly announced the new hierarchy on February 24, 2008. As usual, the chosen date was fraught with symbolism—commemorating the first battle of Cuba's War of Independence in 1895. Not suprisingly, the post-Fidel political firmament would be led by Raúl, soon to be seventy-seven, who was installed as the country's new president. The other big winners were also on the sclerotic side: men well into their seventies, even eighties. In a rich swath of irony, on the very same day that Cuba's geriatric soldiers were rewarded for their loyalty, Hollywood bestowed the Oscar for Best Picture to *No Country for Old Men.* Ninety miles from the U.S. it was official: Cuba had become the country of, well, the *oldest* men. As thousands of its young fled for *La Yuma* (Cuban slang for the U.S.), the old generals traveled up the Cuban food chain of command. Following in the footsteps of Fidel, there would be no retirement prior to the grave.

Nevertheless, it quickly became apparent that there were significant differences between the brothers' management styles. Over the previous decade, Raúl had won nods and points for being generally more mindful and empathetic than his brother over the plight of most Cubans. In 1994, I asked Fidel Castro if he had heard a certain joke popular in Cuba. "What are the triumphs of the Revolution?" The requisite answer being: education, health care, and sports. "And what are the failures of the Revolution?" followed by the punch line: "Breakfast, lunch, and dinner." To my surprise, Castro laughed. Then he said, "When you have too much breakfast, lunch, and dinner, it's bad for your health." The master spinner had instantly turned hunger into a virtue. In contrast, Raúl assured an unruly, angry crowd during the 1994 *balseros* crisis, when thousands fled the island, that he felt otherwise. "Beans are more important than cannons," he said, in a rare public display of emotion.

Nor did Raúl share the depth of his brother's anti-Americanism. In an oft-quoted burst of fury from a 1955 letter to his *compañera* Celia Sánchez, Fidel had written of his larger intentions. "I swore that the Americans would pay dearly for what they are doing here. Once this war is over, I will start a longer and bigger war; a war I am going to wage against the Americans. I realize this is my true destiny." Indeed, Fidel realized his "destiny," defining Cuban nationalism as a realm without U.S. influence. While his brother held steadfast to his isolationist vision, Raúl, a student of economic globalization, had slowly and reluctantly come to see reconciliation with the U.S. as necessary and inevitable.

Soon after assuming power as acting president in August 2006, Raúl offered an olive branch to the U.S., suggesting it was time to turn the page. First he cautioned the U.S. that it had to forgo "impositions and threats" in its approach to Cuba, then hastened to assure the world that "on the contrary, we have always been disposed to normalize relations on an equal plane." Clearly, he had gone too far: within days Fidel threw water on the proposal in his column, underscoring that *his* remained the final word.

Still, the early months of Raúl's ascension were notable for a welcomed series of diplomatic moves and a climate more receptive to reform. Cuba signed two important human rights agreements it had previously resisted. Raúl would meet with Cardinal Tarcisio Bertone, the Vatican's secretary of state and the pope's emissary, laying the groundwork for a future papal visit. Of course, Fidel had greatly benefited from Pope John Paul II's historic mass in Havana in 1998 and thus was a booster of a repeat papal performance.

Being in his brother's shadow had long suited Raúl. For decades, he had contentedly occupied the second power slot, the reflected glare off his brother being more than ample for him. But Fidel's insistence on remaining co-ruler following his "retirement" quickly became Raúl's burden. The younger Castro had hoped to introduce the economic model of socialized capitalism popularized by China and Vietnam— but Fidel kiboshed its implementation.

"Raúl Castro still has not had an opportunity to demonstrate what he thinks because his brother Fidel is there and still spews his opinions," Pablo Milanés, the popular balladeer, told the *Miami Herald* blog "Cuban Colada" in 2008, expressing a widely held view among Cubans. With his brother's insistent meddling, Raúl's honeymoon at the helm was a brief one. Cubans were willing to give him the benefit of the doubt and eager to make him the repository of their hopes. Then disappointment set in.

Raúl Modesto Castro Ruz, the youngest son of Ángel Castro and Lina Ruz, was born on June 3, 1931. His natural playfulness made him his mother's favorite, but not his father's, who was impatient with his son's unruliness. Initially, Raúl followed the academic trajectory of his brothers, Ramón and Fidel, attending La Salle Academy in Santiago, where he was nicknamed *el pulguita*—the flea. Unlike Fidel, Raúl was indifferent to school—with the exception of sports. "He boarded with us at La Salle when he was about five," Fidel recalled in 2005. "Raúl then was a bit spoiled. Sometimes I had to scold him, but Ramón came to his defense."

As his mother's indulged, pet child, Raúl lacked the discipline of his siblings. A toddler troublemaker, he relied on his extravagant charm to fend off parental wrath. Fidel reminisced in his 2007 autobiography, "When I went home on vacation, I heard nothing but complaints from our parents. I told them: 'Give me the responsibility, and I'll take care of him.'" Early in their lives, Fidel became his brother's mentor. "I gave him some books to read. He became interested. I aroused his interest in studying." All the Castro siblings confirm the close bonds between the two brothers. "Fidel was always an influence on Raúl," their sister Juanita told me. "They were very close, in spite of the age [difference]. They've always been very close."

Raúl did not return to La Salle but transferred to a small military prep school in Santiago. He would tell friends that it was the only school that he enjoyed attending. Like Fidel and Ramón, he was later enrolled in the Jesuit-run Dolores School in Santiago in his young teens and then went on to the prestigious Colegio de Belén in Havana.

Fidel, with his keen intellect, rigorous discipline, and titanic ambitions, excelled at school. Raúl majored in social sciences at the University of Havana, but was an unremarkable and discontented student. Sometime in his third year, in 1952, prior to graduation, he dropped out. For a period, he returned to Birán and worked alongside his father and his brother Ramón, who was also an indifferent student. The amiable Ramón, known as Mongo, had two passions that he pursued his entire life: farming and skirt chasing, leavened with a healthy thirst for rum. He left politics to his brothers.

While at the university, Raúl became involved in the Cuban Communist Party. At that time, the Party played a small but active role in the country's politics. In March 1953, Raúl attended a Communist Party conference in Vienna, Austria, as a delegate from Cuba. Upon his return, he was arrested and detained briefly by Batista's intelligence service. "The police kept one of his diaries," recalled Jesús "Chucho" Montané, a veteran comrade. "I went to see him while he was in jail and he told me all his experiences on his trip. He was very enthusiastic." (On the other hand, Fidel had an uneasy relationship with the Cuban Communists, who never trusted his maverick instincts. The Party would decide, in the end, to forge an alliance with Batista.)

"I wanted to travel and I thought it would be a good opportunity," Raúl told *Chicago Tribune* correspondent Jules Dubois in 1958 when he was fighting in the Sierra. "I offered to pay my own passage if they would let me go, and they accepted me. So off I went. . . . I also visited Budapest on the trip. I would go to China if I had the chance, because I like to travel and I want to see the world. But this doesn't mean I'm a Communist."

Fidel claimed credit for his sibling's early ideology: "Raúl was already quite left-leaning," Castro said in 2005, then added, in seeming contradiction, "Actually, I was the one who introduced him to Marxist-Leninist ideas." Regardless, Raúl was a dedicated Communist, and would remain so until the mid-1980s when he foresaw the collapse of the Iron Curtain.

Fidel was certainly sympathetic toward Marxism, but he convinced his brother that publicly identifying with the Soviet Communist Party at that time would be political suicide. "We were reading Lenin and other socialist writers," Fidel remarked during his 1953 Moncada trial testimony. "Anyone who doesn't is an ignoramus." At twenty-six, Fidel was arrogant and flippant, but his political instincts were impeccable. All in good time, he sagely advised his younger brother.

On July 26, 1953, Raúl joined his brother's quixotic and doomed assault on the Moncada barracks, one of the principal Army garrisons that housed Batista's soldiers, in Oriente. "He wasn't counted as one of the leaders of our movement," Fidel told Lockwood in 1964. "He went to Moncada as just another soldier." Although this was hardly the case, Raúl deferred to his brother. After their shared incarceration—twenty-two months in the forbidding Isle of Pines Prison—their partnership was inviolable.

Following their release from prison in May 1955, Fidel and Raúl and their bearded followers—known as *barbudos*—fled to Mexico, where they plotted their return to rout Batista. Over time Raúl proved himself to be an intrepid and brave warrior. He was a superb marksman, gifted at military strategy, and ruthless with enemies. It was Raúl who first met an eager Argentine recruit named Che Guevara and introduced him to his brother in Mexico City in July 1955. "Raúl and Che were very close, although sometimes they argued," reminisced Fidel. "But Che never argued with me, he never disagreed with me; nor did Raúl." Such assertions are verifiably untrue, but it suited Fidel to suggest that Raúl was the inflexible hardliner and that he, Fidel, was the pragmatist, with a more elastic and worldly cosmology. "And on some issues they were a little, shall we say, radical—Raúl more than Che," added Fidel, for good measure.

The brothers' role playing of their hero/villain parts began early in their collaboration and seemed to work for both. But it was an arrangement that favored Fidel, who benefited richly from Raúl's willingness to be the front man or fall guy for tough, unpopular policies that he had, in fact, brainstormed. "Everybody says Raúl is the bad guy and Fidel is the good guy," Juanita Castro explained to me in 2002. "But these are roles they took at the beginning of the Revolution. It's not true—maybe the opposite."

Nor was Fidel above humiliating his brother. At one meeting in 1959, soon after Castro had seized power, a debate ensued about halting the ongoing summary executions of suspected *batistianos*. Raúl Castro and Che Guevara had assumed key operational roles in the purge in which several thousand Cubans were sent *al paredón*—to the firing squad. (Estimates range from five hundred to five thousand.) According to a participant at the meeting, after a majority of the newly installed revolutionary leaders voted to establish a modicum of legal rights for the accused, Raúl objected.

In his bitter memoir *Family Portrait with Fidel,* the former *fidelista* writer Carlos Franqui who defected in 1968, described how the meeting devolved into a telenovela: "Suddenly, Raúl stood up and without asking permission to speak, shouted to Fidel, 'this is a lot of shit!' Everyone froze. Fidel, with a threatening look, turned to his brother and said, 'Tell [everyone] you are sorry and take back what you said.' To this Raúl responded in a way no less surprising than his first outburst; he burst into tears. From tragedy we went to melodrama. No one uttered a word. There seemed to be a serious rift between the Castro brothers. I tried to pull the fat out of the fire by saying that Raúl had simply used an expression that was just a bit strong, more in tone than in intention. Raúl begged our pardon. . . . I do have two memories of that meeting—Raúl's expletive and his answer to the official telegram [to halt the executions]: 'It came too late. Last night we shot the last prisoners.'"

From 1955 to 1965, Raúl was more than a hardliner; he was his brother's henchman. Throughout the guerrilla war in the Sierra, Raúl did not hesitate to execute suspected informers—usually peasants—regardless of the exculpatory merits of each case. Like Fidel, he erred on the side of vengeance, assumed the worst of his enemies, and took no chances. Such choices remained his credo until he felt confident that the Revolution had defeated Batista and any U.S. attempt to rescue or re-impose the former status quo.

After taking power in 1959, Fidel continued as his brother's tutor in matters big and small. Fidel encouraged Raúl to increase his political profile but Raúl was mortified by public speaking. As a young man, he had a thin, reedy voice that threatened to go mute when he was in front of assembled gatherings. "Fidel sent him to a voice teacher for speech therapy to improve his elocution," said a general from Santiago who worked under him. Regardless, he avoided giving speeches, and when compelled to do so, he never improvised, but read from a prepared and decidedly brief text. "As a point of fact, I am not used to making frequent appearances in public, except at times when it is required," Raúl reminded an audience in 2006. "I have always been discreet; that is *my* way. . . . [And] I am planning to continue that way."

Raúl Castro had a long and arduous learning curve. He would learn his limitations but grow confident in his talents. He clearly suffered from comparisons to his movie-star *caudillo* brother throughout the 1960s and '70s. "Fidel knew every side of Raúl: the Communist, the obedient follower," said Franqui, ". . . the neurotic suffering from little brother complex." The dissident writer Franqui, who frequently clashed with Raúl, claimed the younger Castro once raged at him, "Nobody offends Stalin when I'm around!"

Yet veterans who saw the best and worst of the brothers generally agree with the assessment of José Luis Llovio-Menéndez, a senior official in the Sugar Ministry who defected in 1982. "If I had to have an enemy of the two," said Llovio-Menéndez, who died in 2002, "I would prefer to have Raúl, because Fidel never forgets nor forgives. Raúl will allow rehabilitation, and [he] can forgive and move on."

While Fidel Castro thought of himself as the father of his country, Raúl was content to run the country's Armed Forces and to look after the extended, often fractious Castro family. In contrast to Fidel, an unsentimental man obsessed by politics and ideas, Raúl enjoyed a life filled with friends, outside interests, and deep loyalties within the FAR as well as the family. Raúl was the toastmaster at weddings and the negotiator of divorces. He sent the birthday gifts and attended interminable graduation ceremonies. He is sentimental, voluble, and quick to tears. "Raúl was the favorite of my mother, and the favorite of mine because he was so tenderhearted," said Juanita Castro. "With the family he is very, very good."

Within the Castro clan, Raúl was always the point man for intrafamilial crises and emergencies. In 1959, young Fidelito Castro was in a near-fatal car accident and rushed to the hospital. At the time, his father was being interviewed on the popular American news program *Meet the Press* at a television studio in Havana. At one point in the interview, the moderator asked Fidel if he would like to attend to his son in the hospital. Journalist Jack Skelly, who grew up in Banes, Cuba, near the Díaz-Balarts, recalled that Fidel declined the invitation and continued with the interview. "And Fidelito was almost dying," said Skelly, who ran to the hospital and found Raúl there comforting Fidel's wife, Myrta. Because of his instinctive empathy, the Castro clan is loyal and protective of Raúl, who has served as their reliable go-to guy.

Inclined toward negotiation, Raúl forged the reconciliation between Myrta Díaz-Balart and Fidel in 2000 and ironed out the tensions between Fidelito and his father around the same time. And it was Raúl who stayed in close contact with Myrta, expediting her various visits to Cuba and attending to her medical care.

Juanita Castro has lived in Miami since October 1964. After her mother's death in 1963, she told her brothers that she wanted to visit their younger sister Emma in Mexico City. Once out of the country, however, she soon denounced the Revolution she had once ardently supported and—implicitly—her brothers. She had been deeply distraught over the confiscation of private property and the imposition of Soviet-style socialism. On a personal level, she was furious with Fidel for his casual disparagement of their father in several media interviews in the early 1960s. During a marathon meal cum interview with Lee Lockwood, Fidel referred to their father as being a "*latifundista* [a wealthy landowner] . . . who exploited the peasants" and who "played politics for money." Sitting at the dinner, Raúl initially challenged his brother about the amount of land owned by their family, but in the end deferred to him.

In counterpoint to Raúl's position as the Castro family patriarch in Havana, Juanita established a similar role for herself in Miami. Her comfortable Coral Gables home is a sanctuary for visiting family, including the discreet sojourns of her sisters, as well as assorted nieces, nephews, and cousins—a fair number of whom have quietly settled in South Florida. She remains in close contact with all her sisters:

Agustina, the youngest, and Angelita, the eldest, both of whom live in Havana; and their sister Emma, who has lived her adult life in Mexico. Juanita is a retired pharmacist and successful businesswoman. Ironically, like thousands of her fellow exiles, she sends money and medical supplies to her relatives, regardless of their being Cuba's first family.

In 1955, Raúl returned home, without Fidel, to visit their parents in Birán after their release from prison. Learning of their father's death the following year, Raúl wrote to his mother from Mexico with aching tenderness.

> Dear Mom,
>   In moments like this, what can I tell you? Only that I have an immense desire to see you and that I love you more than ever. No matter what, you will always have a son that eternally adores you.
>   Your Raúl

The same day he wrote Juanita.

> With our father's death, I know that you are suffering greatly. The time and my spirit did not allow me to write you sooner. Finally, it is now possible; I am sending you a photo and with it all my affection. Fill yourself with strength and valor. I hope to be able to see all of you soon.
>   I love you always,
>   Your Raúl

According to Juanita, Raúl was inconsolable after their mother's death in 1963. "Raúl was very affected by her death. He had been her favorite because he was so caring," she told me in 2001. Contrary to a popular myth that Fidel remained at work when Lina suffered a heart attack at Juanita's home in Miramar on 7th Avenue, both brothers ran to Lina's side. However, Raúl stayed by his mother's body at the house and huddled with family members for consolation. He traveled by train with the family to Birán with the casket of their mother in tow. Fidel flew to Oriente, then met his siblings at the train station when they arrived. He paid his respects at their home in Birán, where their mother was laid out, but left soon after her funeral.

At the time of his mother's death, Raúl was a young parent himself. A few weeks after the 1959 victory, he had married Vilma Espín Guillois, the daughter of a prominent family in Santiago, Cuba's second-largest city and once its capital. Espín came from privilege, culture, and considerable wealth; her father, José Espín, was an executive at the Bacardi Rum Company. "We had an easy life," Vilma told me in 1994, "but we had principles." She did postgraduate work at MIT in chemical engineering in 1955, encouraged by her father, who had hoped it would distract her from revolutionary politics. It didn't.

Espín dropped out of MIT after several months, according to Tom Gjelten in his account *Bacardi and the Long Fight for Cuba.* On her way back to Cuba, she alighted in Mexico City to meet the celebrated revolutionary brother duo. Espín promptly fell in love with Raúl, who was equally besotted, spent three days with him, and returned to Havana as their comrade in arms. Later she joined the Castros in the Sierra Maestra. "At the time, I was the head of the underground for all of the province of Oriente," she told me at her office at the Cuban Women's Federation. "The role of women was very important. Women were tortured, women were assassinated." A close confederate of the martyred revolutionary Frank País, Espín had impeccable revolutionary bona fides. When reminiscing about the revered País, whose photograph hung on the wall just behind her desk, Espín suddenly, and uncharacteristically, broke into tears.

After the Revolution, she founded and served as president of the Women's Federation. More significantly, she stepped into the unofficial role as Cuba's First Lady and held that position until her death at seventy-seven on June 18, 2007.

The couple had one son, whom they named Alejandro in tribute to Fidel's nom de guerre. Alejandro Castro Espín followed in his father's footsteps into the Army, rising to the rank of colonel with a vast intelligence portfolio that covers China. Raúl and Vilma also had three daughters. One of Raúl's daughters, Mariela, is married to an Italian photographer and has traveled widely throughout Europe. His other two daughters are both married to high-ranking officers in the FAR. Déborah, their eldest, was given Vilma's revolutionary code name while their youngest, Nilsa, nicknamed Nilsita, was named in honor of Vilma's beloved, deceased sister.

A delicately strung, zealous revolutionary, Nilsa Espín had attended the 1953 conference on Communism in Vienna with Raúl. Like Vilma, Nilsa also applied for a U.S. visa to study at MIT. But because of her attendance at the Vienna conference, she was denied entry to the U.S. Nilsa fell in love with and married a fellow ideologue, Rafael Rivero Pupo. While the Espíns were Oriente aristocrats, Rivero came from a humbler background.

When Nilsa decided she wanted to attend the Sorbonne in Paris, the Espín family paid for Rivero's tuition to the esteemed university. Nilsa evolved into a fearless guerrilla fighter who adopted the nom de guerre of Madame Curie; she was a founding member of the 26th of July Movement. Her husband, also a revolutionary zealot, was elevated to the rank of captain. After the rebels seized power, the couple spearheaded a "revolutionary reeducation" program run out of the old Batista barracks, Camp Columbia, which Castro renamed Liberty City.

Rafael Rivero became an important liaison between the Soviets and the Cubans. Although never publicly reported, the speculation among Havana's chattering class was that the Soviets had became dissatisfied with Rivero's performance during the Cuban Missile Crisis of October 1962.

Those thirteen days in October, in which the world's superpowers hovered at the precipice of mutual destruction, marked Fidel Castro for life. He sent Soviet leader Nikita Khrushchev a letter urging a nuclear strike on the U.S. if Cuba were attacked. "I say this because the imperialists' aggressiveness has become extremely dangerous," wrote Fidel during the drama, well-recounted in Michael Dobbs's *One Minute to Midnight*. "And if they do indeed perform an act so brutal, that would be the moment to eliminate that danger forever, in an act of the most legitimate self-defense. However hard and terrible the solution might be, there is no other."

Castro was despondent for months when Khrushchev dismissed his advice and negotiated directly with President John F. Kennedy, leaving him out of the loop entirely. Castro may well have found in Rivero a scapegoat for his immense frustration. Whether or not at the behest of the Russians, as was rumored, Castro fired Rivero in 1965.

What followed was a surreal, Chekhovian moment in Cuban history. A devastated Rivero took his life by shooting himself in his office. There are two versions of what happened next: Nilsa, who routinely carried a machine gun slung over her shoulder, discovered his body in his office at Camp Columbia—then took her own life. In Carlos Franqui's version, the double suicide hews closer to the operatic plotline of *Tosca*: a grief-stricken Nilsa ran to Raúl Castro's office and shot herself in front of her brother-in-law.

Soon after the Revolution, Raúl and his family settled into a sprawling seventh-floor apartment in Nuevo Vedado, not far from the historic Colón Cemetery in Havana. Later he moved to a country-style mansion with sweeping grounds and assorted farm animals known as La Rinconada, not far from Fidel's family home. While relatives and foes attest to his love of family, Raúl was hardly the faithful husband. But like his brother Fidel, he conducted his affairs with a degree of courtliness and discretion.

According to relatives of Celia Sánchez, Fidel's political and personal partner until her death in 1980, Raúl was the patriarch to a parallel family. A long-term affair with a pretty assistant in the FAR begun in the 1960s, they say, produced at least one son, named Guillermo, in the early 1970s. A light-skinned, blond child, Guillermo would later study medicine, according to the Sánchez relations who met him socially. They also believe that Raúl sired a second younger son—though it is unclear whether the boy shared the same mother as Guillermo or was the son of another liaison.

Raúl would have other significant affairs. One was with a Bulgarian woman who lived in Havana. Later he had a long infatuation with a Colombian nurse. According to a colonel in the FAR, many government elites believed that Raúl was involved in the 1980s with the First Secretary of the Party in Matanzas, a woman who went on to enjoy an important political career. Another attractive young woman in the Ministry of Commercial Affairs caught Raúl's eye in the 1990s. Raúl's romantic life was not dissimilar to that of his brothers, Fidel and Ramón, or for that matter, their father, Ángel. He was a Cuban man of a certain generation for whom extramarital liaisons were almost de riguer. The difference lay in Raúl's deeply felt passion for fatherhood and in his esteem for his wife.

By the mid-1980s, Raúl's marriage to Vilma had settled into a familial partnership and friendship. Some insiders said they lived separately for more than twenty years. But throughout his dalliances, he remained respectful of Espín and her public role as First Lady of the country. He was at her side at family celebrations and tragedies, and stood beside her at official events and receptions.

Following her diagnosis of cancer in 2004, Raúl was scrupulously attentive to her needs. Her death in 2007, by all accounts devastated him. He wept profusely at her memorial in Havana and at the interment of her ashes in Santiago's Mausoleum of the Frank País Second Front. In an ironic bookend, Fidel, who had been too preoccupied to attend Vilma and Raúl's wedding, was too ill to attend her funeral.

Over time, the Nilsa-Rivero suicide drama was quietly erased from Cuba's revolutionary memory, never having made it into its history books. The sensational double suicide rocked Cuba's revolutionary elite, but suicide is not an anomaly in Cuba—either before or after the Revolution. Indeed, Cuba has the highest rate of suicide in Latin America, and is among the highest in the world. One factor is the country's unforgiving, scorched-earth, winner-take-all political culture.

Cuban nationalism from time immemorial has conflated the rhetoric of self-sacrifice into traditional slogans such as *"Cuba Libre o Muerte!"* Fidel Castro ramped up the patriotic tropes into one simple revolutionary slogan: *Patria o muerte*—country or death. The history of these kamikaze, suicidal invocations is richly documented in *To Die in Cuba* by Louis A. Pérez Jr., who references suicide as a "Cuban way of death."

One might imagine this phenomenon has something to do with the Cuban partiality toward over-caffeination, rum, and telenovelas. A proclivity toward excess may be another contributing factor, but suicide is so ingrained in the "national sensibility," according to Pérez, that long ago it "passed from the unthinkable to the unremarkable."

Another factor was the depth of brutality experienced by successive segments of the population at the hands of the island's colonizers. An estimated one-third of the Indians living in Cuba committed suicide during Spain's brutal conquest of the island in the early 1500s. Many did so by leaping off the steep cliffs overhanging the Yumuri Valley in Oriente. Likewise, African slaves and Chinese indentured workers seeking escape from their barbarous masters took their lives in staggering numbers, "a plague of suicides," as one bishop described it. The name of the third-largest city in Cuba, Matanzas—meaning "massacres"—speaks to the blood debts incurred on the largest island in the Antilles.

Like the Indians and the Africans and the Chinese before them, Cubans regarded subjugation by the Spanish as intolerable. Suicide offered an escape—death with honor. In the celebrated and mournful ballad *"La Bayamesa,"* the narrator describes how she burns her Bayamo home to the ground rather than surrender it to the Spanish. In fact, dozens of towns and cities—including Las Tunas, Guáimaro, and Banes—were torched by their citizens between 1896 and 1898.

"The practice of suicide is the sole, and, of course, definitive Cuban ideology," the exile author Guillermo Cabrera Infante wrote. José Martí, the frail poet of the Revolution, would charge off on horseback into the Spanish for a guaranteed death, having written that the war for independence was "a conflict that can only end in victory or the grave." Mariana Grajales, celebrated as "La Madre de La Patria," sent her husband and eleven sons off to fight for independence. Though only two sons survived, she said her only regret was not having more sons to give to her homeland.

Such is the island's siren song of suicide that the great American poet Hart Crane made two attempts during vacations there. When he was sixteen, he had a failed suicide attempt on a visit to the Isle of Pines; in 1932, following a dissolute night in Havana, he dove into the sea from his ship and drowned.

Cubans continue to take their lives in record numbers—in their homeland and in exile, according to Pérez. The men usually do so by hanging or by gunshot, the women, in a macabre turn, often burn themselves. Inarguably, the failures and disappointments of the Cuban Revolution augmented the despair felt by some. Among the most notable post-Revolution suicides was Osvaldo Dorticós Torrado, Cuba's first president during the early days of the Revolution, who shot himself in 1983; and Haydée Santamaría, the heroine of Moncada and an esteemed government official. Santamaría famously sent a bold and irrefutable message when she leaped to her death on July 26, 1980, the twenty-seventh anniversary of the Moncada attack.

Curiously, the statistics for suicide are roughly the same for Cubans in exile: Former Cuban president Carlos Prio Socarrás shot himself through the heart in Miami in 1977; the novelist Reinaldo Arenas took his life in Manhattan; writer Calvert Casey did the same in Rome; and Miguel Ángel Quevedo, the brilliant editor of *Bohemia,* committed suicide in Venezuela. In June 2008, Pedro Díaz-Lanz, the intrepid former *fidelista* who became the first chief of the Revolution's air force before defecting to the U.S., shot himself in the chest at the age of eighty-one. Two of his siblings also took their lives—one in Havana and one in Miami.

Indeed, it was a suicide that propelled the Castro brothers to political prominence. Humiliated by a political miscalculation, presidential aspirant Eddy Chibás shot himself during the live broadcast of his popular radio show in 1951. The death of Chibás cleared the political stage for a little-known student leader from the backwoods of Oriente. His name was Fidel Castro.

While the blight of suicide has skipped over the Castro family, alcoholism has not. To varying degrees of debilitation, it has afflicted most of the males in the family from its patriarch, Don Ángel, down through all his sons, and on to a number of grandsons. Don Ángel was known to be both hardworking and hard-drinking. Ramón, the eldest of Lina's brood, still amiably hits the bottle. Of Lina's three sons, Fidel has been the most controlled drinker, imbibing with abandon and then swearing off it for periods, but rarely appearing to lose control. Of the siblings, Raúl has been the most disabled by booze—forcing him to spend a good deal of his adult life thinking about *not* drinking.

Of the two co-ruler brothers, Raúl is more classically Cuban: partial to excess, he laughs hard, weeps, dances, sings, and regales friends with corny jokes. When China's president, Hu Jintao, visited Havana in November 2008 bearing millions of dollars in aid and trade agreements, Raúl serenaded him with a folk song. Out of the public spotlight, he is gregarious and spontaneous and knows how to have a good time.

"Raúl is normal, in the sense of being a regular guy—not like Fidel," said Gioconda Belli, the Nicaraguan novelist and former Sandinista. "And he has a very good sense of humor." Belli remembers Raúl as an "unpretentious" man who enjoyed an emotional range and level of personal comfort seemingly unavailable to his brother. An attractive woman, Belli's charms were not lost on Fidel—who pursued her without success.

In November 1979, Belli was part of Nicaragua's delegation sent to Algiers to celebrate the former French colony's independence. In lieu of Fidel, Raúl led Cuba's delegation, which included Gabriel García Márquez and other luminaries of the Left. "Raúl was down to earth, smart, and not preachy," said Belli. Unlike Fidel, he is not a scold nor sententious. Yet he is well versed in politics and—to a lesser degree—cultural issues. At one point, Belli joined Raúl for an extended meeting with General Vo Nguyen Giap, Vietnam's soldier-hero of the 1968 Tet Offensive, for a discussion on the intersection of the military with the political. (Raúl happily returned to Algiers in July 2009 en route to the NAM Summit in Egypt.) They also discussed how "to stop the honor killings in Algiers and the clash between the old *cultura* and the new. And [Raúl] talked a lot about his daughters and wife."

Being the adored, favorite child of his mother made Raúl especially comfortable with women. He is charming and flirtatious—in a way that is endearing and not threatening. His sisters and three daughters have always sung his praises; so, too, have both wives of Che Guevara. Even Alina Fernández, a harsh critic of Fidel, has paid tribute to Raúl's familial caring and authenticity.

But Raúl is also a man's man—as demonstrated by the loyalty he engenders from his subordinates. For years, he was known for his nights and weekends with close friends—carousing, drinking, and attending cockfights. Raúl's empathetic emotional trajectory and soft spot for family runs parallel to his role as The Enforcer. A former CIA analyst, Brian Latell, describes Raúl as pivoting between two personas: Raúl the Terrible, responsible for summary executions after the rebels routed Batista, and Raúl the Compassionate, the sentimental family man.

Outside the family, aggrieved parties often appeal to Raúl as well.

When the relatives of a celebrity political prisoner sought clemency and "home leave" for him, they appealed to Raúl. It was a delicate and tricky matter, owing to the fact that the children of the former official-turned-prisoner had fled the country.

The imprisoned officer's relatives reminded Raúl of earlier days and better memories when the families had vacationed together. When not entertaining visiting Soviet cosmonauts, Raúl had gleefully played with their children on the beach as if he were a child himself. The relatives stressed that they understood the utmost importance of discretion, assuring Raúl they would neither make public statements nor rail against the government. They sought only peace for their family, they assured him.

Raúl was moved and persuaded. The former officer was first allowed weekly home leave, then released from prison but not allowed to leave the country. Family members have honored their word—and not spoken out publicly on the matter. It was not the most satisfying resolution, but by Cuban standards, it was considered a happy ending.

CHAPTER TEN

All the King's Men

The sudden, near-fatal illness that sidelined Fidel Castro in the summer of 2006 triggered a seige of intense political jockeying within every organ of the Cuban government. The Councils of State and Ministers, the Army, the National Assembly, and, most especially, the Politburo of the Communist Party became cauldrons of quiet deal making and agitated horse trading. In private home restaurants known as *paladares* and cars—less vulnerable to surveillance by state security—the wrangling could be fevered. Most upwardly mobile technocrats saw the wisest course as being one in which they appeared devoted to Fidel while enhancing their relationship and bona fides with Raúl. Those who had skipped military careers began to experience pangs of regret.

When the newly minted, reconfigured political hierarchy was announced in February 2008, the coveted number two slot was awarded to José Ramón Machado Ventura. A seventy-eight-year-old former medic, Machado was barely known outside of Havana and unrecognizable to most Cubans. If he was known for anything it was for his nimble surgical skills as a guerrilla, demonstrated when he extracted an M1 bullet slug out of the left foot of Che Guevara with a razor blade.

For his unswerving loyalty and revolutionary commitment, Machadito, as insiders call him, was given the vice presidency of both the Council of State and the Council of Ministers. Machado's political career had begun as an early leader in the Cuban Communist Party. He was also a founder of the Frank País Second Front during the Revolution and was devoted to Vilma Espín, Raúl's late wife. At her funeral, Machado delivered an emotional eulogy extolling her virtues as Raúl cried softly. "She lives within us," he told the assembled mourners.

Machado was once regarded as a no-nonsense problem solver on issues as varied as health care and sugar quotas. He had served as the Revolution's first minister of health until 1967 and set up Cuba's once-estimable, but presently eroded, health-care system. A rigid hardliner, his ascension was distressing to reformers. Others with a historical memory pointed out that he shared a name with another Machado in Cuban politics. The previous one, General Gerardo Machado, president of Cuba from 1925 to 1933, had also been a revolutionary hero in his youth. He later acquired a reputation as a cattle thief. His rule was marked by ruthlessness and brutality in matters large and small—from assassinations to banning conga drums.

José Ramón Machado had a curious background for a Communist. Throughout the 1950s, he had been a devout Baptist who attended church every Sunday. His conversion to Marxism-Leninism, however, was equally fulsome. "One advantage of choosing Machado, who is one year older than Raúl, is that he would not be seen by the younger group as a likely contender for the succession to Raúl," observed the Harvard scholar Jorge Domínguez, who calculated that "the median birth year for this top group [of new leaders] is 1936." Francisco Hernandez, president of the Cuban American National Foundation, noted that Machado was once known as "*'Pedrusquito,'* which is the Cuban version of Fred Flintstone, *el hombre de las cavernas* [caveman], or a troglodyte." Few Cubans under the age of forty had ever heard of José Ramón Machado, which may have been the point.

All the big winners in the first post-Fidel hierarchy were *históricos*—the old guard—promoted from within the ranks of the Party or the Army, some known for their personal relationships with the Castro brothers going back to the 1950s. One vice president of the Council of Ministers is José Ramón Fernández, a former *comandante* and brigade general born in 1925. Another is Health Minister José Ramón Balaguer, born in 1930.

General Julio Casas Regueiro, who had been Raúl's chief aide for decades, was named his replacement as Defense Minister of the Armed Forces. General Casas had spearheaded the reformation of the Army and had served as the Cuban equivalent of a CEO at MINFAR, transforming its vast financial empire from a moldy bureaucracy into a lucrative moneymaker. According to military scholar Frank Mora, formerly of the National War College, Casas oversaw an extraordinary reorganization of the Army after slashing its budget in half in 1990. He did so by downsizing its numbers from a bloated two hundred thousand to a trim fighting force of fifty-five thousand fifteen years later. At the same time he placed almost one million Cubans on call as militia reservists.

Continuing at the Ministry of the Interior (as the country's spymaster in chief) would be General Abelardo Colomé Ibarra, born in 1939.

Both Casas and Colomé have been lifelong, stalwart *raulistas,* operating as the left and right hands of the younger Castro for two decades. Known as Furry, Colomé has enforced discipline and loyalty to the Castros throughout the government's labyrinthine bureaucracies. All five men eschew the limelight and the media, scrupulously maintaining low personal profiles, a trait supremely valued by the Castros.

Other hardliners joined Machado, Colomé, and Casas as Council of State vice presidents: Juan Almeida Bosque (born in 1927) and Esteban Lazo Hernández (born in 1944), a Communist Party strict constructionist. Almeida and Lazo are Afro-Cubans, and thus representative of two-thirds of a population that is either mulatto or black. They would later be joined by another Afro-Cuban, Ricardo Cabrisas, born in 1937, who was named a Vice President of the Council of Ministers. Eight women, almost all Afro-Cubans, were named to the thirty-one-member Council of State, but were regarded more as token appointments. None of the eight women was given a portfolio of a national stature.

Dr. José M. Miyar Barruecos, known to all as Chomy, was initially reappointed Secretary of the Council of State, a sinecure he had held for thirty-plus years. Viewed almost as a surrogate Castro brother, Chomy, who is Raúl's age, tended to Fidel's personal computer and private e-mail. A shutterbug, he has photographed Fidel and his family for decades.

Lest anyone have any doubts, Fidel Castro let it be known that he had presided over the National Assembly's 2008 selections: "That's not because I demanded to be consulted," he wrote from his sickbed, protesting a tad too much. "It was the decision of Raúl and of the principal leaders of the country to consult me."

The announcement of the new order of ancient kingmakers brought instant dismay from pundits, think tanks, and talk shops in the U.S. and abroad. Their distress delighted Fidel.

The big losers were the under-sixty crowd, mistrusted by the *históricos* as being too green and unreliable in matters of national security. "Raúl wants to be a Brezhnev, not a Gorbachev," said CANF's Hernandez, "and he wants an Andropov to succeed him, certainly not a Gorbachev. These men will use repression and liberalization 'pragmatically' as needed to secure internal stability." Several critics, such as Jaime Suchlicki at the University of Miami, were quick to compare Raúl unfavorably with China's post-Mao reformer, Deng Xiaoping.

Among the losers was the reform or pragmatist flank. Carlos Lage, the executive secretary of the Council of Ministers, who favored limited economic reform, was considered a dark horse candidate to replace

Raúl as first vice president. Optimists even dared to dream he would be given the presidency, while Raúl continued running the all-powerful Army. Although Lage initially retained his post as one of the five vice presidents of the Council of State, his loss to a Party apparatchik like Machado signaled grim tidings for those aching for change. The fifty-seven-year-old Lage did, however, hold on to his high-profile post as Executive Secretary of the Council of State—for one more year.

Felipe Pérez Roque, forty-three, who served for eight years as Fidel Castro's chief of staff before becoming foreign minister in 1999, also did not improve his standing—an inauspicious omen. A Fidel bulldog loyalist, Roque, like Lage, remained on the Council of State for another year. In 2001, he had famously lunged for the microphone when Fidel Castro fainted durung a speech, and shouted "Viva Fidel! Viva Raúl! Viva la Revolución!" It was an outburst that the brothers Castro may have felt was too much or too soon. Unlike Lage, Pérez Roque was not especially well liked. Nor did Pérez Roque's slavish devotion to Fidel bode well in the new Raúl era. The failure of Lage and Pérez Roque to secure promotions or recognition in Raúl's new government disappointed foreign diplomats and reform-hungry Cubans. Worse was to come.

The more durable survivors were Culture Minister Abel Prieto, a fifty-eight-year-old ponytailed novelist who is seen as the most liberal member of the Politburo, and National Assembly President Ricardo Alarcón, Cuba's most visible politician, aside from Fidel. While Alarcón remains a senior counselor on U.S. issues, he's had a dicey personal relationship with the Castros. Alarcón, born in 1937 in Havana, was part of the urban underground resistance, not the guerrilla wars in the Sierra. He is an urbane intellectual, fluent in English, and is not entirely to the liking of the countrified Castros. Both Prieto and Alarcón have managed to hold on to their respective turfs, but won no new ground or special dispensations.

Ramiro Valdés, a year younger than Raúl, however, continued his phoenix-like ascension within the Cuban firmament. In the first weeks following Fidel's illness, Valdés was given the newly created Ministry of Information and Communications, with a vast portfolio covering the internet and all phone, satellite, and cable transmissions inside Cuba.

In his previous incarnation as the founder and chief of the Ministry of the Interior, the fearsome Valdés had even dared to tangle with Raúl Castro. In 1986, he was forced out of the Politburo. Valdés spent his government exile profitably, studying computer science and the emerging internet technology while remaining a player in the Communist

Party. In 1996, he became president of Grupo de la Electrónica, placing him front and center in the burgeoning information market. In 2002, Chino Figueredo, a retired general and close friend of Valdés, assured me in a chat, not far from Valdés's swank home in Atabey, that "Ramiro may have been out of sight *but he was never out of power.*" Domingo Amuchastegui, a former intelligence official, agreed. "Valdés spent fifteen years retooling himself, carving a niche for himself," observed Amuchastegui. "And now he is Cuba's telecom CEO."

Notwithstanding his earlier turf skirmishes with Raúl, Valdés remained a blue-blooded Castro loyalist. He is one of the surviving quartet who sailed on the *Granma* in 1956 and fought at the Moncada and in the Sierra (the others are Fidel, Raúl, Juan Almeida, and Pedro Miret Prieto). He was made chief of Fidel's personal security in the early 1960s, a post in which he was credited with thwarting numerous assassination attempts. Valdés was the architect of the much-feared G2, the original Revolutionary Political Police Force, charged with rooting out counter-revolutionaries.

He also led Cuba's crusade, El Nuevo Hombre, or the New Man, of the 1960s. Known as UMAP (the Spanish acronym for its full Orwellian title: Military Units to Aid Production), the "rehabilitation" program culminated with the internment of those deemed to be "undesirables." The first mass roundup in Havana in 1961 was directed by Valdés, who declared homosexuality to be "contrary to revolutionary morality." In the 1960s "Ramiro Valdés represented, with Raúl Castro, the most inflexible, coercive, and repressive strains within the Revolution," wrote Llovio-Menéndez. "A small man, physically off-putting, with a dry, penetrating voice and a goatee, Valdés was known as narrow-minded, pretentious, and bitter. He surrounded himself with MININT functionaries who knew all the slogans and shared his vindictiveness."

The leadership selections continued the pattern established since the *Comandante*'s illness: toggling between re-entrenchment and openings. Change, masked as continuity, would proceed. But any and all change would adhere to Fidel's dictum as laid down in 1961: "*Dentro de la revolución, todo. Fuera, nada.*" ("Inside the Revolution, anything. Outside the Revolution, nothing.") The referees of the "inside" and "outside" zones remained, as always, the Castro brothers.

The Castros' capriciousness as referees was resoundingly demonstrated one year later when twenty of Cuba's preeminent political lights were summarily fired from their jobs and sent packing. The March 2, 2009, announcements were described by most commentators as a purge or a soft coup and brought to mind Fidel Castro's oft-quoted vow, or more precisely a breach of it, that "the Revolution would not eat its own."

The most stunning casualties of the purge were Foreign Minister Felipe Pérez Roque, who had served in his post for almost ten years, and Carlos Lage, Cuba's point man on the economy for the previous two decades, credited with rescuing the country's finances after the Soviet Union's patronage ended. Also shown the door was Fernando Remírez de Esteñoz, former chief of the U.S. Interests Section, who had deftly guided Cuba during the Elián González saga and had been elevated to the highest ranks of the Party's Secretariat and charged with attending to international affairs.

Pérez Roque was replaced by his own deputy, Bruno Rodríguez Parrilla, formerly Cuba's ambassador to the United Nations, while Lage was replaced by General José Amado Ricardo Guerra, a trusted officer in the Army and a confidant of Raúl Castro.

Otto Rivero Torres, who had championed Fidel's pet campaign, "The Battle of Ideas," was booted from his post on the Council of Ministers. His replacement was none other than Ramiro Valdés. The veteran economic minister, José Luis Rodríguez García, was also dispatched, then succeeded by Marino Murillo Jorge, Minister of Internal Commerce.

One major name shuttled to the sidelines was José Miguel Miyar Barruecos, who was removed as secretary of the Council of State. In this case, however, Miyar Barruecos, who had spearheaded Cuba's biotechnology programs, was reassigned to a respectable new slot—as Minister of Science, Technology, and the Environment. His replacement at the Council of State was Homero Acosta Álvarez, a close ally of Raúl and Machado.

While the shakeup ranked among the most significant since the Castros had come to power in 1959, the electric announcements were casually communicated on national television at the end of the afternoon news hour. Following the weather and sports reports, the program anchor simply rattled off the names of several of the more prominent victims and their replacements, then turned to other topics.

Fidel Castro, however, made clear that the changes were no trifling matter. In his "Reflections" published the next day, he assured readers that he had been consulted about the dismissals. The infirm *Comandante* did not thank his comrades for their years of service to the country. Instead he upbraided Lage and Pérez Roque, who had served at his beck and call on a 24/7 basis for decades, for having been corrupted by "the honey of the power—for which they had known no sacrifice—[and which] had awakened in them ambitions that led them to an unworthy

role." Such a repudiation meant only one thing: confessions and punishment would be coming. Indeed, hours later, both men penned the
requisite mea culpas, addressed to the man had who sacked them.

"Compañero Raúl," wrote Lage, "I recognize and assume all responsibility for my errors. My ousting has been very just. Be assured that I
will always serve the Revolution and will always remain faithful to the
Communist Party, to Fidel, and to you." Pérez Roque went further and
announced he would be stepping down from all his posts in the Council of State, National Assembly, and the Party's Central Committee as
punishment for his transgressions. "I fully recognize that I committed errors that were broadly analyzed in a meeting [with the Political
Bureau]. I assume my full responsibility for them," Pérez Roque wrote.

Exactly what "errors" the men had committed was never stated
or explained. But their sudden expulsions and show-trial confessions
mirrored that of Carlos Valenciaga, Fidel's executive assistant, who
had been sacked in December 2008; former foreign minister Roberto
Robaina, who was ousted in 1999; and Carlos Aldana, who was forced
out of his high-profile Party post in 1992.

A familiar face to Cubans, Valenciaga had announced to the world
that Castro had undergone a dire medical crisis in 2006. Personally
groomed by Fidel, the thirty-five-year-old had rocketed to the top of
the Cuban political firmament. He was a deputy in the Council of State
and a member of the Central Committee since 1993. Since 1999, he
had been Chief of Communications for Fidel before he was relegated
to *Plan Pijama,* as forced retirement of government officials is known.

Some said Valenciaga was under house arrest, accused of vague corruption charges such as giving his girlfriend a state-owned laptop. Others
said he had committed the cardinal sin of showboating or appropriat-
ing power. Worse, he had thrown himself a boisterous birthday party
in September 2006 while Fidel hovered "between life and death," in
the words of Raúl. His replacement was Lt. Colonel Rolando Alfonso
Borges, a humorless hardliner whose title spoke for itself: Chief of the
Central Committee's Department of Ideology.

Cuban officials, speaking under anonymity, told the *New York Times*
that Pérez Roque and Lage had become self-important and had communicated to their foreign counterparts "false expectations about how
the country would change." Their fate was sealed after secretly recorded
tapes of them, along with their friend Fernando Remírez of the Party's
Secretariat, confirmed Raúl's doubts that the men were insufficiently
respectful toward their superiors.

In the *Times'* account, the trio had been surveilled at the home of

Conrado Hernández, a Cuban who served as the liaison to business-men in the Basque region of Spain. On the tapes, the men had casually dissed Machado Ventura as being a "living fossil" and a "dinosaur," and even fired off a few jokes about Fidel's health and Raúl. Cuban officials contended that Hernández, who was arrested on February 14, 2008, had made the tapes to pass on Spanish intelligence, a claim Spain vehemently denied. Jesús Gracia, a former Spanish ambassador to Cuba, said the charges made no sense, adding that "this story about tape recordings is typical of Raúl's secret services."

The men had also been videotaped at the home of Lage's cousin, Raúl Castellanos Lage, a cardiologist at the Institute of Vascular Cardiology. The doctor had quipped at one dinner that it would have been "a service to *la patria*" to let Machado die when he was treated for a heart problem at his hospital. "The nation would have been better off," scoffed Castellanos, who was also tossed in the pokey and charged with treason. As it turned out, about a dozen officials—all appointed by Fidel—had been under government surveillance for more than a year prior to their sacking. Subsequently, nine hours of videotape of the victims' indiscretions was shown to selected Party elders. Evidently, Raúl's inner circle felt it needed to justify a lightning-bolt purge that had decimated Cuba's leadership, putting out its best spin for imprisoning some of their brightest stars for making ill-considered jokes.

The 2009 shakeup recalled a previous purge in the mid-1960s known as *La Dolce Vita*. The scandal of *La Dolce Vita* (The Sweet Life), as it was dubbed by Fidel after the then-popular Fellini film, claimed the careers of more than a hundred government officials, many of whom were sent to UMAP camps to cut sugarcane all day.

In both the 2009 and 1966 purges, the charge was unspecified corruption; the actual crime, however, was harboring personal ambition and dallying a bit too long in the spotlight.

There was another element that resonated with the past: Ramiro Valdés had been the architect of *La Dolce Vita* and likely had a hand in the surveillance of those demoted in 2009 through his Information Ministry. After all, Valdés had fully reingratiated himself into the good graces of Raúl and had traveled to Russia with him just a month earlier. He was also a beneficiary of the expulsions—having scored another portfolio for himself as well as a seat on the Council of Ministers.

Cubanologists—often more skilled than Kremlinologists—quickly noted that the heads that rolled belonged to *fidelistas* as opposed to *raulistas* and that the internal shuffle fully consolidated power within Raúl's Armed Forces. "It's the military, the generals who are now even more powerful perhaps than Machado Ventura," the oft-jailed dissident Óscar Espinosa Chepe told the AP's Will Weissert.

Those promoted to replace the disgraced officials shared several factors. Most were either in the military or allied with the Army in some fashion and tended to be older—many in their seventies. The majority, like the Castros, came from Oriente, not Havana. And all of them assiduously dodged center stage or were of sufficiently low wattage not to eclipse either Castro.

One foreign investor, who was in Havana at the time, pointed out that "the military never trusted the civilians." He noted that the police presence during the week of the government shakeup was massive. "There was a policeman behind every tree," he said, adding, "and those were the visible ones. Many more were invisible."

Many of the officials sent to Cuba's Siberia were on the youngish side and tended to be reform-minded, but not all. They were technocrats, pragmatists, or intellectuals, and *all* were associated with Fidel. "You know, there are two Castros," Raúl Castro told President Michelle Bachelet of Chile during a 2009 visit. "We are not the same."

Harvard scholar Jorge Domínguez, who happened to be in Havana during the government shuffle, said, "There are many oddities . . . but if I were to emphasize one among several, it is that Raúl Castro finally has *his* government."

When the smoke cleared and the dust settled, many were left wondering how Ricardo Alarcón, of the National Assembly, and Abel Prieto, of the Ministry of Culture, had survived. Three months later, Fransisco Soberón, credited as founder of the Young Communist League and the Committees to Defend the Revolution, was also out: the president of the Central Bank "resigned" from all responsibilities, including his posts in the Council of State and the Party's Central Committee. The writing was on the wall: No one should feel safe.

The talking points issued to reporters and visitors in Havana suggested that the dismissals were merely Raúl's mission to streamline the government to make it more effective, with a "more compact and functional structure." Certainly, Raúl was intent on safeguarding the country's institutions; he had entrusted the Army, the Party, and the Councils of State and Ministers to men whom he had known since the 1950s or '60s. In turn, they would protect the Castro dynasty.

After all, it is entirely possible that Raúl's son, Colonel Alejandro Castro Espín, might choose to succeed his father, or possibly Déborah's husband, Colonel Luis Alberto Rodríguez López-Callejas, or even, down the road, Raúl's grandson, Raúl Alejandro Rodríguez Castro.

Oddly enough, for having orchestrated a singularly tone-deaf government purge, Cuba was preoccupied by the U.S. reaction. According to Jorge Domínguez, "The Foreign Ministry was emphasizing that there is no change, and in particular there is no change to its good disposition, to respond to whatever Washington may propose. . . . I was truly struck with how closely they are calibrating to expectations regarding U.S. policy."

"Obviously this was a purge," said military expert Frank Mora, "but one that concentrated on the economic team, with the exception of Remírez, Pérez Roque, and Lage, who were punished for garnering too much spotlight within and outside Cuba."

While most of the offenders will go on *Plan Pijama*—that is, staying at home and not showing their face at work, Mora pointed out that "they could be rehabilitated." He notes cases such as Ramiro Valdés, Fidelito Castro, and Marcos Portal. The difference, however, is that the latter two are Castro family members and Valdés is a *comandante*, with titles and privileges not shared by the current crop of demotees. "This is *raulismo*," concluded Mora. "Raúl being Raúl."

Allied with Ramiro Valdés to preserve the status quo is Machado Ventura. Both men have long been power players in the Communist Party and both have synergy and personal history with Raúl Castro. With men like Casas, Colomé, Machado, and Valdés guarding the fort, Raúl Castro will not have to worry about betrayal. Raúl has learned that in a system that favors supplication and flattery, there is always concern about whom to trust. On occasion, he has been woefully mistaken. In the late 1980s and early '90s, Raúl saw some of his most trusted lieutenants—a four-star general and a *comandante*, as well as his own personal secretary—abandon him and the Revolution. The system had failed him.

In 1991, Colonel Jesús Renzoli, Raúl's secretary of twenty-plus years, defected to the U.S. Not only had Renzoli enjoyed ongoing access to Fidel and Raúl Castro, he was the former chief of the Second Secretariat from 1983 to 1990. A noted Russia expert, he was in charge of Cuba's military mission to the USSR from 1990 until his defection, and served briefly as ambassador to the Soviet Union. As Raúl's and Fidel's Russian language translator, Renzoli was privy to *all* of their conversations with the Soviets.

With his family in tow, Renzoli drove across Russia's western border into Finland, then beelined directly to the American embassy in Helsinki. He was immediately whisked to the United States, where he was debriefed by the CIA's famed Cuba hand, the late Dan Lynch, who found him to be an impeccable source. For several years, Renzoli struggled to get his footing in the U.S., and at one point worked for Home Depot. But in 1995, Renzoli, a man of considerable acumen and intellect, began a second career at the World Bank.

There were—before and after Renzoli—other important defections. General Rafael del Pino Díaz, deputy chief of staff of the Cuban Defense Ministry and former chief of the Cuban Air Force, remains the country's highest-ranking defector. In May 1987, General del Pino commandeered a small training plane, with his family on board, to Key West's Naval Air Station. MININT Colonel Filiberto Castiñeiras (who fled in 1993) and MININT's Domingo Amuchastegui (1994), were also high-value defectors. Likewise, Alcibíades Hidalgo Basulto, formerly Cuba's ambassador to the United Nations and chief of staff to Raúl Castro, arrived in 2002 with much to impart.

According to RAND Corporation analyst Edward Gonzalez, who interviewed Renzoli in June 1994, two factors motivated Cuba's top Russian expert to defect. One issue was Renzoli's fear that Cuba might not survive the loss of its Russian patron and its $4 billion subsidy to the island. The impact would slash Cuba's economy by more than one-third. And without the enactment of significant reforms—moves he knew Fidel Castro would resist—Renzoli believed the Cuban economy was doomed.

He was not alone in his thinking. At a meeting of the Politburo in 1987, Renzoli reported that Fidel vehemently rejected a suggestion made by Raúl and General Abelardo Colomé to allow a safety valve for political dissent. By 1990, Raúl Castro's politics had been somewhat moderated by realism. "Renzoli said that Raúl had been struck by the phenomenal impact in Poland by the Solidarity movement throughout the 1980s," recalled Gonzalez. So much so that he met with General Wojciech Jaruzelski, the country's last Communist president, to discuss his fears that no institution in Poland could save its socialist system at the rate state control was unraveling. (When a billboard war broke out between Cuba and the U.S. in 2006, one of the messages displayed on the electronic banner above the U.S. Interests Section in Havana was a quote from former Polish president and founder of Solidarity, Lech Walesa: "Only in totalitarian societies do governments talk and talk at their people and never listen.")

But Fidel shared none of his brother's interest in reforms. As far as he was concerned, perestroika (reform) and glasnost (openness) had brought down the Soviet Union. "Fidel believes in his soul that if you lose control, you lose everything," said Amuchastegui. Still, with Cuba's economy crumbling like a stale cookie, Fidel ceded much of the country's financial woes to his brother. The Revolutionary Armed Forces (FAR) took over many of the day-to-day businesses in Cuba. Under Raúl, the FAR created and still runs the popular farmers' markets. Its cash cow, however, is tourism, which the FAR runs through its subsidiaries, GAESA and Gaviota, both of which are populated with Castro family members.

Raúl had long been impressed with what he has called "the Chinese model," as well as "the Vietnam solution." He traveled to China in November 1997 "to learn more about China's experience in economic construction," according to Amuchastegui, who said he himself left Cuba because of his disillusionment with *fidelismo,* but not with socialism. During his visit, Raúl "spent long hours talking to Zhu [Rongji], China's architect of economic reforms under Jiang Zemin." Raúl was so taken with the Chinese program that he invited Zhu's chief adviser to Cuba. In Havana, Zhu's guru enthralled a host of senior officials and Army officers over several days of meetings. In the end, however, Amuchastegui said the would-be reformers ran into a problem: "There was one person who refused to [sign on]: Fidel Castro."

The idea had been to support limited entrepreneurism and pro-market reforms while shoring up the monopolies of the Army. Renzoli witnessed more than one argument between the brothers over these issues. "There were knock-down, drag-out fights that had Raúl in tears," he told Gonzalez. The writer Norberto Fuentes, who defected in 1994, also got an eyeful: "Their arguments were a sight worth paying to see."

According to Gonzalez, Renzoli underscored that regardless of their many feuds and rifts, "Raúl was totally loyal to Fidel." Nor did Fidel ever doubt his brother's commitment to him. Renzoli also laid to rest the insistent viral rumor of Raúl's being gay. In the 1950s, the younger Castro was dubbed *"La China Roja"* by his enemies for having an effeminate, oriental cast to his features and for his long hair. Newspaper cartoons in Miami during the 1960s depicted Raúl as wearing lipstick and women's clothes. Renzoli dismissed the notion, asserting that his former boss was resolutely heterosexual.

Renzoli had also been stung by the national anxiety and shock over the Ochoa–de la Guardia affair of 1989, a scandal that rocked Cuban society. Eleven top officials of the Ministry of the Interior were tried and convicted of narcotics trafficking and corruption. There is little doubt that the drug charges had some merit (Colombian drug lord Pablo Escobar had been in Cuba in February 1989 seeking to buy surface-to-air missiles), but they were not the sole issue. Some in the *commentariat* felt that the more serious crime of General Arnaldo Ochoa, whom Renzoli greatly admired, had been to advocate for reform.

Domingo Amuchastegui disagrees. "I was not surprised at all. I was in Angola for two years with Ochoa. I adored Ochoa when I was in my twenties and would have given my life for him then. But they had lost everything they stood for. Ochoa and Tony [Antonio de la Guardia] were operating like rogues who believed they were untouchable."

After a Soviet-style televised mock trial, four top military men were executed, including the popular and recently decorated Ochoa, whose revolutionary credentials dated back to the Sierra, and the charismatic Antonio de la Guardia. Seven others were jailed for lengthy terms, including de la Guardia's twin brother, Patricio, and Castro's trusted right hand, General José Abrantes, who headed the Ministry of the Interior.

At the trial, Raúl Castro appeared on live television and gave an emotional speech that rambled on for three hours, unprecedented for him. Some believed he was drunk, others said he was exhausted, and a few said both were the case. All agreed that the entire affair had been a miserable and shattering experience for him. Thereafter, trial coverage was edited before being shown on Cuban television, and Raúl never again publicly addressed the subject.

In a bizarre twist, the children of the late American fugitive Robert Vesco maintained that it was their father "who dropped the dime" on Tony de la Guardia. Vesco had made the stunning transition from Wall Street high roller and financier to Richard Nixon in the 1960s, to economic adviser to Fidel Castro in the 1980s. Likewise, the daughter of de la Guardia charged that it was her father who had warned Castro about Vesco's unsavory dealings with drugs and money laundering.

In 2008, a former Cuban counterintelligence agent named Ernesto Borges Pérez (who was sentenced in 1998 to thirty years in jail for passing secrets to the U.S.) gave a prison interview to Radio Martí. Borges said that Vesco had been involved in the narcotics trade with Colombian kingpin Carlos Lehder—but on the orders of Fidel Castro. Between 1983 and 1984, Vesco had been dealing drugs from Nicaragua and later had laundered money for the Cuban government, Borges said. One former Vesco associate confirms that Vesco once rescued Lehder by boat at his Norman's Cay retreat in the Bahamas just as U.S. marshals and DEA agents arrived to arrest the drug smuggler.

In 1996 Castro abruptly ended his hospitality toward the fugitive tycoon, whose funds had been mostly depleted—much of it spent in rent to his hosts. Vesco was charged with seeking to defraud Cuba's biotechnology company, LABIOFAM, and was sentenced to thirteen years in prison. He served a good deal of it in a prison on the eastern end of the island.

Released in 2005, Vesco lived in vastly reduced circumstances while coping with miserable health. A lifetime chain-smoker, Vesco died of lung cancer on November 23, 2007, at the age of seventy-one, according to the *New York Times*. His Cuban mistress and later his wife, Lidia Alfonso Llaguer, videotaped his final days in the hospital. He was buried in a nameless plot in Havana's famous Colón Cemetery in El Vedado. In the end Vesco had become a Cuban morality fable—a swindler who was no longer needed by his hosts. Worse, he was a man who knew too much.

On March 12, 1998, sometime after midnight, a Russian-made Lada swerved out of control in the Miramar section of Havana, killing its driver. The man behind the wheel, and the sole occupant in the vehicle, was Manuel Piñeiro Losada. Better known as "Barba Roja" for his mangy carrot-red beard, Piñeiro had been Cuba's legendary spymaster for thirty-plus years and a Castro confidant going back to their days in the Sierra. Piñeiro had headed up the Ministry of the Interior and later the Party's Americas Department, the branch of Cuban intelligence charged with exporting and fomenting revolution.

Cubans have several predilections, not the least of which is a passion for conspiracy. Hence, notwithstanding perfectly coherent explanations for the crash—Piñeiro was a heavy drinker and a diabetic, not to mention a lousy driver—the rumor mill quickly concluded that Piñeiro's accident was, *claro*, no accident.

Taken to the grave with him, went the reasoning, were thirty-five years of secrets, plots, and intrigues; the inside track on the de la Guardia scandal; the Vesco mess; and the identities of Cuba's agents around the globe. Then Jorge Masetti, a former Barba Roja operative, fled into exile and wrote a memoir that offered tantalizing glimpses into Piñeiro's murky demimonde in the 1970s and '80s, created at the behest of Fidel Castro.

Masetti chronicled life in Cuban training camps and indoctrination programs for would-be guerrillas. Upon graduation, he globe-trotted through Angola, Peru, Mexico, Costa Rica, Argentina, the Congo, Colombia, and Chile, seeking to topple "imperialist regimes" while sowing the seeds for socialist paradises.

While in Managua, he met the dashing Cuban intelligence chief, Colonel Tony de la Guardia, who secured weapons for the Sandinistas and fought alongside them. Masetti fell in love with de la Guardia's winsomely pretty daughter, Ileana, leaving his wife and four children to marry her.

Masetti's enchantment with the Castros ended with the de la Guardias being tossed in jail with General Ochoa. Convinced that they would survive by cooperating with government prosecutors, the de la Guardia brothers had instructed their family not to seek outside attorneys or media to spotlight their plight. According to Masetti, "Fidel personally visited Tony in his cell for three hours and asked him not to name any of his superiors during the trial. Everything had to 'stay in the family.'" But to the shock of Cuban society, four officers were executed by firing squad and the others given long prison sentences. "It was a revolutionary version of *Alice in Wonderland*," Masetti wrote acidly. "First the verdict, then the trial."

Some maintain that Raúl Castro was the driving force behind the trial and the executions, eager to consolidate MININT's power under himself and the Army. But most scholars concur with Fidel's biographer, the late Tad Szulc, that the executions "would not have happened without [Fidel] Castro deciding it." Nevertheless, Raúl played the badcop role once again while Fidel the Wizard remained behind the curtain directing the trial and executions. Unlike Fidel, who betrayed no emotion, Raúl was visibly shaken for months by the calamitous drama.

Raúl Castro is not the apparatchik he was in 1959. Nor is he the orthodox Party hardliner he once was.

Over the last twenty years, Raúl has evolved from being his brother's enforcer into a socialist reformer of sorts. His transformation came not from instinct or virtue but rather out of a Darwinian imperative of survival—for Cuba and for himself. "In the 1980s, Fidel and Raúl would argue about perestroika and the country's economic problems," said Norberto Fuentes. "Raúl was, and remains, in favor of perestroika, and to an extent, he believes in glasnost."

More than anyone, Raúl Castro knows how close his government came to extinction—not by external threats but by sheer economic miscalculation, inefficiency, corruption, and dependency. A protracted economic crisis followed the loss of Cuba's Russian patron in 1990. Fidel euphemistically dubbed this time "the Special Period," to describe the precipitous drop in the standard of living after the Soviets stopped funding the island. It was a time in which Cubans grew visibly thin (a few were said literally to have eaten their dogs) and every neighborhood on the island was plagued by electrical blackouts, the dreaded *apagones,* in which entire cities would go dark.

In 1994, after four years without its annual Soviet subsidy, Cuba had just about run out of cash. Over the summer, forty thousand desperate Cubans fled to the U.S. in flimsy boats. At the height of the *balsero* crisis, on August 5, 1994, thousands of angry stone-throwing citizens descended on the Malecón, the seawall bordering Havana. Known as *El Maleconazo,* it was among the most significant protests on the island since 1959, and led to the largest exodus after the Mariel boat lift of 1980.

The protests had begun after Cuban authorities intervened in the hijacking of a ferryboat, preventing it from sailing on to the U.S. To quell the escalating crisis, Fidel Castro himself went down to the Malecón, arriving in his jeep. He assured the crowd that no citizens would be prevented from leaving if they so chose. In a testament to his charisma, coupled with fear of retaliation, the furious mob suddenly began chanting, "Viva, Fidel!"

At the same time, one European company waited nervously for Cuba to pay its long-overdue bill. The company, which supplied the island with a good deal of its oil, much of it on credit, was losing patience. "We decided there would be no more deliveries, unless they paid some of their back bills," recalled a senior executive, observing that the major oil companies like Exxon and Mobil already had bailed on Cuba and had terminated deliveries.

It wasn't long before the executive received a phone call from a senior Politburo official. "He begged us to deliver. We had a tanker with about seventy thousand gallons of oil sitting in Havana Harbor, but we told them there would be no more credit," the executive said. "He told me that Fidel was on the Malecón himself personally supervising the *balseros.* There was general panic throughout the country. We finally relented— realizing it was their last chance—and allowed our tanker to deliver."

The tanker docked in Matanzas to avoid the exodus of boats setting off from Havana. The executive then waited at a protocol house in Miramar, giving the Cubans till the weekend to make payment. "We told them, 'No check, no more deliveries,'" he said. By Sunday afternoon, no check had arrived. The executive packed his bags and notified his partners that payment had not been made and business with Cuba would have to be terminated. At four in the afternoon, a few minutes before the businessman was due to leave, he looked out and saw a government car pull up. Finance Minister Carlos Lage stepped out, hurried into the house, and personally delivered the check, rescuing the island from imminent darkness.

• • •

While 1994 was the nadir of Cuba's economic crisis, it was hardly the end of it. The country survived the worst, but it continues to struggle to pay its bills. And until economic dividends begin to trickle down to the kitchen table, Cuba will continue to hemorrhage young people, who have despaired of seeing promised reforms. At the same time, Cubans are having fewer children—Cuba's population is actually decreasing. More than half of Cuba's population of 11.5 million is under forty-five years of age, eight million of whom were born after the Revolution in 1959. And they are hungry for change and opportunities. While 51 percent of the country is mixed race or mulatto, the 11 percent who define themselves as black tend to have a lower standard of living. Once the Revolution's most reliable stalwarts, many blacks have joined the ranks of dissidents.

Men under the age of forty make up the majority of those who have fled Cuba, including an estimated eighty thousand Cubans who left the island for the U.S. between 2005 and 2008. (Estimates of those who have died in the crossing between 1959 and the mid-1990s range from sixteen thousand to seventy-seven thousand.) Fatalities still occur, but the numbers have decreased in the last decade, since human smuggling operations have grown more sophisticated, employing faster and better-built boats.

Some of Cuba's most famous and gifted youth have joined the exodus, including television personality Carlos Otero, who left with his entire family in 2007 during a trip to Canada and promptly signed a Miami television deal. Likewise, the popular musician Isaac Delgado fled north, as did the gifted pianist Alfredo Rodríguez, and the actress Susana Pérez, as well as scores of touring musicians, dancers, athletes, and artists. In March 2008, seven members of Cuba's soccer team defected after a meet in Tampa, followed two months later by a rising baseball star, nineteen-year-old Dayan Viciedo, who slipped into the U.S. via Mexico. Yurisel Laborde, an Olympic bronze medalist in judo, and a half dozen ballet dancers also defected.

In April 2008, reggae star Elvis Manuel and four fellow travelers drowned when their boat capsized in stormy weather halfway between Havana and Key West. The tragedy did not deter Yamil Jaled, the television star, who showed up in Miami in August 2008. Add to this the alarming number of Cuban doctors sent abroad as goodwill ambassadors but who never return home. The loss of so many of Cuba's best and brightest has created a brain drain that could impact the country for decades, perhaps a generation.

Even some of the privileged children of Raúl's innermost circle have fled. Division General Leonardo Andollo was made second in command of the general staff of the FAR in 2001 and is a trusted *socio* (pal) of Raúl. In 1994, the general's twenty-year-old son, Ernesto, a kickbox champion, joined the armada of young Cubans fleeing the country for better opportunities in Miami. It was a scandalous defection for the government and a searing embarrassment for the family. For several years, General Andollo refused to speak with his son.

In 1997, a rapprochement between father and son was negotiated with the approval of Raúl Castro. Ernesto visited the family in Havana and returned to Miami—his visa arranged by Raúl. Ernesto's sister, Deborah Andollo, a world champion depth diver, told me in 1998 that the image of Raúl as the humorless apparatchik was preposterous. "He's not like that at all," she said, and described him as a man partial to practical and cornball jokes. Her mother, sitting with us, nodded her head in agreement.

Nor is General Andollo alone among Raúl's men to have endured a family defection. Andollo's son was soon joined in Miami by none other than the namesake of Ramiro Valdés, Ramirito. Moreover, some of the Castro grandchildren have opted to live in South Florida, including the two sons of Agustina. For several years, Fidel declined to grant his youngest sister a visa to visit them, a source of bitterness for Juanita at the time. "My youngest sister wants to come and visit her two sons, who have been here five years," she told me in 2002. "And she's a woman who really loves her sons, worries about them. My sister has to wait for a special permit to be allowed to travel here." The visa was eventually granted, and Agustina spent six weeks in South Florida.

Other blue-chip defectors from the ruling elites include Annabelle Rodríguez, the daughter of the late Carlos Rafael Rodríguez, the Cuban Communist intellectual who was part of the Castro inner circle and government until his death in 1997. Rodríguez lives in Madrid, where she edits *Cuba Encuentro,* a lively journal of exile dissent. Her sister, Dania Rodríguez García-Buchaca, is married to General Julio Casas Regueiro, Raúl's right-hand man.

Indeed, one useful prism through which to view the Cuban Revolution is that of the divided family. High on the list of the Revolution's casualties is the Cuban family. From the Castro/Díaz-Balart clan to the relatives of Elián González or Luis Posada to the last rafter to have coasted ashored in Key West—all have experienced rancorous separation and loss. Puzzled observers of Cuban politics often ask why this conflict has been so inured to resolution. The answer, in part, lies in the sundered Cuban family.

Not everyone has a successful defection. In 1981, Carmen Vallejo, the daughter of the renowned medic-turned-revolutionary, René Vallejo, tried to defect during a trip to Finland for medical care. Vallejo arrived in Sweden by ferry but, to her horror, the socialist government of Olof Palme turned her back to the Cubans. Since then, she and her family have been unable to travel and are treated as pariahs. Her mother, once Fidel's secretary and translator, lost her job—as did Vallejo's husband. Among a host of indignities, their home was spray-painted with the word *gusanos,* meaning "worms," Cuban slang for counter-revolutionaries.

Likewise, "Juan Juan" Almeida, an outspoken attorney and son of famed *comandante* Juan Almeida, was incarcerated in Villa Marista, State Security's dreaded headquarters, for attempting to leave the country in 2006.

Dr. Hilda Molina, a renowned neurosurgeon, had a similar fate. Once she questioned the efficacy of Cuba's health-care system in the early 1990s, she became persona non grata.

Molina's son left for Argentina in 1994 but she was prohibited from joining him or even visiting her grandchildren. Despite a concerted international campaign on her behalf, the government denied her a visa, contending that Molina's training and talents were national patrimony. By publicly criticizing the state, she, Almeida, and Carmen Vallejo crossed the invisible line. And in Castro Cuba that is unforgivable. (In June 2009, Molina was granted a visa to visit her ailing ninety-year-old mother, a mercy credited to the lobbying of Argentina's President Kirchner.)

On the other hand, Ramón Castro's sons have spent considerable time in South Florida visiting other Castro relatives, who live there quietly. Relatives can come and go with one proviso: that they say or do nothing that could embarrass their family or country.

The same taboo has applied to any exile seeking to make visits to or to return to their homeland. Each year, a small but significant number of exiles return to live in Cuba—something one might call reverse *balseros.* Most return because their expectations were unrealistic or because they found life in the U.S. a daunting challenge. In Cuba, life is harshly constrained, but the bare basics of food, health, and education are assured. In the U.S. they have to work. Among the returnees have been two elderly aunts of the late exile leader Jorge Mas Canosa, who schemed for years to get them out. After a brief period in the U.S., the two aunts decided the hustle and bustle of Miami was not for them and returned to their seaside hometown in central Cuba.

• • •

The human traffic between Miami and Havana naturally prompts talk. Who is or is not a spy is a topic never far from any conversation on either side of the Florida Straits. From the raised eyebrows of *habaneros* to the bloviators on Calle Ocho radio stations, mistrust and suspicion have been the very perfume of the twin Cuban capitals.

In the spring of 2003, when the Cuban government rounded up and arrested seventy-five dissidents and writers, Cubaphiles were abuzz over the curious omission of one of the country's most famous dissidents, Elizardo Sánchez Santa Cruz. The reason was soon forthcoming: Cuban intelligence had cooked up a more delicious humiliation than prison. In August 2003, two writers allied with government intelligence published a slender book titled *El Camajan,* which literally translates as the name of a type of chameleon but usually refers to an opportunist or person who cannot be trusted. The book described Sánchez as an informant for state security.

Sánchez, then a fifty-nine-year-old self-described "socialist-democrat," who heads the Cuban Commission on Human Rights and National Reconciliation, seemed as shocked as everyone else. Denying the charge, he said, "You can believe the totalitarian regime or believe me." And there were reasons to believe him, not least of which was the many years he had spent behind bars in Cuba. Since his release in 1991, his home, phone, and contacts have been under constant surveillance.

When the incendiary charges of *El Camajan* met with skepticism, the Cuban government released more evidence of Sánchez's alleged collaboration with them: a 1998 videotape of a colonel in the Ministry of the Interior embracing Sánchez and pinning a medal on him. Sánchez conceded that he had fallen into a trap, perhaps owing to too many cocktails or poor judgment, and offered a possible explanation: he had been meeting with government officials to facilitate his human rights work.

Most reformers continued to work with Sánchez. Vladimiro Roca Antúnez is a well-known dissident and the son of Communist Party founder Blas Roca. He was released from prison as a condition of President Jimmy Carter's 2002 trip to Havana. "In the worst of cases, Elizardo was a government agent," reasoned Roca. "But in that case, he obviously didn't do the work the government wanted him [to]. Otherwise they wouldn't have done what they did." It's hardly an overwhelming vote of confidence, but amid the daily betrayals and intrigues that suffuse Havana and Miami society, there will always be doubt.

No matter what the facts may turn out to be, the book had precisely the impact the master schemers at the Ministry of the Interior had in mind. It sowed a deeper level of distrust and suspicion among dissidents—and ordinary Cubans. This is the corrosive legacy that will far outlast the failures and successes of Fidel and Raúl Castro.

The Revolution, once celebrated by a million exultant Cubans dancing in the street, has become, with each passing year, more of a somber reckoning than a celebration. In 2009, it had almost a funereal feeling, as heads of state arrived to visit the ailing Fidel, who was too ill to greet them. The streets were unusually dense with police, and harassment of suspected dissidents was frequent.

Cuba is hardly the first authoritarian state to dabble in the smoke-and-mirrors disinformation game—but its officials are masters. Unable to make dissent vanish, such regimes invariably seek to discredit their dissidents instead. The apartheid government of South Africa and the Stalinist elders of East Germany were peerless in this art. In fact, the Cuban intelligence apparatus is modeled on the Stasi, the nefarious East German security organ.

Spying and deception have a curious history in Cuba. Even before the reign of dictator Fulgencio Batista, informers were known as *chivatos,* or "stool pigeons," the term still used today. The Castro government fine-tuned the tradition with Committees for the Defense of the Revolution (CDRs), local watchdog groups that specialize in neighbors informing on neighbors. Typically the offenses involve petty infractions such as black market trading, and the accusations are often motivated by envy. Since the loss of Cuba's Soviet patron, the CDR system has lost some of its clout, as virtually every Cuban—CDR officials included—is doing something on the sly to survive.

Nevertheless, informing is pervasive in post-revolution Cuban society. During a trip to Havana in 1995, I visited a *santero* popular with the intelligentsia. *Santeros* are the priests of Santería, the widely practiced Afro-Cuban religion of the country, and like their Catholic counterparts in the confessional, they are expected to keep confidences. I mentioned my evening with the *santero* at a dinner in Miami a week later. "Oh yes, I know him very well," a newly arrived Cuban told me. Her mother, an official with the Ministry of the Interior, "debriefed" the *santero* every Friday.

Nevertheless, Fidel Castro has waxed indignant over the surveillance methods practiced by other governments, notably the U.S. In a column published in July 2008, he fulminated over the recent passage of the Foreign Intelligence Surveillance Act (FISA), which provided immunity to telecommunications companies that assisted Washington's wiretap program. "Something that offends people's sensitivities, in any social system, is disrespect for privacy," Castro wrote.

For his part, Castro sanctioned the surveillance of not only foreign officials, but of Cuba's own leaders and diplomats. Juan Manuel Reyes-Alonso, who defected from MININT in 2000, was a graduate of M8, which targeted government ministries with an eye on overly ambitious young cadres. Another surveillance organ, dubbed *Control Interno, Número Uno,* authorizes the audiotaping and videotaping of Cuba's top officials. It is an operation known to government officials, and is intended to instill self-censorship. Nevertheless, officials have been known to be careless—and have paid dearly.

Among Internal Control's biggest prey was the young, gregarious Foreign Minister Roberto Robaina, who was sent into "rehabilitation" in 1999, then banished from the government.

The specifics of Robaina's spectacular fall were not made public until May 2002, when a videotape was aired to eighty thousand of the Party faithful. In it, Raúl Castro said he had warned Robaina, "I am not going to allow people like you to muck up this revolution three months after we of the old guard disappear."

Robaina's crime was twofold: he had advised his Spanish counterpart, Foreign Minister Abel Matutes, on how best to bring up the touchy topic of human rights with Fidel Castro. His second sin was having appeared to be politically ambitious. On the videotape, Raúl Castro says he summoned Robaina to his office and read him the transcript of a telephone conversation Robaina had had with Matutes: "You looked like a star. You made a very good impression," Robaina said of his meeting with Fidel. Matutes responded: "The conversation I'm going to have with you will also be very good. You've always been my candidate." Those simple words would doom Robaina. "What the hell 'candidacy' are you talking about, Robaina?" Raúl demanded of the foreign minister, who had been handpicked by Fidel only five years earlier. "What the hell did you talk about with that man? . . . Who did you inform about that? Isn't that disloyalty? One talks to the enemy, Robaina, but one doesn't advise him."

Robaina knew what awaited him when Raúl reminded him of the sad final act of Carlos Aldana's career. In 1992, Aldana had been a Castro favorite, the head of the Communist Party's Department of Ideology and Department of International Relations. Invariably, Aldana was referred to as the third most powerful man in the government. "Aldana had ambitions to become Cuba's [Mikhail] Gorbachev," Raúl Castro reminded Robaina, citing the last Soviet president, whom the Castros blame for the demise of the USSR. "I knew that—and one day I told [Aldana] that if Cuba ever produced a Gorbachev, we would hang him from a *guácima* [tree]." Raúl continued, recounting for Robaina how Aldana had "turned pale. . . . Later I called him into my office and squeezed him. He fell apart. He wept and revealed everything." Robaina fared considerably better than Aldana, who endured a protracted period of *desgracia* and *Plan Pijama* before reportedly being allowed to teach school. Following detention in a military rehabilitation camp on the outskirts of Havana, Robaina was dispatched to clean up Almendares Park and other beautification projects. He would eventually turn to the number one sideline of Cubans post-prison: painting.

Dissidents, of course, are priority targets of government surveillance. Perhaps the most disquieting revelation of the quickie trials of the seventy-five dissidents conducted in May 2004 was the discovery that twelve of the most dedicated members of the ranks were, in fact, informers for state security. The writer Martha Beatriz Roque was sent to prison based on the account of her voluble assistant, whom she trusted even with her computer password. Other dissidents learned that the waiters who served them when they dined with visiting diplomats were MININT agents. Even their visits to the residence of the U.S. Interests Section's top diplomat were closely surveilled. "Today, I can tell the world that I'm really an agent, Agent Tania," announced a jubilant Ophelia Cojasso, who for years served as the president of a group known as the Opposition Human Rights Party.

Perhaps the most notorious double agent was Nestor Baguer, the beguiling president of Cuba's Independent Press Agency. A kindly looking octogenarian, partial to berets, Baguer was the scion of an aristocratic landowning family. He was also one of Cuba's most prized informers. As Agent Octavio, Baguer informed on his fellow journalists for forty years. In Helen Smith's documentary *La Verdad?* Baguer lamented that turning in his friends was "the hardest part" but that revolutionary duty came first. In any event, he added, about his prey, "They're not journalists, they're information terrorists." Baguer passed away in 2004 at the age of eighty-four, not long after he was awarded state honors for his decades of betrayal.

Some in Washington puzzled over why a canny strategist like Fidel Castro would blow the cover of a dozen agents, a significant loss to any security apparatus. Evidently, Castro could not resist crowing. Many of the informers had been welcome visitors at the office and residence of James Cason, the chief of the U.S. Interests Section. From 2002 to 2005, Cason enthusiastically encouraged dissident activity, at the behest of the Bush administration.

"There's a saying here that in Cuba, you can't have a conspiracy against the government," said Lucia Newman, CNN's Havana bureau chief in 2003, "because in order to conspire, you need at least two people. And once you have more than one, you don't know who to trust."

Vicki Huddleston, chief of the U.S. Interests Section in Havana from 1999 to 2002, recalled a visit to the home of Raúl Rivero, a champion of the Revolution turned dissident. "As I walked out of Rivero's house," recalled Huddleston, "I saw state agents removing their antenae from the top of their car parked outside his house." (Rivero was among those sentenced to twenty years for his writings in 2004 but won release after an international campaign to free him.) On another visit to a dissident in Camagüey, Huddleston was told upon her arrival that the family had already been visited by state security agents. In 2008, five years after they left Havana, her husband, Bob Huddleston, found a small microphone or tracking device in his overnight travel kit.

In May 2008, Cuban television broadcast a news "exclusive" based on an elaborately orchestrated sting operation. The fruits of the surveillance revealed that dissidents like Martha Beatriz Roque and Laura Pollan of Ladies in White had been receiving regular cash payments from exile groups in Miami. Roque was said to have received $1,500 a month, ferried to Cuba by none other than the chief of the U.S. Interests Section, Michael Parmly.

It was not the first time Castro had televised the trophies of Cuba's espionage prowess. In June of 1987, Major Florentino Aspillaga Lombard, a suave forty-year-old who headed up Cuban intelligence in Prague, left his office and rendezvoused with his teenage girlfriend. The two drove two hundred fifty miles—crossing the border into Austria and not stopping until they arrived at the American embassy in Vienna. Safely ensconced in the embassy's majestic Hapsburg-era building, Aspillaga told the marine on duty that he was defecting.

CIA station chief James Olson, who later became chief of counterintelligence at the Agency, remembered the day vividly. "It was a beautiful Sunday afternoon and I was home with my family," he said, when one of the embassy marines called and informed him of the walk-in, or defection. "Vienna was the walk-in capital of the world," said Olson, adding that "many walk-ins were low level and not especially important." Olson left his home to meet with the defector. "I saw a Latino-looking gentleman and a teenage girl, who I thought was his daughter, sitting in the reception area." An embassy marine handed him two Cuban passports.

His initial conversation with Aspillaga was inauspicious. As Olson did not speak Spanish, he tried to engage his nervous visitor in English, French, and German, without success. Aspillaga, however, spoke a little Russian and quickly communicated to Olson that he was a man of considerable importance who was growing impatient. "He motioned for me to come close to him and then whispered in my ear," said Olson. "He starts to rattle off a list of names of CIA case officers—covert agents. And that got my attention real fast."

Olson realized he was conversing with one of the master spooks of Cuba's intelligence organ known as the DGI, the acronym for the General Intelligence Directorate (Dirección General de Inteligencia). He promptly summoned a Spanish-speaking agent to the embassy and arranged for Aspillaga and his girlfriend to be given a nearby safe house.

Aspillaga was the polar opposite of Jesús Renzoli, who would defect five years later. Aspillaga had abandoned his wife and family in Vienna and was bereft of "any ideological element," according to Olson. "He was a 'let's cut a deal' kind of guy."

Indeed, Aspillaga cut himself a rich deal: he was paroled into the U.S. and fast-tracked to citizenship with a generous resettlement package of cash, education, and security, along with the usual defector resettlement plan. But it was worth every penny.

"As we got the results of the debriefings," said Olson, "it was shock therapy, the rudest wake-up call you could ever have." Over the next few months, Aspillaga told his CIA counterparts that "every Cuban agent recruited by the Agency over the past twenty years was a double—pretending to be loyal to the United States while working in secret for Havana," according to Tim Weiner's history of the CIA, *Legacy of Ashes*.

"It was devastating, to be quite honest about it," said Olson. "Fidel Castro controlled our entire program. We had been so desperate to have on-island sources that we had put up with low-level peddlers who were all double agents, who gave us almost nothing from 1960 to 1987. I'm ashamed of it." Weiner summed up the debacle: "The Agency came to realize—slowly and quite reluctantly—that their entire record against the Cuban service for decades had been unblemished by success."

There were several reasons for such a colossal failure. One was that the CIA's counter-intelligence office had been "decimated by Jim Angleton," said Olson, referring to the paranoid CIA chief who undermined its authority and credibility. "If we had recruited one solid DGI officer, we would have been on to them," said Olson. A second reason was that the Agency's Latin American desk often did its own counter-intelligence and was inclined to justify its own assets and not concede a problem.

The debacle was the genesis for the Agency creating the Asset Validation System (AVS) in the early 1990s, which screens all operatives. But it was too late for the Agency's Cuba Desk. Indeed, for almost fifty years, CIA intelligence on the island had been negligible. "We've really had nobody and nothing since then," said one former State Department official. "It's why the CIA has been wrong about just about everything."

The third problem, explained Olson, was Philip Agee, the renegade former CIA spy who freelanced for the DGI. "Aspillaga told us that Agee was on their payroll and had done very well by them." It was Agee who approached an inexperienced CIA officer in Mexico City and requested confidential files, claiming that he was asking on behalf of the inspector general of the CIA. "And he got some stuff," said Olson. "It tells you how good the DGI was in the late 1980s." Agee, who ran a Cuban travel agency and was partial to Panama hats, died in Havana in 2008.

Once the Cubans got wise to the fact that they had lost Aspillaga, they turned their loss into a propaganda victory party. Weeks later, they began broadcasting a seven-part television documentary that boasted of their cache. Featured in the series was footage of their surveillance of American agents picking up and leaving "dead drops"—secret but commonplace locations to pass on clandestine materials to their Cuban counterparts. "One of their agents sent a taunting letter to his U.S. handler in secret writing, saying he was a *doble* all along, and how much he loved the Revolution and all that," recalled Olson.

There was also a splashy exclusive in *Bohemia* magazine featuring interviews and photos with the supposed U.S. agents, who were in fact, double agents. Likewise, *Moncada*, the magazine of MININT, ran extensive coverage of Cuba's various conquests and dupes. Even the Museum of State Security on Fifth Avenue in Havana mounted a special display of the trophies and fruits of Cuba's masterful spy service.

"In the spy wars, they were winning one hundred to one," said Saul Landau, "up until Ana Belén Montes [the former senior analyst at the Defense Intelligence Agency, who had been spying for Cuba from 1985 to September 2001]." The U.S., of course, made a big deal about the Cuban Five—members of a network caught spying on exile groups in Miami and sentenced to long prison terms. However, retired State Department staffer Walter Kendall Myers, seventy-two, and his wife, Gwendolyn, seventy-one, arrested in June 2009 and charged with having spied for Cuba for thirty years, were regarded as quite serious. Like the Cuban Five and Belén, the affable, gregarious Myers worked pro bono, evidently motivated by political sympathy.

"The Cuban agents were very tough, dedicated, and disciplined," said Olson, who now teaches at Texas A&M University. "I list the DGI and Stasi as the best intelligence services I worked against. They were trained by the KGB, but it was a case of the students outshining the teacher. What the Cubans did was a masterpiece—one of the finest achievements in intelligence history. They duped us for more than twenty-five years."

The Castro brothers had a motive for periodically broadcasting the trophies of their spycraft. They had a message for both citizens and visitors: be careful what you say; we may have compromising data on you. One Cuban security official, Delfín Fernández, who defected in 1999, claims there is surveillance of foreign diplomats, businessmen, even visiting movie stars with sophisticated listening devices and hidden video cameras. Fernández said that he personally spied on Jack Nicholson, Leonardo DiCaprio and supermodels Naomi Campbell and Kate Moss.

Recruitment for Cuban state security is aggressive, as I learned firsthand. In 2000, I made one of numerous visits to the Cuban Interests Section in Washington. Such visits and supplications are de rigueur for reporters seeking press visas to cover Cuba. In short, it is a begging ritual, and American reporters have been known to promise all manner of things, short of singing the "Marseillaise" standing on their heads.

On this occasion the official I met with was an amiable, savvy man of middle age, whom I'll refer to as Benito. He met me in the lobby of the Interests Section, a formerly genteel mansion on 26th Street NW that has seen better days. But instead of leading me to his office upstairs, Benito asked me to follow him, taking me on a circuitous route, down one flight of steps, then out the back door to the rear yard, and over to the northern side of the grand home where the garbage cans were lined up. As I followed him, I remember looking up at the utility poles and wondering about the tangled morass of phone and cable wires above us. Suddenly he looked at me and asked, "Ana Luisa, would you like to come and work for us?"

A vague dizziness fell upon me. Perhaps I misunderstood him, I thought. Then I heard myself say, "Not in this lifetime." The words shot out of my mouth faster than I knew my brain could possibly work. The genial Cuban paused a moment, showed no reaction, then kept on walking, leading me back inside. I left the mansion feeling a general numbness. Since then, I've wondered how many others had been propositioned in that side yard. And how many nodded affirmatively.

I hasten to disclose that I once gave a talk on my book *Cuba Confidential* at the CIA. I had been invited to address its Cuba Desk and other Cuba policy officials in the National Security Agency, State Department, and the military as part of the Agency's hosted series with authors of foreign policy books. As I was leaving, one of the Cuba analysts told me that he "would be delighted" to speak with me whenever I visited Cuba. On that occasion, it made a certain sense, being the Central Intelligence Agency, after all. Of course, the U.S. Interests Section in Havana also doubles as the eyes and ears for the intelligence community. Until the election of Barack Obama, both sides derided each other's Interest Sections as nests of spies.

When the post–Fidel/Raúl Castro years arrive, Cuba will likely undergo a process similar to East Germany's, where the files on ordinary citizens collected by the Stasi leaked out like time-delayed explosions. "The way it worked was they get a little bit on everybody," said Jorge Tabio, who left Havana in 2000. "It might be something you've done wrong, and they put that in their files. Then when the person does something they don't like, they have something on them." At which point, they can be reeled back to do the State's bidding.

Some of MININT's files, like those of the Stasi, undoubtedly will contain malicious disinformation yielded from personal vendettas, revenge seekers, and petty grievance collectors.

All of which promises to make reconciliation among Cubans in the post-Castro era all the more challenging.

CHAPTER ELEVEN

Calle Ocho at Foggy Bottom

While the combatants on both sides of the Cuba war have been known to literally kill their opponents, the preferred method is political assassination. Although the Cubans excelled in this, their enemies in the U.S. were not slouches. The 2005 confirmation hearings of John R. Bolton to be U.S. ambassador to the United Nations were keenly illustrative of how such battles were waged.

In 2001 George W. Bush appointed Bolton as undersecretary for arms control and international security at the Department of State, also known as Foggy Bottom for its neighborhood and intrinsic bureaucracy. Bolton's appointment had been jiggered by Vice President Dick Cheney over the objection of Secretary of State Colin Powell and the foreign policy establishment. Cheney had his reasons. During the disputed 2000 recount in Florida, Bolton played an important supporting role for the Bush-Cheney ticket. Poll workers tabulating presidential ballots in South Florida said they remembered Bolton squaring off against them with a drop-dead one-liner: "I'm with the Bush-Cheney team, and I'm here to stop the count." Subsequently, Cheney told an audience at the American Enterprise Institute, a conservative think tank in Washington, that Bolton deserved "anything he wants" in the new administration.

Bolton, however, proved to be somewhat like his message on the nature of Cuba: risky and rogue. In March 2002, retired U.S. Army General Barry McCaffrey had twelve hours of meetings with Fidel and Raúl Castro, and came away convinced that Cuba was not a national security problem. "They represent zero threat to the United States," said McCaffrey, who had served as President Clinton's drug czar. "Indeed, I see good evidence of the opposite. I strongly believe that Cuba is an island of resistance to drug traffic and . . . I don't believe they are harboring terrorist organizations." McCaffrey's views were endorsed by retired Marine Corps General Charles Wilhelm, former commander in chief of the U.S. Southern Command, and Marine Corps General Jack Sheehan, former U.S. Atlantic Command commander in chief. The three generals, Vietnam veterans all, advocated changing U.S.-Cuba policy to engagement, focusing on military-to-military contacts and deeper cooperation on narcotics and counterterrorism.

Bolton was not pleased. In May 2002, he told the American Enterprise Institute that the administration believed that Cuba was developing deadly biological materials and exporting the technology to enemies of the U.S. Therefore, Cuba would be noted on the administration's "beyond the axis of evil" list, along with Syria, North Korea, and Libya. There was just one problem: no reliable supporting data. The CIA had determined that, unlike North Korea, Cuba did not pose a threat. (Interestingly, in 2008 the Bush administration dropped North Korea, despite its arsenal of nuclear weapons, from the State Department's terrorism list.)

According to Richard Clarke, appointed to the post of national coordinator for counterterrorism in 1998, a review conducted in the late 1990s concluded that the island country was not a danger to the U.S. Cuba was kept on the list of state sponsors of terrorism, he said, solely because of domestic political considerations.

However, Bolton's confirmation hearings revealed that those who had the temerity to challenge the seemingly confected new evidence discovered themselves in Bolton's crosshairs. Among them was Fulton Armstrong, the national intelligence officer for Latin America on the National Intelligence Council (NIC), which is housed at CIA's headquarters in Langley. The NIC represents the entire intelligence community, including the NSA, CIA, and DIA, as well as the State Department's Intelligence and Research Unit and all military intelligence. Armstrong's long career included serving as director for Inter-American Affairs at the National Security Council before assuming the top slot on Latin American intelligence. "Fulton was known for his deep analytic tradecraft— looking at the weaknesses and strengths of all evidence through a very rigorous process," noted one CIA official.

Armstrong's position was that Bolton was entitled to his own personal opinions, but that he could not state that they were consistent with the findings of the intelligence community. Indeed, the NIC had concluded the opposite: that Cuba's biological weapons research did not represent a threat to the United States.

In what appeared to be a breach of National Security Agency etiquette, Bolton insisted on seeing top-secret NSA summaries of raw transcripts of conversations of Latin American leaders with U.S. officials. Bolton's critics charged that he wanted to learn the identities of certain individuals, such as Armstrong, in order to embarrass them.

Also on the enemies list was State Department chief bioweapons analyst Christian Westermann, who tangled with Bolton about his research into alleged Cuba germ warfare. During the hearings, Westermann testified that after he sent the CIA an e-mail proposing corrections in Bolton's speech, he was "berated" by Bolton.

Unhappy with the Armstrong team's conclusions, Bolton and Otto Reich (another Bush appointment and a hardliner on Cuba) campaigned to have Armstrong removed from his post. Insinuations were made that Armstrong was "soft" on Cuba, even disloyal to U.S. interests. Secretary of State Colin Powell and CIA Deputy Director John McLaughlin, however, according to one CIA source, "went to the wall" to protect Armstrong and Westermann. Armstrong asked for and received an assignment overseas, and in 2008 he retired from the CIA.

Realizing Bolton would not be confirmed by Congress, George W. Bush arranged a recess appointment for him (as he had for Reich as well), thus circumventing congressional approval. When his one-year recess appointment expired in 2006, and Bolton was unable to secure the votes for confirmation, he resigned.

The case of military scholar Alberto Coll was equally telling. Coll had been a deputy assistant secretary of defense during the George H. W. Bush administration and a dean at the U.S. Naval War College. But in 2005, a slander campaign accusing him of espionage and a politically motivated criminal prosecution tarnished his career.

For most of his life, Coll had been a Republican conservative and an anti-Castro hardliner. When he was six years old, he watched as his father was taken from home to serve nine years in a Cuban prison for his opposition to Castro. At the age of twelve, the younger Coll fled Cuba in a propeller-engine plane. He would not see his family again for ten years. Although he did not know English upon his arrival, he went on to win a full scholarship to Princeton, earn a law degree at the University of Virginia, and teach at Georgetown University—before becoming a senior Pentagon official.

Handsome and articulate, Coll was a rising star in the defense establishment. In 1987, the late exile leader Jorge Mas Canosa sought to recruit him to serve as executive director of the Cuban American National Foundation in Washington.

But a decade later, Coll committed the unforgivable: he had slowly come to believe that the U.S. embargo of Cuba was a doomed policy. Once he made those views public, his enemies decided that marginalizing Coll would not suffice; he had to be destroyed. His adversaries were now long and deep in the Bush Cuba-policy team, according to Coll's friends, and were said to include Bolton and Reich; Dan Fisk, deputy assistant secretary of state for Western Hemisphere affairs; and Representative Lincoln Díaz-Balart.

The opportunity came in January 2004. Six months earlier, Coll's eighteen-year-old daughter, Celia, had been killed in a car accident, a loss that shattered Coll. Around the same time, his own father became terminally ill. One State Department colleague described Coll as appearing "almost catatonic." Another recalled Coll telling him that "the color has drained from my life."

Perhaps seeking consolation, Coll decided to visit Cuba, which he was legally allowed to do for either research or visits with relatives. He noted on his visa that he would be seeing an aunt, which he did. But he also had a romantic liaison with a girlfriend from his childhood and did not note the rendezvous on his visa. It was the kind of white lie of omission committed routinely by thousands of Cuban exiles after the Bush administration instituted onerous restrictions on travel.

The liaison was discovered, Coll believed, through secret wiretaps of him by the Justice Department, performed at the behest of the hardliners in the administration. "Who ordered the intelligence collection against Alberto Coll?" a senior CIA official asked rhetorically. "It wasn't ordered by the Agency [CIA]. It appears to have come from [the] administration." Inarguably, Coll had exercised poor judgment, considering that he held a national security clearance. His enemies insisted that a romance with any Cuban national had to be a recruitment ploy of Cuban intelligence. Coll's friends, however, pointed out that the childhood friend was a woman with a background in the arts, singularly uninterested in politics.

Unbeknownst to most Americans, Cuba-related investigations are allowable under the Patriot Act because Cuba remains on the list of state sponsors of terrorism. Hence the FBI could well have put Coll under surveillance. Calls to the Justice Department and State Department seeking a comment about the Coll case were not returned. However, the prosecuting attorney, Lee Vilker of the U.S. Attorney's Office in Rhode Island, where Coll lived and worked, pointed out that surveillance of Coll could also have been "theoretically" possible through the Foreign Intelligence Surveillance Act of 1977.

What is known is that throughout 2004, FBI agents interviewed many of Coll's friends and associates and subpoenaed a travel agency in Cambridge, Massachusetts, for all of his travel records. With legal bills surpassing $100,000 and the prospect of a protracted trial, Coll pleaded guilty to making a false statement on a federal form. He faced five years in prison and a $250,000 fine.

In the hope that Coll would receive the maximum penalties, his enemies launched a media campaign in Miami a week prior to his sentencing. On May 20, 2005, Carlos Saladrigas, an exile leader from a distinguished political family, received a call informing him that Coll had just been "arrested for being a spy for Cuba." Saladrigas learned that other prominent exile leaders, as well as reporters, had received the same phone call.

Although the story was entirely bogus, multiple versions of it soon showed up in the Miami media. TV America, a popular Spanish-language cable channel, ran three nights of programming devoted to the Coll story that suggested he was a spy. The vilification continued into the pages of *El Nuevo Herald*—with one "congressional source" opining that "this is something more than a trip to Cuba," then comparing Coll to the case of Ana Belén Montes, the Defense Intelligence Agency official found guilty of espionage in 2002. Coll told me that he was certain the source was Representative Lincoln Díaz-Balart, who had argued that there were other high-value agents at the level of Belén Montes. If someone such as Coll could turn against the U.S. embargo, the reasoning went, it surely meant he was a spy.

Jaime Suchlicki, the director of the Institute for Cuban and Cuban-American Studies (ICCAS) at the University of Miami, stepped forward to ratify the congressman's suspicions, adding that he would "not rule out that Coll was collaborating with the Cuban government." Suchlicki's views have rarely been at odds with Miami exile congressional representatives, who have secured millions of dollars in funding from the United States Agency for International Development (USAID). The ICCAS, in turn, has generally endorsed their policy of isolating Cuba.

El Nuevo Herald also published a commentary by Ernesto Betancourt, a former director of Radio Martí, that seemed to reprimand Coll's deceased daughter for her plans to spend a year studying at the University of Havana. Others said they had been tipped off about Coll by Frank Calzón, director of the Center for a Free Cuba, another major recipient of USAID monies. Calzón declined comment on the matter.

Coll's case was an interesting counterpoint to that of Jorge Castañeda, Mexico's former foreign minister and a well-known intellectual. In February 2008, Mexico's *El Universal* published an article in which the former head of Mexican intelligence charged that Castañeda had been a Cuban agent from 1979 to 1984. Castañeda, who had been a leftist in his early years, vehemently denied the charge, noting, accurately, that the intelligence chief had been charged with being part of an auto theft ring. The Castañeda story, however, barely made a ripple in the Miami firmament. The difference in treatment was due to the fact that Castañeda had been steadily migrating over to the center-right of the Cuba debate since the late 1990s, garnering anti-Castro bona fides with his criticism of the Cuban government. In his case, whether the charge was true or not was irrelevant.

Judge Ronald Lagueux was unimpressed by both the attacks against Coll and the state's case. In June 2005, Lagueux imposed the minimum penalties allowed by law: a $5,000 fine and one-year probation. From the bench, he cited Coll's "distinguished and stellar career" and stated his hope that Coll "will be able to pursue his career in various ways despite this conviction." Likewise, the Virginia bar refused to revoke Coll's law license, levying its minimum sanction of a one-year suspension.

Coll's enemies had hoped to prosecute him for something far more serious than a travel violation. But unable to find any evidence of espionage, they settled for a smear campaign. As petty as the charge was, the Coll affair served a more important purpose for them: an object lesson for others. If a former Defense Department official could be brought to his knees, working-class exiles in Hialeah, Florida, and Union City, New Jersey, who slipped into Cuba to visit families did not stand a chance.

"We recognized this was not the crime of the century, and that's why we recommended the lowest possible punishment," said Vilker, the U.S. attorney deputized to handle the case. "This is something we never do."

The sorry Coll affair was back in the news in August 2008, when Chris Simmons, a lieutenant colonel formerly employed by the Defense Intelligence Agency, showed up on Miami television. Simmons, who is closely allied with Roger Noriega, George W. Bush's assistant secretary of state for Western Hemisphere affairs, appeared on the Spanish-language television program *A Mano Limpia,* promising to "name names" of Cuban spies.

Simmons casually cited Cuba scholars Gillian Gunn and Marifeli Pérez-Stable without evidence or specific charges, and rehashed the allegations against Coll. While Simmons called himself a counter-intelligence Cuba expert, he was unable to speak Spanish on the program and required a voice-over translation. He was also flogging a book he hoped to write on the topic. Simmons even made a return visit to the show, offering up more names. The second time, the scholars

Lisandro Pérez and Julia Sweig and family reconciliation activist Silvia Wilhelm were added to Simmons's ever-expanding list of traitors. Wilhelm responded in December 2008 by filing a lawsuit for malicious defamation against Simmons.

Phillip Peters of the Lexington Institute, a libertarian research group, blasted Simmons as "a smear artist" on his blog "The Cuba Triangle" and pointed out the speciousness of his methodology. "Simmons noted that Coll has the same alma mater, the University of Virginia, as convicted spy Ana Belén Montes," wrote Peters, "which establishes a 'trend of certain universities that are associated with Cuban intelligence.' By my count, there are 20,356 students enrolled now at the University of Virginia. Better get busy, Colonel."

Simmons was a natural performer in the Miami echo chamber of casual slander, gossip, and off-the-record, unattributed items. He appeared to have been the source as well for a book called *Enemies* by *Washington Times* writer Bill Gertz, that referred to Coll as "an apparent spy."

Because he was now a felon, Coll lost his security clearance, which effectively sabotaged any future military career, barring a presidential pardon. Still unsatisfied, Coll's foes campaigned to cancel the documentaries on international affairs that he hosted on the History Channel, and pressured the Naval War College to dismiss him. (Fortunately for Coll, he was later offered a position at DePaul University College of Law as director of its European Legal Studies Program.)

The Cuba war had produced its Captain Dreyfus.

In June 2004, in preparation for the election season, the Bush administration announced a new get-tough policy on Cuba. Drafted by a team of seasoned hardliners and issued as an executive order, the policy ended most educational travel to Cuba, sliced remittances to relatives on the island to a paltry three hundred dollars every three months, and limited family visits for exiles to once every three years. Neither illness, death, nor funerals were grounds for an exception, and visits were allowed only to parents or children. Aunts, uncles, and cousins no longer qualified as "family."

In its pursuit of maximum isolation of Cuba, the administration halted most cultural and religious visas to the island as well. The restrictions imposed on the island were even harsher than those levied on regimes such as North Korea, Iran, Burma/Myanmar, or Sudan. Typical was the denial of visas for three Cuban scientists hoping to attend a U.S. conference on coral reefs in the summer of 2008. A spokeswoman for the State Department Bureau of Western Hemisphere Affairs explained to the *Miami Herald* that "under the Patriot Act, visa applications from Cuba, which is a state sponsor of terrorism, are subject to special screening procedures, and it will generally mean they take longer."

The policy grew out of a five-hundred-page report from the administration's Commission for Assistance to a Free Cuba that made the case for regime change in Cuba. Created in the fall of 2003, the commission sought to address several concerns. One was that support for the embargo and its torchbearers was flagging. Some of the report's authors hoped that the prewar interventionist policies implemented in Iraq might be replicated in Cuba—with perhaps the same outcome.

The Bush administration's hard line on Cuba posed a dizzying array of problems for policy makers at State. In 2008, days before Chinese tanks rolled into Tibet, killing scores of monks and civilians, the State Department dropped China from its human-rights violator list. Cuba, however, remained on the list. The turn of events brought to mind the 2004 assessment of Lawrence Wilkerson, formerly Colin Powell's chief of staff, that the U.S.'s relationship with Cuba was the "dumbest policy on the face of the earth. It's crazy."

There were several explanations for maintaining a counterproductive policy that spanned almost half a century. While genuine passion and ideology, along with human rights concerns, motivate most exiles, there was also an anti-Castro cottage industry that richly benefited from the protracted antagonism. The eight years of the Bush presidency were the golden goose for a cadre of ideologically hardline entrepreneurs and their organizations.

In 2008 alone, the U.S. Agency for International Development and the State Department doled out a whopping $45 million of taxpayer largesse to groups charged with fostering democracy in Cuba, such as the Center for a Free Cuba and the International Republican Institute. In March 2008, Felipe Sixto, a special assistant to President Bush, and the White House's chief liaison with exile leaders, resigned amid charges that he had embezzled nearly $600,000 of USAID grant money. The thievery took place while Sixto was chief of staff at the Center for a Free Cuba (CFC) and was employed at the White House. The matter, which involved a scam shortwave radio contract, was referred to the Justice Department by Frank Calzón, who headed the CFC. In December 2008, Sixto pled guilty to stealing from a federally funded program and repaid the money to the CFC.

The center was just one of several exile groups with peculiar accounting procedures. According to a report compiled by the Cuban American

National Foundation (CANF) in 2008, just 17 percent of the $65 million of USAID funds intended for "direct on-island assistance" between 1996 and 2006 made it to Cuba.

Instead, recipients of taxpayer-financed federal grants aimed at "democratizing" Cuba spent 83 percent on their own salaries, travel, administrative, and paperwork expenses, according to CANF, the largest exile group in the U.S. "Cuba's embattled opposition finds itself with little material support from the United States," the CANF report concluded, "as a result of the misdirection of tens of millions of dollars in U.S. funds."

After the Sixto scandal broke, USAID temporarily halted some of its 2008 funding for Cuba programs while it investigated the embezzlement at the Center for a Free Cuba and suspicious credit card spending at the Miami-based Grupo de Apoyo a la Democracia (Support Group for Democracy). But in a surreal twist, according to a 2008 Government Accountability Office (GAO) report, USAID renewed payments of the frozen funds to both before the inquiry was completed. The total haul for the Grupo de Apoyo between 2000 and 2008 came to $10.9 million, according to the GAO, while $7.2 million was doled out to the Center for a Free Cuba between 2005 and 2008.

USAID had, in fact, dropped $83 million on anti-Castro groups between 1996 and 2008, inspiring the Cuban government to call its beneficiaries "mercenaries of the empire." Another GAO report found that grantees spent unusual sums of money on items such as cashmere sweaters, Godiva chocolates, and other dubious luxuries for dissidents in Havana. Moreover, just 5 percent of the grants between 1995 and 2005 were awarded on the basis of standard-issue competitive bidding.

Matters were equally dismaying at Radio Martí and Television Martí. The International Broadcasting Bureau spends around $35 million in taxpayer funds annually on Radio and Television Martí, which transmit Spanish-language broadcasts to Cuba. Since 1983, a half billion dollars has been spent on the Martís.

In 2006, 2007, and 2008, the GAO found all manner of funny business at the Martís. Known in Miami as *"botellas"*—meaning literally "bottles," but slang for pork-barrel sinecures—the stations have long operated as gift baskets for Miami's political elite. For a period, the fathers of Miami's congressional representatives Ileana Ros-Lehtinen and Lincoln and Mario Díaz-Balart, who champion funding for the stations, had their own shows on Radio Martí.

Because the Cuban government jams both stations' transmissions, Congress approved $10 million in 2006 to buy TV Martí its own airplane from which to beam its signal. The Bush team also assigned a C-130 military plane to fly around Cuba beaming Radio and TV Martí at the cost of an additional $18 million. Nevertheless, listenership and viewership numbers have declined as the Martís' programming has become more shrill since their 1996 move from Washington to Miami. Evidently, Cubans are keen for uncensored news of the world and their country, but get all the screeds they need homegrown.

The 2007 GAO report found that the Martís had awarded more than $1 million in contracts to Miami's TV Azteca and Radio Mambí—the latter renowned for its deep bench of anti-Castro bloviators, to aid transmission, bypassing federal contract-bidding procedures. More dubiously, and perhaps in contravention of the Martí charter, the two stations were running Martís' programming locally.

Radio Martí's partiality for tirades prompted the Cuban dissident group Agenda for Transition to write the State Department in early 2009 requesting "urgent changes." Vladimiro Roca, the group's spokesman, complained that the programming had become increasingly Miami-centric to the point that listeners turned it off in sheer boredom. "[It] is so bad and so uninteresting to the Cuban people that no one listens," said Roca. "Eighty percent of the station's programming is about the local agenda in Miami." Roca's group suggested "returning the station's headquarters to Washington, which is where it should be and from where it never should have moved."

A GAO report issued in February 2009 went further—concluding that just 2 percent of Cubans listened to or watched Martí. It determined that the Martís were run with little transparency, and that the hiring of "talent" suggested favoritism—and hardly passed the smell test.

Representative William Delahunt, who requested the report, noted that in 2007 a TV Martí executive had been sentenced to twenty-seven months in prison for taking $100,000 in kickbacks. The GAO also pointed out that the director of the Office of Cuba Broadcasting had hired his nephew as the OCB's chief of staff. Assessing TV Martí's dismal viewership numbers, Delahunt described the broadcaster as "a TV station in search of an audience."

A similar pattern of waste, excess, and political agenda was found in the Office of Foreign Assets Control (OFAC), a division of the Treasury Department. The primary mandate of OFAC is to enforce sanctions against countries harboring terrorists. But a 2007 government report found that 61 percent of the office's investigations dating back to 2000 had been aimed at just one target: Cuba. Between 2000 and 2005,

OFAC penalties for violations of the Cuban embargo represented more than 70 percent of all penalties the office imposed. In the last year of the Clinton administration, there were 188 Cuba cases filed by OFAC. The Bush administration more than tripled that in its first year, meting out penalties to 788 parties.

In 2004, a congressional hearing revealed that tax dollars earmarked for the war on terrorism had been spent on tracking unauthorized travelers to Cuba. OFAC acknowledged at the hearing that it had just four employees searching for the funds of Osama bin Laden and Saddam Hussein, as opposed to more than twenty full-time investigators charged with hunting down suspected violators of the embargo. American taxpayers had also picked up the tab for OFAC's prosecution of a seventy-five-year-old grandmother from San Diego who took a bicycling trip to Cuba, an Indiana teacher who delivered Bibles, and the son of missionaries who traveled to the island to spread his parents' ashes at the site of the church they'd founded fifty years before.

Curiously, the informers of these "crimes" were often other exiles. In a uniquely Cuban permutation, some exiles seeking freedom in the U.S. have imported with them a culture of suspicion and denunciation. To a relative degree, a segment of hardline exiles succeeded in replicating a variant of Cuba's informer-denunciation system in Miami. The worst offenders have mimicked the CDR committees of Cuba by reporting neighbors or enemies to the police, FBI, OFAC, or U.S. Customs.

The restrictive Bush policies had been a triumph for Representatives Mario and Lincoln Díaz-Balart and Ileana Ros-Lehtinen. Lincoln Díaz-Balart suggested on Miami television in 2004 that the assassination of Castro might not be a bad idea. Ros-Lehtinen went further. In a 2006 British-produced documentary on Castro, she declared, "I welcome the opportunity of having anyone assassinate Fidel Castro and any leader who is oppressing the people." It was not the diplomatic language typically invoked by the ranking minority member of the House Committee on Foreign Affairs.

But politicians in South Florida often operate from a different rule book, one closer to the standards and political ethics of Latin America. A prime example was the fate of the North-South Center. The public policy center, led by Ambler H. Moss Jr., focused on Latin American and Caribbean affairs and was considered a jewel in the crown of the University of Miami. While the university has a long history of politicized academia—beginning with its hosting of the CIA's anti-Castro station JM/WAVE, the North-South Center was a small mecca for a politically diverse group of freethinkers.

The center included several professors who concluded in published papers that the U.S. embargo of Cuba was shortsighted and ineffective. One of its faculty members was Max Castro, who also wrote spirited columns in the *Miami Herald* in which he lampooned U.S.-Cuba policy. This did not sit well with the Díaz-Balarts, who in 2003 whirled into action. According to several UM faculty, the brothers saw no reason why federal funds should assist a center that was at odds with their policy goals on Cuba. Despite support for the center from Senator Bob Graham, a Democrat, the brothers reportedly decided simply to defund it. Asked why they would seek to dismantle an esteemed educational facility, Representative Mario Díaz-Balart was quoted as saying: "Three reasons: Max Castro. Max Castro. Max Castro."

The vendetta did not end there. The dean of UM Arts and Sciences, along with the faculty selection committee, then recommended Castro to another post in Latin American studies. Mysteriously, that teaching post was soon eliminated. Not long after, the *Miami Herald* terminated Castro's column. Further testament to the clout of the Díaz-Balarts was the naming of the building housing the law school at the University of Florida in honor of their father and grandfather Rafael Díaz-Balart, both ministers in the Batista government. A road off Le Jeune Boulevard in Coral Gables was also named for them.

While George W. Bush's ramped-up Cuba policy appeased the old guard in Miami known as *el exilio histórico,* it was derided by numerous U.S. allies. It also bombed with the dissidents in Cuba that it purported to assist. "This new package of measures once again shifts the center of attention toward a confrontation between the Cuban government and the United States," said Osvaldo Payá, who spearheaded the esteemed Varela Project, a grassroots organization that seeks electoral and economic reforms. "It's Cuba versus the United States, all over again. Those who led this [Cuba Commission report] looked into their own needs, rather than those of Cuba and the peaceful-opposition movement."

One of many people affected by the travel restrictions was Carlos Lazo, a Cuban-American combat veteran in the Army National Guard. Sgt. Lazo, who has two sons in Cuba, spent a year in Iraq as a combat medic, notably during the siege of Fallujah.

In June 2004, on his first R & R reprieve from Iraq, he flew to Miami in the hopes of visiting his teenaged sons. Even though Lazo arrived days before the new Bush restrictions went into effect, he was banned from taking the trip. He returned to Iraq for another assignment not knowing if he'd survive and see his sons again. Upon his return, he learned that he had to wait until 2006 to visit his children. "The administration that trusted me in battle in Iraq does not trust me to visit my children in Cuba," he said.

A frustrated Lazo flew to Washington to meet with congressional leaders on the Hill. He was particularly keen to meet with Cuban-American lawmakers, who he assumed would be sympathetic to his plight. But only Senator Mel Martinez of Florida and Representative Bob Menendez, the Democratic congressman from New Jersey, were willing to talk.

Representatives Lincoln and Mario Díaz-Balart refused to meet the sergeant and dispatched staffers to keep him at bay. Their colleague, Ileana Ros-Lehtinen, was equally hospitable. "I tried to talk to Ileana, but she didn't want to talk to me," Lazo told *Herald* columnist Jim DeFede.

By July 2008, U.S.-Cuba policy began to assume a definable madness when Representitive Lincoln Díaz-Balart learned about an upcoming trip to Havana of fourteen Little Leaguers from Vermont and New Hampshire. The preteen boys were looking forward to playing baseball with Cuban teens in Havana. Planning for the trip had been trying and arduous, according to their coach, Ted Levin, who said it took "twenty months and three rejections before OFAC approved the trip." At that point, Díaz-Balart demanded an emergency meeting with Bisa Williams, coordinator for the State Department's Office of Cuban Affairs, and Barbara Hammerle, deputy director of OFAC. The agenda was simple, wrote Díaz-Balart: "the very troubling granting of a Treasury/OFAC license to a Little League team to travel to Cuba in August."

But the intransigent congressman, used to having things his way as George W. Bush's tutor on Cuba policy, found himself facing off against a half dozen incensed legislators from New England. Vermont's lieutenant governor, Brian Dubie, and its two senators, Patrick Leahy and Bernard Sanders, strongly backed the trip, as did New Hampshire's senators, Judd Gregg and John Sununu, both Republicans. Leahy said he balked at "the idea of the government telling ordinary Americans, let alone Little Leaguers, where and when they can travel. If the president can go to China at taxpayers' expense, these kids ought to be able to go on a privately paid trip to Cuba to play some baseball." Díaz-Balart fired back in a statement that "a sporting event is not an appropriate way to respond to the ongoing torture of political prisoners," to which Leahy responded: "He should pick on somebody his own size."

By some miracle—or perhaps owing to the embarrassment of the Little Leaguers' plight appearing in Al Kamen's *Washington Post* column—OFAC did not rescind the licenses.

• • •

By mid-2008, Raúl Castro had unveiled a series of reforms—from loosening restrictions on private farms to greater access to the internet and tourism facilities. All told, Raúl's initiatives had garnered generally positive reviews within Cuba and from abroad. The Bush administration, however, greeted the 2008 reforms with its trademark disdain, calling them "minimal and insufficient." Even Cuba's new program for home ownership, arguably the cornerstone of capitalism, was dismissed as insignificant.

"They're cosmetic," sniffed Dan Fisk, the National Security Council's senior director for Western Hemisphere Affairs, who emphasized to reporters the über-tyranny of the Castros. Nevertheless, Fisk and his fellow Cuba hawks recognized that the ground was moving quickly beneath them, as America's allies rallied around Raúl Castro and his nascent reforms. "We would hope that the international community, and I say that in the large terms, recognize that this isn't real change; this isn't fundamental change in the nature of the system," said a dismayed Fisk.

In April 2008, a routine State Department briefing devolved into agitprop theater and then comedy. Pressed on the Bush administration's response to Raúl Castro, spokesman Sean McCormack sought to limit the conversation. Several reporters pressed him for more detail: "They have to become a full-on U.S.-style democracy all at once or you are not going to be happy?" asked one reporter. "Don't you get points for incremental changes?" shouted another journalist. The exchange went from lively to surreal—and offered a telescoped mini-forum of fifty years of U.S.-Cuba policy.

McCormack: . . . You don't get points for transitioning power from one dictator to another . . . well, we're just looking for something. And what we have thus far is nothing.

Question: So you don't think—you don't think reforms are possible?

McCormack: What does it amount to? . . . You have a situation now in which a handful of people who have been in place for the past several decades determine the direction of this country, what happens in the country, whether or not people can express their opinion freely in the town square, which they cannot. That situation qualitatively has not changed from, you know, today to ten years ago to twenty years ago.

Question: So are you talking about Cuba or China?

Question: Or Saudi Arabia?

At which point the briefing room broke into laughter. A palpably discomfited McCormack muttered, "Okay," exhorting his audience for a respite.

In May 2008, George W. Bush, whose approval rating had dropped to the lowest of any U.S. president since polling began, weighed in: "Cuba will not be a land of liberty so long as free expression is punished and free speech can take place only in hushed whispers and silent prayers." It was a fine sentiment, but one expressed for just one country: Cuba. Bush then took an unprecedented action, speaking directly by videoconference with dissidents, thus guaranteeing that the level of hostility between the two countries remained stratospherically high.

Bush's videoconference caller was Martha Beatriz Roque, arguably the most outspoken critic of the Castros, and as such a favorite of the administration. The dissident told National Public Radio that she had stayed up all night to prepare her remarks. But what she had to say did not please the White House. To its chagrin, she advised the president to lift restrictions on family travel and remittances to Cuba.

It was hardly the message that hardliners wanted to hear. Miami's political leadership had begun to fret that Raúl's incremental reforms in Cuba could, in fact, alter the status quo for all concerned, themselves included. To ensure that change would not come to pass, Florida's lawmakers scrambled to push through legislation that would cripple travel agencies and airlines that provide travel to Cuba. Signed into law by Governor Charlie Crist, the 2008 Sellers of Travel Act required travel agents to pay up to $275,000 to fund investigations of themselves for potential irregularities regarding flights to Cuba. If enacted, the stipulated fees would have put some airline charters out of business.

Representative David Rivera hailed the legislation as an "antiterrorism bill." A bewildered Maria Teresa Aral of ABC Charters told Agence France-Presse she saw it another way: "You are giving them money to investigate yourself?" A Florida judge, equally nonplussed, halted the legislation pending review and in April 2009 a federal judge struck the new law from the books. Eight months earlier, another federal judge overturned a second Rivera initiative that had forbidden academics working in Florida from using private funds to travel to Cuba.

Zealots had more success with another venture: banning a children's book entitled *A Visit to Cuba*, along with its Spanish-language edition, *Vamos a Cuba*, from Miami's elementary schools. The slim illustrated volume was part of a series aimed at introducing children to their counterparts around the world—including several countries run by authoritarian governments. All the books passed muster with the Miami-Dade

County School Board—with the exception of the one on Cuba. Noting that Cuba's children were shown in the book with smiles on their faces, as opposed to weeping over food shortages, the board voted to ban the volume. The issue soon landed in the courts at the cost of millions of dollars in legal fees. Never mind that the Miami school district was mired in debt and had to shutter classrooms and lay off teachers. *Por fin*—at last—hardliners had found a crusade, and they were taking it all the way to the Supreme Court, whatever the cost.

In the Sunshine State of Florida, electoral fraud long preceded the recount saga of 2000. In some counties it dated back to the first days of statehood in 1845. In the twenty-first century, the state sustains several political cultures. The Panhandle, Tallahassee, and Jacksonville have more in common with the South, notably Georgia and Alabama. The counties at the southern tip often borrow electoral and political traditions from Latin America. Hence, election funny business tends to differ in the two regions. In the southern counties, notably Miami-Dade, absentee ballot fraud is a perennial.

Governor Charlie Crist came to office in 2007 as an amiable Republican centrist promising reform of the state's election system. During the 2000 and 2004 elections, skittish touch-screen machines offered everything but a receipt. Crist promised to fix them, then had second thoughts. Crist's admirable early efforts went into slow motion once he set his sights on the GOP's vice presidential slot, then settled for being John McCain's campaigner in chief for the state.

Crist did ban the touch-screen machines, but in the same bill he also moved up the Florida primary. The latter caused plenty of mischief for the Democratic Party, culminating in a painful, expensive food fight between Hillary Clinton and Barack Obama.

Most contentious was the state's felon policy. Until 2007, felons who had served their sentences were banned for life from voting (barring a clemency hearing), even for such petty offenses as possession of marijuana or vandalism. In 2000, 600,000 former inmates were unable to vote, a figure that swelled to an astonishing one million by 2008, according to the American Civil Liberties Union (ACLU). Roughly 60 percent of Florida's ex-felons are African-Americans, 85 percent of whom were incarcerated for crimes related to personal drug use.

Quite a few of them found themselves on the felon "purge lists" created by former Florida secretary of state Katherine Harris and her equally nimble successor, Glenda Hood. However, many on the notorious lists had never committed a crime. To his credit, Crist changed the law to assist reinstatement of voting rights for most nonviolent offenses. But according to the ACLU, which sued the state on the issue, ex-inmates were never apprised of their status. As a result, some 96,000 eligible voters, likely in the Democratic column, were unable to vote in 2008.

Mindful of the peculiarities of the Floridian playing field, Democrats turned out a small army to do battle in November 2008. With an eye on the state's twenty-seven electoral votes, Barack Obama's campaign dispatched 350 paid staffers to the state; they, in turn, registered 700,000 more voters than Republicans. Eleven field offices were set up in Miami alone. "The Democrats are showing a Republican level of discipline this year, even staying on message," Miami columnist Jim DeFede said during the campaign. "They have money to burn and they are burning it."

Since the tenure of Governor Jeb Bush, it has been a tough slog for Democrats in Florida. In 2005, Bush's Republican-controlled legislature limited early voting hours to eight hours during the work week and eight hours on the weekend. In 2008, early voting began on October 20 and was unusually heavy, with many waiting on lines three to four hours. Despite pleas from election officials to extend voting hours, Governor Crist argued that that was outside his legal purview. Democrats countered that Jeb Bush had changed voting-hour schedules in 2002. One week before election day, Governor Crist changed his mind—perhaps after checking his own declining approval numbers. Polls were kept open—and busy—twelve hours daily with extra weekend hours. It would be the largest turnout in the state's history.

The trickiest piece in Florida's political puzzle was the Cuban vote, otherwise known as the Third Rail. There are roughly one million Hispanic registered voters in Florida, of which half are Cuban-Americans. Once a rock-solid GOP constituency, the Cuban exile vote still packs a punch, but there have been noteworthy shifts and defections since 2000.

While most exiles are decidedly anti-Castro, the bitterness of the first wave that left Cuba between 1959 and 1965 is not generally shared by younger and newer arrivals. More than half of the Cuban-Americans in the United States arrived after the 1980 Mariel boat-lift exodus. Of this group, 75 percent have family in Cuba. According to several polls conducted by Florida International University, the South Florida *Sun-Sentinel,* and by Bendixen & Associates, this group tends to view themselves primarily as economic, not political, refugees. For them, family comes first, then issues of personal liberty. High on their agenda was unfettered travel and the ability to send unrestricted funds to their families.

In 2004, the unpopularity of the Bush travel policy cost the Republican Party an estimated 17 to 20 percent of exiles who voted either Independent, Democratic, or not at all. Thereafter, Democratic and Independent registration in Dade and Broward counties swelled with first-time Hispanic voters. Damian Fernandez, provost of the State University of New York at Purchase, saw the shift in registration rolls as a yellow blinking light for Republicans in 2008. "I think the wise policy for anyone," Fernandez said, "is to be tough on the government but soft on the people. Let families travel, let people send their money, let people connect." Andrés Gómez of the University of Miami described the change among exiles as "the politics of passion giving way to the politics of reason."

In 2008, Miami's Republican congressional representatives faced serious challengers—a first. The weekly alternative paper the *Miami New Times* was so encouraged by polls on voting patterns that it gleefully (and falsely) headlined one feature story the "End of the Díaz-Balart Dynasty." In fairness, the Miami congressional races had tightened—with the Democratic challengers advocating the end of limits on travel and remittances for Cuban-Americans. The platform, of course, was sheer heresy to the Díaz-Balarts and Ileana Ros-Lehtinen. And as the Díaz-Balarts happen to be the former nephews of Fidel Castro and the sons and grandsons of well-known Cuban politicians, there is little sunlight within their ranks between the personal and the political.

As the congressional contests narrowed, the incumbents availed themselves of every weapon in their considerable arsenal. Because the political trio and their allies control many of the levers of power in Miami, their influence was felt in media markets, law enforcement, even the courts. They also could count on the beneficence of the National Republican Congressional Committee, which poured millions into the races, as did the U.S.-Cuba Democracy PAC, a lobbying group dedicated to preserving the embargo. Since 2004, the Cuba PAC has doled out about $2.5 million, the lion's share to Republicans. But other favored recipients include Florida's Democratic representatives Debbie Wasserman Schultz and Kendrick Meek, both of whom gave tepid and belated support to their fellow Democrats. Senate Majority Leader Harry Reid and Joe Lieberman also have done quite well with Cuba PAC money.

Some polls over the summer had Raul Martinez, the fifty-nine-year-old colorful former mayor of Hialeah, a working-class enclave north of Miami, in a squeaker race with Lincoln Díaz-Balart for the Twenty-first Congressional District. The burly, larger-than-life Martinez had reliably delivered the pork to constituents during his twenty-four years as Hialeah's mayor. Democrats were thrilled when Martinez won the surprise endorsement of the *Miami Herald*.

In the Twenty-fifth District, Lincoln's younger brother, Mario Díaz-Balart, forty-six, battled Joe Garcia, the forty-four-year-old chief of the Democratic Party in Miami and the former executive director of CANF. In 2002, as chair of Florida's House Redistricting Committee, Díaz-Balart had cherry-picked his own district, in what could only be described as one of the great gerrymandering triumphs in recent history. Then he ran for the seat and won. Six years later, the district had changed, with Republican voters moving out and non-Cuban Hispanic voters—who tend to vote Democratic—moving in. Still, Díaz-Balart was the incumbent, with a fulsome war chest and the attendant perks.

Joe Garcia's challenge was initially considered a long shot, but he proved to be a talented candidate—adroit in fund-raising and indefatigable on the campaign stump. He let it be known he was not going to allow his "Cuba cred" to be questioned. "I'm not going to be out-Cuban-ed," warned the sound bite–savvy Garcia, who had been mentored by the late Jorge Mas Canosa. While Martinez had the grassroots organization and name recognition, Garcia received the largesse of many exile businessmen, formerly faithful to Republicans, who fretted that Cuba would soon be big business.

Ileana Ros-Lehtinen was never in a horse race. She faced off against Annette Taddeo, a forty-year-old Colombian-American businesswoman. Taddeo was an attractive challenger, but a political neophyte. Ros-Lehtinen has represented the Eighteenth District since 1989, the longest tenure of the three, and has been the most effective in delivering constituent services. Nevertheless, Taddeo began the campaign with a 31 percent trail, and ended up with 42 percent of the vote.

Florida's exile politics are a blood sport, and anyone who makes it into the final gladiator rounds will not be wearing a halo. That said, the 2008 congressional contests stunned even seasoned Cubaphiles, who likened them to death matches. "The last time the Díaz-Balarts were removed from power, it took a revolution and we ended up with Fidel Castro," prophesied Joe Garcia a week before the election. "They will have to be crowbarred out of here."

Democrats would not forget that only ten years earlier, Miami's mayoral election had been overthrown for a host of irregularities. One such violation involved a certain Manuel Yip, who had "voted" for Republican Xavier Suárez. In fact, it was the fourth time Yip had "voted" since his own death. But most of the fraud that has dogged Florida has centered on absentee ballots. In the 1998 mayoral election, approximately five thousand absentee ballots were found to be fraudulent. Some folks were unaware they had voted, some did not live in the country, and (naturally, being Miami) some were dead. In addition, many of the ballots had the same witness. One Miami vegetable peddler had witnessed more than seventy absentee ballots. And some of the city's poorest had been paid ten dollars to vote for Suárez.

Not unreasonably, Democrats were wary that Republicans might reprise some moves from the old playbook. They were not entirely disappointed. In late October, not long after absentee ballots arrived in the mail, a gentleman calling himself "Juan" arrived at the Hialeah homes of several supporters of Raul Martinez. "Juan" offered the voters assistance in filling out their ballots, then promised to deliver the ballots to the elections office. "Juan" had been dispatched by callers claiming to work for Martinez. In fact, neither "Juan" nor his dispatchers worked for Martinez or the Democratic Party; and no one knew what happened to the ballots.

The *Miami Herald* traced the phone number given to the duped residents. The number turned out to be that of a consultant who worked for Lincoln Díaz-Balart but who misidentified himself several times, in just one phone conversation, as working for Díaz-Balart's Democratic rival. Three voters told the *Herald* that their initial contact came from a female caller whose phone number belonged to Sasha Tirador, who supervised a phone-bank operation for David Custin, a political consultant retained by the Díaz-Balart brothers.

One misled voter summoned Jeff Garcia, the campaign manager for Raul Martinez, who was able to videotape "Juan" along with his car and license plate. Another mysterious visitor named "Angel," purporting to be from Miami-Dade's election supervisor's office, was also videotaped. Cornered by a Raul Martinez volunteer, "Angel" said he was employed by the Díaz-Balart office. A quick-thinking Jeff Garcia then delivered affidavits from the duped voters to the State Attorney's Office and reminded reporters that misrepresentations by telephone are violations of federal law.

Cesar Gonzalez, Lincoln Díaz-Balart's spokesman, told me that the fraud allegation was "a ludicrous charge coming from a desperate campaign." The Martinez camp thought otherwise and consulted with high-powered Miami lawyer Michael Band, formerly of the State Attorney's Office. Martinez's people also made sure the "Juan" story appeared on the local television news. Those wise in the ways of Miami, however, were not holding their breath. Miami-Dade State Attorney Kathy Fernandez Rundle has never been known to be proactive in investigating cases that might incur the ire of Miami's political or business elites.

There were other factors that augured poorly for the Democratic challengers. For all intents and purposes, they were denied any meaningful debates with their opponents and were shut out of several media markets, notably a few crucially important radio stations. Meanwhile, most Americans remained clueless that the fight for Florida was being waged in a parallel universe, a good deal of it via Spanish-language media.

Radio Mambí, which claims to be the number-one Spanish-language radio market in South Florida, did not allow Democrats to appear or advertise on its shows, according to party staffers and candidates. One Obama campaign official, requesting anonymity, described Radio Mambí as an attack machine against the candidates, operating as "a 24/7 McCain–Díaz-Balart infomercial." Univision's influential television station, he said, also had a "decided Republican bias."

Radio Mambí is run by the Calle Ocho kingmaker Armando Pérez Roura, formerly a champion of Fulgencio Batista until his rout in 1959. Pérez Roura went on to enjoy a long radio career under Fidel Castro, not leaving Cuba until 1968. Once in Miami, he reinvented himself again as a man with a microphone and a mission to identify those insufficiently anti-Castro. Anyone who aspired to power in Miami regarded his show as a necessary pit stop. Such power appears to have rewards. When Pérez Roura's son was arrested for selling large quantities of narcotics in 2004, as he had been in 1984, charges against him were mysteriously reduced, then dismissed by State Attorney Fernandez Rundle, who is a frequent guest on Pérez Roura's show.

Over the years, Pérez Roura has maintained a hospitable welcome to some of the most notorious characters in the exile firmament. Disgraced politicians—even convicted terrorists—are regularly heard on Mambí, which bills itself as La Grande. During the campaign, Pérez Roura interviewed John McCain and offered unlimited air time to the Díaz-Balarts and Ileana Ros-Lehtinen. Other guests on his show derided the Democratic challengers, suggesting that their election would amount to a Red Plague, soft on Communists and Islamic terrorists. Almost daily, Pérez Roura referred to the Democratic presidential candidate as "Barack Hoooo-sein Obama"—delectably drawing out the syllables of his middle name.

Pérez Roura was complemented by the virtuoso gifts of media personality Ninoska Pérez-Castellón, who cohosts a morning show with him, goes solo in the afternoon, and offers another on Miami television. "That's three shows daily she has to campaign against me," fumed Martinez during the campaign. "She is a full-time Raul Martinez basher and she will say anything to help the Díaz-Balarts." His fellow Democrat Joe Garcia was piqued that the Federal Communications Commission had not looked into the matter. "Ninoska attacks me twenty-four hours a day, every single day," said Garcia, "and I have complained to Univision [Mambí's parent company]."

At the other end of the radio dial, two maverick pro-dialogue exile radio hosts, Max Lesnik and Francisco Aruca, learned that their shows had been canceled by their stations. The left-leaning hosts were told they were being replaced by sports coverage. Both men, who relish taunting Miami's leadership, claimed it was political pressure, not ratings, that led to their dismissals.

But the coup de grâce in the election season was delivered via television. One Díaz-Balart commercial began with a mug shot of Raul Martinez and the word "GUILTY" running across the screen. What the commercial did not tell viewers was that Martinez's conviction had been reversed on appeal. Nor did viewers learn that the 1990 extortion charges against him had been leveled by an acting U.S. attorney named Dexter Lehtinen. Lehtinen happened to be the husband of Ileana Ros-Lehtinen, who stepped in and took the congressional seat that Martinez was thought to have locked up.

Raul Martinez responded in kind with his own attack ads. One charged Díaz-Balart with accepting money from an indicted Puerto Rican politician, and with employing "a pay to play scheme," charges denied by Díaz-Balart. Mario Díaz-Balart's ads sought improbably to tie Joe Garcia to the collapse of Enron. "You can still do the Big Lie in Miami," said Garcia. "And get away with it. This is a town where the basic institutions have collapsed." Mario Díaz-Balart did not return calls seeking a response.

Joe Garcia responded by zeroing in on the Achilles' heel of the Díaz-Balarts: Fidel Castro. His most memorable ad began with circus calliope music and a red-lettered "WARNING" on-screen that "Any similarities between the following characters is . . . a family thing." The next image was Fidel Castro gesticulating wildly, with red-lettered text below him reading "Cuban dictator Fidel Castro." Next came Mario Díaz-Balart making virtually the same gestures with the text below him reading "U.S. Rep. Mario Díaz-Balart." The third visual was the scowling face of Mario's brother Lincoln Díaz-Balart. The images repeated: Fidel, Mario, Lincoln. Then the message appeared on screen: "This November . . . let's end the family circus. Vote against Fidel's nephews."

It was a clever commercial that entertained and edified viewers—but did not quite do the trick. Garcia lost to Mario Díaz-Balart 53 to 47 percent. The attacks on Raul Martinez were far more deadly, reducing his once-held lead to a loss of 58 to 42 percent.

In the overcaffeinated precincts of Miami-Dade, conspiracy perfumed the air through the summer and right up through election night. More than one Obama staffer told me that Republican operatives were directing phone banks to urge folks to call in to the powerful Spanish-language talk shows and accuse Obama of being a *comunista* or a *marxista.*

One popular topic on Miami talk radio was Obama's background as a "community organizer," which was likened to running a CDR, a neighborhood watch group in Cuba renowned for their snitching. Joe Centorino of the State Attorney's Office told me he was not surprised to hear of such doings in Dade. "But what's the crime here?" he responded. "Remember that not all dirty tricks are illegal."

Obama knew he faced a steep climb in Cuban Miami for several reasons. First was his stated willingness to negotiate with Cuba, with just a few preconditions. Second, he was a Democrat in Republican territory. Third was his skin color, usually indicated by tapping two fingers against one's forearm. Some referred to him as *"el negro,"* others alluded to the *"nube negra"* (the black cloud). There was much teeth gnashing among Democrats about race innuendo, but pollster Sergio Bendixen predicted that racism was not as strong an element in *la comunidad* as it was reputed to be.

John McCain promised that if elected he would continue the Bush policy of isolating Cuba. The Arizona senator had morphed into an anti-Castro hardliner quite suddenly. In 2000, he had said he would support normalizing relations with Cuba, even with the Castros still in power. "I'd be willing to do the same thing we did with Vietnam," said McCain.

In keeping with his new philosophy, McCain selected a team of Cuban-American hardliners to advise him on Latin America including Adolfo Franco, formerly assistant administrator of the troubled U.S. Agency for International Development, and Otto Reich. In August 2008, Lincoln Díaz-Balart was tapped to be both McCain's tutor on the region and his spokesman.

McCain's campaign correctly assumed it would carry a majority of *el exilio histórico,* constituting about three hundred thousand older, whiter exiles, by offering a recitation of various anti-Castro mantras. Still, he carried the burden of a poll-dead president, whose party was destined to be routed in the Senate and the House. Moreover, even exile hardliners tend to be social progressives, supporting bilingual education, expanded Social Security and Medicare spending, and fewer immigration controls. McCain's vice presidential choice of Sarah Palin, a Christian-right conservative who favors teaching abstinence and creationism, was a poor fit for most Cubans. To boot, the Iraq War, championed by McCain-Palin, was as unpopular on Calle Ocho as it was in Times Square.

To bolster its bid, the McCain camp made much of Barack Obama's former relationship with Bill Ayers, the Weather Underground bomber turned university professor invariably described as an "unrepentant terrorist." Obama had met Ayers some twenty-five years after Ayers was charged, but not convicted, for his Weatherman activities. As the election spiraled into its final weeks, the Obama-Ayers connection became the centerpiece of the McCain-Palin campaign. Sarah Palin mentioned Ayers at virtually every appearance, and McCain brought up Ayers in the last presidential debate.

As it turned out, McCain had his own "terrorist friend" problem. During Palin's Florida campaign tour, in which she steadily invoked Obama's "terrorist friend," she conspicuously skipped over Miami. Local cynics said it was not by accident that Palin failed to appear in the state's most populous city, where the definition of *terrorism* can be quite elastic.

In late July, while campaigning for McCain in Miami, Senator Joe Lieberman met with the wife of convicted bomber-assassin Eduardo Arocena and vowed to pursue a presidential pardon on his behalf. Arocena is the founder of the Cuban exile paramilitary Omega 7, renowned for a string of bombings and murders from 1975 to 1983. Arocena was convicted of forty-two counts pertaining to conspiracy, explosives, firearms, and destruction of foreign government property within the United States. He is serving a mandatory life sentence in federal prison in Indiana.

Among Arocena's targets were New York's Madison Square Garden and John F. Kennedy International Airport, where Omega 7 planted a suitcase bomb intended for a TWA flight to Los Angeles—in protest of the airline's flights to Cuba. The plane would have exploded if not for the fact that the bomb went off on the tarmac prior to being loaded. Other targets included New York City's Avery Fisher Hall, where bombs shattered three floors of windows; the ticket office of Aeroflot, the Soviet airline; and the Cuban Mission to the United Nations. There was an attempted assassination of Cuba's ambassador to the UN, Raúl Roa García. Arocena was also convicted of the murder of a Cuban diplomat in New York and the 1979 killing of Eulalio José Negrín, who had advocated diplomacy with Cuba. Negrín was machine-gunned down as he stepped into his car in Union City, New Jersey, in front of his thirteen-year-old son.

Nevertheless Lieberman, who at the time was said to be McCain's choice for vice president, and later, for his secretary of state, was caught on tape (viewable on YouTube) promising Miriam Arocena he would seek a pardon for her husband. "It's my responsibility, it's my responsibility. I will carry it [the pardon request] back. I will carry it back," Lieberman told Arocena just before addressing a group at a McCain event. "I think of you like you were my family. . . . I'll do my best."

Another vocal champion of an Arocena pardon was Roberto Martín Pérez, who campaigned with McCain and made a radio commercial for the candidate. He and his wife, radio host Ninoska Pérez-Castellón, an executive director of the Cuban Liberty Council, were among McCain's most dedicated supporters. Pérez-Castellón was quick to point out that the council did "not endorse candidates," because of its nonprofit status, but that directors and members were free to campaign in their personal capacities. It was a distinction that eluded Raul Martinez, Joe Garcia, and Annette Taddeo.

On May 23, 2008, Barack Obama delivered a speech to the Cuban American National Foundation at the Jackie Gleason Theater in Miami Beach. "John McCain's been going around the country talking about how much I want to meet with Raúl Castro, as if I'm looking for a social gathering," Obama told the crowd. "That's never what I've said, and John McCain knows it. After eight years of the disastrous policies of George Bush, it is time to pursue direct diplomacy, with friend and foe alike, without preconditions." Inside the hall, the event was sold out. Outside, to the surprise of many, there were neither protests nor riots. History had been made. "The watershed event here," said Damian Fernandez, provost of Purchase College, "is the open discourse on Cuban politics for the first time ever in Miami."

The presidential outcome, of course, was the ultimate watershed. Barack Obama carried Florida in part by capturing 38 percent of the Cuban-American vote, surpassing the gold standard set in 1992 by Bill Clinton, who garnered 30 percent of the exile vote. Obama even snared about 10 percent of Republican voters. Pollsters for both campaigns were especially impressed that Obama won about half of the Cuban-American vote under the age of forty-four. "That's the first sign of a shift in the Cuban-American electorate that I've seen," said Dario Moreno, who polled for Republican candidates.

"I will immediately allow unlimited family travel and remittances to the island," Barack Obama promised on the campaign stump. To that end, he assembled a policy team made up of seasoned veterans of the Cuba wars that favored initiating engagement with Havana.

"Change," as Obama vowed, was indeed finally coming to Miami.

CHAPTER TWELVE

The Graveyard Shift

In October 2008, Raúl Castro granted his first interview as president of Cuba—and one of the very few he has ever given. The lucky recipient was not one of the dozen or so accredited reporters based in Havana. Nor was it a journalist who has covered the Miami/Havana beat, nor one of the hundreds of representatives from media organizations and academia who have filed requests with the Foreign Ministry. Rather, Raúl Castro's first interlocutor was the actor/director Sean Penn, who periodically weighs in on politics.

Penn had just winged in on a Venezuelan military jet from Isla Margarita, the picturesque island near Caracas, after spending two days with a convivial Hugo Chávez. With Penn were writer Christopher Hitchens and historian Douglas Brinkley, whom the film star had invited to accompany him, presumably to lend gravitas to his efforts. The three hoped to reprise their luck with Raúl Castro and, according to Penn, seemed to have been promised as much.

But the gods, in the form of Fidel, who orchestrated the event, chose only the movie star. Penn had met the *Comandante* in 2005, and the two quickly took a shine to each other. Moreover, Penn became fast friends with Chávez—of whom he was wont to say, "Chávez may not be a good man, but he may well be a great one." Penn was now "eager for an interview with [Raúl] the new president," according to his account of the trip published in *The Nation*.

Typically journalists, myself included, who have secured interviews with Fidel wait months or years or more. That was not the case for Penn, however, who said he made a phone call, and the very next day had his request granted. The Castros had not miscalculated: Penn proved to be as accommodating and charitable as Oliver Stone in his sunny documentaries of Fidel.

Raúl Castro was a gracious and amiable host, but he made clear, through his translator, that the interview was not his idea. "'Fidel called me moments ago," he told Penn. "He wants me to call him after we have spoken. He wants to know everything we speak about. I never liked the idea of giving interviews. One says many things, but when they are published, they become shortened, condensed. The ideas lose their meaning.'"

As it turned out, Raúl thoroughly enjoyed himself and passed seven hours chatting with his guest. He joked that he could now rival his brother in garrulousness. "You are probably thinking, 'Oh, the brother talks as much as Fidel!' It's not usually so."

Raúl also passed on one anecdote that his brother no doubt would have preferred remain unsaid. "You know, Fidel once had a delegation here, in this room, from China: several diplomats and a young translator. I think it was the translator's first time with a head of state. They'd all had a very long flight and were jet-lagged. Fidel of course knew this, but still he talked for hours. Soon, one [sitting] near the end of the table, just there, his eyes begin to get heavy. Then another, then another. But Fidel continued to talk. Soon all of them, including the highest-ranking of them, to whom Fidel had been directly addressing his words, fell sound asleep in their chairs. So Fidel turns his eyes to the only one awake, the young translator, and kept him in conversation till dawn."

Raúl revealed one substantive point to the film star: that he was open to meeting with president-elect Barack Obama in "a neutral place"—outside the U.S. or Cuba. Raúl warned that Obama would have to dodge assassination attempts on his march to the White House, but should he arrive in the Oval Office, Raúl was amenable to discussions. "Perhaps we could meet at Guantánamo," he quipped, interjecting his trademark irreverent humor. "And at the end of the meeting, we could give the president a gift . . . the American flag that flies over Guantánamo Bay."

Raúl's evolution from Marxist-Leninist to wary pragmatist owed its origins to the collapse of Soviet communism. But two years into his tenure, matters became complicated by what Fidel Castro described as the collapse of capitalism—as global markets sputtered erratically from Washington to Beijing to Moscow. At home, Raúl confronted the detritus of nearly a half century of economic failure in Cuba.

Another urgent problem was crime. Since the Special Period, the euphemism employed to describe the time of acute hardships endured in the wake of the Russian pullout in 1990, desperate Cubans have become accustomed to stealing what they need or, in some cases, simply want. Since 2000, there has even been a spike in violent crime—all the more alarming for a country long regarded as one of the safest. In February 2009, a fifty-nine-year-old Spanish priest, beloved for his work with prisoners and the indigent, was found stabbed to death. Five months later, another priest, age seventy-four, was found murdered. Residents in Havana have reported burglaries in which all contents were stolen, along with building materials such as plumbing ripped out of walls.

To many Cubans, the Special Period is in its twentieth year. True, the island's tourist economy scored its peak performance in 2008, up by 13.5 percent with 2.4 million visitors, generating about $3 billion in revenue. Benefits, however, have not been felt in a meaningful way by most Cubans.

Beginning in late 2007, something rare and brave occurred in Cuba: ordinary citizens took the law into their own hands in a rapid-fire series of protests. Following the reported rape of three women, students at the University of Oriente in Santiago staged a sit-in in September 2007. According to one professor, the school's dean was detained by the students. There had been previous demonstrations to protest crime on campus, as well as a petition that some five thousand students signed. Other complaints targeted the lack of quality food, paper, books, and computers in classes, and the plethora of substandard housing.

But mindful that it was student protests like these that led to the 1959 Cuban Revolution, the government resisted the impulse to put down the demonstrations militarily. Instead, it sent representatives to meet with the students and acquiesced to several of their demands, notably security on campus and the dismissal of the dean.

However, when students in Cienfuegos soon after organized a protest rally seeking greater civil liberties, they did not receive the kid-glove treatment of their counterparts. Five student protestors were arrested, as were other student dissidents throughout the island. Orlando Gutiérrez, who heads the Miami-based Directorio Democrático Cubano (Cuban Democratic Directorate) that monitors dissident groups inside Cuba, reported that eight of the student leaders in Santiago were later quietly expelled from the university.

"The government is afraid of the students," said one former Cuban diplomat who lives in Havana. "And it worries them that it happened in Santiago, in Oriente [the birthplace of many rebellions], of all places. They are worried about the students and also about reform factions in the FAR, including those who have been kicked out or 'retired out' of the Army."

In January 2008, National Assembly chief Ricardo Alarcón was confronted by students at an elite computer school. A widely circulated, secretly recorded videotape showed a defensive, unprepared Alarcón being peppered with complaints about Cuba's one-party elections, the lack of work opportunities, and the inability to travel outside of Cuba. Students complained that many basic goods—including toiletries and clothes—are sold in convertible currency meant for tourists and foreigners, making some necessities inaccessible to state employees, who are paid in Cuban pesos, which are worth much less.

The students were also angry about laws prohibiting them from entering state-run hotels, limiting internet access and foreign travel. "Why can't the people of Cuba go to hotels or travel to other parts of the world?" Eliécer Ávila, a teenage student, asked. Alarcón ducked questions about the internet and called travel "a privilege," not a right. When he was their age, before the Revolution, he said, he wasn't able to enter Cuba's luxury nightclubs or exclusive beaches. "I never set foot in the Tropicana, nor Varadero [the beach resort]," he parried, evidently missing the point. "You know why? Because my father didn't have the money to pay for it!"

In April 2008, a sit-in took place in a park near the Plaza of the Revolution by ten women of the dissident group Las Damas de Blanco (Ladies in White) who, as their name suggests, always wear white. The group conducts silent marches down Havana's Fifth Avenue, beginning at the historic Church of Santa Rita de Casia to protest the imprisonment of family members (dissidents were rounded up in what is known as the Black Spring of 2003, when seventy-five writers and activists were imprisoned). "We are here to demand the release of our husbands and won't leave until they are free or they arrest us. We have waited long enough; we want to talk to the new president," said Laura Pollan, a spokeswoman for the group. Such public protests are rare. In short order, the women were hauled off by police and escorted back to their homes.

Also of note was an unauthorized concert of Carlos Varela. The well-regarded *nueva trova* singer is known for his thinly veiled protest songs such as "Guillermo Tell" (William Tell), interpreted as an unflattering parable about Fidel. For penning such ballads, Varela has often been denied permits to perform, notwithstanding his immense popularity. Despite not having a permit, a huge crowd descended on the Havana venue, having heard of the concert by word of mouth. Not long into Varela's performance, the crowd broke into a bellowing chant of *"Libertad!"*—Freedom! Some of the fans were wearing white bracelets imprinted with one word: *cambio,* or change, a phenomenon begun in late 2006.

The government took notice and posted an article on *Granma*'s website warning that "there will be no space for subversion in Cuba." It made good on its threat and ramped up the harassment and arrests of dissidents. Jaime Suchlicki of the University of Miami warned of a likely "Tiananmen Square showdown" that the United States needed to prepare for. But other Cubaphiles found the analysis a woeful misreading, noting that the majority of dissatisfied Cubans tend to flee, not fight. "There may be another Tiananmen Square," scoffed one U.S. Cuba Desk diplomat. "But it will happen in Tibet, not Havana."

In August 2007, Raúl Castro issued a two-hundred-page decree directing Cuba's three thousand state-run companies to comply with a new system he called *perfeccionamiento empresarial*. It would be a quasi neo–free market system using the management style of the private sector and applying those practices to state-run enterprises. The goal was to attack the endemic inefficiency and corruption in the country's bureaucracy by granting more localized control to managers and workers. More significantly, the new system stipulated that salaries and payment would be based on merit and achievement—not on simply showing up and moving paperwork around (or as is more often the case, *not* showing up). Conceptually, at least, it was revolutionary—a system Fidel Castro would once have castigated as counter-revolutionary.

In June 2008 a banner headline ran across the top of the state-run newspaper, *Trabajadores* (Workers), defining Raúl Castro's credo for his new government: "The key is in *perfeccionamiento empresarial*"—perfecting the state company system. The headline was Raúl's salvo warning that a new business model would be put in place, not unlike that of the Armed Forces. Speaking to the National Assembly, he drove home the need for reform, even jesting about the sorry state of Cuban economics: "We cannot hope that two plus two are five. Two plus two are four," he said, setting up his punch line. "Sometimes, actually, in socialism, two plus two comes out to three."

The economy took an unforeseen thrashing during the summer of 2008 when four deadly hurricanes— Fay, Gustav, Hanna, and Ike (ranging from category 2 to category 4)—leveled much of Cuba. Cyclonic winds up to two hundred miles an hour terrorized the island, leaving a half million people without shelter or schools and a third of the population without electricity. Much of the sugar, citrus, and tobacco crops were destroyed, with estimates of the damage reaching $10 billion. Among the worst hit were the western province of Piñar del Río, the eastern tip of Baracoa, and the small southwestern Isla de la Juventud (Isle of Youth), where Fidel Castro compared the wreckage of Gustav to that of "a nuclear blast." Raúl, however, was conspicuously absent from the scene. Unlike his brother, who would have been on the front lines rallying morale, Raúl did not emerge until several weeks later when he quickly toured devastated Isla de la Juventud.

Much of the goodwill and capital Raúl had accrued was lost by his nonperformance following the catastrophic storms. Doubts and misgivings had been steadily piling up—much of them in response to his disappointing hires. Confronted by Cuba's flaccid economy, he instinctively turned toward its multilayered bureaucracy rather than creating new initiatives. At public receptions and press conferences, he often seemed awkward, unprepared, with a tendency for malapropisms. Little of Raúl's personal charm—so evident in his private life—endured in the glare of the spotlight. Indeed, being front and center as a public figure seemed to unnerve him.

Prior to the siege of storms, Cuba had defaulted on its trade credit debt to Japan and had seen the price of its chief commodity, nickel, plummet to eight dollars per pound (down from its high of twenty-five). The hurricanes, among the worst in the island's history, were the coup de grâce of what William LeoGrande of American University called "a perfect economic storm."

Dissidents Martha Beatriz Roque and Vladimiro Roca delivered an urgent letter to George W. Bush at the U.S. Interests Section in Havana, asking that limits on travel and remittances be rescinded "for at least two months" to relieve some of the hardship from the storms. The appeal pulled at the heartstrings of most exiles—but not those of Miami's incumbent congressional representatives. They closed ranks around a Bush administration plan allowing aid to be sent *only* through authorized relief groups, not through Cuba's governmental relief agencies.

As it had done since 1959, Cuba declined any U.S. funds sent with conditions. Again pride trumped need. In any event, Cuba could depend on aid, without restrictions, from Venezuela, China, Brazil, and its newly energized ally, Russia.

The Russians moved quickly and generously to ship supplies to the besieged island. Their motives, however, were not entirely altruistic. The Putinites in Moscow, riled by NATO expansion and conflict with the Republic of Georgia, were eager for a military partner and a beachhead in the Western Hemisphere. "Cuba has a very important geostrategic situation," Andrei Klimov, the deputy chairman of the State Duma's Committee on International Affairs, remarked. "If America installs ABM [antiballistic missile] systems near our borders, Russia too may deploy its systems in those states that will agree to take them." There was another lure for the Russians: reestablishing Lourdes. The quaintly named former Soviet intelligence collection site and listening post in Havana had been shut down in late 2001 after saber rattling from cold warriors in the Bush administration. It was the largest Russian signal intelligence site abroad, strategically located to easily eavesdrop on military and civilian voice and data transmissions relayed by satellites. The site had been eyeballed by China, which deepened its relationship with Cuba in the years after Russia retreated.

In late September 2008, Hugo Chávez alighted in Havana for a brief mentoring session with Fidel Castro—en route to high-level talks in Russia and China, in which, presumably, Lourdes was on the agenda. He was met at José Martí Airport by Raúl, a veteran student of both Communist powers, but it was Fidel whom Chávez most depended upon. "Castro has been a teacher for me," Chávez told Hitchens, Brinkley, and Penn. "Not on ideology but on strategy." Upon his return to Caracas five days later, Chávez slipped back into Castro's hospital suite to debrief his mentor on the progress of his trip.

Soon after, with one eye riveted on Washington, Cuba said it had decided against allowing Russian missiles on its soil. At least for the time being. Russian president Dmitri Medvedev visited Havana at year's end and the red carpet was once again unrolled for Cuba's former patron. An array of investments in Cuba were announced—from tourism and mining to energy.

Notwithstanding natural catastrophes and an economy running almost on life support, Raúl Castro's ascension to power coincided with a geologically propitious moment: the discovery of oil in Cuba's northern waters. According to the U.S. Geological Survey, the North Cuba Basin—in the deep waters of the Gulf of Mexico—has somewhere between 4.6 billion and 9.3 billion barrels, as well as 1 trillion cubic feet of natural gas. First discovered by Repsol YPF, the Spanish oil company, in July 2004, five of the oil fields have been determined to be of high quality. Cuba moved quickly to divvy up the 74,000-square-mile area into fifty-nine exploration blocks, then invited foreign oil conglomerates to bid.

Among those who have signed deals with CUPET, Cuba's state-run oil company, are Repsol; Brazil's Petrobras; PDVSA of Venezuela (which has also committed to modernizing Cuba's refineries and land-based oil wells); India's ONGC Videsh; Norway's Nordsk Hydro; Vietnam's state energy cartel, Petrovietnam; Malaysia's state-run Petronas; and Canada's Sherritt International Corporation. Also in place are Russian and Chinese joint ventures. But by mid-2009, Cuba had sold just

twenty-one of its fifty-nine sea blocks of offshore rights because companies remain gun-shy about doing business with a country mired in debt.
Two Canadian companies, Sherritt International and Pebercan, Inc., are
owed more than $500 million.

Down the road, however, Cuba could well be in the enviable position
of having its own oil reserves, as well as natural gas and vast fields of
sugarcane suitable for producing ethanol. If and when their oil spews
forth, Cuba could transform itself from being a beggar importer to
being energy sufficient. In five years' time, the island theoretically could
become an exporter reaping as much as $5 billion annually from oil and
ethanol. "If proven, and after a three- to five-year development period,
these reserves could produce about three hundred thousand barrels per
day of oil," said Jorge Piñón, former head of Amoco Oil in Latin America. Meanwhile, Raúl enjoys the ongoing benevolence of oil czar Hugo
Chávez—who cheerfully supplies the island with roughly one hundred
thousand barrels a day at terms that would rival those of Santa Claus.

Optimists and spinners such as Chávez suggested that Cuba's discovery of black gold warranted its membership in the elite club of oil
monopolists. "Cuba could join OPEC [Organization of Petroleum
Exporting Countries]," Chávez crowed in 2008. Piñón offered a more
nuanced perspective: "My view is that for now Cuba's oil potential is
more of a politically strategic value than an economic financial balance
of payment benefit," he said. "It would make a future Cuban government free from any possible Venezuelan influences." In other words, if
and when its oil is pumped to the surface, Cuba would be free to show
Chávez the door should Havana so choose.

Since the beginning of Fidel's slow fade to black in July 2006, Cuba's
robust cultural arena has been rife with partisan warfare and conflicting agendas. Alternating cycles of openness and repression have been
the watchword in Cuban culture, state run and otherwise. In December
2007, the Oscar-winning German film *The Lives of Others* was shown in
Havana. The film, which explores the searing nature and costs of informing, was given no advance publicity. Yet more than a thousand Cubans
queued up for hours to attend the two screenings. Audience members
streamed out and, in murmured conversations, noted the pointed parallels between the East German Stasi and Cuba's state security services.
Most remarkable was the fact that the film was shown at all.

While human rights activists applauded the surprise screenings, they
were dismayed by other developments. Beginning in early 2007, some
of the country's most divisive zealots from the 1960s and '70s appeared

on state-run television. Topping the list was Luis Pavón Tamayo, chief of the National Cultural Council from 1971 to 1976. Working closely with MININT chief Ramiro Valdés, Pavón spearheaded the campaign to ferret out and marginalize writers and artists judged to be insufficiently revolutionary. Virtually all homosexuals made Pavón's list, thus ensuring they would not be published or produced for a decade or more.

Almost immediately, Havana's vocal and well-organized intelligentsia sprang into action. Writers such as César López, novelist Pedro Juan Gutiérrez, Reina María Rodríguez, and filmmaker Senal Paz struck back, using the internet to protest and communicate with each other and the State. "This is an attempt to revive the darkest period for Cuban culture," said Reynaldo González, a noted writer. Antón Arrufat, the acclaimed playwright, told Reuters his story: "I lost my job and was sent to work in a library basement for nine years tying parcels of books with string. I was not allowed to publish for fourteen years." The writer Miguel Barnet, a member of the National Assembly not known for taking risks, also joined the protest.

Catalyzed by the internet, Havana's *nomenklatura* engaged in an intensely cathartic, sometimes chaotic conversation conducted, to a large degree, on the website of the Ministry of Culture (www.cubarte .cult.cu). Even Eliades Acosta, the Party's Central Committee point man on culture, weighed in about the need to democratize society and ameliorate the fears of citizens about speaking out. "It was astonishing on a gazillion levels," observed writer Achy Obejas, who tracks culture in Havana. "People asked that it be published in *Granma* so *cubanos a pie*—Cubans on the street—could read it."

Criticism of Pavón was so fast and furious that the government shut down Cubarte for three days. Punishments were meted out to some. Eliades Acosta's article vanished from the website, and he was later dropped from the slate of those running in the upcoming election for the National Assembly, where he had long enjoyed a seat.

Members of the National Association of Cuban Writers and Artists (UNEAC) demanded a meeting with Culture Minister Abel Prieto, also a novelist, and with the heads of Cuban television (ICRT). Some four hundred young Cubans protested outside Casa de las Américas, the government-run cultural organization that fosters the arts in Latin America, claiming they had been barred from the meeting. Nevertheless, they were pleasantly surprised by the outcome.

Following the meeting, UNEAC issued a communiqué in which the ICRT acknowledged that it had been "a mistake" to broadcast programs featuring reviled figures from Cuba's dark past. The dramatist Arrufat asked for more, including an investigation and reckoning about the Revolution's darkest days. "A debate should be opened up now about that period of Pavón's tenure," Arrufat told EFE, ". . . which to date has not been done."

Later in the year, several prominent intellectuals appeared on the state-run television show *Open Dialogue.* "We had accustomed ourselves to not debating," said Alfredo Guevara, the former director of the Havana Film Festival and a trusted friend to both Castro brothers since their student days. "We answered Fidel with silence," he said elliptically, adding that for dialogue to begin, "Raúl had to come." The government did not concede defeat, but Luis Pavón was not seen again on television. It was a victory that spurred intellectuals and dissidents to continue to push the envelope.

At the next Havana Arts Biennial, performance artist Tania Bruguera did just that: inviting ordinary Cubans onstage to use the microphone and say what was on their minds. Quite a few unleashed their unhappiness with the state's limits on freedom. The artist left disposable cameras on the floor for audience members, thus documenting the event. Not surprisingly, Biennial officials were furious.

Rafael Hernández, the editor of *Temas,* a culture review in Havana, said his country was at the crossroads. Society, the intelligentsia, and even some in the government were hungry for change, he said, and were contemplating new paradigms of socialism. The Party leadership and the Army, however, were another story. "Our big problem is that we are losing our youth," said Hernández. "They are leaving in record numbers. And this is serious."

Despite shortages of computers and limited access to the internet, the blogosphere is alive in Cuba and often manages to get news in and out of the island. Moreover, the country has spawned several notable bloggers who write along the razor's edge. Yoani Sánchez, a petite, dark-haired woman, has written a blog since 2006 called "Generación Y." (The blog's name is a nod to the thousands of Cubans bestowed names beginning with "Y" such as Yociel, Yanisleidi, Yoandri, Yusimí—hybridized names reflecting the influence of the country's former Russian patrons in the 1970s and '80s. With an estimated million visitors monthly—mostly from outside Cuba—Sánchez's blog is a diary of the daily trials and travails of life in Havana, from food shortages to a dissident uncle imprisoned during Cuba's Black Spring of 2003. "The Internet is a gray area the Cuban government hasn't figured out how to regulate yet," Sánchez told *BusinessWeek.* After writing her blog entry on her home computer, Sánchez loads it onto a flash drive, then runs over to an internet center and uploads its contents to www.desdecuba .com, which hosts an online magazine and five other dissident blogs.

Sánchez does not shy away from confrontation. At one point, she urged the resignation of Fidel Castro and suggested that what Cuba needed was a leader who was "a pragmatic housewife." At a public forum, she challenged Mariela Castro, Raúl's daughter, about limited personal freedoms. Cognizant of the perils to herself, she is betting that the government will reform—not out of virtue, but because it has no choice.

In March 2008, the government blocked access to her blog, a tactic invoked periodically. (ETECSA, a Cuban joint venture with Telecom Italia, is the sole internet and phone provider.) When Sánchez was able to get back online, she blogged with a vengeance: "So, the anonymous censors of our famished cyberspace have tried to shut me in a room, turn off the light, and not let my friends in." A few months later, *Time* magazine listed her in its "100 Most Influential People."

Not long after, Fidel Castro weighed in on the blogger-dissident, noting that her "affirmations are divulged immediately to and by imperialism's mass media." Without mentioning her by name, he chastised writers who "assume the job of those who undermine" the state. He threw a sharp jab at Madrid's press corps, which had recently given a journalism prize to Sánchez, colorfully dissing it as a trophy of "the neocolonial press of the ancient Spanish metropolis that awards them." Sánchez did not retreat. "Revolutions don't last half a century," she wrote in a posting about the fiftieth birthday of the Revolution. "They always expire, trying to make themselves eternal. . . . Nothing will manage to raise it from the tomb and bring it back to life. Let it rest in peace."

There will be other cyber revolutionaries down the road who will doubtless find ways to get their messages online. The government knows this. "In the street, at jobs and in neighborhoods, there's some flexibility in terms of repression and expression," Ahmed Rodríguez, a freelance reporter, told the *Miami Herald*. Rodríguez, who heads up a news agency called Youth Without Censorship, continued: "People have lost a little bit of their fear—not all of it." He allowed that change had occurred following Raúl Castro's call for more debate. He cited as evidence the fact that Cuban television had broadcast the stunning footage of King Juan Carlos of Spain upbraiding Venezuelan president Hugo Chávez in 2007. "There it was, clear as day, on Cubavisión, the king telling Chávez to shut up. In the past, we would never have been allowed to see that."

Along with writers and artists, musicians—even banned groups—

have begun downloading their offerings on computers in hotels or state-run internet shops. But they remain mindful that such liberties could vanish on a dime with Ramiro Valdés at the helm of the Ministry of Information and Communications. "Ramiro is again very powerful. And very feared," said one former diplomat who insisted on speaking a few blocks away from his Vedado home. Following the announcement of Valdés's appointment in 2007, Cubans became more cautious about their phone and e-mail communications, some abandoning e-mail except for mundane messages. At a 2008 international conference, Valdés said he would seek to replicate the Chinese model of censorship and described the internet as "the bucking bronco of new technologies [that] can and must be controlled."

Valdés and his fellow *históricos* were doubtless chagrined at the screening of *The Lives of Others* and the subsequent airing on Cuban television of the baseball documentary *Out of This League*. The film featured Cuban baseball legend Orlando "El Duque" Hernández, who fled to the U.S. in 1997 after being barred from playing in Cuba. Previously, Hernández had been the sinew behind Cuba's beloved and triumphant team, Los Industriales. In the U.S., he instantly became a star pitcher for the New York Yankees and lasted nine seasons in the major leagues. "I am not a traitor," Hernández told the camera emotionally. "I am an Industrial."

Throughout 2008, several significant meat-and-potato reforms were announced. Cubans would soon be able to own and have title to their homes for the first time since the Revolution. Previously homes and apartments could only be traded, in what is known as the *permuta* system, a complex trading scheme that allowed Cubans to swap residences with each other. It has been a system susceptible to corruption but one that has endured and adapted to Cuban socialism. It is run by *corredores,* real-estate brokers who generally operate on tips. Money is not supposed to change hands by law, but typically does.

Raúl Castro said that he would like to see ordinary citizens—90 percent of whom hold title to their homes—own them, with the attendant benefits. "It would provide a source of taxable income for the government, and its effect on the cash-starved populace would be just as profound," wrote David Adams in the *St. Petersburg Times*. Not to mention the pride of ownership.

Caps on state salaries, usually about ten dollars a month, were also removed, offering some incentive for workers. Computers, DVD players, and Nintendo games became available for sale. For the first time,

ordinary Cubans were given access to cell phones and allowed to purchase rice cookers, car alarms, video machines, microwaves, large-screen
television sets, toasters, and air conditioners. Many such appliances had
been banned in the early '90s when Cuba's economy bottomed out and
there was insufficient energy to power them.

Raúl and his men also promised to overhaul the country's antiquated
transportation system, investing $2 billion in new roads, infrastruc-
ture, bridges, and the *autopista*—the main highway that runs through
Cuba. Other than the ubiquitous *cacharros*—the gas-guzzling U.S.
jalopies from the 1950s—most Cubans depend on public transportation. For decades that meant waiting around on street corners for a
diesel-spewing, eighteen-wheeler Russian-made bus known as a *cam-
ello* (camel) that hauled as many as four hundred passengers, most of
whom stood or hung out its windows. In 2008, some three thousand
new buses from China appeared in Havana, replacing most of the *cam-
ellos*. Private taxi services were allowed in in 2009.

On the kitchen front, Raúl called the island's inability to feed itself "a
national security issue." Cuba imports 70 percent of its food while millions of acres of arable land are unused. In 2007 the country spent more
than $1.5 billion on imported food products and roughly $2.5 billion
in 2008. Almost $500 million of its imports came from the U.S., which
ironically, despite the embargo, is Cuba's fifth-largest trading partner.
To remedy Cuba's food crisis, individual farmers are now permitted
to cultivate up to ninety-nine acres of government land and keep their
profits.

Raúl Castro's team also tackled one of the island's thorniest problems: the banning of its citizens from hotels and tourist facilities, long
a source of bitterness, particularly among blacks. Cubans now have
access to hotels and can rent cars. Of course, precious few Cubans can
afford such luxuries. While about two-thirds of the population have
access to dollars—via families abroad or the black market—a weekend
in a Varadero Beach hotel is as likely for them as a trip to the moon.
However, a brunch at a hotel with a day at a pristine tourist beach is
not so remote. Moreover, having the right to have access to such luxuries—however out of reach—resonates on deep psychological and sym-
bolic levels.

The hotel issue had been problematic. When Fidel Castro restarted
the island's tourism economy in the early 1990s, Cubans were initially
allowed into hotels. Not long after, the U.S. charged Cuba with sex trafficking and prostitution, the latter being rampant. Partly in response,
the government banned citizens from tourist facilities, fomenting an

enduring and smoldering bitterness among Cubans. Critics of the policy aptly derided it as "tourism apartheid." "I built hotels and then I couldn't get close to them," a thirty-two-year-old construction worker complained to Reuters. "Now I can't go because they're expensive, but at least they don't prohibit me." Cuba's young prostitutes—or *jineteras*—are also back in droves, able to ply their trade at hotels with less government interference.

In the first days of December 1958, Ginger Rogers and George Raft opened Meyer Lansky's spanking new, divinely decadent $14 million Rivera Hotel to sellout crowds. Two weeks later, Fidel, Raúl, and their *barbudos* marched on Havana with a promise to end gambling, the Mafia, and sin, replacing them with wholesome tropical Marxism.

Fifty years later, it was more or less back to square one minus the gambling—except that the Cuban Army, not the mob, would be running matters. But reviving tourism will not be a walk on the beach, as it were. Jane Bussey, editor of the magazine *Latin Trade,* points out that the island's Caribbean neighbors have long benefited from the U.S. embargo and the many trade agreements that exclude Cuba. "They have privately joked, 'Gracias, Fidel,'" said Bussey, "because Cuba's isolation has meant more tourist dollars for them." Keen to snare more of the lucrative market, the Army is ramping up the country's tourism sector to make it more competitive with other Caribbean getaways.

The modest, but appreciated, reforms of Raúl and his men have extended beyond tourism. The government relaxed some media controls and expanded television coverage to include one channel offering twenty-four-hour programming from foreign networks such as Telesur, Discovery Channel, Television Española, and Venezuelan TV. Cubans now watch a diverse array of American shows, including *The Sopranos, Grey's Anatomy,* and quite a bit of CNN.

Cuba's often capricious justice system underwent some fine tuning as well. In 2008, Raúl Castro commuted all but three death penalty cases to thirty years in prison and initiated discussion to abolish the country's death penalty. There remain, however, about 205 political prisoners, some of whom are repeatedly arrested on Kleenex-flimsy charges.

Wayne Smith, the former head of the U.S. Interests Section in Havana during the Carter administration years visits, Cuba several times a year. Throughout 2008 and 2009, he said, he observed a tangible shift on the island and heard "a guarded but general optimism." Others were more cautious in evaluating the depth of reforms. Phillip Peters of the Lexington Institute, pointed out that "these measures do not tackle the big problems of growth, new jobs, and fixing the purchasing-power problem that affects most Cubans."

Nevertheless they are significant moves for a change-phobic political culture. "Changes are already happening," said one Cuban Communist Party official, adding a proviso: "Don't expect to see any announcements in *Granma*. That will never happen." In other words, he seemed to be saying, Raúl needs to operate under the radar—without publicity—at least while his brother is still alive.

Indeed, the ailing Fidel continued to weigh in to reproach those advocating rapid reforms. In an April 2008 column he entitled, "Do Not Make Concessions to Enemy Ideology," Castro warned that "people must be very careful with everything they say, so as not to play the game of enemy ideology." He went on to lay blame for Cuba's moribund economy on the Russians. "The Special Period was the inevitable consequence of the disappearance of the USSR, which lost the ideological battle and led us to a stage of heroic resistance from which we still have not wholly emerged." Then Castro sternly advised his successors to "meditate hard on what you say, what you affirm, so you don't make shameful concessions." A second column by the waning leader chastised would-be reformers: "Going in reverse is not going forward."

One step that resonated as a back-to-the-future leap came with the announcement that the Communist Party would meet in late 2009 to hold its first congress since 1997. The surprise announcement signaled two shifts: the Party was being given parity with the Army, and second, hardliners, who dominate Party policy, were elbowing out moderates. Moreover, several *históricos,* who happen to be generals, were promoted within the Politburo and given expanded portfolios, including Ramiro Valdés, Ulises Rosales del Toro, and General Álvaro López Miera, vice minister for defense, along with Salvador Valdés Mesa, president of the Cuban Workers Federation.

Three years into the long dying of Fidel Castro, it was clear that Raúl would not govern through the force of personality as his brother had, but through the country's dominant institutions: the Armed Forces and the Communist Party. That pragmatism would supplant charisma was evident at Raúl's first major speech on July 26, 2008, in Santiago, to mark the fifty-fifth anniversary of the Revolution. At just forty-five minutes long, the speech was a dry, by-the-numbers tribute to his brother's achievements and a brief litany of planned infrastructure projects for the future. Stirring and inspirational it was not. The speech had been vetted by Fidel, as Raúl himself confirmed. And lest anyone forget that Cuba remained a co-presidency, looming behind the diminutive Raúl was an immense banner of his brother and mentor—smiling, fist raised, beaming down on the assembled with maximum Fidel-wattage intensity.

"The Cuban people don't need more charisma," argued Lissette Bustamante, a journalist who traveled in Fidel Castro's entourage for five years until her exile to Madrid in 1992. "Cubans have been saturated in charisma. The quota was long ago surpassed." Bereft of aspirations to be *comunista* or *socialista,* materially deprived Cubans, she said, were now unabashedly *"consumista."*

The Peruvian novelist and political conservative Mario Vargas Llosa saw changes occurring in Cuba, but in slow, micromanaged increments. "Fidel's death will bring about a psychological change," said the writer. "The reforms are being introduced timidly by Raúl Castro and his team because he realizes that if Cuba is to survive, it must evolve."

But the *raulistas* saw their future another way. The maintenance and security of the government came first and foremost. Suspected dissidents would be rigorously monitored and periodically arrested. Private complaining would be tolerated, public dissent was at one's own risk. No one knew this better than the Afro-Cuban dissident Jorge Luis García Pérez, known as "Antúnez," who had spent seventeen years in prison before finally winning his freedom in 2007. On July 4, 2008, he was arrested for the fifteenth time since he'd been released—an average of about one arrest a month. That same weekend, an estimated two hundred dissidents were picked up around the island to prevent them from attending the annual Fourth of July party at the residence of the chief of the U.S. Interests Section. "Raúl Castro's strategy is to create a mirage of change for the international community to mask the fact that acts of repression are increasing," Antúnez told the *Herald.* "They arrest you and let you go tomorrow to hide the sense that there is a wave of repression. I'd call it a 'wave lite.' It's different, and we don't know what lengths it will reach."

In August 2008, the arrest of Gorki Águila, the provacateur lead singer of the punk-rock group Porno Para Ricardo, generated swift condemnation. After a one-day trial, the anarchist protest singer was released with a warning and a 600 peso fine, roughly $28. Interviewed by *El País,* Águila attributed his release to the fact that state security "didn't expect that I would have so much support." Águila said he was preparing to record a song about Raúl, adapted from one that he had written about Fidel. It would be called *"El Comandante II."* Águila compared his prison release to a set of Russian wooden matroyshka dolls. "You come out of a small jail, only to go into a slightly larger one, and so on. I am now in a larger one, but there's always the risk I'll fall into the smallest doll." He did—and was arrested again in early 2009.

The Castros are the dynastic royal family of Cuba. Scattered throughout government portfolios and ministries are an array of relations—uncles, nieces, and cousins—who are well known among the chattering classes but not to the average Cuban. Raúl's daughter, Mariela Castro Espín, forty-seven, has stepped into her late mother's role as Cuba's unofficial First Lady. Soon after Vilma's death, she assumed her mother's position as the head of Cuba's Federation of Women and as spokesperson for the family.

A passionate advocate for gay and transgender rights, she heads the National Center for Sex Education (CENESEX). Once the family rebel, Mariela leans toward progressive liberalism and has chosen a decidedly bohemian lifestyle. She is married to an Italian photographer with whom she has two children; she also has a son from a previous liaison with a Chilean whom she did not marry. She has the perspective of an intellectual who has traveled widely and lived abroad.

High on her ambitious agenda is the legalization of same-sex marriage and the inclusion of sex-change surgery for transgenders in the Cuban health-care system. Her critics point out that the system barely meets basic, minimum needs.

Her priorities, such as gay rights, have put her at occasional loggerheads with *históricos* and with Cuba's Catholic Church. In June 2008, *Palabra Nueva,* the monthly magazine of the Archdiocese of Havana, published an editorial in response to her work: "Respect for the homosexual individual, yes," it concluded. "Promotion of homosexuality, no." But Mariela Castro's influence is undeniable and her allies include Minister of Culture czar Abel Prieto. "I think that marriage between lesbians, homosexuals can be perfectly approved, and that wouldn't cause an earthquake in Cuba, or anything like that," Prieto said to the astonishment of his elders in 2008.

Prieto's comments would have precipitated an earthquake in the early 1960s, when thousands of gays were hauled off to detention centers and jails. Such thinking represents a sea change for Cuba politically and culturally.

Certainly a same-sex wedding held in the courtyard at CENESEX in 2007—replete with veils, rings, and kisses—between two young women, ages nineteen and twenty-eight, never would have occurred without Mariela Castro's advocacy. Nor would the screening of *Broke-*

back Mountain, the gay-themed Oscar-winning drama, have taken place without her lobbying. In May 2008, she convened a one-day conference entitled "International Day Against Homophobia," and gave a fiery speech on the subject. Not long after, the Ministry of Health authorized state-funded sex-change surgery for twenty-eight Cubans.

Raúl's feisty daughter is willing to speak boldly on other issues. She has urged the end of the odious and costly travel and emigration restrictions for Cubans. "I think we should grant permission to all those who want to leave," she told *La Vanguardia,* a Spanish newspaper, in 2008. Cubans are allowed to compete for visas to leave the island, but as she conceded, the process is a daunting obstacle course that entails "a great deal of difficulty."

Mariela's older sister, Déborah, maintains a lower profile while working as an adviser to the Minister of Education. Déborah's son, Major Raúl Alejandro Rodríguez Castro, however, holds a singularly important post: ensuring the personal security of his grandfather, the president.

Raúl has always understood that he is a transitional figure who will likely lead his country for another five years until his early eighties. "He's going very slowly," said Domingo Amuchastegui, a former intelligence officer who worked with both Castro brothers. "He would go faster if a certain person left the scene. It's been a shared interim. And as usual, they are having a tug of war on every single issue."

Raúl's mission, says defense expert Frank Mora, "is regime survival" and leading Cuba from "being less a country of *caudillos* and more a country of institutions—albeit nondemocratic institutions run by *raulista* technocrats." Of these institutions, Raúl's Army, the FAR, will remain the central organ of the government and the prototype for other businesses. It is now Cuba's über-company.

However, Fidel Castro's concerns about "a generational problem" in Cuba's leadership were prescient and all too relevant. Raúl Castro has chosen and prepared his grave site—outside Santiago where the ashes of his wife were spread. At the Mausoleum of the Frank País Second Front, Raúl's name is already embossed on a plaque next to Vilma's, mounted on an immense boulder ringed by royal green palms and the Micara hills.

Sometime in the next decade, many of Fidel's and Raúl's septuagenarian appointments will be dead or gone. Their governing bunker mentality will presumably exit with them. A new tier of leaders, mostly men, but also some women, in their fifties, who have already assumed their places in government ministries and the Army, will replace them. These relatively young Turks are committed nationalists; most are committed socialists and *raulistas,* until that proves to be a disadvantage. But precious few are *fidelistas.*

Worth watching among the technocrats are Jorge Luis Sierra Cruz, the young Minister of Transportation, as well as Manuel Marrero Cruz, a forty-five-year-old colonel, who heads up the lucrative Ministry of Tourism. Marcos Portal, the former Minister for Basic Industries, has re-emerged after an auspicious political debut followed by a sudden tumble in 2004. *Granma* cited Portal's "self-sufficiency [and] undervaluing the advice of other experienced colleagues" as the problem.

Daniel Erikson, a Cuba analyst with Inter-American Dialogue, notes that Portal rehabilitated himself and is now regarded as an expert who knows Cuba's business ventures inside and out. This could make him a figure to be reckoned with in the future if Raúl elevates managers over ideologues. Portal is also family. Portal's wife is Tania Fraga Castro, the daughter of Angela Castro, the eldest sister of the Castro brothers; Fraga Castro is a high-ranking official in the Ministry of Health.

While some have benefited from nepotism, others have suffered. Often there is a roller-coaster ride—first a surfeit of privileges followed by a sundering crash, which occasionally is followed by a resurrection. Honor killings, in the metaphorical sense, are part of the Revolution's political culture. Once a member of a family falls *en desgracia,* the entire family is tainted, to varying degrees. Carlos Lage's family had been especially well placed throughout the government. His scientist brother, Agustín Lage, head of Havana's prestigious Center of Molecular Immunology, had been a prime mover in Cuba's biotechnology program. Until the unceremonious sacking of their father, Lage's sons, César Jr. and Carlos Lage Codorniu, seemed poised for political stardom. The junior Carlos Lage was president of the University Students Federation (FEU) in 2007, the prized post that once guaranteed a smashing political career.

Fidel Castro sought but failed to be elected president of the FEU when he was a student leader at the University of Havana. Since the Revolution, Fidel assiduously mentored future FEU presidents, several of whom have transited into his inner circle: Carlos Lage was FEU president in 1975, a post also held by Carlos Valenciaga, later Fidel's personal secretary, while Felipe Pérez Roque likewise orbited from the FEU to become Fidel's secretary, culminating in his appointment as Foreign Minister.

But Raúl Castro, an anti-intellectual who dropped out of the university in his sophomore year, never attributed great value to the FEU. What was the springboard to power under Fidel appears to have become the kiss of death in the era of Raúl. Indeed, it was Raúl who dismissed Robaina, Valenciaga, Lage, and Pérez Roque (all but Robaina were former FEU presidents) and sent them packing into Cuban political oblivion.

Curiously, none of Fidel's own children appears destined for a major political career. Nor have any of his sons gone into the country's Armed Forces. Inheriting their father's intellectual bent, Fidel's sons have favored professions in medicine and the sciences. Fidel's brood, according to several accounts, are friendly but not especially close with Raúl's children. One exception is the close relationship between Fidel's son, the well-liked Antonio who heads up the baseball league, and his cousin Alejandro.

The legacy factor is strongest in Raúl Castro's clan—whose members can be found in virtually every ministry. Raúl's son-in-law, Colonel Luis Alberto Rodríguez López-Callejas, married to Raúl's daughter Déborah, is chief executive officer of GAESA, the business arm of the Army. The clout and prestige of Rodríguez, whose father was a division general and now heads the Cuban Defense Information Study Center, cannot be overestimated. "There are higher-ranking generals in the Army, but few come close to having his influence," says Frank Mora. "He is the most important entrepreneur in the Army."

Another important player is Raúl's son, Alejandro Raúl Castro Espín, a colonel in MININT with a critical portfolio. The younger Castro heads up intelligence collection and also serves as Cuba's point man and liaison with China. He is an accomplished politician, though very much in the low-profile mold of his father. Down the road, he will likely step into a more public role. He occupies a far more strategic position than his cousin, Fidel, a sixty-year-old physicist who is the scientific adviser to the Council of State.

Every New Year's Day a caravan of banner-festooned jeeps and trucks leaves Santiago de Cuba, re-creating Castro's eight-day victory march across the island in 1959. In 2009, to mark the fiftieth anniversary of the Revolution, the Caravan of Victory was slated to be a blowout, celebratory party. But with Castro confined to his convalescent suite, the festivities were downgraded to a more subdued commemoration.

Standing in for Fidel was his firstborn child and namesake. As a tow-headed photogenic nine-year-old, Fidelito had been at his father's side during the historic journey that culminated at Camp Columbia, the military barracks in Havana. Father and son have a marked physical resemblance to each other, but in temperament Fidelito is closer to that of his mother. Like Myrta Díaz-Balart, he has no passion or appetite for politics. Nevertheless, he was thrilled to repeat the experience of the caravan, calling it "the happiest day of my life." Still, the differences of a half century were stark. In 1959 the caravan was surrounded by hordes of jubilant Cubans, which was not the case in 2009. In contrast to his father, Fidelito's appearance generated no electricity with the small but polite crowds that came out to see him, mostly out of curiosity. In 1959 Castro had assured the cheering crowds, "This is not a dictatorship," promising that "the day that the people do not want us, we shall leave."

With the inauguration of President Obama, the forty-eight-year-old U.S. embargo of Cuba began its death spiral. The megaphone diplomacy that had defined much of U.S.-Cuba policy, with its demand for "regime change," simply ceased.

Had Senator John McCain won the 2008 election, the standoff between the U.S. and Cuba, a superpower and a Caribbean island, could well have stayed on course—frozen in the Cold War realities of the 1960s. Instead, the views of exile hardliners have received a less hospitable hearing in the Obama Oval Office. The Cuban Liberty Council, the fiercely hard-right exile group, no longer arranges the place settings at the White House on Cuban Independence Day. Replacing it are the CANF and the Cuba Study Group, an exile organization led by pragmatic Cuban-American businessmen.

Representative Lincoln Díaz-Balart, who as George W. Bush's quarterback virtually dictated policy and staffing regarding Cuba, also has been retired. In his place are now two other Cuban-American lawmakers: Senator Bob Menendez and Representative Albio Sires, both of New Jersey, not Miami, and both Democrats. The two Jersey legislators do not support ending the embargo, but have acceded to loosening travel restrictions for Cuban-Americans and to some quiet diplomacy with the island. Nevertheless, Menendez nearly overplayed his hand in March 2009 when he put a hold on a billion-dollar omnibus spending bill because of several Cuba provisions. While Menendez succeeded in limiting changes to Cuban travel and agriculture policy for a period, there were costs. "Menendez may have frittered away a lot of capital with Obama over a trifling issue," said former NSC Cuba adviser Richard Nuccio.

For the first time since 1960, hardliners have to compete with other exiles and interests who demand unfettered travel to Cuba and those who want to see the embargo lifted. The latter remains a tall order. As written, the Helms-Burton Act of 1996 snatched away the presidential prerogative of terminating the embargo with a signature—and

granted it to Congress. The law also precludes the U.S. from rescind-
ing the embargo *if* either Castro brother is at the helm. Although the
Obama team is neither able nor inclined to lift the embargo entirely, it
can encourage its allies in Congress to begin the process of dismantling
Helms-Burton, the behemoth legislation that is laden with all manner of
mischief and special-interest prohibitions. Many of the very exiles who
once demanded its enactment now want it terminated—an irony too
rich to be lost on anyone.

Contrary to popular myth and public misunderstanding, the president does have a wide array of tools that will allow him to recali-
brate Cuba policy. With a 2009 Brookings Institution poll showing an
unprecedented majority (55 percent) of Cuban-Americans opposing
continuation of the embargo, and 79 percent viewing it critically, the
administration will have the wind in its sails to act.

Obama's team will likely end travel restrictions to Cuba, first for
Cuban-Americans, then for cultural and educational groups, and finally
for the general public. They also promptly lifted the "communications
embargo" on Cuba, thus repealing limits on programming of television,
radio, internet, and computer sales. Quietly, they encouraged the Organization of American States and other hemispheric councils to invite
Cuba back into the fold.

Down the road, the administration will consider restoring the status
of the "interests sections" in each other's capitals to formal embassies
or may decide to appoint a special envoy to Cuba. They will expand
existing military agreements, especially those policing narcotics. And if
the prevailing winds favor them, they will quietly delete Cuba from the
State Department's list of state sponsors of terrorism.

It is a safe bet that Obama will compel Radio and Television Martí
to professionalize its content and bidding practices. The administration may also choose to bring the profligate stations back under the
umbrella of the Voice of America to keep a closer eye and ear on them.
While another $20 million has been requested by USAID and the State
Department to fund Cuba programs for 2009, the Obama team will
slow the gravy train and review its recipients and their programs more
thoroughly. The new scrutiny from Washington was apparent by May
2009 when the administration took a bite out of the Martís' budget,
forcing the stations to reduce costs and staffing.

The U.S. Navy base at Guantánamo Bay at the eastern tip of the
island remains a playing card on the table for both Washington and
Havana. Upon taking office, Obama pledged to shut down the prison
holding terror suspects there. But the underlying, century-old issue

concerns the base itself, established in 1903. For fifty years, the Castros, in protest to the affront to Cuban sovereignty, have not cashed a single check for Guantánamo's lease—about four thousand dollars a year. "We will begin to insist on the base's closure with greater determination," Raúl Castro said shortly after Obama took office. In the past, he noted, "we slightly downplayed our demands for the base's closure so as not to discourage the [global] campaign urging the closure of the prison camp." In the end, Raúl reminded the world that the "the territory [must] be returned to its legal owner—the Cuban people." He pointed out his own strategic analysis as consolation to the U.S.: "The base has no military value for [the Americans]. From a military point of view, it's a real mousetrap."

An array of factors augur well for some dramatic shifts. American oil companies, agribusiness, and the Chamber of Commerce have intensified their lobbying of the president and Congress, arguing that the U.S. can no longer afford its grudge match with Cuba. They will hammer away at the fact that the Emerald Island, just ninety miles south of Key West, Florida, is now an oil and energy producer. They will cite studies that conclude that the lifting of the embargo would result in $5 to $13 billion in annual revenue for the U.S. As a sweetener for embittered hardliners, they will point to the estimated $2 billion in annual growth to Florida's economy, along with tens of thousands of new jobs. They will contend that, with each passing day, the United States becomes more and more irrelevant to the economy, politics, and future of the largest country in the Caribbean.

To make their case, they will point out certain undeniable, historical facts. One may be as unpalatable as it is true: that after a half-century showdown with a tropical island, the greatest superpower in history will likely walk away empty-handed.

Fidel Castro swore he would never surrender, and he was true to his word. "I am prepared to reenact the famous Hundred Years' War—and win it," he warned in a letter fifty-five years earlier. Rage he did—until the very end.

LIST OF ACRONYMS

CUBAN GOVERNMENT

MININT: Ministerio del Interior (Ministry of the Interior), intelligence

MINREX: Ministerio de Relaciones Exteriores (Ministry of Foreign Affairs)

MINFAR or **FAR:** Fuerzas Armadas Revolucionarias (Revolutionary Armed Forces)

CEN: National Executive Committee

GAESA: Grupo de Administración Empresarial, or Business Administration Group, a division of MINFAR

DGI: Dirección General de Inteligencia (General Intelligence Directorate), division of MININT

CDR: Comités de Defensa de la Revolución (Committees for the Defense of the Revolution)

CIMEQ: Centro de Investigaciones Médico-Quirúgicos (Center for Medical-Surgical Studies)

CIMEX: Comercio Interior y Mercado Exterior (Domestic Trade and Foreign Market), Cuba's largest business conglomerate, made up of eighty companies, and created in 1989

CUPET: Cuba Petróleo, Cuba's state oil company

UNEAC: Unión de Escritores y Artistas de Cuba (Union of Cuban Writers and Artists)

ICRT: Instituto Cubano de Radio y Televisión (Cuban Institute of Radio and Television)

ETECSA: Empresa de Telecomunicaciones de Cuba (Telecommunications Company of Cuba)

PCC: Partido Comunista de Cuba (Communist Party of Cuba)

FEU: Federación de Estudiantes Universitarios (University [of Havana] Students' Federation)

CEID: Centro de Estudios de Información de la Defensa (Center for Defense Information Studies)

CENESEX: Centro Nacional de Educación Sexual (National Center for Sex Education)

LABIOFAM: Laboratorios Biológico Farmacéutico (Biological Pharmaceutical Laboratories)

ICAIC: Instituto Cubano de Arte e Industria Cinematográfico (Cuban Film Institute)

279

UMAP: Unidades Militares para Ayuda a la Producción (Military Units to Aid Production)

VENEZUELA

DIGEPOL: Venezuelan intelligence until 1974
DISIP: Servicios de Inteligencia y Prevención (Directorate of Intelligence and Prevention Services), Venezuelan intelligence after 1974
PDVSA: Venezuela's state oil company
ICICA: Investigaciones Comerciales e Industriales, Compañía Anónima (Commercial and Industrial Research Agency), Luis Posada Carriles's security agency

UNITED STATES

OFAC: U.S. Treasury Department's Office of Foreign Assets Control
JTTF: Joint Terrorism Task Force (for South Florida)
FISA: Foreign Intelligence Surveillance Act
GAO: U.S. Government Accountability Office
DOJ: Department of Justice
DHS: Department of Homeland Security

MILITANT EXILE GROUPS

CORU: Coordinadora de Organizaciones Revolucionarias Unidas (Coordination of United Revolutionary Organizations)
MIRR: Movimiento Insurreccional de Recuperación Revolucionaria (Insurrectional Revolutionary Recovery Movement)
Omega 7
Cuban Power

SPOOKS, PLOTTERS, POLITICIANS & THE LAW

MILITANTS AND FELLOW TRAVELERS

Orlando Bosch (1926–), aka Señor Paniagua, Carlos Sucre, Pedro Peña: 1976— founder of CORU

Luis Posada Carriles (1928–), aka Comisario Basilio, Bambi, El Solo, Lupo, Ramón Medina, Juan José Rivas López, Louis McClaud

Gaspar Jiménez: Captured with Posada in 2000; found guilty in attempt on Fidel Castro in Panama; pardoned in 2004, pardon rescinded by Panama in 2008

Pedro Remón: Captured with Posada in 2000; found guilty in attempt on Fidel Castro in Panama; pardoned in 2004, pardon rescinded by Panama in 2008

Guillermo Novo: Convicted in Letelier/Moffitt assassination; found guilty in attempt on Fidel Castro in Panama in 2000; pardoned in 2004, pardon rescinded by Panama in 2008

Frank Castro: Founding member of CORU, lives in Dominican Republic

Ignacio Novo: CORU and Condor operative; part of Letelier/Moffitt assassination

José Dionisio Suárez Esquivel, aka El Charco de Sangre (Pool of Blood): member of CORU; convicted in Letelier/Moffitt assassination, released in 2001 after serving eight years; lives in Miami

Virgilio Paz Romero: Member of CORU; convicted in Letelier/Moffitt assassination, released in 2001, served 10 years, lives in Miami

Valentín Hernández: Member of CORU; murdered Luciano Nieves in 1975; fugitive until capture in 1977, released in 2006; lives in Fort Myers, Florida

Eduardo Arocena: Serving life sentence for 42 counts related to Omega 7 bombings, 1975 to 1983

Freddy Lugo: Posada employee found guilty of planting explosives in 1976 Cubana bombing, convicted 1986, incarcerated 1976 to 1993, served 16 years, released in 1993

Hernán Ricardo: Posada employee; found guilty of planting explosives in 1976 Cubana bombing, convicted 1986, incarcerated 1976 to 1993, served 16 years, released in 1993

Andrés Nazario Sargén: Former chief of Alpha 66, died in 2004

Osiel González: Posada cohort in failed Castro assassination attempt in Ecuador in 1972; secretary general of Alpha 66

Antonio Veciana: Cofounder of Alpha 66 with Eloy Gutiérrez Menoyo; renounced militancy in 1990s

Hector Cornillot Llano: Member of CORU; cohort of Bosch; convicted in 1972 of bombing Air Canada office in Miami Beach; released in July 2001, served 23 years

Rafael Hernández Nodarse: Bay of Pigs veteran; media tycoon based in Honduras; friend and patron of Posada

José Antonio Llama: Former director of the CANF turned whistleblower; charged in 1997 plot against Castro; acquitted

Ángel Alfonso Alemán: Former Cuban political prisoner; charged in the Esperanza caper to eliminate Castro; acquitted

Osvaldo Mitat and Santiago Alvarez: Posada's longtime cohorts; pled guilty in 2006 to illegal possession of false passports and firearms

Ernesto Abreu, Rubén Darío López-Castro, and José Pujol: Pled guilty in 2007 to obstruction of justice for refusing to testify against Posada

Francisco "Paco" Pimentel: Cuban exile businessman and collaborator of Posada

Arnaldo Monzón Plasencia: Executive director of CANF in New Jersey, active in covert operations; died in 2000

POLITICIANS

George H. W. Bush: Director of CIA 1975–1977; president of U.S. 1988–1992

George W. Bush: President of U.S. 2000–2008

Jeb Bush: Governor of Florida 1998–2007; head of Florida GOP; business partner of Armando Codina; business associate of fugitive Miguel Recarey

Prescott Bush: Father of George H. W. Bush; senator from Connecticut; shareholder in West Indies Sugar Company

Fulgencio Batista: President of Cuba from 1933 until January 1, 1959

Hugo Chávez: Former army colonel in guerrilla war; president of Venezuela 1998–present

Fidel Castro Ruz: President of Cuba 1959–2008

Raúl Castro Ruz: President of Cuba 2008–present

John F. Kennedy: President of U.S. 1960–1963

Robert Kennedy: U.S. attorney general 1960–1964

Carlos Andrés Pérez aka CAP: President of Venezuela 1974–1979 and 1983–1993; Minister of the Interior in early 1970s

General Augusto Pinochet: President of Chile 1973–1990

Peter Vaky: U.S. ambassador in Venezuela, 1976

Otto Reich: Ambassador to Venezuela 1986–1989; Iran-Contra participant

Ileana Ros-Lehtinen: Miami congresswoman (18th District), elected in 1989

Lincoln Díaz-Balart: Miami congressman (21st District), elected in 1992

Mario Díaz-Balart: Miami congressman (25th District), elected in 2002

Mireya Moscoso: Panamanian president 1999–2004; pardoned Posada and cohorts in 2004; pardon rescinded in 2008 by the Torrijos government

Martín Erasto Torrijos: President of Panama 2004–present

SPOOKS

David Atlee Phillips (1922–1988): CIA officer for 25 years; chief of Cuban operations 1968–1969; later chief of CIA's Western Hemisphere Division

E. Howard Hunt (1916–2007): In early 1970s, CIA Latin American and Cuban operative; Watergate burglar

Porter Goss: CIA operative 1959–1972; director of CIA 2004–2006

Erasto Fernández: Venezuela's DIGEPOL chief; recruited Posada in 1971

Orlando García: DISIP chief through 2000; responsible for CAP's personal security

Ricardo "El Mono" Morales Navarette: DISIP officer, CIA asset, FBI informer; killed in 1982 in Miami

Rafael Rivas-Vásquez: Analyst for DISIP 1972–1994; chief of DISIP from 1989

General Manuel Contreras: Pinochet's chief of DINA, Chile's secret police; headed up Operation Condor and Dirty War; serving 25 sentences totaling 289 years in prison for kidnapping, forced disappearance, and assassination

Félix Rodríguez: Posada's former comrade from Bay of Pigs; directed covert Iran-Contra operation in El Salvador

Lieutenant Colonel Oliver L. North: National Security Council member who directed the Iran-Contra mission

Donald Gregg: Former CIA, George H. W. Bush's national security adviser and point man on Iran-Contra

Fabian Escalante: Cuba's former chief of intelligence

Joaquín Chaffardet: DISIP official until 1974; later Posada's business partner and attorney

THE LAW

Eugene Propper: U.S. attorney charged with investigating the Letelier/Moffitt assassination in 1976

Dennis Ramdwar: Trinidad and Tobago's deputy police commissioner in 1970s and '80s

Diosdado Diaz, Luis Rodriguez, and George Kiszynski: Members of Joint Terrorism Task Force based in Miami (mid-'90s to 2002)

Hector Pesquera: FBI special agent in charge of Miami Bureau from 1999 until December 2003

Ed Pesquera: Assigned to lead FBI investigation in Miami office on Posada case in 2003

Kendall Coffey: Former U.S. attorney; represented Santiago Alvarez

Eduardo Soto: Posada lawyer

David Sebastian: Posada paralegal

Arturo Hernández: Posada lawyer

Felipe Millan: Posada lawyer

Judge William Abbott: U.S. immigration judge in Posada case in 2005

Judge Norbert Garney: Texas magistrate in Posada case in 2005

U.S. District Judge Kathleen Cardone: Presiding federal judge in the Posada case in El Paso, Texas

Marcos D. Jiménez: U.S. attorney for the Southern District of Florida, 2000–2005

Alexander Acosta: U.S. attorney for the Southern District of Florida, 2005–2009

U.S. District Judge Peter Sheridan: New Jersey federal judge in Posada case

Raoul Cantero: Attorney for Orlando Bosch and Jorge Mas Canosa; appointed to Florida Supreme Court by Jeb Bush; resumed private practice in 2008

Alberto Gonzales: U.S. attorney general, 2005–2007

Michael Mukasey: U.S. attorney general, 2007–January 2009

Eric Holder: U.S. attorney general, January 2009–present

John W. Van Lonkhuyzen: 2007–2009, Justice Department Posada prosecutor

Edward Nucci: 2005–2006, Justice Department Posada prosecutor

David Deitch: 2006–2007, Justice Department Posada prosecutor

Paul Ahern: 2007–2008, Justice Department Posada prosecutor

Rebekah Sittner: 2009, Justice Department Posada prosecutor

Omar Vega and Jorge González: 2005–2009, members of Miami FBI Joint Terrorism Task Force

TIMELINE

March 10, 1952	Gen. Fulgencio Batista stages a military coup, seizing the presidency of Cuba.
July 26, 1953	Fidel Castro leads 134 followers in a failed attack on the Moncada military garrison in Santiago. Seventy are killed. Fidel and Raúl Castro are sentenced to 15 years but are released in May 1955 due to an amnesty granted political prisoners.
January 1, 1959	Fidel Castro's forces defeat those of Batista in eastern and central Cuba. Batista flees to the Dominican Republic and later Portugal.
May 17, 1959	The Cuban government enacts the Agrarian Reform Law, which limits land ownership to 1,000 acres.
March 17, 1960	U.S. president Eisenhower secretly orders CIA director Allen Dulles to train Cuban exiles for an invasion of Cuba.
July 5, 1960	All U.S. business/commercial property in Cuba is nationalized.
October 19, 1960	U.S. imposes an economic embargo on Cuba prohibiting all exports except foodstuffs, medicines, medical supplies.
April 16, 1961	Castro defines the Cuban Revolution as being socialist.
April 17, 1961	1,300 U.S.-supported Cuban exiles invade Cuba at the Bay of Pigs. Two days later, Castro claims victory.
January 1962	Cuba is suspended from OAS (Organization of American States).
September 26, 1962	Congress passes a joint resolution whereby the president has the right to intervene militarily in Cuba if U.S. interests are threatened.
October 2, 1962	The U.S. government tightens the embargo. All ports are closed to nations that allow their ships to carry arms to Cuba (and other restrictions).
October 18–29, 1962	Cuban Missile Crisis; President Kennedy announces that there are nuclear missile sites in Cuba; orders a naval blockade of the island.
October 28, 1962	Radio Moscow announces that the Soviet Union has accepted a proposed solution, and has agreed to remove its missiles from Cuba. Premier Khrushchev's letter to President Kennedy is broadcast.

February 8, 1963	The Kennedy administration further tightens the embargo and makes most travel to Cuba illegal for U.S. citizens. All Cuban-owned assets in the United States are frozen, including an estimated $33 million in U.S. banks.
October 1965	More than 3,000 Cubans leave in a boat lift to the U.S. after Castro announces that those who want to leave for the U.S. can depart from the port of Camarioca.
November 6, 1965	Cuba and the U.S. agree to airlift for Cubans who want to go to the United States, the onset of the Freedom Flights program, which enables 250,000 Cubans to come to the U.S. by 1971.
November 2, 1966	President Johnson signs into law the Cuban Adjustment Act, facilitating Cubans who have reached the U.S. to reside there legally.
September 8, 1969	Cuba expels Associated Press correspondent Fenton Wheeler. In retaliation, Washington prohibits Cuban news bureaus in the U.S., except for those on UN property.
February 15, 1973	U.S. and Cuba sign an anti-hijacking agreement, the only formal agreement between the two countries. But Cuba formally revokes the agreement four years later.
July 10, 1974	The embargo is loosened to allow the import of low-value gifts. In addition, the U.S. Treasury Department eases travel-related restrictions.
September 28, 1974	Senators Jacob Javits (R-NY) and Claiborne Pell (D-RI) travel to Havana to meet with Castro—the first visit to Cuba by elected officials of the U.S. government since diplomatic relations were severed in 1961.
November 1974	Assistant Secretary of State William Rogers and Assistant to the Secretary of State Lawrence Eagleburger conduct secret normalization talks with Cuban officials in Washington and New York. The talks end over Cuba's intervention in the Marxist revolution in Angola.
March 18, 1977	U.S. government lifts prohibition on travel to Cuba and allows U.S. citizens to spend $100 on Cuban goods during their visits.
April and May 1977	The United States and Cuba sign agreements on fishing rights and maritime boundaries. The two countries also agree to open "interests sections" in each other's capitals.
January 9, 1978	The U.S. Treasury Department allows U.S. residents to provide relatives in Cuba with no more than $500 in any three-month period.
November– December 1978	The Committee of 75, a group of exiles, are chosen to negotiate with the Cuban government. Cuba releases 3,600 political prisoners.
April 1980	Mariel boat lift; a flotilla of refugees (eventually numbering 125,000 over five months) begins an exodus for the U.S.
December 1, 1981	President Reagan secretly authorizes the CIA to support operations against leftist insurgents in Central America.
April 9, 1982	Charter air links between Miami and Havana are halted by

the U.S. government. Ten days later, the U.S. government reinstitutes the travel ban.

May 24, 1983   Assistant Secretary of State Thomas Enders meets with Ramón Sánchez Parodi, the head of the Cuban Interests Section, to request that Cuba take back nearly 800 imprisoned *Marielitos*.

May 20, 1985   Congress passes legislation creating Radio Martí, named after Cuban patriot José Martí, to broadcast news to Cuba. The Cuban government immediately jams the signal.

November 19, 1987   The United States and Cuba conclude a new immigration pact that reinstates the 1984 agreement in which Cuba agreed to accept the return of *Marielitos*.

January 26, 1990   Cuban television starts broadcasting *CNN World Report*, a weekly CNN news series. Cuba is one of the first countries to sign on to broadcast this report.

March 23, 1990   The U.S. launches its first test of TV Martí. After broadcasting to Cuba for three hours, it is jammed by the Cuban government.

December 1991   Collapse of the Soviet Union ends aid for Cuba estimated at $5 billion a year.

October 15, 1992   Congress passes the Cuban Democracy Act, sponsored by Representative Robert Torricelli (D-NJ) in the House of Representatives and Senator Bob Graham (D-FL) in the U.S. Senate. The legislation, commonly known as the Torricelli Bill, prohibits foreign-based subsidiaries of U.S. companies from trading with Cuba and U.S. citizens from traveling to Cuba, among other prohibitions.

November 6, 1993   Cuba announces it is opening state enterprises to limited private investment.

July–September 1994   Following Castro's declaration of an open migration policy, a new boat lift begins. Some 35,000 fleeing Cubans, or *balseros*, set sail for the U.S. Ends when the Clinton administration agrees that legal migration to the U.S. will be a minimum of 20,000 per year.

October 5, 1995   President Clinton announces measures to expand people-to-people contacts between the U.S. and Cuba and to allow U.S. nongovernmental organizations to fund projects in Cuba.

February 1996   Cuban MiGs shoot down in international airspace two civilian aircraft belonging to the Miami-based group Brothers to the Rescue, killing four. President Clinton suspends charter travel to Havana and has Congress approve legislation to use a portion of the $100 million in frozen Cuban assets in the U.S. to compensate the families of the victims.

March 12, 1996   Clinton passes the Cuban Liberty and Democratic Solidarity (Libertad) Act, also known as the Helms-Burton Act. The legislative behemoth codifies the U.S. embargo and enacts penalties on foreign companies doing business in Cuba, permits U.S. citizens to sue foreign investors who make use of American-owned property seized by the Cuban government, and denies entry into the U.S. to such foreign investors. The legislation also bans U.S. imports of sugar from any foreign country that buys sugar or molasses from Cuba, and reduces American contributions to the World Bank and other financial institutions if they loan to Cuba.

July 16, 1996   President Clinton suspends enforcement of specific Title III provisions of the Helms-Burton Act, which permits suits to be filed in U.S. courts against foreign investors who are profiting from U.S.-claimed confiscated property. Suspension continues every six months hence.

November 13, 1996   Angered over Helms-Burton, Britain, Germany, and the Netherlands for the first time cast their ballots against the United States at the annual vote in the UN General Assembly on the U.S. embargo of Cuba.

February 12, 1997   The Clinton administration approves licenses for U.S. news organizations to open bureaus in Cuba.

January 21–25, 1998   Pope John Paul II visits Cuba.

March 20, 1998   The Clinton administration announces new measures allowing direct flights between Havana and Miami, and allowing Cuban-Americans to send up to $300 every three months to island relatives through licensed brokers.

November 12, 1998   Thirty years after it was kicked out of Cuba, the Associated Press, the world's oldest news service, receives approval to reopen its Havana bureau.

November 25, 1999–
June 2000   On Thanksgiving Day, six-year-old Elián González is found in the Straits of Florida clinging to an inner tube. For six months U.S. relations with Cuba are tested during the bitter struggle over returning Elián to his father in Cuba.

December 12, 2000   U.S. and Cuban officials begin another round of talks on immigration issues.

June 23, 2001   Castro faints during televised speech, setting off speculation about his health and successor.

2000–2008   President George W. Bush assembles a Cuba team that recalibrates U.S. policy to one of confrontation, vastly tightening restrictions on Cuba.

October 2004   Castro falls forward during speech, breaking kneecap and arm.

July 31, 2006   Cuban government announces that Fidel Castro has fallen gravely ill.

February 2008   Raúl Castro officially takes over the presidency from his brother.

April 17, 2009   President Barack Obama announces "a new beginning with Cuba."

June 3, 2009   The OAS lifts its forty-seven-year suspension barring Cuba.

Sources include data from the Associated Press, BBC, Reuters, PBS, and the *Miami Herald*.

TEAM RAÚL

Raúl Castro, as President of Cuba, is both the chief of state and head of government. His roles include being the President of the Council of State, President of the Council of Ministers, and leader of the Armed Forces. Fidel Castro has stayed on as the president of the Communist Party.

Under Raúl Castro, the Armed Forces (MINFAR) and the Cuban Communist Party, notably its Politburo and Secretariat, are the country's most influential institutions. The National Assembly plays a lesser role.

Pres. of the Council of State	Raúl Castro Ruz, Gen.
First Vice Pres. of the Council of State	José Ramón Machado Ventura
Vice Pres.	Juan Almeida Bosque, Commander of the Revolution
Vice Pres.	Julio Casas Regueiro, Gen.
Vice Pres.	Abelardo Colomé Ibarra, Gen.
Vice Pres.	Juan Esteban Lazo Hernández
Sec. of the Exec. Comm. of the Council of State	Homero Acosta Álvarez
Pres. of the Council of Ministers	Raúl Castro Ruz, Gen.
First Vice Pres.	José Ramón Machado Ventura
Vice Pres.	Ricardo Cabrisas Ruiz
Vice Pres.	José Ramón Fernández Álvarez
Vice Pres.	Ulises Rosales del Toro, Div. Gen.
Vice Pres.	Ramiro Valdés Menéndez, Commander of the Revolution
Vice Pres.	Jorge Luis Sierra Cruz
Vice Pres.	Marino Alberto Murillo Jorge
Sec. of the Exec. Comm. of the Council of Ministers	Brig. Gen. José Amado Ricardo Guerra

SENIOR OFFICERS OF ARMED FORCES

Commander in Chief of FAR	Raúl Castro, Army Gen.
Minister of FAR	Julio Casas Regueiro, Corps Gen.
Minister of the Interior	Abelardo Colomé Ibarra, Corps Gen.
First Vice Minister of FAR	Leopoldo Cintra Frías, Corps Gen.
Vice Minister and Chief of General Staff of FAR	Álvaro López Miera, Corps Gen.
Vice Minister of FAR	Ramón Espinosa Martín, Corps Gen.
Vice Minister of FAR	Joaquín Quinta Solá, Corps Gen.

MEMBERS OF THE POLITBURO OF THE CUBAN COMMUNIST PARTY (PCC)

First Secretary of the Communist Party Central Committee
Fidel Castro Ruz

Second Secretary of the Communist Party Central Committee
Raúl Castro Rúz

First Vice President of Councils of State and Ministers
José Ramón Machado Ventura

Minister of FAR
Julio Casas Regueiro, Corps Gen.

Minister of the Interior
Abelardo Colomé Ibarra, Corps Gen.

Vice Minister of FAR
Álvaro López Miera, Corps Gen.

Minister of Information and Communications
Ramiro Valdés Menéndez, Commander of the Revolution

First Vice Minister of FAR
Leopoldo Cintra Frías, Corps Gen.

Vice Minister of FAR
Ramón Espinosa Martín, Corps Gen.

Vice President of the Council of State
Juan Esteban Lazo Hernández

President of the National Assembly
Ricardo Alarcón

Vice President of the Council of State
Juan Almeida Bosque, Commander of the Revolution

Minister of Public Health
José Ramón Balaguer

Director of the Finlay Institute
Dr. Concepción Campa Huergo

Minister of Basic Industries
Yadira García Vera

Minister of Culture
Abel Prieto Jiménez

Minister of Agriculture
Ulises Rosales del Toro, Gen.

Minister of Transportation
Jorge Luis Sierra Cruz

Ambassador to Angola
Pedro Ross Leal

Chief of Communist Party in Havana
Pedro Saez Montejo

Member of the Secretariat of PCC
Misael Enamarado Dager

Minister of Higher Education
Miguel Díaz-Canel Bermúdez

Secretary General of the Cuban Workers Federation
Salvador Valdés Mesa

NOTES

Interviews are dated when of some significance—historically or politically. With most subjects or sources, multiple interviews or conversations were conducted over several years.

PREFACE

New Yorker, May 3, 1993. Cartoon by Robert Mankoff.

PART I

INTERVIEWS

David Adams, Miami
Luis Aguilar León. Miami: December 13 and 14, 2000
Fulton Armstrong, Washington, DC
Sonia Baez, Havana
Bernardo Benes, Miami
Natalia Bolívar. Havana
Jerry Brown. Havana and Santa Clara, Cuba: August 14, 2000
Guillermo Cabrera Infante. London: August 1996
Fidel Castro. Havana: October 16, 1993; January 3 and 4, 1994; July 26, 2000
Juanita Castro. Miami: December 11, 2000; April 18, 2002
Raúl Castro Ruz. Encounters in Havana on January 3, 1994; August 14, 2000
Steven Clemons, Washington
Efraim Conte, Miami
Luis Conte Agüero, Miami
Amb. Jeffrey Davidow
Rep. William Delahunt, Washington
Jack Devine, former chief for Latin America, CIA. New York: September 17, 2000
Rafael Díaz-Balart. Miami: October 8, 2001
Daniel Erikson
Vilma Espín. Havana: December 22, 1993; January 2, 1994
Heine Estaron
Mark Falcoff
Michael Fuchs
Lourdes García-Navarro

Col. Sam Gardiner, Washington
Edward Gonzalez
Barbara Walker Gordon. Washington: March 3, 2002
Alfredo Guevara. Havana: January 3, 1994; July 22, 2000
Amb. Paul Hare
Amb. Vicki Huddleston
Kirby Jones
Saul Landau
Salvador Lew, Miami
Father Amado Llorente. January 25, 2001
Lee Lockwood. January 16, 2001
Rosario Moreno, Miami
Leon Morgenstern, MD
Achy Obejas
Jim Olson, former chief of counterintelligence, CIA
Phil Peters
Kevin Phillips
José Rodríguez Feo. Havana
William D. Rogers, former assistant secretary of state for inter-American affairs, 2002–2005
John Ryan
Carlos Saladrigas
Conchita Sarnoff. August 2006
Marjorie Skelly Lord. Miami: November 4, 2001
Amb. Michael Small
Oliver Stone, Santa Monica, CA
Julia Sweig
Tad Szulc. January 12, 2001
Jorge Tabio, Havana
Ginger Thompson
Isabelle Walker

FILMS

Fidel, Estela Bravo documentary, 2001.
Comandante, Oliver Stone documentary, 2003.
Looking for Fidel, Oliver Stone documentary, 2004.

DOCUMENTS/REPORTS

Daily Press Briefing, December 18, 2007, Tom Casey, deputy spokesman. "Castro's Comments." Washington, DC.
Gonzalez, Edward. "Cuba: Clearing Perilous Waters." RAND, 1996.
Joyce, Mark. "Brother in Arms: Transitioning from One Castro to Another in Cuba." *RUSI Journal,* October 2007.
McCormack, Sean. State Department News Briefing, December 4, 2006.
Morgenstern, Leon, MD. "Malignant Diverticulitis Diverticular Disease: Management of the Difficult Surgical Case." Williams & Wilkins, 1998.
Morgenstern, Leon, MD; Robert Weiner, MD; Stephen L. Michel, MD. "'Malignant' Diverticulitis: A Clinical Entity." January 19, 1979.

Morgenstern, Leon, MD; Tatsuo Yamakawa, MD; Meir Ben-Shoshan, MD; Harvey Lippman, MD. "Anastomotic Leakage after Low Colonic Anastomosis." *American Journal of Surgery*. June 19, 1971.

BOOKS

Bardach, Ann Louise. *Cuba Confidential: Love and Vengeance in Miami and Havana*. New York: Random House Vintage, 2002.

Bardach, Ann Louise, and Luis Conte Agüero. *The Prison Letters of Fidel Castro*. New York: Avalon, 2006.

Blanco, Katiuska. *Todo el tiempo de los cedros: Paisaje familiar de Fidel Castro Ruz*. Havana: Casa Editorial, April, 2003.

Bonachea, Ronaldo E., and Nelson P. Valdés. *Revolutionary Struggle: Vol. 1 of the Selected Works of Fidel Castro*. Boston: The Massachusetts Institute of Technology, 1972.

Castro, Fidel, with Ignacio Ramonet. *Fidel Castro: Biografía a dos voces*. New York: Random House Mondadori, 2006.

———. *Fidel Castro: My Life*. London: Allen Lane, 2007.

———. *Fidel Castro: My Life*. New York: Scribner 2008.

Coltman, Leycester. *The Real Fidel Castro*. New Haven: Yale University Press, 2003.

Conte Agüero, Luis. *Cartas del presidio*. Havana: Editorial Lex, 1959.

De la Cova, Antonio Rafael. *The Moncada Attack: Birth of the Cuban Revolution*. Columbia, SC: University of South Carolina Press, 2007.

DePalma, Anthony. *The Man Who Invented Fidel: Castro, Cuba, and Herbert L. Matthews of the New York Times*. New York: Public Affairs, 2006.

Erikson, Daniel. *The Cuba Wars*. New York: Bloomsbury Press, 2009.

Fernández, Alina. *Castro's Daughter: An Exile's Memoir of Cuba*. New York: St. Martin's Press, 1997.

Fidel y la religión: Conversaciones con Frei Betto sobre el Marxismo y la teología de liberación. Havana: Editorial Si-Mar S.A., 1994.

Franqui, Carlos. *Diary of the Cuban Revolution*. New York: Viking Press, 1980.

———. *Family Portrait with Fidel*. New York: Random House, 1984. (Translated by Alfred MacAdam.)

Geyer, Georgie Anne. *Guerrilla Prince: The Untold Story of Fidel Castro*. Kansas City: Andrews & McMeel, 1993.

Gjelten, Tom. *Bacardi and the Long Fight for Cuba*. New York: Viking, 2008.

Gonzalez, Edward. *Cuba Under Castro: The Limits of Charisma*. Boston: Houghton Mifflin, 1974.

Gonzalez, Edward, and David Ronfeldt. *Castro, Cuba, and the World*. Los Angeles: RAND, 1986.

Gott, Richard. *Cuba: A New History*. New Haven: Yale University Press, 2004.

Infante, Guillermo Cabrera. *Mea Cuba*. Plaza & Janés Editores, 1992.

Kushner, Rachel. *Telex from Cuba*. New York: Scribner, 2008.

Lockwood, Lee. *Castro's Cuba, Cuba's Fidel*. New York: Macmillan, 1967.

Matthews, Herbert. *Revolution in Cuba: An Essay in Understanding*. New York: Scribner's, 1975.

Miná, Gianni. *An Encounter with Fidel*. Melbourne: Ocean Press, 1991.

Montaner, Carlos Alberto. *Los Cubanos: História de Cuba en una lección*. Miami: Brickell Communications Group, 2006.

Pérez, Louis A. Jr. *Cuba in the American Imagination.* Chapel Hill: University of North Carolina Press, 2008.

Phillips, Kevin. *American Dynasty.* New York: Viking, 2004.

Quirk, Robert E. *Fidel Castro.* New York: W.W. Norton & Company, 1993.

Ros, Enrique. *Fidel Castro y el gatillo alegre: Sus años universitarios.* Miami: Ediciones Universal, 2003.

Skierka, Volker. *Fidel Castro: A Biography.* Maine: Polity Press, 2004.

Symmes, Patrick. *The Boys From Dolores.* New York: Pantheon, 2007.

Szulc, Tad. *Fidel: A Critical Portrait.* New York: Avon Books, 1986.

Thomas, Hugh. *Cuba or the Pursuit of Freedom.* New York: Da Capo Press, 1998.

———. *The Cuban Revolution.* New York: Harper & Row, 1971.

ARTICLES

Fidel Castro Ruz: "Reflections" by the Commander in Chief/or Comrade Fidel in *Granma*:

"Gestures That Are Impressive," April 27, 2009.

"Trapped by History," April 24, 2009.

"Pontius Pilate Washed His Hands," April 24, 2009.

"The Summit and the Lie," April 23, 2009.

"Obama and the Blockade," April 22, 2009.

"Delirious Dreams," April 21, 2009.

"The Secret Summit," April 20, 2009.

"Officers with Sound Beliefs," April 16, 2009.

"Does the OAS Have a Right to Exist?" April 15, 2009.

"Days That Cannot Be Forgotten," April 14, 2009.

"On the Blockade, Not One Word Was Said," April 14, 2009.

"News of Chávez and of Evo," April 13, 2009.

"Meeting with Barbara Lee and Other Members of the Black Caucus," April 8, 2009.

"The Seven Congress Members Who Are Visiting Us," April 7, 2009.

"Lies in the Service of the Empire," March 26, 2009.

"It Had All Been Said," March 25, 2009.

"The Facts Are Proving Me Right," March 23, 2009.

"Glory to the Good!" March 23, 2009.

"We Are the Ones to Blame," March 20, 2009.

"More News on the Agonies of Capitalism," March 13, 2009.

"The Agonies of Developed Capitalism," March 12, 2009.

"Healthy Changes Within the Council of Ministers," March 3, 2009.

"The Article by Chávez," February 13, 2009.

"Meeting with Chilean President Michelle Bachelet," February 12, 2009.

"Rahm Emanuel," February 9, 2009.

"Deciphering the Thinking of the New President," January 29, 2009.

"The Eleventh President of the United States," January 22, 2009.

"The Unjustifiable Destruction of the Environment," December 16, 2008.

"Sailing Against the Tide," December 2, 2008.

"The Great Crisis of the 1930s," December 1, 2008.

"Dimitri A. Medvedev," December 1, 2008.

"Meeting Lula," October 31, 2008.

"The Worst Choice," October 30, 2008.

"Economic Illiteracy," October 26, 2008.

"The Russian Orthodox Church," October 21, 2008.

"We Are and We Should Be Socialists," October 4, 2008.

"A Subject to Reflect On," October 2, 2008.

"The Democratic Socialism," September 26, 2008.

"Bush's Self-Criticism," September 25, 2008.

"The True Story and the Challenge of the Cuban Journalists," July 3, 2008.

"The McCain Tour and the Manifest Destiny of the U.S. Fourth Fleet," June 30, 2008.

"The Empire's Hypocritcal Politics," May 25, 2008.

"Martí's Inmortal Ideas," May 22, 2008.

"Two Hungry Wolves and a Little Red Riding Hood," May 18, 2008.

"Yankee Response in the Hemisphere: The Fourth Fleet of Intervention," May 4, 2008.

"An Acid Test," April 30, 2008.

"Our Spirit of Sacrifice and the Empire's Blackmail," April 24, 2008.

"The Living and Dead," April 22, 2008.

"Peace and Prosperity," April 20, 2008.

"Making Concessions to Enemy Ideology," April 15, 2008.

"Bush, War and the Tooth-and-Nail Struggle for Survival," April 6, 2008.

"Bush in Heaven (II)," March 22, 2008.

"Bush in Heaven (I)," March 22, 2008.

"Chávez Visit," March 8, 2008.

"The International Criminal Court," March 6, 2008.

"Christians Without Bibles," March 2, 2008.

"Premature Death," March 1, 2008.

"I Hope I Never Have Reason to Be Ashamed," February 28, 2008.

"Who Wants to Be in the Garbage Dump?" February 22, 2008.

"What I Wrote on Tuesday 19," February 21, 2008.

"Message from the Commander in Chief," February 18, 2008.

"The Republican Candidate (Part Five and Last)," February 15, 2008.

"The Republican Candidate (Part Four)," February 14, 2008.

"The Republican Candidate (Part Three)," February 12, 2008.

"The Republican Candidate (Part Two)," February 11, 2008.

"The Republican Candidate (Part One)," February 10, 2008.

"An Example of Good Communist Behavior," January 7, 2008.

"Antonio Maceo: The Bronze Titan," December 8, 2007.

"A People Under Fire," November 29, 2007.

"Bush, Hunger and Death," November 22, 2007.

"Oil Costs and Development," November 19, 2007.

"The Conversation with Chávez," November 19, 2007.

"The Ideological Waterloo," November 15, 2007.

"The Summit Debate," November 12, 2007.

"The Value of Ideas," November 10, 2007.

"The Elections," October 23, 2007.

"A Silent Complicity," October 10, 2007.

"The Empire's Illegal Wars," October 1, 2007.

"Aznar's Silence," September 29, 2007.

"Deliberate Lies, Strange Deaths and Aggression to the World Economy," September 18, 2007.

"The Empire and Its Lies," September 11, 2007.

"Submission to Imperial Politics," August 27, 2007.

"Remembering Chibas, 100 Years After His Birth," August 25, 2007.

"The Empire Tastes an Unprecedented Moral Defeat," August 22, 2007.

"The Empire and the Independent Island (Parts IV and V)," August 17, 2007.

"The Empire and the Independent Island (Parts II and III)," August 16, 2007.

"The Empire and the Independent Island (Part I)," August 15, 2007.

"The Brain Drain," July 17, 2007.

"Bush, Health and Education," July 14, 2007.

"World Tyranny," July 7, 2007.

"The Killing Machine," June 30, 2007.

"The Good Lord Protected Me from Bush," June 28, 2007.

"A Reflection on My Reflections," June 22, 2007.

"Vilma's Struggles," June 20, 2007.

"The Tyrant Visits Tirana," June 11, 2007.

"Bush's Lies and Cons," June 7, 2007.

"Bush in the Sky," March 22, 2007.

Abend, Lisa. "Idalmis Menendez—Insight from Fidel Castro's Former Daughter-in-Law," *Miami Herald,* December 20, 2006.

Anderson, Jon Lee. "Fidel's Heir," *New Yorker,* June 23, 2008.

Aznárez, Juan Jesús. "Castro's Main Defect Is That He Was Brought Up Like a Gangster," *El País/Herald Tribune,* April 25, 2007.

Bardach, Ann Louise. "Conversations with Castro," *Vanity Fair,* March 1994.

———. "The Long Goodbye," *Financial Times,* November 10, 2007.

———. "Oliver Twist," *Slate,* April 14, 2004.

———. "The Spy Who Loved Castro," *Vanity Fair,* November 1993.

Boadle, Anthony. "Cuba's Castro Ridicules Gaffe-Prone Bush," Reuters, February 14, 2004.

———. "Raúl Castro Calls for More Policy Debate in Cuba," Reuters, December 20, 2006.

Brody, Jane E. "Let the Mind Help Tame an Irritable Bowel," *New York Times,* September 2, 2008.

Bussey, Jane. "Many Ask: Can Economic Links Be Forged Anew?" *Miami Herald,* May 19, 2002.

Isla, Wilfredo, and Frances Robles. "Fidel Castro's Towering Shadow dures," *Miami Herald,* August 1, 2008.

ael. "Brand Cuba," *Wall Street Journal,* March 11, 2008.

and M. A. Menéndez. "The Economic Power of the Castro Broth-16, June 24, 2001.

Fidel Rumors Swirl, Our Newsroom Plan Awaits," *Miami Her-2009.

ith Entourage, Is Spotted on Strolls," *New York Times,*

gencies Distracted by Focus on Cuba," *New York 07.*

McBride, Joseph. "The Man Who Wasn't There," *Nation,* July 16–23, 1988.

———. "Where Was George," *Nation,* August 13–20, 1988.

Martínez, Yolanda. *"Temen por salud de Fidel," Reforma,* August 13, 2007.

Menendez, Ana. "Dictating May Be Good for Your Health," *Miami Herald,* April 25, 2007.

Ojito, Mirta. "Cuba Reaps Goodwill from Doctor Diplomacy," *Miami Herald,* August 17, 2008.

Reyes, Gerardo. *"Acusan de fraude a ex nuera de Fidel Castro," El Nuevo Herald,* July 15, 2008.

Rodriguez, Andrea. "Argentine Prez: Fidel Castro 'Believes in Obama,'" Associated Press, January 21, 2009.

———. "Castro Looks Frail, Alert in New Photos," Associated Press, January 16, 2008.

Snow, Anita. "Castro Quips After Bush Speech That He Survived Assassination Because of God's Protection," Associated Press, June 28, 2007.

———. "Cuba Perks Show a Post-Fidel Touch," Associated Press, September 9, 2007.

Stephens, Sarah. "U.S. Policy 'Disserves' the Cuban People: Pity Carlos Gutierrez, Our Secretary of Commerce," *Huffington Post,* February 22, 2007.

Sweig, Julia E. "Fidel's Final Victory," *Foreign Affairs,* January/February 2007.

Vulliamy, Ed. "In the Last Act of Castro's Cuba, a Search Is on for a New Beginning," *Observer,* January 20, 2008.

"Cuban Journalists Say U.S. Denied Them Visas," Associated Press, September 29, 2008.

"Cuba's Castro Looks Healthy in New Video," Associated Press, September 22, 2007.

"Fidel Castro puede regresar al gobierno si asi lo desea," EFE, November 17, 2008.

"Hugo Chávez Visits Fidel, Raúl Castro," Associated Press, March 8, 2008.

"Troops Mobilized After Castro's surgery; Castro Health Crisis," *Miami Herald,* April 4, 2007.

"U.S. Dismisses Overture from Raúl Castro," EFE, December 4, 2007.

PART II

INTERVIEWS

Lazaro Albo. Miami: August 17, 2006

Ángel Alfonso Alemán. New Jersey, San Juan, Puerto Rico: April 27, 1998

Antonio Jorge Alvarez. Washington, Miami: May 5, 13, and 24, 1998

Bernardo Álvarez, Venezuela ambassador to the U.S. Washington, DC: August 2006

Matthew Archambleault. July 18, 2007; August 29–31, 2005

James Bamford. December 17, 2001

E. Lawrence Barcella Jr., assistant U.S. attorney in Letelier prosecution. July 24, 2007

Don Bohning, Miami

Adriana Bosch. Miami: March 13 and May 24, 2006

Karen Bosch. Miami: May 24, 2006

Orlando Bosch. Miami: March 13 and May 24, 2006

Ana Carbonell, chief of staff to Lincoln Díaz-Balart. May 1, 2008

Luis Posada Carriles. Aruba: June 15–18, 1998; El Paso, Texas: September 1, 2005

Joaquín Chaffardet. El Paso, Texas: September 1, 2005
Kendall Coffey, attorney. Miami
Carter Cornick. July 22, 2007
Rep. William Delahunt, Washington
Jack Devine. New York: September 17, 2000
D. C. Diaz, Miami
Gustavo Diaz
John Dinges
Alfredo Durán, Miami
Eduardo Encinosa. Miami: March 3, 2002
Blake Fleetwood, Washington
George Freeman, *New York Times* counsel
Gaeton Fonzi, Miami
Gilberto García. August 28, 2007; September 13, 2007
Orlando García Jr. Miami: July 20, 2006
Osvaldo García. Betheseda, MD: July 22, 2006
Rolando García. Betheseda, MD: July 22, 2006
Robert Gelbard, Washington, DC
Arnaldo Gonzáles Fermin. Isla Margarita, Venezuela: May 8–11, 1998
María González. Miami: June 27, 2001; October 11, 2001
Osiel González. Miami: August 18, 2006
José Alfredo Gutiérrez Solana. Union City, NJ: May 1998
E. Howard Hunt, Miami: June 1, 1998
Tom Julin, Hunton & Williams
George Kiszynski, Miami
Peter Kornbluh
Mario Martínez Malo. Miami: June 1, 1998
Raúl Masvidal. November 25, 1994; December 6, 1994; May 30, 1998
Alberto Milián. Miami: April 11, 2002
Gustavo Moreno. June 2, 1998
Roseanne Nenninger. El Paso, Texas, and New York: 2005
Judy Orihuela, press officer for Miami office of FBI
Miguel Pereira, federal prosecutor. San Juan, Puerto Rico: April 26, 1998
José Pertierra, attorney for Venezuela
Hector Pesquera, FBI special agent in charge. Puerto Rico: April 28, 1998
Ricardo Pesquera, attorney. San Juan, Puerto Rico: April 27, 1998
Paco Pimentel. New York City: June 1998
Eugene M. Propper, U.S. attorney in Letelier case. July 22, 2007
Dennis Ramdwar, chief of police for Trinidad and Tobago. August 1 and 15, 2006
Rich Rivera, Union City, NJ
Luis Rodriguez, Miami
Colonel Manuel Rodríguez-Madrid. Isla Margarita, Venezuela: May 5, 1998
William D. Rogers, former assistant secretary of state for inter-American affairs
Salvador Romaní. Miami: August 18, 2006
Néstor Sánchez, former CIA, Department of Defense. April 26, 1998
David Sebastian, paralegal for Posada. Miami: 2005–2007
Eduardo Soto, attorney. Miami: 2005–2006
Wayne Smith, Washington, DC

Frank Sturgis. Miami: March 20, 1993
Richard Thornburgh. Washington DC
Antonio Veciana. Miami: July 14, 2006
George Volsky
Jay Weaver

DOCUMENTS/REPORTS

"Additional Defendants Plead Guilty to Obstruction of Justice in U.S. Investigation of Luis Posada Carriles." Department of Justice, December 13, 2007.

"Castro Weighs in on Posada Case." Official Cuban Government translation of Fidel Castro's speech. July 26, 1998.

Committee on Foreign Affairs, U.S. House of Representatives. Staff Report. Congressional Hearings: House Judiciary Committee Holds Hearing on Department of Justice Oversight. Witnesses: Attorney General Alberto R. Gonzales, Rep. Bill Delahunt, D-MA. May 10, 2007.

"Examples of Controversial Pardons by Previous Presidents." A Report Prepared by Minority Staff, Committee on Government Reform, U.S. House of Representatives. April 20, 2001.

Exclusion Proceedings for Orlando Bosch Avila. U.S. Department of Justice, Office of the Associate Attorney General, Washington, DC. January 23, 1989.

Fax from Luis Posada from El Salvador, signed "Solo." August 1997. Given to A. L. Bardach.

FBI memo from J. Edgar Hoover to State Department concerning briefing of George Bush. November 29, 1963.

Handwritten notes (three pages) from Luis Posada Carriles, given to A. L. Bardach on June 18, 1998.

House Select Committee on Assassinations documents from *National Security Archive Documents*:

Cable from Secretary of State Henry Kissinger. "Subject: U.S. Position on Investigation of Cubana Airlines Crash," October 1976.

CIA/FBI memorandum of Luis Posada Carriles. June 9, 2005.

CIA, anti-Castro activities, Luis Posada. June 18, 1995.

CIA, anti-Castro activities, Luis Posada. August 16, 1995.

CIA, documents on Roland Otero. October 14, 1977.

CIA signature sheet on Luis Posada. September 26, 1970.

DEA outside contact report. January 25, 1978.

Deposition of Otto J. Reich before the Senate Select Committee on Secret Military Assistance to Iran and the Nicaraguan Opposition. July 15, 1987.

"Documents Linked to Cuban Exile Luis Posada Highlighted Targets for Terrorism." Edited by Peter Kornbluh. May 14, 2007.

FBI interview of Orlando Bosch on August 22, 1963, re: MIRR bombing attack on a Cuban sugar mill.

"Public Diplomacy and Covert Propaganda: The Declassified Record of Ambassador Otto J. Reich." Edited by Thomas Blanton www.gwu.edu/~nsarchiv/NSAEBB. March 2, 2001.

Report of the Congressional Committees Investigating the Iran-Contra Affair, excerpt. November 13, 1987.

Review (1996) of FBI files on Luis Posada. June 22, 1978.

Review (1997) notes on Luis Posada, anti-Castro activities. June 28, 1978.

State Department and Intelligence Community Involvement in Domestic Activities Related to the Iran-Contra Affair. September 7, 1988.

State Department memo from Melvyn Levitsky to Donald P. Gregg. "Subject: Responses by Vice President Bush to Telegrams Regarding Orlando Bosch." June 8, 1988.

Interview with Orlando Bosch and Luis Posada with Blake Fleetwood. San Juan de los Moros Prison, Venezuela: March 1977.

Interview with Luis Posada, during Caracas incarceration. June 17, 1978.

Interview with General Orlando García Vázquez. June 12, 1978.

Interview with Orlando Bosch by Andrés Oppenheimer. October 18, 1991.

Interview with Jorge Mas Canosa by Andrés Oppenheimer. September 20, 1991.

Interview with Luis Posada Carriles, Office of the Independent Counsel. Conducted by the FBI in Honduras. February 3, 1992.

Interview with Gerardo Hernández by Saul Landau. U.S. Penitentiary, Victorville, CA. April 1, 2009.

Letter to HSCA from Robert L. Keach re: Luis Posada et al. December 20, 1977.

Meeting with informant re: Orlando Bosch and Luis Posada. May 31, 1978.

Minority staff, Committee on Government Reform, U.S. House of Representatives. April 20, 2001.

Periodic file summary on Luis Posada and Cesario Diosdado. March 3, 1978.

Transcript of interview by Peter R. Bernal with Antonio "Tony" Calatayud, *Entrevista con Tony Calatayud.*" WRLN-TV. August 9, 1998.

U.S. Comptroller General Office report. "White Propaganda."

U.S. District Court for the District of Puerto Rico Court Transcript, *United States of America* v. *Ángel Manuel Alfonso et al.* October 30, 1997.

U.S. District Court for the District of Puerto Rico Court Transcript, *United States of America* v. *Ángel Manuel Alfonso et al.* April 29, 1998.

U.S. General Accounting Office. "Report to Congressional Requesters, State Departments's Administration of Certain Public Diplomacy Contracts. October 1987.

BOOKS

Alonso, Julio Lara. *La verdad irrebatible sobre el crimen de Barbados*. Havana: Editora Politica, 1986.

Bamford, James. *Body of Secrets: Anatomy of the Ultra-Secret National Security Agency*. New York: Doubleday, 2001.

Bohning, Don. *The Castro Obsession: U.S. Covert Operations Against Cuba 1959–1965*. Washington, DC: Potomac Books, 2005.

Bosch, Adriana D. *Orlando Bosch: El hombre que yo conozco*. Miami: Editorial SIBI, 1988.

Branch, Taylor, and Eugene M. Propper. *Labyrinth*. New York: Viking Press, 1982.

Corn, David. *Blond Ghost: Ted Shackley and the CIA's Crusades*. New York: Simon & Schuster, 1994.

Didion, Joan. *Miami*. New York: Pocket Books, 1987.

Dinges, John. *The Condor Years: How Pinochet and His Allies Brought Terrorism to Three Continents*. New York: The News Press, 2004.

Dinges, John, and Saul Landau. *Assassination on Embassy Row*. New York: Pantheon, 1980.

Fonzi, Gaeton. *The Last Investigation.* New York: Thunder's Mouth Press, 1993.

Gómez Estrada, Alejándro. *¡La Bestia Roja de Cuba!* Self-published, 1990.

Herrera, Alicia. *Pusimos la bomba . . . y que!* Caracas, 1981.

Hunt, E. Howard. *Give Us This Day: The Inside Story of the CIA and the Bay of Pigs Invasion.* New York: Arlington House, 1973.

Mallin, Jay Sr., and Bob Smith. *Betrayal in April.* Virginia: Ancient Mariners Press LLC, 2000.

Matthews, Herbert. *Revolution in Cuba: An Essay in Understanding.* New York: Scribner's, 1975.

Pérez Roura, Armando. *Tome Nota.* Self-published, 1995.

Phillips, David Atlee. *The Night Watch: 25 Years of Peculiar Service.* New York: Atheneum, 1977.

Phillips, Kevin. *American Dynasty.* New York: Viking, 2004

Posada Carriles, Luis. *Los caminos del guerrero.* Self-published, 1994.

Rosas, Alexis, and Ernesto Villegas. *El terrorista de los Bush.* Caracas: 2005.

Thomas, Evan. *The Very Best Men. The Four Who Dared: The Early Years of the CIA.* New York: Simon & Schuster, 1995.

Torres, María de los Angeles. *In the Land of Mirrors: Cuban Exile Politics in the United States.* Ann Arbor: University of Michigan Press, 1999.

ARTICLES

Alfonso, Pablo. "Orlando Bosch Denies Blame," *Miami Herald,* September 13, 1997.

Allard, Jean-Guy. "*¡Aquí están las pruebas!*" *Granma Internacional,* May 29, 2007.

———. "Posada Knows Too Much," *Granma,* June 14, 2007.

Anderson, Curt. "Pipe Bomb Found on Truck Belonging to Witness in Posada Case," Associated Press, January 17, 2007.

Anderson, James. "In Barbados, Castro Honors Victims of '76 Bombing," *Miami Herald,* August 2, 1998.

Anderson, Sarah, and Saul Landau. "Autumn of the Autocrat," *IPS Fellow Covert Action Quarterly,* No. 64. Spring 1998.

Alter, Jonathan. "Clinton 's New Life," *Newsweek,* April 8, 2002.

Bachelet, Pablo. "U.S. House Hearing Focuses on Posada," *Miami Herald,* November 16, 2007.

Bardach, Ann Louise. "Our Man's in Miami," *Washington Post,* April 17, 2005.

———. "Scavenger Hunt: E. Howard Hunt Talks," *Slate,* October 6, 2004.

———. "Twilight of the Assassins," *Atlantic,* November 2006.

———. "Why the FBI Is Coming After Me," *Washington Post,* November 12, 2006.

Bardach, Ann Louise, and Larry Rohter. "A Bomber's Tale." *New York Times,* July 12 and July 13, 1998.

———. "A Cuban Exile Details Horrendous Matter of Bombing," *New York Times,* July 13, 1998.

———. "Cuban Exile Leader Accused in Plot on Castro," *New York Times,* August 26, 1998.

———. "Life in the Shadows, Trying to Bring Down Castro," *New York Times,* July 13–14, 1998.

———. "A Plot on Castro Spotlights Exiles," *New York Times,* July 14, 1988.

Barry, John. "CIA's Man at the Bay of Pigs," *Miami Herald,* July 16, 1998.

Branch, Karen. "Help Bosch, Shun Ties to Castro," *Miami Herald,* June 30, 1988.

Bonilla, Efrén. *"El presidente dice que el ex-embajador Charles Ford el que le hizó la solicitud,"* *Tiempo,* August 30, 2008.

Bussey, Jane. "The Remaking of Venezuela's Justice System," *Miami Herald,* March 6, 1998.

Caldwell, Alicia A. "2 Plead Guilty in Cuban Militant Case," Associated Press, November 17, 2007.

Campbell, Duncan. "Bush's Decision to Bring Back Otto Reich Exposes the Hypocrisy of the War Against Terror," *Guardian,* February 8, 2002.

Cancio Isla, Wifredo. *"Diario cubano divulga supuestas llamadas de Posada sobre bombas,"* *El Nuevo Herald,* May 12, 2007.

Cawthorne, Andrew. "Cuba Puts Elderly Exiles on Trial for 'Invasion,'" Reuters, September 21, 2000.

Chardy, Alfonso. "Indictment Against Posada Reinstated," *Miami Herald,* August 15, 2008.

———. "Militant Cuban Exile Honored," *Miami Herald,* May 2, 2008.

———. "Posada Says Castro Is Persecuting Him," *Miami Herald,* August 31, 2005.

Chardy, Alfonso, and Jay Weaver. "FBI's Cuba Trip Draws Rebuke," *Miami Herald,* May 4, 2007.

Chardy, Alfonso, Oscar Corral, and Jay Weaver. "FBI, Cuba Cooperating on Posada," *Miami Herald,* May 3, 2007.

Corral, Oscar, and Alfonso Chardy. "Flashback: Posada Speaks to Herald," *Miami Herald,* May 17, 2005.

Dillon, Sam. "Cuban Exile Waging 'War' under New Identity," *Miami Herald,* October 21, 1986.

Ducassi, Jay, and Ana Veciana-Suarez. "Miami Votes to Let Bosch Have His Day," *Miami Herald,* March 25, 1983.

Epstein Nieves, Gail. "Bosch's Alleged Role in Havana Bombing," *Miami Herald,* April 13, 2001.

Fleetwood, Blake. "I Am Going to Declare War," *New Times,* May 13, 1977.

Garvin, Glenn, and Frances Robles. "Panama Suspect Has Ties to Dade," *Miami Herald,* November 21, 2000.

Gaynor, Tim. "Castro Talks of Murder Plot at Panama Summit," Reuters, November 17, 2000.

Gemoules, Jack. "County's New Boss: Avino," *Miami Herald,* June 3, 1988.

James, Ian. "Castro Foe Denies Financial Backing," *New York Times,* July 14, 1998.

Kimery, Anthony L. "In the Company of Friends: George Bush and the CIA," *Covert Action,* Summer 1992 (Number 41).

Kleinnecht, William, and Juan Forero. "Cuba Implicates N.J. Businessman," New Jersey *Star-Ledger,* November 8, 1998.

Kwitney, Jonathan. "The Mexican Connection," *Barrons,* September 19, 1988.

Lacey, Marc. "Political Memo: Resurrecting Ghosts of Pardons Past," *New York Times,* March 4, 2001.

Landau, Saul. "Investigate Posada's Statements," *Miami Herald,* August 3, 1998.

McBride, Joseph. "George Bush, C.I.A. Operative," *Nation,* July 16, 1988.

———. "Where Was George," August 13–20, 1988.

Marquis, Christopher. "Foundation Flexes Clout in Fighting Off Allegations," *Miami Herald,* July 31, 1998.

Pertierra, José. "Posada Carriles: Extradite or Prosecute," *CounterPunch*, May 19, 2006.

Powell, Robert Andrew. "A CANF-Do Attitude," *New York Times*, May 23, 1996.

Reyes, Gerardo. "Bosch's 'Mix': Ingredient for Trouble?" *Miami Herald*, June 12, 1993.

Rice, John. "Castro Steals Show with Death Plot," Associated Press, November 18, 2000.

Robles, Frances. "Cuba: U.S. Funneled Money to Dissidents," *Miami Herald*, May 19, 2008.

———. "Exiles Deny Plot on Castro," *Miami Herald*, December 15, 2000.

Romero, Simon, and Damien Cave. "Venezuela Will Push U.S. to Hand Over Man Tied to Plane Bombing," *New York Times*, January 23, 2009.

Russell, Dick. "Little Havana's Reign of Terror," *New Times*, October 29, 1976.

Siegel, Robert. "Posada Charges Dropped, Venezuela Fumes," NPR: *All Things Considered*, May 9, 2007.

Van Natta, Don Jr. "Cuban Exile Group Plans Lawsuit against *Times*," *New York Times*, July 17, 1998.

Vasquez, Michael. "Judges: Miami Fire-Fee Attorney Acted Reprehensibly," *Miami Herald*, August 9, 2007.

Weaver, Jay. "Serious Legal Questions Loom for Posada," *Miami Herald*, February 25, 2008.

———. "Weapons Surrender Lightens Jail Time," *Miami Herald*, June 7, 2007.

Williams, Carol J. "Pressure Grows to Prosecute Cuban Exile: Dismissal of Charge Against Admitted Terrorist Stirs Outrage," *Los Angeles Times*, May 10, 2007.

Wilson, Catherine. "Convicted Terrorist Bosch Sent Bombs to Cuba," Associated Press, April 12, 2001.

Zeitlin, Janine. "Cuban Painters and Fugitives: Luis Posada Carriles and José Dionisio Suárez Esquivel Show Their Stuff and Tell Their Stories," *New Times*, November 1, 2007.

"Anti-Castro Exile Renounces Terrorism," Associated Press, July 24, 2001.

"CANF and Luis Posada Carriles," *Miami Herald*, July 16, 1998.

"CANF Leaders Subpoenaed in Castro Assassination Plot," *Miami Herald*, December 3, 1997.

"Castro Visits His Father's Spanish Home," *New York Times*, July 29, 1992.

"Cuba Accuses Salvador of Harboring Potential Killer," Reuters, November 18, 2000.

"Cuba Publishes Book on Anti-Castro Activist Posada Carriles," EFE, November 22, 2007.

"Cuban Exile Group Holds Memorial for Victims of 1976 Plane Bombing," *Miami Herald*, October 7, 1996.

"Cuban Exile Says He Lied About Link to Bombings," *Sun-Sentinel*, August 3, 1998.

"Cuban Exile Says He Lied to Times about Financial Support," *New York Times*, August 4, 1998.

"Cuban Exile's Lawyer Accuses Castro of Framing His Client," Dow Jones Newswire, December 14, 2000.

"El Club Big Five de Miami tiene dos nuevos socios," *El Duende*, May 29, 2007.

"Felony Charges Take a Powder," *New Times*, July 15, 2004.

"Judge Tosses Indictment of Cuban Militant Luis Posada Carriles," *Fox News,*
    May 8, 2007.
"Panama: Exile Says Aim Was Castro Hit," *Miami Herald,* January 13, 2001.
"Recaudarán fondos para defensa legal de Posada Carriles," El Nuevo Herald,
    April 24, 2009.
"Univision Says Exile Group Was Present During Bomber Interview," Bloomberg
    News Service, July 15, 1998.
"Venezuela to Ask Panama to Extradite Cuban Exile," Reuters, December 21, 2001.

PART III

INTERVIEWS

Jonathan Benjamin Alvarado
Domingo Amuchastegui
Déborah Andollo. Tarara, Cuba: January 24, 1997
Merri Ansara
Gustavo Arnavat
Michael Band
Gioconda Belli
Jane Bussey
Lissette Bustamante
Frank Calzón
José de Cardenas, USAID. January 5, 2009
Tony Castell, Havana
Juanita Castro. December 11, 2000; April 18, 2002
Fidel Castro Ruz. Havana: October 16, 1993; January 3 and 4, 1994
Max Castro
Raúl Castro Ruz. Encounters on January 3, 1994; August 14, 2000
Joe Centorino
Steven Clemons
Kendall Coffey. March 3, 2002
Jake Colvin
Alberto Coll. June 2005
Efraim Conte
Darrel Couturier
Amb. Jeffrey Davidson
Jack Devine
Rafael Díaz-Balart. October 8, 2001
Jorge Domínguez
Daniel Erikson
Vilma Espín. Havana: December 22, 1993; January 2, 1994
Damian Fernández, Miami
Chino Figueredo, Havana
Jess Ford, GAO investigator: TV and Radio Martí
Norberto Fuentes, Miami
Jeffrey Garcia
Joe Garcia, Miami

Robert Gelbard, Washington DC
Paul Giongliania, Public Affairs, CIA
Andrés Gómez
Alberto Gonzalez Casals, Washington, DC
Cesar Gonzalez, spokeman for Lincoln Díaz-Balart. October 20, 2008
Pedro Gonzalez, Miami
David Gootnick, GAO investigator: USAID. Cuba
Barbara Walker Gordon
Amb. Jesús Gracia
Graciela de la Guardia. Havana: October 8, 1995; January 4, 1998
Ileana de la Guardia. Miami: October 1995
Mario de la Guardia. Havana: October 8, 1995
Patricio de la Guardia. Havana: October 20, 1997; July 2000
Alfredo Guevara. Havana: January 3, 1994; July 22, 2000
Orlando Gutiérrez
Francisco "Pepe" Hernandez
Rafael Hernández, editor of *Temas*. Stockholm, Sweden
Amb. Vicki Huddleston
Kirby Jones
Salvador Lew
José Luis Llovio-Menéndez. New York, Miami: 1994–2000
Lee Lockwood. January 16, 2001
Frank Manitzas
Raul Martinez
Marcíal Milián, political officer of U.S. Interests Section. May 2006
Molly Millerwise, OFAC Treasury Department
Alejandro Míyar
Carlos Alberto Montaner
Frank Mora
Rosario Moreno, Miami
Donald Nixon. Tustin, California, 1996, and Havana, 1995
Richard Nuccio
Achy Obejas
Jim Olson, former CIA chief of counterintelligence. July 16, 2008
Marifeli Pérez-Stable
Phil Peters
Jorge Piñón
Portia Palmer, USAID. January 5, 2009
Anibel Quevedo, Havana
Manuel Rocha, U.S. Interests Section. Havana: October 2, 1995
Carlos Saladrigas
Portia Siegelbaum
Howard Simon, ACLU
Jack Skelly
Wayne Smith
Julia Sweig
Tad Szulc
Nelson Valdés

René Vasquez Díaz, Stockholm, Sweden
Barbara Vesco. Winter Gardens, FL: 1995
Dan Vesco. New York: October 9, 1995
Dawn Vesco. 1995
Patricia Vesco. Winter Gardens, FL: 1995
Lee Vilker, U.S. attorney in Coll case. 1995
Tim Weiner
Kevin Whitaker, State Department
Carol Williams

DOCUMENTS/REPORTS

GAO—"Continued Efforts to Strengthen USAID's Oversight of U.S. Democracy
Assistance for Cuba." November 2008.
GAO—"U.S. Democracy Assistance for Cuba Needs Better Management and Over-
sight." November 2006.
Cuba: Raúl Castro's National Assembly Speech (Text). BBC Worldwide Monitor-
ing: July 2008.
"The Cuban Rafter Phenomenon: A Unique Sea Exodus." University of Miami:
2004.
Domingo Amuchastegui. "FAR: Mastering Reforms." Cuba in Transition, Vol. 10.
Association for the Study of the Cuban Economy: 2000.
"Focus on Cuba," Staff Report, Cuban Transition Project. Issue 46: August 11,
2006.
Gonzalez, Edward. "Cuba: Clearing Perilous Waters." Los Angeles: RAND, 1996.
Joyce, Mark. "Brother in Arms: Transitioning from One Castro to Another in
Cuba." RUSI Journal, October 2007.
Mora, Frank O. "Cuba's Ministry of Interior: The FAR's Fifth Army." Bulletin of
Latin American Research, Vol. 26, No. 2, 2007.
———. "Generations in the FAR General Officer Corps: Backgrounds, Experiences
and Interests." Cuban Affairs Quarterly Electronic Journal. April 2006.
———. "Young Blood: Continuity and Change Within the Revolutionary Armed
Forces." Cuban Affairs Quarterly Electronic Journal. April 2006.
U.S. Department of State, Daily Press Briefing by Sean McCormack. April 18, 2008.
Werlau, Maria. "Fidel Castro, Inc.: A Global Conglomerate." Cuba in Transition.
ASCE: 2006.
Werlau, Maria, and Armando Lago. The Cuba Project. Free Society Archive: 2008.

FILMS/ VIDEO

Charlie Rose. Interview with Deputy Secretary of State John D. Negroponte, April
25, 2008.
"Cuban State Council Announces Cabinet Reshuffle (BBC/Cubavision TV). March
2, 2009.
¿La Verdad? Documentary by Helen Smyth, 2006.
Looking for Fidel. Documentary by Oliver Stone, 2003.
638 Ways to Kill Castro. Documentary by Dollan Cannell, 2006.
Shoot Down. Directed by Cristina Khuly, 2007.

BOOKS

Anderson, Jon Lee. *Che Guevara: A Revolutionary Life*. New York: Grove Press, 1997.

Bardach, Ann Louise, co-editor. *The Prison Letters of Fidel Castro*. New York: Avalon, 2006.

Bardach, Ann Louise. *Cuba Confidential: Love and Vengeance in Miami and Havana*. New York: Vintage, 2002.

Blanco, Katiuska. *Todo el tiempo de los cedros: Paisaje familiar de Fidel Castro Ruz*. Havana: Casa Editorial, April 2003.

Castro, Fidel, with Ignacio Ramonet. *Fidel Castro: Biografía a dos voces*. New York: Random House Mondadori, 2006.

Castro, Fidel, with Ignacio Ramonet. *My Life*. New York: Scribner, 2007.

Dobbs, Michael. *One Minute to Midnight: Kennedy, Khrushchev, and Castro on the Brink of Nuclear War*. New York: Knopf, 2008.

Fernández, Alina. *Castro's Daughter: An Exile's Memoir of Cuba*. New York: St. Martin's Press, 1997.

Franklin, Jane. *Cuba and the United States: A Chronological History*. Melbourne: Ocean Press, 1997.

Franqui, Carlos. *Diary of the Cuban Revolution*. New York: Viking Press, 1980.

———. *Family Portrait with Fidel*. New York: Random House, 1984. (Translated by Alfred MacAdam.)

Fuentes, Norberto. *Dulces Guerreros Cubanos*. Spain: Editorial Seix-Barral, 1999.

Gjelten, Tom. *Bacardi and the Long Fight for Cuba*. New York: Viking Press. 2008.

Gonzalez, Edward. *Cuba Under Castro: The Limits of Charisma*. Boston: Houghton Mifflin, 1974.

Gonzalez, Edward, and David Ronfeldt. *Castro, Cuba, and the World*. Los Angeles: RAND, 1986.

Guillermo, Alma. *Dancing with Cuba*. New York: Pantheon, 2004.

Latell, Brian. *After Fidel*. New York: Palgrave, 2005.

Llovio Menéndez, José Luis. *Insider: My Hidden Life as a Revolutionary in Cuba*. New York: Bantam Books, 1988. (Translated by Edith Grossman.)

Lockwood, Lee. *Castro's Cuba, Cuba's Fidel*. New York: Macmillan, 1967.

Mallin, Jay Sr. *History of the Cuban Armed Forces*. Reston, VA: Ancient Mariners Press, 2000.

Marifeli, Pérez-Stable. *The Cuban Revolution: Origins, Course, and Legacy*. New York: Oxford University Press, 1993.

Masetti, Jorge. *In the Pirate's Den: My Life as a Secret Agent for Castro*. San Francisco: Encounter Books, 1993.

Oppenheimer, Andrés. *Castro's Final Hour*. New York: Touchstone, 1992.

Pérez, Louis A. Jr. *On Becoming Cuban: Identity, Nationality, & Culture*. University of North Carolina Press, 1999.

———. *To Die in Cuba: Suicide and Society*. Chapel Hill: University of North Carolina Press, 2005.

Smith, Wayne S. *The Closest of Enemies: A Personal and Diplomatic History of the Castro Years*. Canada: Penguin Books, 1987.

Sublette, Ned. *Cuba and Its Music: From the First Drums to the Mambo*. Chicago Review Press, 2004.

Szulc, Tad. *Fidel: A Critical Portrait*. New York: Avon Books, 1986.

Tattlin, Isadora. *Cuba Diaries: An American Housewife in Havana*. New York: Algonquin, 2003.

Weiner, Tim. *Legacy of Ashes*. New York: Anchor/Doubleday, 2007.

Zito, Míriam. *Asalto*. Havana: Casa Editora, April 1998.

ARTICLES

Adams, David. "Democrats Move Boldly in S. Florida," *St. Petersburg Times,* May 7, 2008.

———. "Where No Homes Sell, Ever," *St. Petersburg Times,* June 4, 2008.

Amuchastegui, Domingo. "Leadership Shows Renewed Interest in Attracting FDI," *CubaNews,* December 2008.

Bachelet, Pablo. "Bush Administration Changing Who Gets Cuba Aid Money," *Miami Herald,* March 30, 2007.

———. "Raúl Castro's Grip Is Firm, Senate Panel Is Told," *Miami Herald,* January 12, 2007.

———. "U.S. Shifting Funds Away from Miami Anti-Castro Groups," *Miami Herald,* March 30, 2008.

Bachelet, Pablo, and Wilfredo Cancio Isla. "Cuba to Make Computers, Microwaves, Other Goods Available to Consumers," *Miami Herald,* March 15, 2008.

Bardach, Ann Louise. "Cuba at the Crossroads," *Washington Post,* February 12, 2006.

———. "50 Years Later, Who Wins and Who Loses," *Washington Post,* January 11, 2009.

———. "The GOP's Bill Ayers?" *Slate,* October 15, 2008.

———. "Hoodwinked," *Slate,* August 26, 2004.

———. "The Inventor of Fidel," *Washington Post,* July 1, 2006.

———. "A Page with a Purpose," *New York Times,* April 13, 2003.

———. "Slander: The Assassination of Alberto Coll," *Slate,* July 11, 2005.

———. "Trouble in Florida," *Daily Beast,* October 30, 2008.

———. "Vesco's Last Gamble," *Vanity Fair,* March 1996.

Boadle, Anthony. "Brazil's Lula Says Fidel Castro Lucid and Healthy," Reuters, January 15, 2008.

———. "Cuban Writers Angered by Resurfacing of Censor," Reuters, January 15, 2007.

———. "Illegal Flow of Cubans to U.S. on the Rise," Reuters, October 1, 2007.

Brown, Tom. "McCain—Out of Touch with Cuban Americans?" Reuters, May 23, 2008.

Bustamante, Lissette. *"Confesiones de la periodista del Fidel Castro,"* El Mercurio, July 26, 2008.

Cancio Isla, Wilfredo. "Cubans' Statement Warns of Frustration," *El Nuevo Herald,* August 25, 2008.

———. "Ex-agent: Escobar Met Cuban Officials in '89," *Miami Herald,* March 12, 2008.

———. "Ex-Castro Ally a Sensual Painter," *Miami Herald,* June 5, 2007.

———. "U.S. Spy Asked to Help Cuba.," *El Nuevo Herald,* April 7, 2008.

Cancio Isla, Wilfredo, and Renato Perez. "Cuba Tapped Phone for Evidence Against Robaina," *Miami Herald,* August 3, 2002.

Castañeda, Jorge. "The Plot Against the Castros," *Newsweek*, March 23, 2009.

Cave, Damien. "U.S. Overtures Find Support Among Cuban-Americans," *New York Times*, April 21, 2009.

Chardy, Alfonso. "Exile Broadcasters Sign Off for Last Time," *Miami Herald*, June 14, 2008.

Cordoba, José de. "Cuban Revolution: Yoani Sánchez Fights Tropical Totalitarianism," *Wall Street Journal*, December 22, 2007.

Crispín, Sarrá. *"Todo mi pueblo se pregunta . . . y yo también,"* Kaos en la Red, April 7, 2008.

David, Ariel. "Italy Seeks Extradition of 139 Suspects in South America's Dirty War," Associated Press, January 10, 2008.

Davis, Charles. "U.S./Cuba: Justice Not So Blind in Politically Charged Cases," *IPS*, January 29, 2008.

DeFede, Jim. "Combat Veteran Fighting 'Cruel' Travel Policy," *Miami Herald*, June 26, 2005.

Erikson, Daniel P. "Charting Castro's Possible Successors," *SAIS Review of International Affairs*, Volume 25, No. 1, Winter-Spring 2005.

Fernández, G., and M. A. Menéndez. *"El poder económico de los hermanos Castro,"Diario 16* (Madrid), June 24, 2001.

Frank, Marc. "Cuba's Aging Leaders Move to Shore Up Revolution," Reuters, March 26, 2008.

———. "Fidel Visible, But Raúl Still in Control of Cuba," *Financial Times*, July 20, 2007.

———. "Havana Spins Revamp of Castro," ABC News, April 24, 2009.

Franks, Jeff. "Cuba Leader Raúl Castro Turns 77 Amid Rising Hopes," Reuters, June 3, 2008.

———. "Shake-up Puts Raúl Castro Stamp on Cuba Government," Reuters, March 2, 2009.

González, Fernán. *"Mariela Castro: 'orgullosa de mi padre,'"* BBC Mundo, September 18, 2006.

Gumbel, Andrew. "Battle for Cuba's Future Is Brewing Behind the Scenes," *Independent*, February 20, 2008.

Krauze, Enrique. "Humanizing the Revolution," *New York Times*, December 30, 2007.

Lacey, Marc. "Report Finds U.S. Agencies Distracted by Focus on Cuba," *New York Times*, December 19, 2007.

———. "Robert Vesco, '70s Financier, Is Dead at 71," *New York Times*, May 9, 2008.

Lacey, Marc, and Jonathan Kandell. "Fugitive Financier Vesco Is Said to Have Died," *New York Times*, May 3, 2008.

Latell, Brian. "The End of an Era," *Miami Herald*, December 10, 2006.

———. "Raúl on His Own," ICCAS, January 2009.

LeoGrande, William M. "Next U.S. President Should Be Ready for Immigration Crisis," *Miami Herald*, September 18, 2008.

Luxner, Larry. "Puerto Rico Eyes Post-Communist Cuba as Potential Trade Partner, Tourism Rival," *CubaNews*, January 2009.

Marin, Mar. "Cuba's Aging Revolutionaries Trying to Pass the Torch," EFE, June 27, 2007.

Marx, Gary. "Cuba Gets Hint of Different Style," *Chicago Tribune*, December 22, 2006.

Menendez, Ana. "Cuba: Same Old Repression in a New Package," *Miami Herald*, June 3, 2008.

Montaner, Carlos Alberto. "One Less Crutch for Raúl Castro," *Miami Herald*, June 26, 2007.

Pacepa, Ion Mihai. "Who Is Raúl Castro? A Tyrant Only a Brother Could Love," *National Review*, August 10, 2006.

Penn, Sean. "Conversations with Chávez and Castro," *Nation*, November 25, 2008; December 15, 2008.

Pérez-Stable, Marifeli. "Chinese-style Reforms Would Be an Improvement," *Miami Herald*, July 5, 2007.

Peters, Phillip. "Will Raúl Castro Reform Cuba's Economy?" *Cuba Policy Report*, September 25, 2007.

Putney, Michael. "Obama's First Step Puts Castro on the Defensive," *Miami Herald*, April 22, 2009.

Radelat, Ana. "Even with Obama, Democrats in Control, Changing Cuba Policy Will Be Tough Sell," *CubaNews*, December 2008.

Rieff, David. "Will Little Havana Go Blue?" *New York Times Magazine*, July 13, 2008.

Robles, Frances. "Cuban Government Undergoes Massive Restructuring," *Miami Herald*, March 3, 2009.

———. "Cuba's Raúl Castro Encourages Criticism," *Miami Herald*, October 2, 2007.

———. "Funding for Free Cuba Is Frozen," *Miami Herald*, July 22, 2008.

———. "Raúl Castro Takes Stage at July 26 Parade," *Miami Herald*, July 26, 2007.

Roig-Franzia, Manuel. "Cuba's Next Generation May Crack Door to Democracy," *Washington Post*, February 22, 2008.

———. "A New Generation Stands by in Cuba," *Washington Post*, February 21, 2008.

———. "Raúl Castro, Leader with a Freer Hand," *Washington Post*, February 20, 2008.

Sanchez, Ray. "Cuban President Raúl Castro Quietly Turned 77," *Sun-Sentinel*, June 4, 2008.

———. "Cuba's President to Be Selected Today: Raúl Castro Considered Leading Choice to Succeed Brother," *Sun-Sentinel*, February 24, 2008.

———. "Dissidents Note Subtle Change in Treatment," South Florida *Sun-Sentinel*, December 16, 2007.

Sardi, Nelson Bocaranda. *"Los Runrunes de Nelson Bocaranda Sardi,"* El Universal, January 15, 2009.

Siegel, Robert, and Marc Frank. "Cuba Eases Restrictions, Aims for Economic Boost," NPR, April 1, 2008.

Smith, Geri. "Imagining Life Without Castro," *BusinessWeek*, March 12, 2008.

Sniffen, Michael J. "Ex-Bush Aide Charged with Theft from Cuba Group," Associated Press, November 26, 2008.

Snow, Anita. "Cuba Deports American Wanted on Allegations of Child Sex Abuse, Pornography," Associated Press, June 13, 2008.

———. "Raúl Castro Attends 13th Birthday Celebration for Cuban Boy Elián González," Associated Press, December 6, 2006.

————. "U.S. Groups Hope Obama Allows More Travel to Cuba," Associated Press, April 26, 2009.

Suchlicki, Jaime. "Is Raúl Castro Ready to Deal?" *Miami Herald,* January 7, 2007.

Urbina, Ian. "Change Means More of the Same, with Control at the Top," *New York Times,* April 5, 2009.

Valdés, Nelson P. "Cuba: Prelude to Succession," Associated Press, February 24, 2008.

Vicent, Mauricio. *"El laberinto cubano,"* *El País,* June 28, 2009.

Weissert, Will. "Changing Cuba: Monster Buses Vanish from Havana Streets," Associated Press, April 18, 2008.

Williams, Carol J. "Luis Posada Carriles, a Terror Suspect Abroad, Enjoys a 'Coming-out' in Miami," *Los Angeles Times,* May 7, 2008.

"Bolivia's Morales Says Fidel Castro Thin But Lucid," Reuters, May 23, 2008.

"Cuban Dissidents Say Colleague Died in Custody," EFE, June 26, 2007.

"Cuba's Raúl Castro on 'Learning' Trip in China," Reuters (Beijing), November 19, 1997.

"Fidel's Niece Says Cuba Reluctant to Release Data on Pedophiles," EFE, January 31, 2008.

"Florida Lawmakers, Travel Agents Row Over Cuba Trips," *Agence France-Presse,* May 2, 2008.

"High-speed Escape," *Economist,* June 14, 2008.

"La hija de Raúl Castro espera más información sobre los destituciones en el gobierno," EFE, March 25, 2009.

"More Cubans Finding the Courage to Speak Out," *Miami Herald,* December 8, 2007.

"More Reforms; More Critical Press; Cubans Living Abroad Meet," Cuba Central Center for Democracy in the Americas, March 21, 2008.

"New Reasons for Cuba Opening Wash Ashore," *Palm Beach Post,* January 5, 2007.

"No Celebrations for U.S. Cubans as Raúl Castro Holds on to Power," AFP, January 23, 2007.

"Nota Official," *Granma,* October 14, 2004.

"Power Shake-up Casts Doubt on Post-Castro Cuba," Associated Press, March 5, 2009.

"Raúl Castro Calls His Brother, Fidel 'Irreplaceable.'" AFP, December 20, 2006.

"Raúl Castro Hints at Changes for Cuba," *Oxford Analytica,* August 6, 2007.

"Rights Abuses Unabated in Raúl Castro's Cuba Group," Reuters, July 5, 2007.

"Subtle Changes May Be in the Books for Cuba, Analysts," AFP, January 23, 2007.

"U.S. Dismisses Overture from Raúl Castro," EFE, December 4, 2007.

"Vesco llevo al narcotraficante Carlos Ledeher a Cuba," Radio Martí, May 29, 2008.

"White House: Cuba Changes 'Cosmetic,'" AFP, April 18, 2008.

"Writers in Cuba Upset Over Re-appearance of Dark-era Censors," EFE, January 18, 2007.

WEBSITES CONSULTED

Along the Malecón: http://alongthemalecon.blogspot.com
Cuban Colada: http://miamiherald.typepad.com/cuban_colada/
Cuban Information Archives: http://www.cuban-exile.com/index.html
Cuban Polidata: http://cubapolidata.com/
Cuban Research Institute/FIU: http://cubainfo.fiu.edu

The Cuban Triangle: http://cubantriangle.blogspot.com/
El Café Cubano: http://elcubanocafe.blogspot.com/
Generación Y: http://www.desdecuba.com/generaciony/
Granma: http://granma.cu/
Institute of Cuban and Cuban-American Studies, University of Miami: www.miami
    .edu/iccas/
Mambi Watch: http://mambiwatch.blogspot.com/
U.S. Interests Section in Havana: http://havana.usinterestsection.gov

INDEX

Council on Foreign Relations, 21
Crespo, Luis, Jr., 161
Crespo, Luis, Sr. "El Gancho," 161
Crist, Charlie, 244, 245–46
Cuba, 81, 92, 143; biological weapons research in, 231–32; biotechnology in, 14, 18, 23, 274; Black Spring of 2003 in, 259, 265; blogosphere in, 265–67; bombings in, 159; Brazil as trading partner of, 69; Bush family relations with, 58–64; Coll's visit to, 233–34; CORU attacks in, 114–15; crime and justice in, 257–58, 269; cycles of openness and repression in, 263–65; death penalty in, 269; declining population of, 218; defections from, 211–12, 218–20; dissent in, 212–13; economy of, xxii, 212–13, 217–18, 257–58, 259, 260–63, 268, 270; energy shortages in, 268; farm ownership in, 243, 268; hardliners and *históricos* vs. reformers and pragmatists in, 48, 77, 202–7, 210, 267, 270, 272; health care in, 21, 202, 220, 272–73; home ownership in, 243, 267; hurricanes of 2008 in, xxi, 260–61; informers in, 222, 224–25, 240; Italian tourist killed in, 155, 162, 168, 172–75; mulatto and black population of, 204, 218; nationalization of property by, 59, 97, 193; 1994 *balseros* crisis in, 187–88, 217; nuclear power program of, 36, 39; oil imports of, 217, 263; oil production and refining in, 65, 69, 71, 142, 262–63, 278; one-party elections in, 259; papal visit to, 33, 92–93, 188; political prisoners in, xx, xxi, 71–72, 269; power shortages in, 217, 268; press visas in, 31–34; prostitution in, xix, 33, 268–69; socialism in, 48, 193, 267, 274; "Special Period" in, 216–17, 257–58, 270; state security services of, 263; suicide rate in, 197–99; suppression of dissent in, 271; tourism in, 36, 55, 65, 187, 258, 269; tourist facilities off-limits to Cubans in, 36, 243, 268–69; tourist hotel bombings in, 101–2, 155, 162, 171, 172, 178; on U.S. state

sponsors of terrorism list, 231–33, 237, 277; War of Independence of, 124; Washington Special Interests Section of, xxi, 22, 32, 72, 207, 228, 229; youth departing from, 187, 218–20, 265
Cuba Confidential (Bardach), 32, 152, 228–29
Cuba Diaries, 21–22
Cubana de Aviación airline bombing, 111, 117–37, 139–41, 151, 153, 155, 158, 160–61, 170, 177
Cuban American National Foundation (CANF), xviii, 62, 106, 147–49, 166–67, 169, 203, 204, 232, 237–38, 248, 254–55, 276
Cuban-Americans, 103, 246; changing attitudes of, xviii, 63, 145–46, 246–47, 277; voting by, 246–47, 254
Cuban Atomic Energy Commission, 36
Cuban exiles, 118, 124, 175, 240
Cuban Five, 162, 227
Cuban Independence Day, 113, 276
Cuban Intelligence, 32, 35, 107, 120, 139, 141, 144, 162, 215, 221, 225–28, 233
Cuban Liberty Council, 62, 148, 167, 169, 254, 276
Cuban Missile Crisis of 1962, 9, 19, 60, 64, 104, 196
Cuban national fencing team, 118–19, 125, 128–29
Cuban nationalism, 188, 197–98, 273
Cuban Revolution: 1998 anniversary of, 33; 2006 anniversary of, 3–4
Cuban Revolution, xxi, 9, 22, 26, 30, 37, 44, 47, 52, 56, 67–68, 70, 74, 76, 77, 79, 82, 84–85, 87, 89, 103, 184, 187, 191, 192, 193, 197, 199, 206, 207, 208, 222, 225, 227, 258, 259, 265, 267, 269, 270, 274; divided families and, 219; fiftieth anniversary of, 266, 275–76
Cuban Women's Federation, 195, 272
Cubarte website, 264
Cuba Study Group, 62–63, 276
Cuba-U.S. relations, xx, 48, 57, 63, 71–72, 75, 142–43, 162, 188, 196, 211, 230–45, 252–55, 276–78; Obama administration and, xxi–xxii, 252, 254–55